Complex Managerial Decisions
Involving
Multiple Objectives

The Wiley Series in
MANAGEMENT AND ADMINISTRATION

ELWOOD S. BUFFA, *Advisory Editor*
University of California, Los Angeles

MANAGEMENT SYSTEMS, SECOND EDITION
Peter P. Schoderbek
OPERATIONS MANAGEMENT: PROBLEMS AND MODELS, THIRD EDITION
Elwood S. Buffa
PROBABILITY FOR MANAGEMENT DECISIONS
William R. King
PRINCIPLES OF MANAGEMENT: A MODERN APPROACH, THIRD EDITION
Henry H. Albers
MODERN PRODUCTION MANAGEMENT, THIRD EDITION
Elwood S. Buffa
CASES IN OPERATIONS MANAGEMENT: A SYSTEMS APPROACH
James L. McKenney and Richard S. Rosenbloom
ORGANIZATIONS: STRUCTURE AND BEHAVIOR, VOLUME I, SECOND EDITION
Joseph A. Litterer
ORGANIZATIONS: SYSTEMS, CONTROL AND ADAPTATION, VOLUME II
Joseph A. Litterer
MANAGEMENT AND ORGANIZATIONAL BEHAVIOR:
A MULTIDIMENSIONAL APPROACH
Billy J. Hodge and Herbert J. Johnson
MATHEMATICAL PROGRAMMING: AN INTRODUCTION TO THE
DESIGN AND APPLICATION OF OPTIMAL DECISION MACHINES
Claude McMillan
DECISION MAKING THROUGH OPERATIONS RESEARCH
Robert J. Thierauf and Richard A. Grosse
QUALITY CONTROL FOR MANAGERS & ENGINEERS
Elwood G. Kirkpatrick
PRODUCTION SYSTEMS: PLANNING, ANALYSIS AND CONTROL
James L. Riggs
SIMULATION MODELING: A GUIDE TO USING SIMSCRIPT
Forrest P. Wyman
BASIC STATISTICS FOR BUSINESS AND ECONOMICS
Paul G. Hoel and Raymond J. Jessen
BUSINESS AND ADMINISTRATIVE POLICY
Richard H. Buskirk
INTRODUCTION TO ELECTRONIC COMPUTING: A MANAGEMENT
APPROACH
Rodney L. Boyes, Robert W. Shields and Larry G. Greenwell
COMPUTER SIMULATION OF HUMAN BEHAVIOR
John M. Dutton and William H. Starbuck
INTRODUCTION TO GAMING: MANAGEMENT DECISION SIMULATIONS
John G. H. Carlson and Michael J. Misshauk
PRINCIPLES OF MANAGEMENT AND ORGANIZATIONAL BEHAVIOR
Burt K. Scanlan
COMMUNICATION IN MODERN ORGANIZATIONS
George T. and Patricia B. Vardaman
THE ANALYSIS OF ORGANIZATIONS, SECOND EDITION
Joseph A. Litterer
COMPLEX MANAGERIAL DECISIONS
Allan Easton

Complex Managerial Decisions
Involving
Multiple Objectives

HD69
.D4 E27

Allan Easton

School of Business
Hofstra University

JOHN WILEY & SONS, INC.
New York • London • Sydney • Toronto

Copyright © 1973, by John Wiley & Sons, Inc.

Library of Congress Cataloging in Publication Data:

Easton, Allan, 1916–
  Complex managerial decisions.

  Includes bibliographical references.
  1. Decision-making. 2. Decision-making—Mathematical models. I. Title.

HD69.D4E27   658.4'03   73-4713
ISBN 0-471-22938-5

Printed in the United States of America

10 9 8 7 6 5 4 3 2 1

to Miriam

Preface and Statement of Purpose

The stream of thought about management and administrative decision-making may be likened to a broad and deep river having two high banks—the east and west.

On the west bank we find encamped the cohorts of the quantitative schools; the mathematical economists, the mathematical psychologists and sociologists, the management scientists, operations researchers, probability theorists, and systems analysts. On the east bank are the practicing managers and administrators, the "seat of the pants" boys, the intuitionists, the descriptive school, the institutionalists, and others with a primarily qualitative orientation.

The west-bank people engage themselves with model building, with developing highly specialized methods for dealing with particularized problems, with furthering the state of their art, and with deriving compact generalizations on an ever-increasing level of abstraction. They obtain their intellectual rewards from contemplating the crystalline beauty of their creations and from their success in deriving far-reaching conclusions from the most parsimonious initial assumptions. On the west bank there is excitement, intellectual ferment, and high morale. A substantial portion of their energy is devoted to the education of neophytes to help carry on the tradition and to enable them to go forth into the world as teachers and practitioners of their always fascinating and sometimes esoteric specialties.

As they gaze across the broad expanse of the river, the west bankers view the goings-on on the east bank with a mixture of contempt, condescension, tolerance, and pity—that these backward natives are incapable of comprehending the quintessential purity, beauty, and truth of the west-bank works.

On the east bank something analogous is happening but with less excitement, flair, and with more contact with the hard realities of the real world. Practitioners are busy, grimly doing the world's work without being able to articulate their methods. They use idiosyncratic, *ad hoc* techniques that are inelegant, nonrepeatable, unexplainable; but the essential work is being done —often well, sometimes botched—but it is being done. The emphasis here is on intuition, good judgment, seasoning, and experience. East-bank academicians concentrate on describing institutions, structure, and process; on developing insights; and on speculating on how to improve judgment and how to impart wisdom to the young.

The attitudes of those on the east bank toward the west parallel those of the west toward the east. East bankers tend to be contemptuous, condescending, and overcritical. They view those on the other side as impractical theorists, arrogant, overbearing, immature, and, if well meaning, then wholly out of touch with the nitty-gritty of the real world with its imponderables and frustrations—a world in which the *ceteris paribus* assumption *never* holds. Some east-bank partisans accuse the west bankers of having engineered a subtle coup, of having captured the banner bearing the words, *Decision Theory*, and of now considering themselves sole defenders of the faith and the only legitimate arbiters of what may be properly admitted under that rubric.

Down on both shores of the river labor the bridge builders, assiduous people who are trying to bridge the chasm that separates the mathematical, model-building orientation of the west bank and the pragmatism of the east. Quickly they discover just how broad that chasm really is; valiantly they labor for microscopic gains. Beginning with east-bank orientation some salt their writings with adaptations of west-bank ideas, simplistic enough to be acceptable to hard-lining east bankers. West-bank bridge builders start from their mathematical viewpoint and work toward popularization, or, as west-bank purists would say, vulgarization or "pablumization."

*   *   *

This book is a serious effort at bridge building with an east-bank viewpoint, in which I attempt to narrow the gap between the seemingly incompatible east- and west-bank approaches by introducing semiquantitative structure and methodology into decision making involving multiple interests and therefore multiple objectives. I have borrowed extensively but selectively from many fields, using the ideas I judged to be the most useful and ignoring those not useful enough for my purpose, too difficult or too abstruse for the target east-bank reader.

We will be dealing throughout this book with the search for the best course of action from among alternative solutions to complex, multiple-objective decision problems. There are two parts to this process: (a) the actual search for the best solution, and (b) the search for the most efficient path to the best solution.*

Practitioners with an east-bank orientation are likely to assign higher priority to part (a) than to part (b). Those with a west-bank point of reference usually reverse these priorities. For them, a more efficient method for reaching the optimum solution will be very much more preferred to a less efficient method, although the end result might be the same with either method.

Of course both parts of the process are important, but in the early stages in the development of the science of decision making involving multiple objectives, the pace of progress toward each end may be unequal. In this book, relatively little attention is devoted to part (b), not because this part of the task is unimportant, but because work in this direction must wait until there is a wider choice of methods for dealing with one-of-a-kind, complex, multiple-objective decision problems than is now on the horizon.

In this volume, I present a number of decision/evaluation/rating models with variations, and I suggest how they may be used in several areas of managerial and administrative activity. It is my hope that business managers, administrators, students of decision making, and other persons interested in this subject will find that reading this material has enhanced their decision-making capabilities.

---

* See Douglass J. Wilde, *Optimim Seeking Methods* (Englewood Cliffs, New Jersey, Prentice-Hall, Inc., 1964), p. 2.

The models and variations contained in the following chapters might be better classified as *prescriptive* rather than descriptive. They are prescriptive in the sense that I show the reader how he *can* make certain kinds of decisions, not necessarily how particular managers actually *do* this part of their jobs. I have selected a number of models because of the important respects in which they resemble real decision processes, but I have conducted no field or laboratory research to ascertain what percentage of real-life decisions are made by which specific method or combination of methods.

In addition to their general usefulness in the areas of managerial and administrative decision making on both the operational and policy-making levels, the materials presented here will be useful in the solution of problems of investment choice for portfolio managers, vendor choice for industrial buyers, rating and evaluation systems for engineering project selection, site selection in plant location, and many others. In fact, any activity that involves the identification, evaluation, selection (or ranking) of competing alternatives on multiple objectives (or criteria) is an area of potential application.

In spite of a proliferation of excellent books and articles on quantitative techniques, the solution of complex, multiple-objective problems in administration and management can be aided in only a limited way by application of rigorous mathematical models* and scientific method. The number and complexity of managerial problems that can be handled by management science methods is growing rapidly, but their number remains a miniscule subset of the set of all possible managerial decision problems. I offer this proposition: with few exceptions, most real-life problems have no unique, complete, and final solution. Most human systems in which decisions must be made are either largely indeterminate or are intricate beyond comprehension.†

Moreover, after making his decision, the manager will rarely know if he made the best choice of available alternatives because he cannot simultaneously compare the accepted and rejected alternatives under controlled conditions. Unlike the laboratory scientist or the design engineer who may be able to structure experimental situations as a means for comparing alternative designs, the real-life decision maker cannot. Many decisions result from unstructured, nonrepetitive situations that change rapidly and unpredictably.‡

Yet managers do make decisions; evaluators do make evaluations; the rating services do issue their ratings with at least a superficial semblance of assurance. Plant location consultants do find satisfactory plant sites; con-

---

* For a study relating to the general applicability of management science techniques to complex decisions, see R. B. Brietenbach, "An empirical study of the applicability of management science within the top management positions of a large organization," *I.E.E.E. Transactions on Engineering Management,* Vol. EM-17, No. 1 (February 1970), pp. 2–10.

† A broad discussion of the limitations of a simplistic world view is contained in Mario Bunge, *The Myth of Simplicity,* (Englewood Cliffs, New Jersey, Prentice-Hall, Inc., 1963).

‡ The decision maker's approach to problems is more apt to be *clinical* rather than scientific. For an explanation of the differences between these two approaches, see the discussion of "convergent" and "divergent" phenomena in C. E. Summer and J. J. O'Connell, *The Managerial Mind* (Homewood, Illinois, Richard D. Irwin, Inc., revised edition, 1969), pp. 25–38.

sumer product evaluation services do discriminate successfully between superior and inferior product offerings; sales managers can distinguish among good, better, and best salesmen. My observations of these phenomena lead me to conclude that, with few exceptions, they do so with the exercise of trained judgment aided only occasionally by the newly developed methods of management science or by the older quantative techniques. In many instances, they rely mainly on trial-and-error experimentation.

It would not be wise to reject or otherwise deprecate traditional methods of decision making as being wholly lacking in validity or effectiveness. Practicing managers and administrators, when interrogated, may be unable to explain how they made their decisions or evaluations; but somehow, even if inefficiently, the world's business is getting done. If a particular manager, in making decisions, uses a mixture of 90 percent art (judgment, intuition)* with 10 percent science, he is probably not doing his job any differently from his opposite number in a competing firm. If all decision makers fumble a bit, some appear to fumble less than others. Some men exhibit the ability to make quite satisfactory decisions (in the pragmatic sense) more often, with less expenditure of time and energy, than others. In a highly competitive environment, 30 percent efficiency is better than 25 percent; a batting average of .300 is better than one of .250. The man who can develop a slight competitive edge, in the long run, can move himself up the ladder of achievement. It is my hope that this volume will help its readers to develop such a competitive edge.

As a practical matter, we seek improvement not perfection. I am convinced that the administrator's decision-making capability can be expanded if large, hard-to-manage problems can be divided into smaller, more manageable subproblems. *My approach, therefore, is to minutely dissect a number of decision models to illustrate how this analytic process can be accomplished.* This detailed examination of decision subprocesses should assist the reader in recognizing similarities between parts of my models and his own favorite methods for dealing with multiple-objective problems. If so, the reader may also uncover unexpected shortcomings or biases in his own methods; or he may gain new understanding of their limitations. Such recognition would form the basis for first a searching reexamination, then an upgrading of technique.

*   *   *

There is growing disenchantment with the practical results of using single-objective decision processes (e.g., cost minimization, profit maximization, return on investment, and so on) and an increasing sensitivity to the deleterious effects on the quality of life and the physical environment produced by narrowly focused, short-time horizon decisions. The application of multiple-objective methods, with the broadening of the decision horizon to encompass social, ethical, political, temporal, and environmental considerations seems more suited to meeting today's challenges.

---

* Two excellent works dealing with the place of judgment in administration are Roy E. Brown, *Judgment in Administration* (New York, McGraw Hill Book Co., 1966), and Sir Geoffrey Vickers, *The Art of Judgment* (New York, Basic Books, Inc., 1965).

I confine my inquiry to a rather limited fraction of decision theory, particularly the area in which judgmental and quantitative methods overlap and in which decisions or evaluations involve multiple objectives and criteria. This book is not an exhaustive treatise on managerial decision making, nor a systematic overview, review, or summary of the many excellent works available on decision theory and management science.*

The organization and structure of this volume can be gleaned from the table of contents. The sequence of development is:

Part I   Introductory matter dealing with multiple interests and other influences that contribute to the complexity of managerial decisions.

Part II   The stages in the decision process beginning with perception of a need for action and ending with the presentation of multi-attribute alternative solutions to the decision problem.

Part III   The treatment of multivalued alternatives in preparation for ranking them in order of attractiveness or classifying them into merit categories.

Part IV   Specific techniques for merit-ordering multivalued alternatives, for finding the best of the lot, or for placing them into merit categories.

Part V   A wrap-up and synthesis.

Throughout this work and particularly in the last part, I provide partial answers to four perplexing questions:

1. Is it possible to devise decision procedures where, in spite of the need to exercise judgment, the procedures can be fully explicated and each step made fully defensible?

2. Why is it that men of good will, presented with identical facts and alternatives in a problematic situation, still arrive at quite different choices of alternatives? What are the stages in the problem-solving process that could give rise to this phenomenon? Where are the forks in the road?

3. Is it possible to break down a class of multiple-objective decision problems so that it can be programmed on a digital computer and thereafter so routinized that complex decisions can be made by computers?

4. Can the decision processes of a particularly skilled administrator be simulated and reproduced so that he can delegate many of his complex decisions to subordinates with reasonable assurance that their decisions would not differ materially from those he would have made under similar conditions?

*   *   *

* For a bibliographic listing of works on several aspects of the theory of decision making see, William T. Greenwood (ed.) *Decision Theory and Information Systems* (Cincinnati, Ohio; Southwestern Publishing Co., 1969), pp. 103–104; 201–202; 359–360; 495–496; 598; 720; 803–804. Also, from a psychological viewpoint see Ward Edwards and Amos Tversky (eds.), *Decision Making* (Middlesex, England; Penguin Books. Ltd., 1967), and see the individual bibliographical listings given by the authors of each article in the collection.

This book is intended for two categories of readers: (1) students of management, administration, and policy making in various fields (e.g., business, hotel, hospital, education, military, public, correctional, and so on) and (2) practicing managers in all levels of organization.

The nature of the subject matter has made the use of some mathematical reasoning and notation unavoidable, but these are used sparingly and on the simplest level possible to develop the underlying ideas. Complete mathematical proofs or derivations of equations have not been presented because of my belief that the book's audience will value clearly written exposition and heuristic developments over mathematical precision and elegance. In all cases where mathematical reasoning beyond college algebra and geometry have been employed, there is a parallel exposition in words of the ideas, concepts, and relationships. The reader who is uncomfortable or impatient with mathematical symbols and equations can skip over them without losing the thread of the arguments.

*   *   *

Sprinkled throughout the text and concentrated at the end of the book are many short and a few long case examples, some of them real, some fictional. My main purpose in offering these cases is to bring to the reader, whether he is a practicing administrator or a student of decision making, realistic situations that are well suited for analysis by multiple-objective decision or evaluation methods. Most of the cases were also designed to be read along with the text as interesting, stimulating, and—above all—entertaining examples of multiple-objective problems that working executives are apt to meet.

Although prison wardens, school superintendants, business executives, ships' captains, military commanders, government officials, and hospital administrators do different kinds of work, they have much in common, too. In particular, they must all contend with the pushing and pulling, the maneuvering, and the pressuring of diverse interest groups, from which there emerge complex problems involving multiple objectives. The cases are provided to demonstrate the ubiquity of multiple-interest, multiple-objective problems in disparate fields.

Many of the cases are fictional, but only in the sense that art imitates nature. To avoid embarrassment to those persons or organizations involved in the real cases, I have changed names, places, settings, and descriptions of the events. Subject to these changes, the nonfictional cases (the imaginary ones are so labeled) are reflections of true happenings.

Several of the cases are so complex and unstructured that it was not feasible, considering the space limitations and the reader's interest span, to present detailed data or exhaustive factual descriptions of the events in the condensed narratives. For this reason the cases can probably not be used to best purpose for development of fully realistic solutions or recommendations of professional caliber. Instead, they should be used for practice in analysis of complex, multiple-interest, problematic situations. Questions are provided with the more difficult cases to guide and aid the reader in this task.

*   *   *

A major portion of the material was conceived, formulated, and prepared while I was teaching business decision making at Columbia University's Graduate School of Business and for a short time when I was engaged in research with the Chauncey Williams Industrial Marketing Research Project at Columbia. I wish to thank my faculty colleagues and my students both at Columbia and at Hofstra for their generous assistance in critically evaluating my synthesis of decision-making principles. I owe a debt to several classes of graduate and undergraduate students who were forced to serve and suffer as captive audiences while I expounded and refined this material.

I also acknowledge an immense debt to my intellectual forebears upon whose work I have liberally drawn. Wherever possible I have made specific citations, but the number of persons whose ideas I have used indirectly is so great, that it was not possible to trace every contribution back to its original source. A blanket acknowledgment and thanks are offered as poor substitutes to those whose names I have omitted.

I offer a special expression of gratitude to Professor Elwood S. Buffa of the Graduate School of Management, University of California, Los Angeles, for his many encouragements and helpful suggestions concerning the organization of this work; and to Dean Harold L. Wattel of the School of Business of Hofstra University without whose prodding and rifle-shot assistance, this work might never have reached print.

West New York, New Jersey and
Hempstead, New York 1973   *Allan Easton*

Contents

II   DECISION ELEMENTS AND MODELS

3   Initiating the Decision Process 54

4   Elementary Decision and Evaluation Models 70

IV *TREATMENT OF DECISION ALTERNATIVES (B)*

APPENDIX

Complex Managerial Decisions
Involving
Multiple Objectives

I. INTRODUCTION AND BACKGROUND

1. Concerning Complex Decisions (A)

The two main ideas developed in Chapter 1 are:

1. *Decisions produce changes which affect multiple interests.*

2. *Important decisions must be defensible even if they are largely intuitive.*

DECISIONS AFFECT MULTIPLE INTERESTS

The Influencer and the Influenced

A large proportion of decisions made by individuals, families, groups, governmental agencies, profit and non-profit organizations will profoundly affect the daily lives of many citizens, interest groups, business firms, and other entities. Of course, the extent and intensity of the impact may be insignificant, if these decisions are about trivial matters; but if the decisions are nontrivial, the influence on others may range from substantial to overwhelming, from beneficial to harmful, or from temporary to permanent.

Nearly all moderately active persons in contemporary society act in both individual and organizational roles. These activists' decisions tend to have far-reaching effects because of their many roles, and within each role, because of the large numbers of other persons and interests that are subject to their influence.

You may recognize Mr. Gordon Roberts as perhaps an extreme but by no means rare example of the influential man (see Box 1–1). Mr. Roberts has

---

Box 1–1   Gordon Roberts, Influential Man

Mr. Gordon Roberts, age 45, B.A., M.B.A., L.L.B., holds an important position as executive vice-president of a large industrial firm. He is also a husband and father of four children; he contributes to the support of several relatives; he is moderately active in the PTA, a political club, his church, and a country club. He serves on the board of trustees of the local hospital, the civic association, a charitable fund-raising organization, and the town boosters club. He belongs to three alumni associations, two professional societies, one fraternal organization, all of whose meetings he attends if time permits. He is an officer in his industry trade association and from time to time serves on industry committees. In addition, if his busy schedule permits, he accepts temporary assignments for worthwhile causes, such as co-chairman of the Community Chest drive. Each of the above roles has its relative importance in Gordon Roberts' life scheme; within each role are levels of influence.

The most demanding is his leadership role with his firm. There he is responsible directly to the president and through him to the board of directors, and indirectly to various classes of security holders. Beneath him on the authority ladder are junior officers, division and department heads, and employees on several lower levels. His job also requires that he be involved with several major customers, some suppliers, an advertising agency, trade unions, competitors, and others. Just how far his influence extends depends on the specific matter he is involved in at any instant of time.

---

several roles and many levels of influence, as is shown schematically in Figure 1–1. If he were to decide, as he often wistfully wishes he could, to

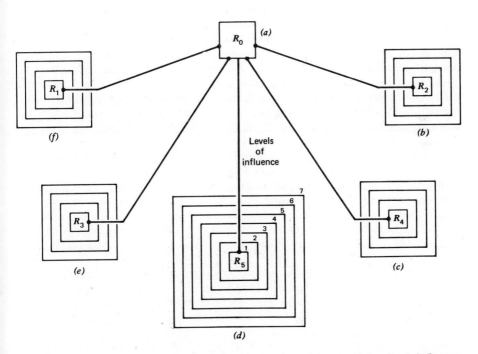

FIGURE 1–1. Gordon Roberts with five of his roles with several levels of influence shown for each role: (a) Gordon Roberts (himself); (b) Gordon Roberts (husband and father); (c) Gordon Roberts (civic association executive); (d) Gordon Roberts (executive vice-president); (e) Gordon Roberts (hospital trustee); (f) Gordon Roberts (trade association executive).

take a two-year leave of absence from his job, and to travel around the world, solo, by oxcart, literally thousands of persons would have their lives affected in some way. It is easy to see, therefore, that many of Gordon Roberts' other decisions, business and personal, may affect a multiplicity of interests.

Not only do active people exert wide influence over many other persons and interests, but they, too, are subject to pressures of multiple influences. Their behavior must be designed to satisfy the many diverse demands made on them; their personal and organizational decisions are mainly determined by both the immediate and potential pressures that they feel. For example, consider the case of Sam Jones, an industrial buyer in Gordon Roberts' firm. Sam has an important job that can affect the profitability of his firm, but he has very limited discretion in setting buying strategy. The engineering department sets forth in great detail the specifications of the items to be purchased and requires that vendors have engineering approval before orders can be placed with them. Delivery dates are set by production control as are the quantities and rates of shipment. Inspection standards are controlled by the inspection department; payments are under the jurisdiction of the accounts payable section. Within these limits, Sam Jones can exercise residual discretion of price determination and choice among approved vendors.

Although Sam Jones' job has many routine aspects, he works under severe pressures. Good business planning requires that purchasing be given adequate lead time to bring in the needed materials, but often adequate lead time is not permitted because of last-minute engineering changes or rejections of incoming material by incoming inspection. Accounts payable may have overlooked paying some invoices and thus may have caused an interruption in deliveries. He may be badgered by the controller's department for permitting the inventory of purchased materials to grow too fast in anticipation of production and then may be criticized by the production manager for not getting materials into the plant soon enough to allow for delays in receiving and stockroom procedures. A representative from the front office clamors for extra savings in purchasing costs to offset a cost rise in another sector of the business. Telephones are ringing all day, people are waiting to see him, expediters are rushing to and fro, and papers are flying; this is a typical day in the working life of Sam Jones. The working buyer habitually wears a harried expression that belies the oft-heard comment, "Those buyers have a soft job. All they do all day is go out to lunch in fancy restaurants with salesmen."

Very important men in Sam Jones' life are the vendors' salesmen. These men use the personal relationship they build up with buyers as part of their sales appeal. Sam is showered with attention by the salesmen. He receives Christmas gifts and, when he permits it, is entertained lavishly. To the salesman, Sam is a "great guy." Sam may be greeted with envy, mistrust, or suspicion by other members of the firm, but by his salesmen, he is made to feel that he can do no wrong. If Sam has ambivalent feelings toward the company, he can always find sympathy and compassion from the vendors' salespeople.

Decisions Produce Changes That Affect People[1]

Individual and group reactions to change can be widely varied depending on how the impact of the changes are perceived. The decision maker may encounter strong, perhaps violent, resistance. At the other extreme, he may be met with enthusiastic acceptance; or he may encounter apathy and outright indifference.

As a first approximation, those who benefit from the changes wrought by the decision can be expected to be less resistant and more accepting; those who consider themselves as worse off, more resistant; those who are relatively unaffected, indifferent. But experience has shown that the foregoing simple expectations are often false. Changes may upset many cherished arrangements and create anxieties and hostility even among those who ostensibly benefit from them. Changes can produce deep-seated psychological responses that cannot be explained by the benefit-contribution disequilibrium alone.

Status relationships are altered. Losses in status, both relative and absolute, actual or potential are unwelcome. Power possessed by individuals and groups may be threatened. This power is cherished and any new arrangement that tends to reduce it will be resisted. The specter of change evokes fears of loss of security and visions of being forced into new and unfamiliar behavior.

Resistance to change can be expected even from persons who, superficially, might appear to benefit.* This may seem irrational to the decision maker who has carefully calculated the benefits to all affected parties, but it should not be totally unexpected. He may have overlooked the possibility that some groups may benefit more than others. Often one group's gain is seen as another's loss even if they both seem better off to the unsophisticated observer. Groups may have strong feelings about parity with other groups, and any change that upsets the parity will be resisted. For example, an employee who has requested a $1000 per annum increase in salary may be delighted when he gets that amount, but when he discovers that one of his fellow employees who until then earned the same salary as he, received a $1500 increase, his glee will turn to disappointment and even anger. The principle of relative deprivation operates when the groups watch each others' gains and losses produced by the change and assess their relative as well as their absolute standings.

Mistrust by the persons affected by the change may cause suspicion about the motivation behind the decision. Simple oversights may be interpreted as coldly deliberate slights. Conspiracy theories gain currency and credence and cause thoroughly beneficial change proposals to be greeted with resistance and outright sabotage.

Although many of the hostile responses to well-intentioned changes may seem completely irrational, the decision maker should not be too quick to

* For an example of how this can happen see Case I-III.

condemn these reactions. The fears may be quite justified if the decision's consequences were insufficiently explored, if important interests were overlooked or given insufficient weight; if there is substantial disagreement on the priorities or urgencies. The individuals and groups who must suffer the impact of the changes may have had more unpleasant experiences with the results of narrowly focused decisions than the man who is making the decision. They may be wiser than he is.

Identify Interests

Aside from the obvious concern for the ultimate impact of a decision, the responsibility one feels for the welfare of the various persons and interests that would be affected is largely a matter of individual or organizational conscience and philosophy. It would probably not be conducive either to good mental health or to effective functioning to become intensely concerned with even the remotest adverse influence. It is easy to see how overconcern could become inhibiting or even incapacitating.

At the other extreme, more undesirable perhaps than overconcern, is the situation in which all interests but one's own are neglected and decisions are made on the narrowest possible grounds with the shortest time horizon. Many real-life decisions are made just this way, and a distressingly large percentage of them are probably followed by "unanticipated consequences."

It is therefore essential to ascertain which interests are important and must be factored into the decision problem, and which may be safely ignored. The only reliable way to answer these questions is, for each decision problem, to identify the multiple interests and to make a reasoned judgment of their relative urgencies.

Undoubtedly, a very difficult part of estimating the impact of decisions on the various interests is to judge the meanings and values others will place on the decision consequences. It would be rash to assume that one person's valuation judgments, the decision maker's, for example, would be sufficiently reliable. It helps immeasurably to develop the ability to understand and anticipate others' reactions, but failing in this superhuman ability, alternative methods must be employed.

The merger and acquisition movement that swept the United States in the 1960s provided many examples of profound changes in corporate ownership that were brought about with financial consideration paramount. The flood of divestitures in the following decade revealed that many of these marriages were ill-conceived; that the partners could not live together in harmony; that they had overlooked important factors in their zeal to exploit the dubious advantages of "pooling of interest" accounting (see Box 1–2).

Box 1–2   A Note on Mergers and Acquisitions

It is quite possible (and indeed it often happens) to effect a corporate merger or acquisition with primary, even exclusive attention given to the interests of the controlling stockholders and the other primary claimants (bondholders, debenture-holders, preferred stockholders, et cetera). Many such mergers have undoubtedly been completed and there is relatively little hard data available on how they fared afterward. One wonders if these marriages were completely successful. Did they live happily ever after? Or were some of them fraught with unanticipated consequences?

After the merger has been completed, after the lawyers, the accounts, the underwriters have interested themselves in other things, the merged organization must still live out its destiny. It must face the process of digestion and realignment of interest group demands. It must deal with at least two sets of claimants from the marriage partners who constitute the components of the merged entity. To avoid bruising internal conflicts, lawsuits, governmental attack, tax problems, dealer dissatisfaction, distributor dissatisfaction, work stoppages, community harassment, loss of personnel to competitors, and the like, all of which sap the vitality of the new entity, defensive measures must be undertaken. Better yet, proper anticipatory planning should precede the actual merger arrangements.

*   *   *

In summary, in instituting organizational change as a consequence of a corporate merger or acquisition, the leadership group may take either the *narrow* or the *broad* view. In the narrow view, the fewest possible alterations in organizational arrangements, benefit distributions, and required contributions are involved. Attention is focused on financial matters, exchange rates, tax considerations, aggrandisement of key executives, or controlling persons. Little time is spent in tracing the effects of the new arrangements on the broader organization or on the claimants, external to the firm, or on indirect or less visible interests. Direct effects of the change are noted, but the more subtle indirect effects are ignored.

In the broader view, the probable effects of the exchange on all of the firm's claimants are considered. Predictions are made on the probable reactions, both immediate and delayed, of claimant groups. Attempts are made to obtain a reasonable compromise that represents "simple justice" for all claimants. The relative positions of the various claimants will not be unacceptably altered. If necessity demands that the interests of one claimant group be downgraded relative to others, contingency measures are planned to deal with the inevitable conflict.

Source. Allan Easton, "Is Organization Theory Helpful in the Study of Corporate Mergers?" in Allan Easton and Arnold Broser (eds.), *Current Problems in Mergers and Acquisitions* (New York, Hofstra University Press, 1970) pp. 122–126.

Public and Quasi-public Hearings

Businessmen tend to be hypercritical about the management methods employed by governmental agencies but, in one respect, public and governmental bodies employ a superior technique for anticipating and resolving intergroup conflict. They use the *public hearing*. In such hearings, all interested parties are invited to state their positions. Although public officials do not always heed the protestations of interest groups, they do become aware of all the contending forces at work in the proposed change. When issues become complex and the decisions affect the lives of many people or firms, the public hearing is probably the most reliable tool for eliciting the meanings of the prospective decision for the parties at interest.

The public hearing technique is not widely used in private, nongovernmental organizations mainly because of the real or fancied need for secrecy, but partial substitutes are sometimes employed. The committee meeting, the staff meeting, the general membership meeting, and the "bull session" are some of the devices used to arrive at an estimate of the probable effects of decisions. However, these substitute techniques will prove inferior to the full-blown public hearing if they tend to be narrowly focused on only a small fraction of the interests likely to be affected by the decision.

IMPORTANT DECISIONS MUST BE DEFENSIBLE

A Formal Defense May Be Required

Don't worry if you are having difficulty in selecting a necktie of the right color and pattern to go with the new suit you have chosen to wear to the stockholders' meeting. You probably will not have to face a court of inquiry that will second-guess your sartorial decisions. But, you must be fully prepared to defend your site-selection decision before a congressional committee made up of disappointed and, perhaps, hostile legislators if you are the chairman of the Atomic Energy Commission and must select a site for the installation of a $350,000,000 particle accelerator.[2] You might someday have to defend yourself in a malpractice suit if you are a physician who has been daring enough to try a controversial new drug on a desperately ill patient. Or, if you are the contracting officer in charge of M-16 rifle procurement and you have awarded the contract for 500,000 rifles to a firm that was not the lowest bidder, you must expect to be challenged and must anticipate being asked why the lowest bidder did not get the contract award.[3]

Many decisions that involve large quantities of money, that may affect human life, that variously affect the well-being of contending claimant groups will require justification and, perhaps, a formal defense. In some kinds of decisions the nature of the circumstances virtually guarantees that a defense must be available for presentation at any time. In the particle accelerator location problem, it is certain that there will be an uproar in Congress no matter where the final site is to be, because of the 100 senators and 435 representatives, there can be no more than two senators and one congressman who will be pleased by the siting choice. An engineer who designs a bridge must routinely submit his design calculations or have them always available for examination as a justification of his material and structural decisions.

Decision Reports and Documentation*

Good professional practice requires that written reports be offered to substantiate recommendations and to justify decisions on weighty matters. These reports should contain a step-by-step explication of the considerations that led to the adoption of the final recommendations and to the rejection of other alternatives. Just how elaborate these documents should be depends, of course, on the importance of the decision and on the custom peculiar to the situation.[4]

In the case of important personal decisions, the formal report is obviously an absurdity. But even here, some pencil and paper work in defining, delineating, and recording the decision steps help in the making of better-reasoned decisions.

In a business or organizational situation, economic considerations require that heedless costs incurred for justification of routine decisions be held to a minimum. It would clearly be too easy to be carried away with the practice of covering one's tracks if an atmosphere of fear prevails, and if written defenses are routinely demanded for all decisions.

Personal Consequences of Hasty Decisions

Almost every organization has formal and informal methods for evaluating the quality of important decisions. These methods may involve reviews by superiors, by outside consultants or auditors, by dissident interest groups, by parties adversely affected by the decision, by peers, or by ambitious subordinates who "second-guess" the decisions. Therefore, it may not be enough that a specific decision produce a workable, good-enough solution, or even a moderately profitable solution. It is necessary, more often than not, that the best possible solution be adopted. It is not wise to succumb to the temptation of adopting the first action that appears to meet the decision objections (see Box 1–3).

Box 1–3   Howard Smith's Savings Proposal

Howard Smith was assigned the problem of making a cost saving in the manufacture of a small appliance, and after some work he presented his superior, Mr. Jarrett, with a proposal that promised a savings of $12,000 per

---

* See Part I Appendix entitled, "Outline of a Decision Report."

month. Mr. Jarrett was delighted with Smith's proposal, and although too busy to check Smith's work, he ordered Smith's recommendations implemented. Smith modestly accepted Jarrett's congratulations on a job well done.

Lurking in the wings was the crafty Arthur Davis, a young designer who sometimes served as Smith's assistant. Davis was ambitious and hoped either to be promoted or to be given Smith's job. Davis studied Smith's working papers and made careful cost estimates on several of the alternatives that Smith had uncovered but had not pursued. He discovered the following:

Alternative Design Change Proposal	Net Savings That Could Be Realized (per Month)
A_1	$55,000
A_2	75,000
A_3	(15,000) loss
A_4	12,000[a]
A_5	80,000

[a] Smith's choice

Davis discovered also that Smith had fully costed out only alternatives A_3 and A_4, apparently then deciding that A_4 was satisfactory. Davis observed that, in fact, Smith had chosen one of the less desirable alternatives, even though the one chosen did result in substantial savings.

Armed with this new insight and detailed cost data on the other alternatives, Davis requested a meeting with Mr. Jarrett. He pointed out to Mr. Jarrett that the company could save an additional $60,000 or $65,000 per month if one of Davis' proposals were adopted.

Mr. Jarrett was impressed with Davis' acuity and initiative and began to wonder if his earlier favorable opinion about Smith was mistaken. He began to wonder if old Smithie hadn't lost some of his flair and ambition. He wondered why Smith hadn't seen the obvious advantages of the Davis proposals. Jarrett thanked Davis and promised him a substantial cash bonus if the proposals produced the promised savings. From that day on, Smith's standing in the firm went into a decline.

The example of "Old Smith" in Box 1–3 has an important moral. The solution to the problem must not only be good, in most instances, it must be demonstrably the best. For when less than the best alternative is selected, the decision maker and his decisions become vulnerable to attack from those who would benefit from showing that better solutions were available than the one adopted if only reasonable care and competence had been employed in dealing with the problem.

Use of Judgment Unavoidable

To say that a decision must be defensible is not to say that judgment may not be used in arriving at that decision. For example, if the chairman of the Atomic Energy Commission had been challenged on the relative weights he had assigned to the several criteria used in evaluating the alternative sites, he could probably have sustained his claim that it was within his discretion to make such judgments. Perhaps he would have been only mildly challenged on his judgments of what constituted relevant criteria for site evaluation. However, if he had used intuitive methods for scoring the alternative sites on the evaluation criteria, he could have expected strong criticism because Congress would expect hard facts and data to be used there.

Thus, there is usually room for the use of intuition or judgment in part of the decision procedure and there is a need for hard data in other parts. A successful defense or justification can better be sustained if the challenging parties are convinced that each was properly used, that the facts were honestly reported, and that the mix of fact and judgment was reasonable.

Preference for Rationality

There is a definite belief in both scientific and administrative circles that rationality in decision making is preferred to nonrationality; that the use of judgment and intuition is undesirable except as a last resort. For rational decisions,[5] the reasoning processes are capable of definition and explication; for intuitive decisions, the thinking processes are either imperfectly understood or completely unknown. Rational decisions are, therefore, easier to explain and defend even if they may really be no better than intuitive decisions.

Since intuitive decisions and, more particularly, impulsive decisions defy analysis, there is a much greater possibility that emotions, biases, attitudes, and predispositions will influence or dominate the process. The decision maker may be victimized by his own "devils," which act to confuse and bewilder him. Deep-seated psychological factors may tend to distort his thinking; he may not take time to consider and absorb important data; he may unknowingly block out important facts. And because decisions of this kind are made inside the psyche, it is not possible to obtain the benefits that would come from subjecting the reasoning process to outside scrutiny.

In spite of their obvious risks, we cannot be certain that intuitive decisions are inevitably inferior to rational decisions, just because of their nonrationality. As the reader will discover for himself, there are many opportunities for the introduction of emotion-laden value judgments and bias into the most "rational" of decision processes. At its best, decision making is as much an art as it is a science, particularly for unstructured policy decisions affecting multiple interests.

And there are great artists in this field as well as inept practitioners. It is quite possible for a skillful and experienced decision maker to make consistently better decisions with his ill-defined intuition than can the novice with the best available scientific methodology. But, of course, all, from the novice to the master, can do better if they use superior methods.

It is the fact that the reasoning process underlying intuitive decisions is unknown (and perhaps unknowable) that accounts for everyone's suspicion and lack of confidence. The executive's subordinates, superiors, and peers may have great faith in his ability without knowing how he works, but others will be unwilling to rely on faith. Instead they insist on documentation, proof, evidence, supporting data, and so on. For example, very few building departments will issue building permits on the strength of the faith in the architect; no court of inquiry investigating a bridge disaster will accept faith as a substitute for detailed design calculations; no congressional committee will accept the contracting officer's choice of the highest bidder's offer over that of the lowest bidder on faith alone.

Thus, there are many circumstances, particularly in an organizational or political setting, where intuitive processes are simply not admissible. In such cases, the ability to skillfully explicate a decision from beginning to end may be saving of lives, assets, reputations, prestige, and personal freedom, even if it should appear that judgment played a substantial part in the handling of the intangibles.

Bias Inevitable

It is rarely possible to make decisions, evaluations, or ratings that are completely free from inherent discrimination of some kind. Bias may be introduced into the process in many ways: when exercising a choice of which criteria to include and exclude, in the quantification of data, in probability estimation, in forecasting outcomes, and in weighing objectives. Many decision subprocesses are subject to subtle or gross bias.

Whether through ignorance or carelessness, many decision makers appear to overlook the inherent bias in their methods. They use the techniques with which they are most comfortable or familiar without any real concern for their fairness. This freewheeling practice may produce unfortunate consequences in exceptional circumstances when the decision maker is called on to defend his decision from attack by advocates of rejected or disfavored alternatives who typically contend that their low scores were the outcome of biased or unfair methods that were maliciously employed to the disadvantage of their clients.

If bias is inevitable, the best the decision maker can do is to make the bias explicit and to account for its effects. Then the consequences of the bias can be better understood and, most important, the decision maker will not deceive himself. This would be no slight accomplishment.

Notes and References

1. For a collection of articles dealing with many aspects of change in an organizational setting, see W. G. Bennis, K. D. Benne, and R. Chinn (eds.), *The Planning of Change* (New York, Holt, Rinehart and Winston, Inc., 1969).

2. See "Hamlet West of Chicago Chosen over 200 Rivals," *The New York Times,* Dec. 17, 1966, p. 1.

3. See "Senators Question Army on Awarding of Rifle Contracts," *The New York Times* September 5, 1968, p. 40.

4. Any good work on technical writing can be used to assist in the preparation of decision reports. For example, see Harold F. Graves and Lyne S. S. Hoffman, *Report Writing,* 4th ed. (Englewood Cliffs, New Jersey: Prentice-Hall, Inc., 1965).

5. For a discussion of rationality in decisions see I. J. Good, "How Rational Should A Manager Be?" *Management Science*, Vol. 8, No. 4 (July 1966), pp. 383–393 and bibliography.

Important Words and Concepts

Multiple interests
Decisions
Individual role
Organizational role
Multiple influences
Levels of influence
Resistance to change
Benefit-contribution disequilibrium
Parity
Principle of relative deprivation
Priorities
Unanticipated consequences
Valuation judgments
Intergroup conflict
Public hearing
Narrowly focused decision
Formal defense
Intuition
Rationality
Bias

Overview of Chapter 1

Decisions affect multiple interests. Nearly all moderately active persons act in both individual and organizational roles. It is essential to ascertain which interests must be given priority and which can be safely ignored, but it is difficult to estimate how others will view the impact of the decision on their own interests. The public hearing or some adaptation are good ways for eliciting the probable impacts on the interested parties. Decisions produce changes and change creates fears and anxieties that produce resistance and hostility. The resistance may seem irrational and unrelated to the actual benefit changes but must be anticipated.

Decisions that involve weighty matters must be defensible. Good professional practice requires that documentation be prepared even if the decision is found to involve exercise of judgment.

Although rationality is preferred to nonrationality in decision making, rational decisions are not necessarily better. The need for explication and for convincing others favors rational methods. Bias appears to be inevitable in many parts of the decision process and, if possible, it should be made explicit to avoid self-deception.

Questions for Review, Discussion, and Research

Review

1. When making decisions, why is each person or organization both the influencer and the influenced?

2. Can you think of any important personal decisions you have made that did not affect persons other than yourself?

3. Can you think of an important business decision you made or observed that did not affect multiple claimant groups?

4. Why do you think people tend to resist change?

5. What is a public hearing and what are its advantages?

6. Why do business firms fail to make use of the public-hearing technique?

7. Under what circumstances do you think a formal defense of a decision would be required?

8. When will a "good enough" decision suffice and when will only the best do?

9. Under what circumstances is the use of judgment and intuition justified when making decisions?

10. Why is there a preference for rationality over nonrationality in decision making?

11. Are rational decisions always better than nonrational decisions?

12. Can you think of any decision methods you have used or have seen used that contain inadvertent biases?

Discussion

1. Do you think Mr. Jarrett was justified in rewarding Davis and losing his good opinion of Smith?

2. Do you think that Sam Jones was justified in his attitude toward his employer and toward the salesmen who call on him?

3. Do you think that firms involved in merger negotiations should go beyond the usual matter of financial exchanges of securities and be concerned with people who do not have a financial stake in the firms?

4. Why should the president of a business firm care what other people think of his decisions?

Research

1. Attend a public hearing in your community and report on the way the interests of the various parties were revealed.

2. Find a particular example of resistance to change and explore the reasons behind the resistance. Interview the people involved and relate their positions to the objectives of the decision.

3. Select a fairly simple decision you have made or have been involved in and prepare an explication and defense as if you were expecting a serious challenge.

4. Examine the details of a past corporate merger that was followed by one or more divestitures. Can you identify any of the basic reasons why these divestitures were necessary?

5. Search among your acquaintances, friends, or family for persons in positions analogous to Gordon Roberts and Sam Jones. Prepare a chart showing the extent of their influence on others and the pressures under which they operate.

2. Concerning Complex Decisions (B)

The four main ideas developed in Chapter 2 are:

1. Assumptions are required about the nature of the decision environment.

2. Decision making involves several kinds of costs.

3. Decisions affect future events, require good timing, are influenced by the decision maker's time sense.

4. Creativity is required for good decision.

THE DECISION ENVIRONMENT

Assumptions Required about the Nature of the System

The state of the system in which decisions are being made and in which their consequences will emerge cannot be fully understood by mortal man. Philosophers disagree in their world views, but practical men must make some assumptions about the nature of the decision environment if they are to make meaningful decisions about matters that will affect the future.

Several of the alternative assumptions that can be made are shown in Box 2–1. The appropriateness of an assumption depends on the decision

---

Box 2–1   Seven Assumptions About the Decision Environment

1. The system is completely random and, therefore, totally unpredictable. Events occur purely by chance and any conceivable outcome is as likely as any other. Prediction is a fruitless endeavor. The decision climate is pure and unrelieved uncertainty and total instability.

2. The system is subject to certain laws which are imperfectly understood and is simultaneously subject to large random influences. Uncertainty

dominates, but some small element of predictability is present and research into the behavior of the system will give worthwhile returns. Some stability can be assumed with a large component of noise.

3. The system is completely determinate and lawful but only a fraction of the independent variables are under the decision maker's control. The controllable variables are well understood, but the others, incompletely Some random influences are present but do not dominate. Improvement of knowledge about uncontrollable variables pays off in better forecasts. The system is stable.

4. The system is completely determinate and all but a few random and uncontrollable variables are under the decision maker's control. However, the system is so complex that complete knowledge is impossible because of limitations of time, money, or manpower. Moreover the system contains nonlinearities and, consequently, the relative composition of the input-action mixes is not preserved in the system output. Efforts made to understand the system pay off with better forecasts. The system is stable.

5. The system is determinate and simple enough so that all possible relationships and variations can be explored and predicted with reasonable expenditures of energy. The input-output relationships are reasonably independent because of system linearity. Random influences in the form of occasional accidents are small and infrequent. The decision climate is one of certainty. The system is stable.

6. The system is assumed to be predetermined by some higher power. Man and his works are subject to powerful forces that cannot be deflected. Intervention is futile because man can never change the outcomes. The decision climate is one of uncertainty, but it can be changed to certainty if there is good prognostication. The skills of soothsayers, fortune-tellers, astrologers, and their modern counterparts are highly valued. The system is stable.

7. The system in its present and future states is optimal because God* in His infinite wisdom and goodness could or would not produce anything imperfect. Any criticism, attack, or overt attempt to alter the system that must now be admitted to be perfect, is irreligious, blasphemous, sinful, subversive, or possibly criminal.

---

* For the word, God, substitute "Our Leader" or "His Highness," et cetera.

---

maker's personal world view; on the political, religious, and social climate in which he functions; and on his knowledge, at the time, of the nature of the forces operating on the decision system. It is not necessary that he adhere rigidly and exclusively to any single assumption; the one that best fits the special circumstances should be chosen.

Forecasting the Decision Environment

Although it is customary to think of a forecast as a prophecy, for decision making purposes it is more realistic to define forecasting as the process for making assumptions about the future. We cannot, at this stage of scientific and intellectual development, reliably predict what the future will bring. Seers, clairvoyants, fortune-tellers, or astrologers do not prove sufficiently reliable nor are their productions generally accepted by those parties whom the decision must satisfy.

What we can do is to prepare scenarios with as much detail as seems appropriate to the occasion, bringing into account as many variables as are deemed relevant, which will describe the state of the world as it might be at some future time. If we employ good and careful methods for preparing our scenarios, we shall more and more frequently produce forecasts that bear some resemblance to the actual events as they unfold.

Based on one or more of these general scenarios, the decision maker can produce specific forecasts about the outcomes of alternative courses of action. Of course, if the scenarios he produces are faulty and bear little or no resemblance to actual events, the predictions based on those scenarios will be useless or wholly misleading.

There may not be a single scenario in which we have complete confidence so it may be necessary to prepare several based on different assumptions about the decision system and the course of future events. In such circumstances, the outcomes of alternative courses of action would be predicted for each alternative future. This idea is shown schematically in Figure 2–1.

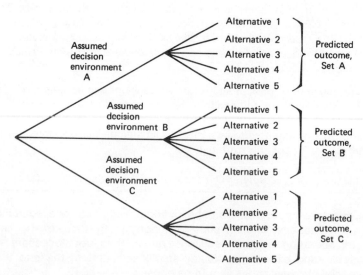

FIGURE 2–1. *A schematic representation of the outcomes of five alternative courses of action in three assumed decision environments.*

General Environmental Factors

Assumptions will also be required on many other environmental factors that in various ways influence the decision climate. A few of them are:

1. Demographic changes.
2. Economic trends.
3. The current business philosophy.
4. Legal and legislative enactments.
5. Social attitudes and practices.
6. Educational trends.
7. Religious attitudes, changes in public morality.
8. War and peace developments.
9. Scientific and technological developments.
10. Political developments.
11. Foreign developments.
12. Health and medical developments.

Claimant Group Demands[1]

Because decisions usually have a broader effect than the expected direct impact, the interests of many claimant groups may require consideration. For example a business firm's decisions may have impact on these groups:

1. Top, middle, and lower management.
2. White-collar, skilled, semi- and unskilled workers.
3. Labor unions.
4. Stockholders and various classes of creditors.
5. Various levels of government.
6. Various classes of professionals.
7. Customers.
8. Suppliers.
9. Local communities.
10. Educational institutions and others.

Or a hospital organization's decisions may have impact on these groups:

1. Medical staff members.
2. Visiting physicians.
3. Nurses of various grades.
4. Semiprofessional and unskilled workers.
5. Administrators and trustees.
6. Donors, fund-raising groups, and volunteers.
7. Categories of actual and potential users.
8. Governmental agencies.

9. Medical insurance firms.
10. Professional societies.
11. Community and political groups.

DECISION-MAKING COSTS

Kinds of Costs

Whether decisions are made by an individual in isolation or by a large task force, the costs associated with the process may be substantial, and may, in fact, be a major determinant of the structure and thoroughness of the process. Although the following list of cost sources is not complete, it does illustrate the extent and variety of decision-making costs.

1. Costs will be incurred by permitting an existing unsatisfactory condition to persist unabated while (a) deciding whether to decide, and (b) while the decision process intended to ameliorate the undesirable condition grinds on to its conclusion. Failure to "stop the flow of blood" may result in large losses while debates go on about the best way to cure the underlying condition.
2. Opportunity costs are present in every situation where decision-making time and capability are limited. There may be more profitable ways to use the scarce time. If so, there will be a cost in terms of income foregone or larger losses incurred by failing to apply the scarce time to more profitable uses.
3. There will be the direct costs associated with the various steps of the decision process including (a) diagnosis, (b) identification of the affected interests, (c) formulation of decision objectives, (d) preparation of detailed specifications and measurement scales, (e) identification of feasible alternatives, and (f) evaluation of alternatives.
4. If a trial-and-error decision process is used, there may be several false starts and decisions implemented that must be rescinded at some expense.
5. If an elaborate defense is required, as for example in anticipation of a court test or a congressional investigation, considerable staff and legal expenditures may be involved.

Limiting Costs

The costs incurred in making decisions must bear some reasonable relationship to the anticipated benefits. A profitable decision is one for which the benefits exceed the cost, but this may not be enough. For a particular benefit level, the cost should be as low as possible; or, conversely, for a particular level of cost, the benefits should be as large as possible.

The allowable costs should also bear a reasonable relationship to the magnitude of the decision, to the length of time the organization will be committed to the decision consequences, and to the ease of making subsequent adjustments should there be unanticipated consequences of an unfavorable nature. Don't make an irreversible, multimillion-dollar decision, one that will affect the lives of many people, with a bare five minutes of contemplation and then spend a full half hour agonizing over your choice of the main course at dinner. It happens that way much too often.

Cost Minimization of Repetitive Decisions

When a personnel manager hires operatives for a production line and uses a test for deciding which applicants to accept or reject, he is exposed to two types of errors:

1. The test will accept unsatisfactory applicants.
2. The test will reject satisfactory applicants.

In the first instance there is the cost of hiring, training, and then discharging unsatisfactory employees. In the second, there is the waste of testing time. By making the test more stringent, he can avoid hiring poor candidates, but he will reject more good people. By making the test more lenient, he will reject fewer good people, but he will accept more potential failures. He seeks a balance that will minimize overall hiring costs.[2]

The United States armed forces have a similar problem with their preinduction physical examinations of potential draftees. If the medical requirements and the accompanying comprehensive examination procedures are very severe, few physically inadequate men will be inducted into the service and some otherwise satisfactory men will be rejected as unfit. On the other hand, if the medical examination is superficial, rarely will a healthy candidate be turned away, but some highly unsuitable men will be inducted and will subsequently be discharged for medical reasons.

In the former case, the cost of medical procedures would be high; in the latter they would be low, but the waste of money for training and clothing candidates with physical defects would be high. According to a story in *The New York Times* for July 28, 1970, the General Accounting Office discovered that the military spent $19.6 million in 1967 and $17.9 million in 1969 for pay, uniforms, and travel for soldiers who were discharged for pre-service defects which, in most instances, could have been detected beforehand by more exhaustive medical examinations. The GAO was unsparing in its criticism of what it characterized as "unnecessary costs" and "waste" of the taxpayers' money.

The military response to this criticism was that the rate of acceptance of candidates with physical defects could be reduced if more comprehensive medical procedures were installed, but the benefits from such a change would probably not be worthwhile in relation to the large cost increases for medical testing. By implication, the military was saying that they had achieved an optimum condition in the testing of potential draftees and that any change either toward or away from greater medical stringency would only raise overall costs.

As these two examples illustrate, there are opportunities for the use of cost-effectiveness and cost-minimization methods with repetitive decision procedures. Unfortunately, when decisions are one of a kind, conventional cost-minimization techniques may not be applicable. For these decisions, it may not be possible to determine which particular method for making the decision is the most economical.

THE TIME FACTOR IN COMPLEX DECISIONS

Decisions Affect Future Events

Every decision that you are making or will make has some influence on the flow of future events. Just as a stone thrown into the water causes ripples that radiate in ever-expanding circles, so a decision implemented today has consequences that spread out over time. With simple decisions, the primary consequences become quickly apparent and the secondary effects may prove to be negligible. With complex decisions on important matters, only a part—perhaps the smallest part—of the effects are promptly apparent to those involved in the decision. By the time the outcomes, responses, counter-responses, and other ramifications become known, the environment will have undergone change, perhaps in accord with expectations, perhaps not. There will always be doubt that the expected outcomes will happen in the environment that was predicted at the time the decision was first made.* One part of the future is determined by the past; the other part is uncertain and unpredictable.

Yet, in spite of the inevitable uncertainty of future events, we must make decisions. We would not endear ourselves to our superiors or to our constituencies if we consistently failed to make the needed decisions because of fear of future uncertainties. The experienced decision maker finds that he must learn to act as if he knows exactly how his decisions will work out. He cultivates an air of quiet confidence, if only to prevent others who depend on his decision-making ability from losing their faith in his ability to cope.

---

* An incident relating to this point is described in Case I-I.

The successful manager has learned that he is not competing against an absolute standard of perfection, but with other equally fallible human beings. He tries to do a better job than the man against whom his performance is being compared.

If his natural caution tells him that his decision, however well intentioned, may turn out badly, he tries to structure the situation so that there will be an opportunity, sooner or later, to take corrective action on the basis of the then current feedback. If it is unavoidable that his decision sets events into motion with little or no chance to make corrective adjustments, he learns to live with his anxieties without permitting them to incapacitate him for the stream of decisions that follow.

He recognizes the need for calm deliberation in considering all stages in the decision process if he knows that his organization must live for a long time with the consequences of his decisions, particularly if they will have weighty impact. He holds himself to limited decisions, whenever possible, and reserves opportunities for reconsideration, especially if the particular decision must be made rapidly or intuitively because of the press of time. He knows that impulsive decisions may be fine for unimportant problems— shall he ride the bus or subway to work, or will he walk? But, impulsiveness may prove disastrous—and is, therefore, indefensible—when he makes decisions with long-lasting ramifications.

Decisions Require Good Timing

Doubt over the correct time to make or implement a decision, to take an appropriate action, or to set plans into motion plays an important part in every manager's working life. The right action taken at the right moment can save the day and deescalate a growing crisis. The same action, applied too soon or too late, can be ineffective, or can even exacerbate an already unsatisfactory situation.

We know very little about what makes for correct timing. The difference between a tennis champion and a merely competent player may lie only in subtle differences in timing of the tennis stroke. The application of a periodic vibration to a mechanical structure can produce wide and perhaps destructive gyrations if the excitation occurs at the resonant frequency of the structure. But the effect is minimal if the frequency of the vibration is far from the natural resonance. Here too, in the mechanical system, timing is the critical factor.

Every employee who has ever wanted to ask his boss for a raise knows the importance of good timing. If his superior is cranky, out of sorts, has just lost a large order, or has just had a quarrel with his wife, his response to the request for a salary increase would probably be less genial than if a time were chosen when he was in good spirits. Executive secretaries owe a large part of their organizational influence to their sensitivity to the moods

of their bosses, and to their ability to provide good timing advice to sup-
plicants.

Successful stock market speculators know the great value of good timing
when buying "long" or selling "short." To consistently buy when prices are
about to fall and to sell when prices are about to rise is evidence of poor
timing. Poor timing causes the hapless investor to replace Bernard Baruch's
advice, "Buy cheap and sell dear," with its obverse, "Buy dear and sell
cheap."

That timing is critical in the affairs of men was recognized by the ancients.
This truth is embodied in Ecclesiastes (see Box 2–2).

Box 2–2   On Correct Timing

   To every thing there is a season, and a time to every purpose under the
heaven;

2. A time to be born, and a time to die; a time to plant and a time to
   pluck up that which is planted.
3. A time to kill, and a time to heal; a time to break down, and a time to
   build up.
4. A time to weep, and a time to laugh; a time to mourn, and a time to
   dance.
5. A time to cast away stones, and a time to gather stones together; a time
   to embrace, and a time to refrain from embracing.
6. A time to get, and a time to lose; a time to keep, and a time to cast away.
7. A time to rend, and a time to sew; a time to keep silence, and a time
   to speak.
8. A time to love, and a time to hate; a time of war, and a time of peace.

Source. Ecclesiastes 3:1.

Many timing decisions lend themselves to precise analysis. The outcome
for alternative time periods or intervals can be predicted and the best time
chosen. For example, the timing of merchandise deliveries for a retailer's
inventory can effect both inventory expense and out-of-stock losses. If he
buys too far ahead, he is faced with storage, borrowing, and insurance costs
that increase as the length of owning time increases. On the other hand, if
he orders too close to demand, he may lose sales because of shortages. He
seeks a delivery time that will produce minimum overall cost.

In other more ambiguous cases, good timing is analogous to good judgment; it comes only from extended training and practice. When a rifleman
shoots at an oscillating pendulum target on a rifle range, he synchronizes his
firing impulse along with the movements of the target. The number of hits
increases as his timing and aim improve. The decision maker also learns
when to take action in a timely fashion.

The Past, Present, and Future Orientations[3]

Decision makers differ in the degree to which their decisions are influenced by their sense of time, by their orientations toward the past, the present, and the future. In the normal person, the three times are usually held in some sort of balance; in other cases, one or two of the three times may tend to dominate.

This phenomenon is illustrated schematically in Figure 2–2. At the top (a) is a pair of curves that represent the time sense at infancy and in early childhood. For the very young, there is no past and no future; there is no history and tomorrow never comes. As the child matures, his perception of the past and of futurity grows. When he reaches maturity his time-sense curve might resemble (e). But there are persons who for deep-seated psychological reasons have unbalanced time perception as is shown in (d) truncated past, (c) truncated future, and (b) both past and future truncated. Boxes 2–3, 2–4, and 2–5 contain profiles of three company employees with

---

Box 2–3   James Martinson—Man with a Fixation Concerning the Past

James Martinson, age 60, is production manager for the Acme Metal Products Company and is an example of an executive whose outlook is dominated by the past. He likes to reminisce about his past successes; today's events are baffling and he deprecates modern methods as pretentious frills. He analyses all present situations in terms of analogies to past experiences. He can often be heard saying, "Why, this problem is just like the one I solved in 1958 when I was manager of the spinning department . . . I suggest we do the same thing for this case. I'll bet it will work out just as well as it did that time."

If Martinson had a bad experience, he is wary of all situations he perceives as being similar. He makes little distinction between what has passed and what is now; and, therefore, never forgives past wrongs. He spends a good deal of time thinking about getting revenge for past injustices.

Martinson's personal investment philosophy is based on the fear of a deep economic depression like the one he lived through from 1929 to 1937. He believes in holding large amounts of cash in anticipation of the stock market crash that will present the same buying opportunities he missed in 1932. He lives an austere life with little or no interest in worldly goods. He believes the future will take care of itself as long as all people practice sound moral principles in their personal, business, and political lives. He loves to attend the meetings of his veterans' association and of the alumni association of his college. He is active in Acme's "old timers" club. When he reads, he prefers historical novels; he despises current events and science fiction. His clothes are old-fashioned because he believes that the old styles are best and the new fashions are "just disgusting." He drives a 10-year-old automobile, which he keeps in superb condition, and buys used cars to avoid the high depreciation and rapid obsolescence associated with new-car ownership.

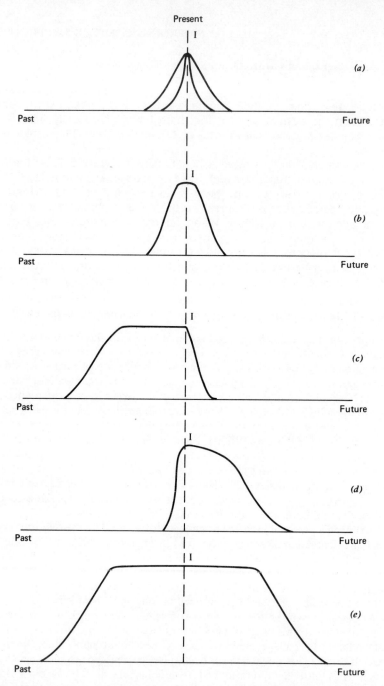

FIGURE 2–2. *Curves for various kinds of time orientation. Vertical scale indicates relative importance, I.* (a) *The inner curve—infancy, the outer curve—childhood;* (b) *the cure for present orientation;* (c) *the curve for past fixation;* (d) *the curve for future fixation; and* (e) *the curve for balanced orientation.*

Box 2-4   Arnold Nestor—A Case of Future Fixation

Arnold Nestor, Acme Products Company's controller, is fixated on the future. He lives in constant fear of having Acme run out of cash. He worries that accounts receivable turnover will be too slow, that raw materials and finished goods inventories will become excessive, that sales will slump, and that expenses will rise. He is constantly trying to upgrade the company's accounts by favoring customers who pay their bills promptly over those who pay more slowly; this in spite of the protests from the sales department.

Nestor worries about the state of the money markets, about meeting interest and sinking fund payments, and about the banks reducing their lines of short-term credit. He believes that the firm should spend its money on real estate to avoid the perils of inflation rather than on plush offices, fancy advertising, and elaborate annual reports.

Like Martinson, Nestor lives an austere existence and saves a large part of his salary for a rainy day. He buys clothes that will not go out of style rapidly; he prefers to spend money on consumer durables rather than on transitory amusements such as the theater, musical concerts, or fine food. When given a choice of compensation arrangements, Nestor chose a deferred plan over larger current income.

Nestor is an avid reader of science fiction but has no interest in history. He believes avidly in astrology and in reincarnation. His religious sect's dogma rests heavily on the idea of an afterlife, resurrection, and other deferred benefits of present sacrifice. Nestor is fond of Martinson and characterizes him as "a fine gentleman of the old school" but ruefully admits that Martinson is awfully hard to convince when it becomes necessary to make a machinery investment with a deferred payoff.

Nestor is chairman of Acme's long-range planning committee and has been praised by Acme's president as "the best damned planner in the company's history."

Box 2-5   Raoul Lagrange—A Case of Fixation on the Present

Raoul Lagrange is Acme Metal Products Company's salesman extraordinaire. Lagrange is a true hedonist; he loves good food and delicate wines; he dresses in the latest fashion. He can usually be found in the latest "in" night spot entertaining a customer in the company of a ravishing "model." Lagrange is contemptuous of both Martinson, whom he calls an old fogey, and Nestor, whom he calls a worrywart. He thinks of himself as one of the "beautiful people."

Lagrange is a supreme optimist and a thoroughgoing pragmatist. He eschews theories and relies on his hypersensitive intuition to tell him how to deal with any situation. He does not worry about the future, but spends every dollar that he earns. He believes that he will always be able to earn his way regardless of the state of the economy. "There is always a place for a good salesman," he says. For Lagrange, history is irrelevant and the future not worth worrying about. "Why worry about what will happen?" he asks. "The Bomb will go boom and we will all be vaporized. One of these days I will be gone, but who knows when and how? Until then, I live."

` Lagrange has several times turned down a promotion to sales manager. He has been completely cheerful about the promotion of a junior and less successful salesman to sales manager and, therefore, to become his superior. "All that planning and record-keeping would drive me up the wall," Lagrange answered when he was asked why he refused the promotion. "I like my job just the way it is. I threatened to quit and go to work for a competitor if they insisted that I take the sales manager's job."

Lagrange refused to participate in Acme's pension plan and employee stock option plan. He expressed a preference for increased current income in place of these deferred compensation devices. His time horizon is short, and he likes to be rewarded in the "here and now" for all of his successes. For Lagrange, the future will never arrive.

---

truncated time senses. Perhaps Martinson (Box 2–3), Nestor (Box 2–4), and Lagrange (Box 2–5) represent extreme examples of individuals whose out-looks on life are dominated by either the past, the present, or the future, and not a balanced combination. But, although they are extreme cases, persons like them are by no means rare. Many persons with recognizably similar tendencies can be found in all large organizations. If these people translate their personal propensities into their organizational decision-making roles, the quality of their decisions will reflect their fixations.*

CREATIVITY IN DECISION MAKING

Decisions Demand Creativity

There are few human activities that demand higher levels of creativity than the complex decision making that involves multiple objectives.[4] No one can be oversupplied with this scarce attribute of personality.

In the decision-making context, creativity involves these factors:

1. The ability to cast off inhibitions, prejudice, fear, and the love of previous solutions.
2. The willingness to open one's mind to new ideas and experiences; to broaden one's perception, to transcend previous limitations.
3. The ability to understand human motivation in its infinite variety.
4. The ability to make novel arrangements from familiar ideas and objects; to improvise.

* See Case I-II for an example of how one executive's short time horizon affected his firm's welfare.

5. The ability to cast aside stereotypes and to recognize that despite superficial similarities, every life situation has its essential uniqueness.

Opportunities for creative exercise abound in each stage of the decision process, but particularly in the following stages.

1. The diagnosis.
2. The identification and statement of objectives.
3. The identification and construction of feasible alternatives.
4. The measurement and prediction of alternative outcomes.
5. The implementation in the face of entrenched resistance to change.

Creativity in Group Decisions

It has become fashionable to deprecate group decisions and to substitute the fantasy of the decision maker who arrives at great and creative decisions in isolation (perhaps floating in a warm bath). Some great decisions may have been generated under these conditions, but in many more instances the decision maker finds that he is "situation bound." He finds that his mind becomes locked in on just a few possibilities and that he is then unable to break out and think of other alternatives or to view the problem in a fresh light. In such circumstances, consultation with others may help him to unlock his situation-boundedness and permits wider-ranging, more creative thought.

Various techniques have been devised for eliciting creative ideas from groups of people acting in concert, for example, Alex F. Osborne's "brainstorming."[5] Experiments conducted in executive training sessions for middle managers show that the number of alternative solutions elicited can be multiplied tenfold with a group working together compared to the average number conceived by men in isolation. Not all the ideas generated in such sessions will be feasible, but a number of surprisingly good alternatives often emerge from a group endeavor that did not appear on any one participant's list.

Executives develop tricks for prodding their creativity which seem to work well for them. Some prefer to leave a problem altogether when they feel blocked and return to it when they are fresher. With the passage of time, the mental set that previously blocked their thought processes may disappear. Others use their associates as "sounding boards." They hear their own ideas discussed and rehashed by the group, and they are able to see their ideas in a different frame of reference.

Notes and References

1. See Allan Easton, "Claimantship versus Membership as Organizational Constructs," *Journal of Human Relations*, Vol. 17, No. 1 (1st Q. 1969) pp.

71–76, and Richard Eells and Clarence Walton, *Conceptual Foundations of Business,* rev. ed. (Homewood, Illinois, Richard D. Irwin, Inc. 1969) pp. 162–187 and bibliography.

2. For a comprehensive treatment of this subject in the context of personnel testing see Lee J. Chronback and Goldine C. Gleser, *Psychoogical Tests and Personnel Decisions* (Urbana, Illinois, University of Illinois Press, 1957).

3. A wide-ranging discussion of time as a factor in human psychology is contained in Joost A. M. Meerloo, *Along the Fourth Dimension* (New York, The John Day Co., 1970).

4. See M. O. Edwards, "Solving Problems Creatively," *Systems and Procedures Journal* (January–February 1966), pp. 16–24 and bibliography for an excellent overview of methods for stimulating and eliciting creativity in individual and group decision making.

5. Alex F. Osborne, *Applied Imagination* (New York, Chas. Scribner & Son, 1963).

Important Words and Concepts

Decision environment
System
Stability
Prediction
Forecasting
Indeterminacy
Controllable variable
System nonlinearity
Scenarios
Alternative futures
Claimant group demands
Opportunity costs
Benefits
Cost minimization
Cost effectiveness
Timing
Past fixation
Future fixation
Present fixation
Truncated time sense
Creativity
Brainstorming
Situation boundedness

Overview of Chapter 2

Assumptions are required about the decision environment, about general environmental factors, and about the interests of various claimant groups. Forecasts are incorporated into scenarios that describe the decision maker's vision of the future state of the environment.

The decision-making process involves costs that must be considered and limited whenever possible. Cost minimization techniques are more applicable to repetitive methods than to nonrecurring types of decisions.

Decisions involve future events; but even if the future is unknowable, decisions often cannot be deferred. Performance in decision making is judged not on the basis of absolute standards but in comparison with other's results and techniques. Decisions require good timing and a proper psychological balance among past, present, and future orientation.

Decision making demands the utmost creativity. Group methods can often be used to raise individual creativity.

Questions for Review, Discussion, and Research

Review

1. Why is it necessary to make assumptions about the state of the decision environment?

2. What difference would it make whether the system were indeterminate or determinate?

3. Is it still possible to make workable decisions if the decision maker is faced with many uncontrollable variables?

4. Why is it necessary or desirable to prepare more than one scenario containing assumptions about the general environment and claimant group demands?

5. Which of these costs do you think would be the greatest: the cost of waiting before deciding, the opportunity costs, the direct costs, or the cost of rescinding an unsatisfactory action?

6. How would you go about trying to limit the costs associated with a particular decision?

7. Why is the user of a selection test always faced with two types of errors?

8. Why do decisions usually affect future events?

9. Everyone knows that the future is unpredictable; how is it possible for managers to make long-term decisions?

10.   What is meant by good timing in decisions?

11.   In what way would a truncated time sense affect an individual's decisions?

Discussion

1.   Do you think that decision making demands more or less creativity than other business activities? Why?

2.   Which of the alternative states of the decision environment do you think is most descriptive of your personal life situation? Why?

3.   Since the personnel manager or the military examiner cannot completely eliminate the two types of selection errors, in your opinion which type of error should be given greater emphasis? Why?

4.   Is it possible to accurately account for all decision-making costs? Why or why not?

Research

1.   Prepare a scenario suitable for a decision to buy a personal residence.

2.   Prepare a report on the differences between the "Fundamentalists" and the "Chartists" in the stock market investment community.

3.   Study a specific decision in an organization to which you have access and prepare a recapitulation of all recognizable decision-making costs.

4.   Select some familiar object (for example, an eggbeater) or some other product category or material and organize a brainstorming session on the possible applications of the object. Before the formal session starts, ask each participant to record his application ideas and compare these lists with the results of the group effort.

CASES *for part one*

APPENDIX *to part one*

CASE I-I
The Davis Company Purchases a Stamping Press

SUMMARY: A decision to purchase a large stamping press has some unanticipated consequences.

The Davis Division of the Standard Metal Products Corp. (name fictitious) is managed by Mr. Avery Timmons, vice-president and general manager. Mr. Timmons has complete profit responsibility and an incentive bonus based on the rate-of-return on total assets used in the division.

After a considerable investigation which included a complete return-on-investment study, Mr. Timmons decided to authorize the purchase of an immense stamping press that would permit the firm to make large savings in factory labor, floor space, and raw materials (because of less waste and spoilage). The division's engineers estimated that the machine would have a useful life of more than twenty years and could be delivered and installed ready for use within two years from the date of issuance of the purchase order. No interruption in the delivery schedules of stampings was anticipated. The financing of the new press was arranged by means of a long-term loan from an insurance company.

Five years after the new machine was installed and used successfully, Mr. Timmons was interviewed by a graduate student doing research in industrial purchasing techniques at the local business school. During the interview these facts emerged:

1. The decision obviously involved a long-term commitment with the expected benefits to be realized over a twenty-year interval.

2. Some of the immediate consequences of the decision became readily apparent: for instance, a reduction of the labor force, savings in raw materials, increased sales and profits, savings in floor space, and the ability to sell stampings at lower prices. In fact, the short-term economic benefits were nearly as predicted by the engineers at the outset.

3. Some of the indirect consequences emerged slowly and several proved to be unpleasant surprises. There was a very high noise level in the vicinity of the new machine which interfered with the work of adjacent departments. Extensive and costly sound and vibration insulation was installed, but the noise and vibration could not be reduced enough for comfort. A long drawn-out court battle erupted when the utility company that supplied the power attempted to construct a larger generating plant and the residents of the area objected. In the interim, because of the large power surges, there were complaints from the nearby residents

about poor television performance. The exasperation of the community was revealed in the form of many broken windows in the plant and offices and many punctured tires on employees' automobiles. Also a powerfully organized community opposition developed to the Davis Division's request for a zoning variance for office space expansion. There was a growing truculence by the labor union that represented the factory workers, and demands were made each year for large severance-pay benefits for laid-off workers.

4.   Later, there was a change in the business climate also. The largest customer for Davis' intricate stampings was faced with unexpected technological developments that necessitated extensive changes in the design of their products. The changes involved substitution of metal castings for many parts that were made by Davis from formed and stamped sheet metal. The level of orders began to slip and slowly approached the point where profits were minimal and the big machine looked like a white elephant. Because of the high fixed charges (interest and amortization of the debt), it was not feasible to take the machine out of service. It was also found that the scrap value of the press was disappointingly small because no ready market existed for such large presses.

At luncheon with the student after the main interview, Mr. Timmons confided that because of his good record of accomplishment with Standard Metal Products, and because his plant was still profitable, his superiors at headquarters had not been unduly critical of the decision to buy the big press. But although his job was not in danger, Timmons ruefully stated that he'd had to sell his boat and had to skip a few vacations because his incentive bonus had been so thinned in recent years.

1.   *What moral can you draw from Mr. Timmons' experience with the stamping press project?*
2.   *Could Timmons have been reasonably expected to anticipate the problems that developed?*
3.   *If you were the Davis Division's chief engineer and you had the benefit of hindsight, what precautions would you recommend to avoid any unpleasant surprises like the ones that happened because of the big press?*

CASE I-II
Conglomerate Corp. Suffers Earnings Drop

SUMMARY: The new president's policy regarding executive promotion and incentive payments causes unexpected difficulties and losses in earnings.

NEWS ITEM

New York: **James Marsden, chief executive of Conglomerate Corp., today announced his retirement as president and his acceptance of the board chairmanship. In Marsden's place, Thomas Carstairs was designated president. Mr. Carstairs was formerly assistant to Mr. Marsden. At the press conference, Mr. Marsden stated that Mr. Carstairs has favorably impressed the board and other company officials with his imagination, competence, and youthful enthusiasm, in addition to his vast knowledge of modern management techniques. This surprise announcement was greeted with scepticism by several business commentators. Davison of** Financial Press **was overheard saying, "The 'Now' generation takes over the executive suite of Conglomerate Corp. Everybody run for cover!"**

POLICY MEMORANDUM—CONGLOMERATE CORP.

From: Thomas Carstairs, President
To: All Division Managers
Subject: Installation of profit-center decentralization

Effective January 1 of next year, profit-center decentralization will be installed throughout the company. Mr. Evans, the corporate controller, will contact each manager to invite him and his financial staff to meetings at which the details of the new program will be described.

The new policy will work as follows:

1. Each of the 125 divisions will be set up as a profit center and will report quarterly on several control factors, but in essence the crucial test of performance will be the profit contribution of the division.
2. Managers will be expected to present their sales and profit

plans along with their capital requirements at the annual planning meetings. If approved by the executive committees of the Groups, these plans will provide the basis for evaluation of managerial performance.

3. Managers will be rewarded on the basis of their profit quota achievement. Generous cash bonuses, stock options, and promotions will be awarded for over-quota performance. Cash awards will be made quarterly subject to review after the end-of-year audit.

4. Each manager will be evaluated annually by the executive committee. After two years on the assignment, each manager will be declared either eligible or ineligible for promotion. Those judged ineligible will be terminated forthwith. Those judged eligible will be given the first available promotional opportunity at headquarters or as manager of a larger division or as a Group executive. The company will pay all relocation expenses for transferred managers. It is expected that this promotion policy will result in the rapid advancement of successful managers. Those who fail to meet our high standards of excellence will have the opportunity to try their skills elsewhere.

NEWS ITEM

New York: **Conglomerate Corp. announces new executive appointment. James Marsden, chairman, today announced the resignation of Mr. Thomas Carstairs and the designation of Mr. Robert Jonas as president of Conglomerate Corp. "Mr. Jonas comes to us with over twenty years of valuable experience, most recently with Amalgamated Corp.," said Mr. Marsden. When questioned about Mr. Carstairs' sudden departure from the company, Mr. Marsden stated that Carstairs had resigned from the presidency at the recent board meeting because of an irreconcilable disagreement over company policy. Mr. Carstairs could not be reached for comment.**

TORRENCE ASSOCIATES, MANAGEMENT CONSULTANTS— CONFIDENTIAL MEMORANDUM

From: Amos W. Torrence, Managing Partner
To: Mr. Martin Bower, Chairman Loan Committee, Worldwide
    Insurance Company, Inc.
Subject: Report on Conglomerate Corp. earnings decline syndrome

In accordance with your instructions I have completed my preliminary inquiry into the earnings decline syndrome of Conglomerate Corp. This confidential report is a first impression; a complete analysis will follow as my staff completes its investigation. My impressions are the results of an interview with both Mr. Marsden and Mr. Jonas. Mr. Carstairs is out of the country and was unavailable for comment.

Of course, in any company as complex and widespread as Conglomerate Corp. any analysis runs the risk of gross oversimplification. There are numerous competitive factors that can account for the good or poor performance of any particular division of so large a firm. However, I believe that many of Conglomerate's difficulties can be explained as being the results of a major corporate reorganization undertaken by Mr. Carstairs in the early years in his incumbency as president. Before that time the company had experienced a steady earnings growth. In fact, Mr. Carstairs' program had what appeared to be immediately favorable results. Table C-I shows the pattern for several years before and after Carstairs joined the firm.

TABLE C-I   Per-Share Earnings

Year	Per-Share Earnings	Year	Per-Share Earnings
1965	$1.00	1970[b]	$1.75
1966	1.05	1971	2.25
1967[a]	1.05	1972	2.75
1968	1.20	1973	2.25
1969	1.50	1974	1.75
		1975[c]	1.25

[a] Carstairs joins Conglomerate Corp. as Assistant-to-President
[b] Carstairs ascends to presidency
[c] Carstairs resigns

Mr. Marsden stated that he was convinced in 1967 that Carstairs would make an excellent replacement for himself. This belief came about because of the favorable results from following Carstairs' recommendations in the years 1967 to 1969. When Carstairs was made president, his reorganization plans were presented to the board, and they were persuaded by Carstairs' confidence and assurance about the correctness of his prescriptions and on the basis of his past performance as Marsden's assistant.

Marsden now feels that this was a terrible mistake, but he is not certain what went wrong.

Mr. Jonas is more certain of his diagnosis of the difficulties encountered by Conglomerate, as you might well expect, since he had no part in the deterioration. This is the gist of his observations and my interpretation of his analysis:

1. Carstairs made a fundamental error in his profit decentral-ization plan. That error was in the two-year evaluation and the "up-or-out" policy. This policy required that the managers all operate with a two-year time-horizon. They had to make their marks in two years or they would be fired.

2. There were a number of undesirable effects of the two-year policy. Managers tended to neglect machine maintenance. When machines broke down, they used the cheapest possible replacement parts with short life. There seemed to be no sense in installing good parts with long life. This would only benefit the next manager and would reduce current earnings. In several plants, managers made union settlements in which there were several annual steps in wage and benefit increases, but the larger steps were to take effect during the next manager's reign. This gave lower current costs and greater reported profits, but passed the onus on to the next manager. There were several instances in which outgoing managers persuaded customers to take on extra-large inventories with the promise that any unsold goods would be returnable. There was no written records of these promises so the auditors did not know that reserves were necessary to offset future returns and profit reductions. These losses were passed on to the next manager. Also a very shortsighted approach was taken to advertising and market research. Only ad campaigns that promised to be immediately productive were undertaken, and marketing research was virtually abandoned. In a few cases, all advertising appropriations were terminated in the last six months of a manager's term of office. This, too, tended to raise his reported profit but to hurt the successor.

3. The foregoing were but a few samples of the unanticipated consequences of building a two-year time-horizon into organizational policy. There are enough difficulties with using profit as a sole measure of managerial performance without adding the two-year gimmick. There were a few more tricks

the managers used to boost their reported earnings, but the above gives you a taste of what went on as a result of Carstairs' policy.

4. Oddly enough, the immediate result of the two-year up-or-out policy was to give earnings a big upward jolt ($1.75 to $2.75 per share in two years) and this early success led to blind complacency on the part of the directors and other executives. No one was willing to argue with success. The declines in 1973 and 1974 were attributed to external business conditions and, although Carstairs was questioned a bit, no one thought to doubt the wisdom of his policies.

5. The first sign of trouble appeared when a number of good managers refused to accept promotions. This puzzled the directors, and some men were called back to headquarters to explain their reluctance. There had been a few earlier cases of refusal to accept transfer, but they had been attributed to the usual family difficulties, reluctance to leave familiar neighborhoods, to take children out of school, and so on. Now for the first time, managers refused transfers to other plants but were anxious to move to headquarters. This eliminated the moving excuse and ultimately revealed the real cause. It became evident that the managers were unwilling to take on jobs that meant cleaning up the hopeless messes left by their predecessors. They all felt that they were being forced to participate in a gigantic liquidation of their divisions, that they would be rewarded for that and punished for doing any long-range planning. The two-year game was good for the first term, tolerable for the second, but impossible for the third.

I tend to concur with Mr. Jonas' version of Conglomerate's difficulties. If one discounts the natural tendency to be overcritical of the errors of a predecessor, the evidence being amassed by my staff, although still fragmentary, supports Jonas' diagnosis.

If that is the case, Conglomerate Corp. will be difficult to turn around. The physical plant is badly neglected, the customer image has been severely damaged, labor relations are severely strained, and distributors are disgusted and highly critical of quality and delivery promises repeatedly broken. In all, the company's situation is badly deteriorated, not beyond redemption perhaps, but the road back will be hard, and earnings can be expected to decline for at least two years until Jonas can turn things around and can restore morale, confidence, and profitability. Whether Jonas is the man for this job, I cannot say at this time. He will need a reasonable time to prove himself. I am encouraged by one step he is taking, however, and that is his "Multi-Variable Early-Warning System." I will include details of this new system in my final report, which should be in your hands in about 90 days.

(signed)   Amos W. Torrence
Managing Partner
Torrence Associates

1. What was there about Mr. Carstairs' "up-and-out" policy that could cause managers to behave the way Jonas said they did?

2. Can you think of any other system of measuring and rewarding managerial performance that would be immune to such difficulties?

3. What do you think Jonas meant by his "Multi-Variable Early-Warning System"?

4. What changes would you suggest in Carstairs' policies that might have prevented or alleviated the problems Jonas reported?

5. What generalization could you develop about the effects of measurement schemes on managerial behavior?

CASE I-III
General Hybrid Microcircuits Gets a New Union

SUMMARY: Both the union organizer and the company management of a technologically based manufacturing firm misread the factory operatives attitudes toward unionization of the plant.

BACKGROUND

General Hybrid Microcircuits Corp. (GHM) was formed in the year 1963 by three engineers who were financed by a group of private investors. The company was adequately financed, well equipped, and well managed. GHM specialized in hybrid microcircuits, used throughout the electronics industry wherever companies sought to adapt their products to the new micro-miniaturization techniques. Hybrid circuits have three principal types of applications: (1) as an interim step between the use of discrete components circuits and full micro-miniaturization, (2) when the special engineering requirements are such that conventional integrated circuit technology is inadequate, and (3) where the small quantity requirements do not justify the high start-up costs associated with high-volume, integrated circuit manufacture.

GHM had carved out a comfortable niche in its markets and had been enjoying steady growth in the small-order business for circuits made to customer specifications. GHM had many competitors with similar or identical products and technology, but few were as successful in meeting the stringent delivery, performance, and quality standards set by GHM's management. Although GHM commanded premium prices, their marketing people spent as much time allocating the plant output among persistent customers as they did in actual sales work.

To increase the production of hybrid circuits is not an easy task. There is a great deal more to raising output than placing equipment on the floor. What is just as important and much harder to do is to develop a force of highly competent and emotionally stable female operatives. A good part of the work involves handling microscopic subassemblies under high-power binocular microscopes where the slightest misalignment or mishandling can cause the ultimate rejection of an assembly or even a completed micro-circuit costing more than $50 apiece.

New operatives undergo a two-week training and indoctrination process and are then moved along into the less demanding jobs. If they show aptitude, operatives are moved from operation to operation, each requiring greater skill than the last until, after a one-year interval, they can conceivably reach top skill. Operatives who reach this top echelon are the elite and are entitled to deference and respect from all, including the top executives of the firm. Operatives who reach a plateau in skill from which they cannot rise further, are either retained at their maximum skill levels or are moved horizontally into subassembly operations of equivalent difficulty. There is a three-month probation period, and new hires who fail to show sufficient promise and the required degree of emotional stability, or who have erratic attendance and promptness records, are released before the end of the trial period.

Throughout the plant there is great emphasis on calm, quiet, cleanliness, order, pleasant manners, and brisk efficiency. All horseplay is forbidden; loud noises, shrieks, or laughing which might cause involuntary hand jerks are not tolerated. The operatives wear lint-free gloves, white nylon smocks, hair bands, and white rubber-soled shoes. A hospital-like air of cleanliness and scientific detachment prevails on the production floor.

The attrition rate for new female operatives is fairly high; fully one-half of the new hires leave before the end of their first year of employment. But after that, the turnover rate is exceptionally low. GHM pays high hourly wage rates, at least 20 percent (on the average) over comparable rates in unionized shops in the locality. After merit raises, the highest-seniority people earn as much as 50 percent more than the highest prevailing wage in other similar shops in the area.

Because the company is fairly small (about 150 employees, of which 100 are production operatives) GHM has very few formal personnel procedures. They rely on high hourly wage rates, careful prescreening, and pleasant working conditions to promote worker morale. The company executives maintain high visibility by walking around the floor in shirt-sleeves and by having lunch with the factory people in the company cafeteria. Everyone sits together at long tables, and there is much good-natured banter between the female workers and the management people. All these factors in combination produce what one operative called, "one big happy family."

REPEATED UNIONIZATION ATTEMPTS FAIL

From the first year of company operation, a number of trade unions with possible jurisdiction tried to induce GHM's production workers to sign membership application cards, but they met with no success. Mr. Firestone had announced as firm company policy that he would recognize any trade union that his employees wanted; but whether or not they chose to join a union, they could expect fair treatment, above-scale wages, and pleasant working conditions. "We do not have to be forced to do the right thing by outsiders," Mr. Firestone constantly reiterated.

Many of the employees who had worked before coming to GHM had reported their experiences in other unionized shops, and these comparisons with the conditions at GHM were enough to discourage vacillators from signing union application cards. At GHM there was very little bickering, petty squabbling, suspicion, unsatisfied grievances, and other unpleasantnesses that the operatives attributed to union shops they had worked in in the past. They found the contrast to GHM so striking that they tended to exaggerate on all counts. Therefore, time and again, after meeting with a sparse or hostile response, the aspiring union organizers abandoned GHM for greener pastures.

THE NEW EXCLUSIVE SUPPLY AGREEMENT

In the spring of 1967, GHM "went public" and the market price of the shares tripled in just a few days after the original offering. At the same time, a large producer of scientific measuring instruments, the RST Manufacturing and Instrument Corp., approached GHM about the possibility of an exclusive supply agreement. RST suggested that GHM set aside 50 percent of their present micro-circuit capacity for RST's needs. Thereafter, additional quantities of a wide variety of circuits for all of RST's new instrument lines would be ordered with long lead times. In addition, RST would make long-term forecasts of their hybrid circuit needs and would guarantee to purchase specified quantities of GHM's hybrid circuits each calendar quarter. Prices would be negotiated for each order, but RST obviously expected substantial price concessions because the firm nature of their commitments and long lead times made the efficient planning of operations more feasible.

After protracted negotiations, an agreement was executed, and there was a celebration party to which all GHM employees, RST executives, the press, suppliers, and other friends of both companies were invited. Mr. Firestone spoke to the assemblage and said that the continuity and stability afforded by the GHM–RST pact would redound to everyone's benefit. RST's president also addressed the gathering and told them that in addition to GHM's fine reputation for quality, dependability, integrity, and engineering excellence, he had been most impressed by its fine employee relations. For these reasons, he said, he was willing to risk "putting all of RST's eggs in GHM's basket." "I know all you wonderful people will not let me down," he said.

The good news was reported in the business press and there was an immediately favorable reaction on the market price of GHM's newly issued shares. By now, because of a special arrangement that Mr. Firestone had made with the underwriters for employee purchases, most of the employees were also small stockholders. All were in a state of euphoria.

MR. GOLDSTEIN'S VISIT

The new contract, along with a rising expectation of greater sales volume, presented GHM's management with the immediate necessity for increasing production capacity. Personnel requisitions were sent to state, city, and private employment agencies. The arduous task was started to fill the training pipeline out of which six months later would come a number of skilled operatives.

One day, on meeting Albert Palmiri, the personnel director, Mr. Firestone inquired about the progress in hiring for the factory.

"It's a funny thing, Mr. Firestone," Palimiri said. "I really don't know how to account for it, but we're getting a much higher caliber applicant than usual. Maybe it's because of the publicity we've been getting. In any event, I expect this time we'll have much less attrition by the end of the probation period."

"That's good," Firestone replied without taking much notice. "That'll save us a few bucks."

About six weeks later Mr. Firestone's secretary, Mary Simmons, called him on the intercom. She said:

"I have a Mr. Goldstein on the telephone. He insists on talking to you about some labor matter. Do you want to talk to him?"

"All right, put him on. . . . Hello, Mr. Goldstein? What can I do for you?"

"Well, I'm glad I finally got through to you directly, Firestone. So far I've talked to three secretaries and a telephone operator. You certainly are well protected," Mr. Goldstein began. "Now that I have you one the telephone, let me tell you my business. I am the field organizer and business agent for the Technical Workers Union of America, Local 5 and, frankly, we have decided to invite your employees into our union. Would you like me to drop into your office to talk more about that?"

"Why not?" Firestone replied. "You know that it has always been our policy to give our people the opportunity to obtain union representation if they want it. So far they just haven't wanted it."

"We'll see about that," Goldstein answered. "I'm glad to hear that you have an open mind on the subject. That's the best way to start. When can I see you?"

"How about tomorrow; first thing in the morning?"

"Good, I'll be there at ten. By the way, Firestone, let's have this first meeting as informal as possible. No lawyers yet, and no tape recorders. I'll come alone too. I'd like to speak with you man-to-man for the first time with no witnesses. O.K.?"

"O.K." said Firestone. "It's a bit unusual, but I suppose there's no harm in that. I'll see you at ten. Goodbye."

The next morning, promptly at ten o'clock, Miss Simmons ushered Mr. Goldstein into the president's office. After a few polite preliminaries, Goldstein began:

"Firestone, I'm glad to talk to you alone this first time. I've heard a lot about you and your methods from my buddies at the Central Labor Council. You have them all frustrated. But now that is all over. I want your shop in my local, and I am now asking you to sign an exclusive bargaining agreement with TWUA Local 5."

"Why should I do that?" Firestone asked. "Show me your membership application cards, and we will petition for an NLRB election. If you win, we will be glad to sign up with your organization. But I don't think you will win."

"It happens that I have about thirty signed cards from all your new employees. Those are from our members whom we encouraged to apply for work when we heard of your recruiting drive. But that is really irrelevant. There will be no election." Goldstein smiled. "We just want you to sign up with us."

"Just like that?" Firestone asked.

"Yes, just like that."

"You must know that what you ask is preposterous," Firestone protested. "Why should I do such a thing if my people don't want a union?"

"People, shmeeple," Goldstein said. "Can't I get the idea through to you? You have to sign with us or you will not be able to continue operating your business. I know all about your new deal with RST Instruments, and the price action of your stock. I'm a stockholder myself. If you insist on being hard-nosed about this matter, your company is in for trouble. How do you think a long strike will affect your delivery promises to RST and the price of your stock? How about the disruption of your delicate production?"

"I guess it wouldn't make things better," Firestone said as he gloomily contemplated Goldstein's remarks.

"Tomorrow morning," Goldstein continued, "there will be a picket line at your doors. I'll bet you a dollar no deliveries get through the pickets. Well, what do you say, do we do things the easy way or the hard way? If you like, we can begin formal negotiations tomorrow morning."

Firestone did not answer and after a few minutes Goldstein rose and said:

"Good day, Firestone. It's been a pleasure meeting you. We'll meet again very soon."

Firestone shook himself to attention.

"Good-bye, Mr. Goldstein. I'm sorry that I don't share the pleasure. Meeting you has spoiled my day."

"Take my advice, Firestone. When faced with the inevitable, relax and enjoy it. Look, here's a list of companies we work with and here's a draft contract. Why not speak with some of these people? They'll tell you that we're not such bad guys to do business with."

Goldstein went out leaving Firestone staring at an open window. The telephone on his desk began to ring. Miss Simmons put her head through the door opening and said:

"Mr. Sabatino is very anxious to talk to you right away."

"Can't it wait," Firestone said. "I've just had a bad shock."

"He's very insistent," she replied.

"Oh, all right, send him in."

Sabatino entered the office and said:

"I'm sorry to press you like this, boss, but what I have to tell you is directly related to Goldstein's visit. I tried to get you on the phone, but Mary held all your calls."

"Well, what happened?"

"We had an incident this morning you should know about." Sabatino said. "When I arrived at the factory entrance this morning I saw a crowd and someone lying on the sidewalk. It was your partner, Robinson. He wasn't unconscious, but he was bleeding from his nose, and he had hit his head on the pavement."

"What happened to Robbie? Was he hurt? Why didn't someone tell me about it?"

"I'm not sure what happened, but I think it was something like this: Robbie saw two men shouting to the girls waiting outside the door, something about joining the union. He grabbed one of the men and told him to get the hell out of there and to stop pestering our employees. One word led to another, and Robbie threw a punch at one of the men and missed. The union man hit Robbie on the nose and knocked him down. A cop ran over and stopped the fight before anyone really got hurt. He asked Robbie if he wanted to press charges, but I stepped in and said no. Robbie had thrown the first punch.

"By now a big crowd had gathered, so I opened the door and led Robbie to the nurse's office. Then we had an ambulance come and take him to the hospital. He has a possible fracture of the nose and concussion."

"Oh, no!" Firestone groaned.

"Oh, yes," Sabatino said. "And you can just bet that carrying Robbie across the floor in a stretcher made a big impression on the girls. They were sure that the mob was going to kill them all. Half of them went home in tears. They all like Robbie, you know, even if he goes off half-cocked sometimes."

"That's just great," Firestone said. "And what did that do to our production?"

"What production?" Sabatino asked. "I'm keeping as many girls as are willing to stay, but I know we're making 100 percent rejects. And with the rumors that are flying, I doubt that we'll be able to get a full crew this week."

"I have more news for you," Firestone added. "Unless we agree to sign up with the TWUA, Local 5, we will have a picket line at the doors tomorrow morning."

"Oh, no!" Sabatino cried. "We are running out of liquid oxygen and some other gases. We were expecting a delivery tomorrow. If there is a picket line, we will not get our deliveries; the drivers are all members of the Teamsters union. Also, we are expecting some electricians and plumbers this week to connect up the new furnaces. They probably will refuse to cross the picket lines too. I don't see how we will ever get those RST orders started."

"Oh dammit," Firestone groaned. "Just when things were going so well for us. Just when we were supposed to start up on the RST circuits. Why did this have to happen at this time?"

"It didn't just happen," was the answer. "I've heard rumors that the union was trying to sign up our people, but I paid no attention. I figured it was just another try and they'd go away and leave us alone like last time. This time it looks like they really mean business."

MEETING BETWEEN FIRESTONE AND LABOR COUNSEL

The next day, exactly on schedule, the promised pickets appeared both at the plant doors and at subway exits and bus stops. Some of the union girls called the other workers at home to persuade them to remain there. All delivery men refused to cross the picket line, and production was virtually at a standstill except for a few in-process operations that could be finished by the few workers who had reported for work.

Mr. David Herold, labor counsel for the Electronics Components Manufacturer's Association, was shown into Firestone's office. After some preliminary conversation the following facts emerged:

1. The union was within its rights to try to unionize the shop.
2. The pickets could not be removed because there was a bona-fide labor dispute. Thirty of the newly hired girls had gone out on strike.
3. The company could demand an NLRB election and the union was certain to lose. But could GHM afford the loss in production, the waste, spoilage, and poor quality that would result in the interim? The entire success of the GHM operation was based on peace and quiet in a low-key environment. There would be no peace or quiet either before or after the election if the union lost.
4. If the union lost this time, they would try again and again. Each time, even if they were unsuccessful, GHM would pay a high price.
5. The simplest course would be for the workers to all sign up with the union. This might cost a little money, but raises were just about due anyhow.

"But," Firestone said. "The people don't want any union. Jean Pilsky called my home last night and told me the girls would back the company 100 percent if we wanted to resist the union. Damn it, Herold, the union could never win in a fair election."

"That is the literal truth," Herold said. "But it doesn't change the essential facts. From what you have told me, I infer that GHM is very vulnerable to attacks of this kind. How you managed to hold off the unions all these years is a mystery to me. Can you afford to pay the price of a knockdown, dragged-out-fight? If your answer is yes, fine—I can begin my part of the battle, and I'm certain we will win this time. But how about next time? Remember, Firestone, as long as your shop is unorganized, you will be the target of every ambitious union organizer in the city. Who knows, you might be attacked by a pinko union next time. Local 5 is not too bad an outfit. I've dealt with Goldstein many times and if you don't try to put anything over on him, he's no worse than any other straight union leader."

"How about one of the business unions? You know, the one that we can sign a 'sweetheart contract' with?"

"Forget it. It's too late for anything like that now. If you wanted to do that, you should have done it years ago."

"Oh, hell," Firestone said. "What can we do to end this mess and get back to normal again?"

"Pray," Herold answered, "that your workers can be persuaded to sign cards with this union. If another outfit gets wind of what's happening, there may be a two- or three-way battle. That would really be a disaster for GHM. I think that the Central Labor Council people will stand by and let Goldstein have the field for himself, but there are one or two maverick unions that won't play ball with the Council unions. Maybe you ought to get your friends in the plant to pass the word around for everybody to sign up with Local 5 right away. If that doesn't work fast enough, I'm afraid you personally will have to appeal to them to sign. I know it's slightly off-color for you to do this, but I can't see anyone filing a complaint against you for doing so."

"Are you sure that's the right thing to do?"

"I can't think of any better solution," Herold replied.

The next day a letter went out to all employees inviting them to another company meeting. The leading speakers were Goldstein for the union and Firestone for the company. Both had the same message: "Sign up today." As the people lined up to obtain their application cards, there was deep gloom on the employees' faces.

THE AFTERMATH

The contract presented to GHM by the TWUA called for exclusive representation, some minor modification in fringe benefits, and an across-the-board wage increase of 10 percent. The agreement was signed by both company and union representatives, but it was promptly rejected by the membership. The wage increase was renegotiated to 15 percent, and again the members would not ratify the agreement. No matter what Goldstein said to the members, they were adamant. They demanded a 30 percent across-the-board increase the first year and 15 percent for each of the next two years, or there would be a strike.

Goldstein met with Firestone and said:

"I can't control these people. They are so mad at you for what they call your sellout, that they refuse to listen to reason. If you don't meet their demands, I'm sure there will be a strike. In fact, there will be a wildcat walkout in the furnace department tonight on the last shift."

"Do something, Goldstein. You're supposed to be a hotshot union leader. Why don't you get some control over the people?" Firestone complained.

"I tried to talk sense to the women, but so far they won't listen to me. I'm afraid if we don't quiet things down very soon, they are going to try to throw Local 5 out and bring in the communist outfit. Then we'll both be in hot water. I'll do one thing for you, however. I think I can get the women to agree that the 30 percent, 15 percent, 15 percent increases will apply only to the people now on the payroll, not to anyone hired after today. In that way the new people can be hired at the old rates. We don't usually like to do that, but these are exceptional circumstances."

"I suppose we'll have to give in," Firestone said. "I'll have to talk things over with my board of directors and my partners, but I don't see how we can remain in business or take care of RST at any reasonable level of prices if we have to raise our hourly rates so high."

"All right, Firestone," Goldstein said. "Call me when you have come to some decision. I'll cooperate with you to the best of my ability. This is a new experience to me, I must admit. I had no idea that the people would turn so hostile to you and the TWUA. Live and learn."

1. *Building on the multiple interests discussion in the text, what do you think went wrong in this incident at GHM?*
2. *What do you think GHM should do at this juncture?*
3. *What do you think Firestone should have done earlier which would have made this incident less costly?*
4. *Are there any ethical issues that this case hinges on? If so, what are they and how do they relate to the facts of the case?*

APPENDIX TO PART I

Outline of a Decision Report

I. *Title Page*
It contains (*a*) name of firm or organization, (*b*) name and position of author(s), (*c*) subject of report, (*d*) persons or entities for whom the report was prepared, (*e*) date of submission, (*f*) whether the report is complete or partial, (*g*) whether or not the report is confidential.

II. *Abstract and/or Summary*
It contains the statement of purpose of report, a summary of important findings, conclusions, and recommendations.

III. *Letter of Authorization and/or Transmittal*
It contains a statement of authorization, the facts of transmittal, signatures of author(s), and concurring authorities.

IV. *Contents, Figures, Charts, and Exhibits*

V. *Body of Report*

    A. General background and the setting in which the problem must be considered, facts bearing on the problem, and necessary assumptions.

    B. The facts and observations that led up to the recognition of the problematic situations; the need for taking action to deal with the situation.

    C. Statement of the diagnosis of the problem and a description of the steps that led to the diagnosis.

    D. Identification of the parties that the solution to the problem must satisfy and other parties that the decision might affect in a substantial manner. The discussion of the relative urgencies of the interests.

    E. Statement of the decision objectives, how they were formulated, and how, if achieved, they will meet the situational demands.

    F. Development of specific criteria on which attainment of decision objectives will be judged. Assignment of numerical weights to reflect the differential importance of the criteria. Justification of the criteria and weight assignments.

    G. Identification of one or more alternatives for dealing with the problematic situation. A discussion of how the alternatives were conceived or developed; why some were rejected out of hand.

    H. Method for evaluation of alternatives.

    I. Factual data, supporting the procedure in (H).

    J. Identification of the best alternative(s) and a discussion of its strength and weakness relative to the others.

    K. Discussion of the merits of the alternative(s) chosen in relation to the interests of all affected parties.

  L. Recommendations for implementation of the chosen alternative, suggestions for follow up, and the identification of possible trouble spots that should be watched;

VI. *Supporting Materials*
They consist of (a) exhibits, (b) citation of sources, (c) computer programs and printouts, (d) data tabulations, (e) photographs, flowcharts, drawings, graphs, (f) bibliography, and (g) credits and acknowledgments.

VII. *Statement of Costs Incurred in the Decision Process*
It includes (a) out-of-pocket costs, (b) purchased and in-house services used, (c) costs incurred by the organization before recommendations can be implemented, and (d) any others.

Notes: 1. Some of the above may be deleted if not appropriate to the particular decision problem, or if the material is confidential and not for circulation.
2. Details of what comprises a full explication of a multiple-objective decision are found in Chapter 17.

II. DECISION ELEMENTS AND MODELS

3. Initiating the Decision Process

The Three main ideas developed in this chapter are:

1. *The decision process begins with a perception of a need for change.*

2. *Diagnosis is the essential second step.*

3. *The third step requires the definition of aims, the identification of affected interests and their relative urgencies, and a determination how goal attainments will be gauged.*

THE FIRST STEP—RECOGNITION OF THE NEED FOR CHANGE

The decision process begins with the perception of the need for change. There may be an intense dissatisfaction with the existing state of affairs or merely an urge for the improvement of a good condition. The motivation for the change may arise within a single individual, or it may be imposed on the decision maker by situational or organizational imperatives. Someone, somewhere, must feel and transmit pressure for a change in the status quo (see Box 3–1).

Box 3–1 Example of Situations That Can Trigger a Complex Managerial Decision

1. While riding in his automobile and listening to the late news, the chairman of the board of the Ex-Amp Corp. hears that the Ex-Amp's president's name was on the passenger list of an airliner that crashed into a mountain with no known survivors.

2. The vice-president and general manager's brother-in-law has just lost his fourth job because of incompetence. The manager's wife asks her husband to find a position in the company for her brother. The brother-in-law is rejected by several company executives as over-priced and incompetent.

3. The sales manager is approached by a fixer who offers to help get large orders from a customer that the sales manager has been unable to break into. A bribe to the purchasing agent and a fee to the fixer will be required.

4. For the third straight year, in spite of steadily rising sales income, the semiconductor products group has reported substantial losses on operations.

This triggering step is flow charted in Figure 3–1 in a somewhat oversimplified form. There is a univariate system (a system in which a single characteristic is being monitored) labeled (A) which has an input and an output. The system's performance (output) is observed by an appropriate mechanism (B) and then is compared (C) with a previously established standard, plan, or other expectation of acceptable system behavior (D). The deviation between the system output and expected performance is monitored (E), and a determination is made through appropriate means whether or not the deviation is tolerable. If tolerable, no action or change is called for, and the decision process is aborted. If excessive, timely and appropriate corrective action is called for, and the decision process begins (F).

Although the corrective action is shown in Figure 3–1 as being another system input, there obviously are other possibilities. The corrective action may involve alterations in the system (reorganization), or it may be deemed necessary to alter the standards, or it may be necessary to redefine what level of deviation from standard is tolerable.

The reference standard against which system performance is being compared may be either static (unchanging) or dynamic (variable with time). The standards may be very explicit as, for example, a body of written rules and regulations or a set of detailed specifications; or they may be implicit as in the case of customary behavior imposed by the rules of etiquette, or a feeling of what is just and fair. The limits of tolerable deviation may be relatively easy to define when standards are capable of strict definition, but the amount and kind of deviation that would be tolerable may be difficult to ascertain when standards are shifting or are vaguely stated.

The change model of Figure 3–1 is much oversimplified because it shows a single-variable system. In most real-life systems about which complex decisions are to be made, there would be multiple inputs, outputs, output samples, standards, deviations to be tested, and corrective actions to be taken.

For a single-variable system, the possibility that there might be a nonlinear relationship between input and output presents no difficulty. But for mutli-variable systems, the presence of significant system nonlinearities may introduce new levels of complexity because of the interdependence between the input-output relationships. Under these conditions, an action might produce one effect on system performance in the absence of other corrective measures, but would produce quite another in their presence. Thus a corrective

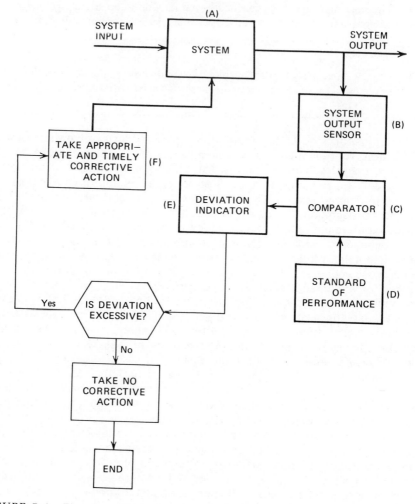

FIGURE 3–1. Flowchart illustrating the perception of the need for taking corrective action that can trigger off a decision in a univariate system.

action intended to reduce system deviations from standard may have quite unexpected results when applied in combination with other inputs.

DIAGNOSIS—THE SECOND STEP

Diagnosis[2] is the essential second step in every change process. It is the act of ascertaining through critical scrutiny, analysis, and insight the causation of the unacceptable state of the system. Our perception of the need for taking action tells us only that the system's performance differs intolerably from expectation, but aside from prodding us into taking timely and appropriate remedial action, the first step just triggers the change process. Diagnosis is next.

In a few decision problems a successful diagnosis virtually completes the problem solution because the appropriate action is obvious once the cause of the difficulty is understood* and suitable alternatives are freely available. This would be true for simple medical diagnoses (a bacterial infection responsive to an ordinary antibiotic in a nonallergic patient), for a simple power failure (replace the fuse or restore the circuit breaker), for a simple automotive defect (remove dirt from the fuel line), and so on.

In other, more complex cases, diagnosis may not point directly to the right solution because there may be many layers of causation.† Thus, treating the direct symptoms may permit a temporary alleviation of an intolerable situation, but new symptoms will pop up in a short time. Thus the physician who prescribes aspirin as a means of alleviating pain may succeed in his immediate objective but, unless the pain is transitory and superficial, the diagnosis and problem solution will not be satisfactory.

Objective of a Diagnosis

The objective of a diagnosis is to pinpoint the system factors that cause unsatisfactory performance. Two main types of difficulty most frequently encountered are:

1. *System Malfunction.* The system once performed acceptably but because of sudden or gradual internal changes, it no longer does. Full or partial restoration of the system to its initial, properly functioning state will reduce the deviation from acceptable performance. *Example:* the president of the firm has suffered a mild stroke which has left him with impaired mental faculties. He can no longer be relied on to make timely and appropriate responses to competitive inroads. *Solution:* replace the president with a more competent chief executive.

2. *System Obsolescence.* The system performs just as it always did and just as its original designers intended, and no internal malfunctions can be detected. But the system no longer has the capability of doing the job that is now required of it. *Example:* technological developments permit direct competitors to produce at lower cost and to undersell us in all of our markets; profit margins are following sales volume and market share in a steady, declining trend. *Solution:* restructure the system to meet new challenges.

---

* For an example see Case II-I.

† See Case II-II.

System malfunction and obsolescence may range from gradual to sudden. The difference between these two extremes lies in the rate of change of system degradation relative to expectation. For example, a sudden power failure causes an interruption of manufacturing operations. A laxness in controlling costs and production quality causes a gradual erosion of profits and a growing customer dissatisfaction. Of the two, the gradual degradation is less traumatic but more malignant because day-to-day deteriorations in system performance may be so subtle that they remain undetected as losses accumulate.

Diagnosis, therefore, involves pinpointing the causation behind a sudden or gradual erosion of system behavior whether the degradation stems from internal malfunction or an inability to cope with new challenges.

Diagnosis an Art

There are many possible paths from the perception of a pattern of clues to the identification of causes. One diagnostician may prefer to trace each symptom separately to its cause; another looks for a pattern in the syndrome of symptoms and seeks ways to alter the pattern. Some decision problems require painstaking, step-by-step analysis; others can be solved by an intuitive flash. Decision makers differ markedly in how they apply their diagnostic ability and technique to finding the causes for symptoms.

A greater knowledge of system logic and function coupled with the skills gained from experience permits speedier diagnosis. When the system is in a state of collapse and losses are piling up at an alarming rate, the ability to make rapid and accurate diagnoses can be of tremendous value in limiting the harmful effects of system failure. This is why specialized diagnostic experts, sometimes called "trouble shooters," are in much demand and often command high fees for their services.

A diagnosis may be partial or complete depending on the urgency of the problem and the personal style or preferences of the decision maker. A partial diagnosis may be necessary in an emergency situation or when the system and its environment have instabilities that preclude a complete search for basic causes or when trial-and-error methods are indicated. A complete diagnosis is more costly in decision maker's time, expert's fees, and losses from the continuation of the undesirable condition. The extent of diagnosis for a particular decision problem must be determined from a balancing of the costs associated with delays in taking corrective action against the costs of taking incorrect action which may have to be rescinded, perhaps more than once.

Diagnostic Technique

Many problems in diagnosis can be attacked successfully by a procedure similar to that described in Box 3–2. The procedure can be elaborated or simplified as the complexity of the problem dictates and the need for documentation indicates.

Box 3–2   Eleven Steps in a Diagnosis

1. Identify the desired (or normal) state of the system and compare it with the exciting state of affairs.

2. Identify and enumerate the symptoms and clues to system inadequacy.

3. Prepare or obtain a set of system diagrams—flowcharts, process diagrams, time sequence charts, and the like—and pinpoint the times and places the symptoms occur.

4. Review any recent changes made in the system structure, process, or environment that may be relevant and relate these changes to the charts obtained in no. 3 above.

5. Prepare a state-of-affairs statement in tabular form, including the answers to the questions: (*a*) What is happening? (*b*) Where is it happening? (*c*) When is it happening? (*d*) How much is happening? (*e*) Are the happenings stable or variable?

6. Prepare a list of tentative inclusive (it could be) and exclusive (it cannot be) hypotheses either symptom by symptom or by pattern. These hypotheses should attempt to explain possible causations.

7. Arrange the hypotheses in order of simplicity or parsimony and test the hypotheses, the simplest first, against the facts developed in no. 5 above.

8. Progressively eliminate hypotheses that fail to conform to the facts of the problem; progressively modify hypotheses as new evidence is obtained and assessed.

9. Continue until a hypothesis that fits all the facts is developed.

10. Devise a test for ascertaining the validity of the final hypothesis.

11. Proceed to the next phase of the decision process.

A Caveat About Diagnosis

Our discussion on diagnosis thus far contains the hidden assumption that the diagnostic process is neutral and does not have any appreciable effect on the problematic situation under examination. This neutrality assumption is shown schematically in Figure 3–2a.

Figure 3–2a shows an observer standing off at a distance (either in the figurative or literal sense) and observing the system's behavior. He devises a number of inclusive and exclusive hypotheses and, through a process of

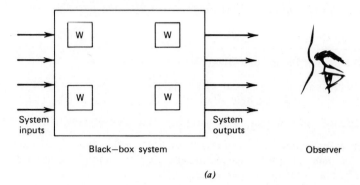

(a)

FIGURE 3–2a. *Schematic representation of an observer examining system outputs and system operations (through one-way windows labeled* W*). Participants of system are either unaware or unaffected by observation.*

elimination, ultimately arrives at the correct diagnosis of the causes of the symptoms. He may be aided in his work by the availability of a metaphorical, one-way window which permits him to study the inner workings of the system without being observed by any of the system personnel. It is assumed that, throughout the diagnosis, the people involved in the malfunctioning or maladapted system are either unaware of the diagnostician's scrutiny or, if aware, are indifferent to it. Obviously this is a gross oversimplification because it is unlikely that the participants will be indifferent or unaware of attempts to submit their shortcomings, real or imagined, to scrutiny.

A bit more realism can be introduced into the conception of the model if feedback links are added as is diagrammed in Figure 3–2b. The observer

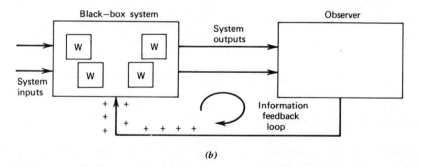

(b)

FIGURE 3–2b. *Schematic representation of system-observer mutual causation. The observer transmits information about his activities to the system, which in turn, produces new outputs that are affected by the new inputs. This mutual exchange continues until a new equilibrium is obtained.*

obtains information about the system behavior as before but he also, either deliberately or inadvertently, transmits information relative to his inquiries and findings back to the system. The system responds to this new input which it adds to others, and the outputs are modified accordingly. The mutual interaction between the observer and the observed continues until a new equilibrium is obtained. If the coupling between the two is loose, the mutuality between the two may be slight, but if the coupling is tight, the diagnostician becomes an integral part of the system, and his diagnostic efforts lose their neutrality.[3]

With the addition of this feedback link, the system participants are no longer indifferent or unaffected by the existence of the observer or by his attempts to pinpoint causation. Just how they might respond to this new and potentially disturbing stimulus is difficult to predict without a knowledge of the particular sets of facts. But respond they will. And, in doing so, they may substantially affect system behavior and thereby make a diagnosis more difficult and make particular diagnoses unsatisfactory.

THE THIRD STEP—DEFINING DECISION OBJECTIVES

Key Questions

The answers to several key questions form the basis for the third step in a large variety of complex decision problems:

Aims. What are we trying to accomplish with this decision? What are our personal, interest group, or organizational aims?

Interests and Their Urgencies. Who are the people, interest groups or organizations we must satisfy with this decision. On whom will there be an impact? What priorities shall we assign to the various interests?

Criteria. How can we gauge whether or not we have accomplished what we set out to do? How can we gauge the degrees of accomplishment? What criteria or standards shall we use to measure goal attainment and interest group satisfaction?

Decision Objectives—Defined

The objectives (synonyms: goals, aims, purposes, intent) of a decision are a set of prescriptive and constraining conditions adopted by the decision maker to permit him to achieve a reasonable compromise of the immediate and potential demands made on him (in his personal or organizational roles) by his direct and indirect claimants.[4]

Examples of prescriptive goals are: (a) to raise profits; (b) to increase market share; (c) to make the company a better place to work; and (d) to become a better citizen. Examples of constraining goals are: (a) actions should not violate any laws; (b) liquidity should be neither too high nor too low; (c) earnings shall not fall below $1 per share.

Ambiguity of Decision Goals

Experience has shown that decision objectives are often ambiguous and are always hard to state clearly and explicitly. Some objectives will be vaguely stated and loosely derived from the decision maker's societal values. Others may be imperfectly rationalized and nonoperational. Many may seem contradictory. Nearly always, goals will be misunderstood by outsiders.

Outside observers may complain that the decision maker acts in a manner inconsistent with his stated objectives. The executive of a firm that professes high regard for the consumer's interests may order the manufacture and sale of shoddy and unsafe products. The loan officer of a bank that advertises its desire to be of service to the local business community may refuse to authorize a loan to save the business of one of the bank's customers. In many cases, the decision maker's behavior is inconsistent with his and his firm's stated objectives because their objectives are really not what they are advertised to be. In other cases, the inconsistency is more apparent than real because there are multiple objectives involved, and the decision is a compromise among them. No single decision goal can be fully attained without damaging the attainment on others.

Goal Priorities

Some objectives will seem to be of overriding importance; others will seem less urgent. Some may seem to be incompatible and a trade-off may be necessary.

The importance of a particular objective may change with time. A convenient way of thinking of these shifting priorities is to postulate an invariant set of goals and to assign a numerical weighting coefficient to each. If a goal is irrelevant or meaningless in a particular situation, it is assigned the weight, zero. If one is more important than another, it is assigned a larger weight.

Changes in the weighting of objectives come about for several reasons:

1. It is beyond the capability of the human mind to consider and evaluate performance on every decision goal simultaneously; some must be sacrificed or ignored, if only temporarily.
2. Goals that are capable of quantification (for example, the profit goal in business) are likely to be given more attention than goals for which quantification is difficult or impossible.
3. Goals that are concerned with the interests of the most powerful, articu-

late, or troublesome interest groups are usually given preference over the goals of the less obtrusive interests.

4. Goals that have a short time-horizon are usually given preference over those involving a long time-horizon.

5. Changes in aspiration levels affect the subjective probability of goal attainment; increases in level of aspiration raise the emphasis placed on affected goals, and vice versa.

The fact that the relative urgency of particular goals changes with time requires that there be a mechanism for providing a periodic reevaluation of goal priorities, particularly when there are repetitive decisions over a long time span.

From Objectives to Decision Criteria

Decision criteria are categories, variables, or attributes on which attainment of decision objectives are to be measured. Criteria may be of the go, no-go type (attributes) or may be of the type that can be expressed as numbers on some sort of measurement scale (variables).

The translation of decision goals into decision criteria may introduce a new set of complications. This happens because no measurement scheme in practice can be completely neutral. Neutrality may be possible in physical systems in the measurement of voltage, light intensity, speed, and time, but neutrality is an elusive goal in human systems.

Measurement criteria can have a profound effect on the behavior of persons who are subject to the measures.[6] For example, if one of the objectives of a decision were to raise the profitability of the firm and the criterion to be used in the sales department were dollars of sales income, we can easily see how salesmen might cut prices to raise sales with the effect of subverting attainment of the profit goal.

The Goal Hierarchy

Like Janus, the Roman god of beginnings, each individual, group, or organization goal has two faces, one *instrumental* and the other *teleological*. The teleological face looks backward toward the origins of all goals, to the attitudes and, through them, to the basic need satisfactions sought by all persons. The teleological face is the answer to the question: *Why—for what purpose?* The instrumental face looks forward toward the external world of behavior and is the answer to the question: *How—how can the purpose be achieved?*

The diagram in Figure 3–3 illustrates the dual nature of goals. It shows a goal chain that begins with attitudes and ends with a specific recommendation for action. If we move from the attitude to goal No. 1 and then toward the higher-numbered goals, we find a sequence of answers to the "how" question. How are we to build up the firm to a substantial size in assets and

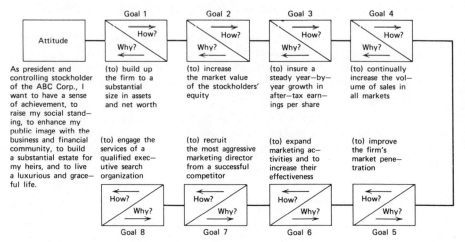

FIGURE 3–3. Goal chain illustrating the fact that each goal has an instrumental as well as a teleological face.

net worth? By increasing the market value of the stockholders' equity. How? By insuring the steady year-by-year growth in after-tax earnings per share. How? By continually increasing the volume of sales in all markets, and so on, until goal No. 8 is reached.

If, in Figure 3–3, instead of beginning with the attitudes, we start with goal No. 7 and move in the opposite direction toward the attitudes, we find a sequence of answers to the "why" questions. Why do we want to recruit the most aggressive marketing director from a successful competitor? To expand marketing activities and to increase their effectiveness. Why? To improve the firm's marketing position. Why? To continually increase the volume of sales in all markets, and so forth. Thus, as a study of Figure 3–3 reveals, each of the goals in the chain has a dual nature: each has both an instrumental and teleological face; each is both a means and an end.

The goal chain (also called a means-ends chain)[7] shown in Figure 3–3 is a linear series without branches. Since there will usually be alternative means (the "hows") for achieving ends (the "whys"), the typical means-ends hierarchy will resemble a tree with branches (or a pyramid if so placed on the page) more than a linear chain. This is illustrated in Figure 3–4, which shows how a single higher-level objective can give rise to multiple, lower-level goals.

Using a Means-Ends Tree

Use of a means-ends tree can often help resolve disputes or confusion about decision objectives. For example, one executive may argue that long-run profitability is the most important goal, but another may argue that service

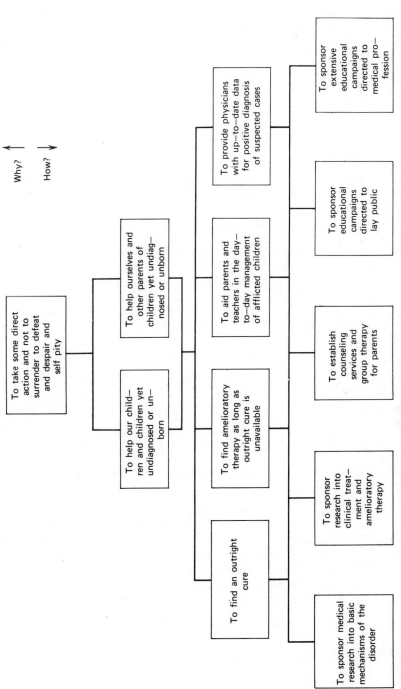

FIGURE 3–4. Four levels of a pyramidal means-ends chain associated with the objectives of the founders of a medical research foundation organized to support research and education leading to greater knowledge of a rare, often fatal, inborn metabolic disorder of children.

Box 3–3   Reconciling Seemingly Contradictory Goals by a Means-Ends Chain

		Achieving a sense of fulfillment
↑		↕
WHY	HOW	Long-run profitability of the firm
↓		↕
		Service to customers

---

to the customer should be paramount, and a third may argue that achieving a sense of self-fulfillment is the highest in importance. Of course, these three objectives are not mutually exclusive, but they are related to each other by a means-ends chain. For example see Box 3–3. Thus, very often the seemingly contradictory goals can be reconciled by recognizing their places on a means-ends goal chain.

The decision maker can often make his identification of complex decision objectives easier if he constructs a means-ends chain for each principle objective. Some of his objectives will be found to fit at an upper level; some at middle levels, and some at lower levels of the chain. Very likely, there will be branch and parallel hierarchies and some overlap because some means will simultaneously satisfy more than one end.

Notes and References

1. I am indebted to Professor William E. Newman of Columbia University's Graduate School of Business for this way of viewing the initiating of the decision process. For a more comprehensive and theoretically complete treatment of the need for taking action, see Alvin I. Goldman, *A Theory of Human Action* (Englewood Cliffs, New Jersey, Prentice-Hall, Inc., 1970).

2. For a more complete treatment of diagnosis in decision making, see C. H. Kepner and B. B. Trague, *The Rational Manager* (New York, McGraw Hill Book Co., 1965) and W. H. Newman, C. E. Summer, and E. K. Warren, *The Process of Management* (Englewood Cliffs, New Jersey; Prentice-Hall Inc., 1967) 2nd. ed., pp. 310–332. Also see J. W. Lorsch and Paul Lawrence, "The Diagnosis of Organizational Problems" in W. G. Bennis, K. D. Benne, and R. Chin (eds.) *The Planning of Change* (New York, Holt, Rinehart and Winston, 1969) 2nd. ed., pp. 468–478.

3. For a more general discussion of this phenomenon, see Magoroh Maruyama, "Mutual Causality in General Systems" in John H. Milsum (ed.), *Positive Feedback* (London, Pergamon Press, 1968), pp. 80–100.

4. Adapted from R. M. Cyert and J. G. March, *A Behavioral Theory of the Firm* (Englewood Cliffs, New Jersey, Prentice-Hall, Inc., 1963), pp. 26–63.

5. Lists of various types of objectives can be found in Bertram M. Gross, "What Are Your Organization's Objectives? A General Systems Approach to Planning" *Human Relations* Vol. 43, No. 4 (April 1964), pp. 205–211, and George A. Steiner, *Top Management Planning* (New York, The Macmillan Co., 1969), pp. 140–195.

6. See V. F. Ridgway, "Dysfunctional Consequences of Performance Measurements," *Administrative Science Quarterly* Vol. 1, No. 2 (September 1956), pp. 240–247.

7. A good discussion of means-ends chains can be found in Manley Howe Jones, *Executive Decision Making* (Homewood, Illinois, Richard D. Irwin, Inc., 1962) rev. ed., pp. 5–25.

Important Words and Concepts

Perception of the need for change
Situational imperatives
Univariate system
Deviation
System input
System output
Corrective action
Reference standard
Static
Dynamic
Nonlinear relationship
Diagnosis
System malfunction
System obsolescence
State-of-affairs statement
Inclusive hypothesis
Exclusive hypothesis
Mutual interaction
Aims
Criteria
Prescriptive conditions
Constraining conditions
Goal priorities
Goal hierarchy
Teleological face
Instrumental face
Means-ends chain

Overview of Chapter 3

The decision process begins with a perception of a need for change. If the deviation between expected and actual system behavior is excessive, corrective action is called for.

Diagnosis is an essential second step. The system may be exhibiting gradual or sudden malfunction or obsolescence. Diagnosis is an art but an orderly procedure, and a full knowledge of the functions and logic of the system can expedite diagnosis. The diagnostician may become part of the system because of mutual interaction between himself and others within the system that is undergoing scrutiny.

The third step involves identifying aims, interests, and their relative urgencies, and setting up criteria on which goal attainment can be measured. Decision goals are often ambiguous, redundant, and of varying urgency. Each goal in a hierarchy of goals has both a teleological (why?) face and an instrumental (how?) face. Seemingly contradictory goals can often be reconciled by arranging them in a means-ends chain.

Questions for Review, Discussion, and Research

Review

1. What are the factors in a situation that can bring about recognition for a need for change?

2. What types of actions may be required to reduce system deviations to a tolerable level?

3. What is meant by the term, diagnosis?

4. Does every problem require the same type of diagnosis?

5. What can happen if the people undergoing scrutiny in a diagnosis know what is happening?

6. How do aims and criteria differ?

7. Why do goal priorities change?

8. How can one deal with shifting priorities?

9. Why are some goals hard to define precisely?

10. What is a means-ends chain?

11. Why is it sometimes useful to think of goals in terms of a goal hierarchy?

Discussion

1. Can you relate the flowchart model of Figure 3–1 to the idea of "management by exception?"

2. In what kinds of situations are we likely to find vague and ambiguous standards for comparison? In what kinds are we likely to find clear-cut standards?

3. In what way would system nonlinearities provide for unpredictability of system response to corrective actions?

4. How does one deal differently with system obsolescence as compared with system malfunction?

5. Do you think that the personal goals of the decision maker will usually coincide with the aims of his firm or organization? Why?

Research

1. Consider the four situations in Box 3–1, can you prepare a list of possible decision objectives, a possible inventory of interested parties and their relative priorities, and a set of decision criteria that might be applicable?

2. Prepare a step-by-step diagnosis of some problematic situation of your choice by using the procedure shown in Box 3–2.

3. Prepare a means-ends chain of decision goals for a problematic situation of your choice.

4. Can you develop a list of problematic situations in which the diagnostic step would be trivial; and a list for which diagnosis would be absolutely essential?

4. Elementary Decision and Evaluation Models

This chapter deals with a number of varieties of decision processes including: single and multistage, focused objective and "muddling-through" types, open and closed-loop models, and satisficing versus optimizing approaches. Basic satisficing and open-loop optimizing models (with elaborations) are presented.

CONCERNING DECISION PROCESSES

Decision, Choice, and Evaluation

As the term, *decision*, has been used thus far in this book it has two meanings. In the broader sense, decision refers to a complex process that begins with the recognition of a need for change and terminates with the adoption and implementation of a particular course of action. An executive would be making a decision when, after discovering that the sales of one product line were falling, he diagnosed the cause and took timely and appropriate action to reverse the decline.

Decision also has a narrower meaning, as a synonym for *choice*. Choice is one step in the decision process. It occurs when the decision maker has completed his evaluation of various alternative courses of action and selects one for implementation. He *chooses* among alternatives or decides which to adopt. For example, a personnel manager examines the qualification of a number of job applicants and makes an accept or reject decision on each candidate.

The word, *evaluation*, refers to another step in the decision process in which alternatives are scored or rated on one or more criteria. If the decision involves multiple criteria, there would be multiple evaluations of each alternative on every criterion. The partial evaluations could then be amalgamated into some sort of index or composite score, one for each alternative. For example, in merit-rating schemes, subjects are rated on a number of performance criteria and the scores are combined into a composite rating which can be used by management for substantiating salary or promotion recommendations.

Single and Multistage Decision Processes

Many complex personal and managerial decisions are, in fact, not single decisions but involve a sequence of subdecisions. For example, a young man who is graduated from high school must decide among many different alternatives (go on to college, get married, join the army, or join the Peace Corps). If he chooses college, then he must choose one or more to apply to; then he must decide which program to register for; then which courses to take, and so forth.

In many instances, the person who initiates the decision process may involve others in the multistage sequence. If a married woman suffering from marital unhappiness seeks some sort of relief, she may choose divorce, separation, counseling, or some other course. If she chooses the divorce route, she must choose a law firm. The firm will choose a legal strategy and a jurisdiction in which the case will be tried. The court of law will make several decisions before arriving at a verdict and the matter is finally resolved.

Focused Objective versus the "Muddling-Through" Type

Multistage decision may be either the focused objective or "muddling-through" types.[2] In the former, the entire sequence is designed to attain an initial set of quite specific goals. For example, the unhappy wife triggers off the multistage sequence leading to a court-awarded divorce, with the express purpose of relieving her unhappiness.

In the muddling-through type of decision sequence, the decision-maker's attention is directed toward the relief of the immediate pressures without attempting to deal with all of the issues involved in the problematic situation. Decisions are made in small pieces with the outcomes affected by the balance of forces pushing the decision maker. At one time objective no. 1 is given overwhelming priority and the others downgraded in importance. When this oversight creates new pressures, other objectives are given precedence until the new pressures are eased. Still later, more pressures erupt, and these, too, are dealt with, ad infinitum. The executive who uses the "muddling-through" approach may find that each subdecision in the seemingly endless chain produces new sets of difficulties so that it appears that he can never rid himself completely of any problem.

Open and Closed Loop Processes

The open-loop decision, in a stable and certain environment, proceeds from recognition of the need for change to implementation of the chosen alternative without trial-and-error experimentation or the testing of the end result against decision aims. An exhaustive analysis of all decision alternatives is required before it is prudent to set events into motion.

A closed-loop decision process involves information feedback which permits a comparison of decision results against aims. Implementation can begin if the comparison shows that the corrective action is appropriate and timely. If not, the process steps can be reiterated until acceptable actions are discovered.

The choice of an open or closed-loop model is most influenced by the nature of the decision environment, the personal propensities of the decision maker, and the time available for the full investigation of all alternatives. Occasionally time and money pressures will prevent adequate consideration of all alternatives. In such instances, closed-loop, trial-and-error methods are probably best. But if circumstances allow, it will usually prove less costly if alternatives are studied and evaluated in a quiet office, on paper, rather than on the firing line with real people and high-cost resources.

Open-loop processes are a necessity when decisions are of great weight and are irreversible. For example, if the ABC Corp. was dissatisfied with its location in the city of New York and wished to explore the possibility of a move to another city, the trial-and-error methods associated with closed-loop methods could not be used. This kind of problem requires extensive analysis of alternative locations before the right one can be found. Once chosen, and the plants relocated, correction of a poor location would be extremely costly. It would be necessary to be right the first time.

On the other hand, if the decision is easily reversible, if the actions can be rescinded with little cost, a closed-loop model might result in lower decision-making costs. For example, Robert Thomas is the office manager of a large retail store chain and his secretary is ready to leave her job to get married. He would prefer to select a new secretary from the company's secretarial pool, and to do this he elects to try candidates on the job for a week's trial to see how proficient each is. If he selects an unsuitable candidate, he can return her to the pool with little or no dislocation. He may try to discover in advance which pool member is most likely to succeed in the new job, but if he is wrong, the error is easily corrected. Extensive investigation into the qualifications and backgrounds of all alternative candidates would be unnecessary and wasteful.

Satisficing and Optimizing Processes

The simplest form of decision process involves the "satisficing"[3] rather than the optimizing approach. The decision maker searches for an acceptable, workable solution, and not for the best possible. He implicitly assumes that when he has found one workable solution to his problem, the marginal gain from further search is less than the further costs of searching for and testing additional alternatives. If he is experienced, skillful, and creative in devising action programs, he may be able to hit on a workable solution on the first try. If the first trial is unsuccessful, further search is made until an acceptable action is found. In using a satisficing approach, the decision maker is always vulnerable to persons who may later uncover a better solution and use the improvement to embarrass him with his superiors.*

* For an example see Box 1–4.

There are two kinds of optimizing approaches: (a) finding the best possible alternative courses of action, and (b) finding which alternative among those available is best. To find the absolute best may be difficult or impossible, because to do so may involve the examination of every conceivable alternative. If the criteria can be described by some sort of mathematical function, mathematical methods of optimization may be applicable.[4] If not, and if the alternatives are multivalued and disparate, mathematical methods may not work.

The second case is more operational, if more limited. It only requires that one discover which of the alternatives offered for test is the best, an easier and usually less costly task than true optimization.

Decision making using open-loop approaches involves the determination of the worth of each alternative. The worth measures can be based either on a ranking scheme or on placing each alternative's index number on a graded scale.

Satisficing methods are not as demanding of accurate measurement. It is only necessary to discover if an alternative meets or exceeds some satisfactory level.

ELEMENTARY SATISFICING MODELS

Simplest Satisficing Model

Figure 4–1 contains a flow chart[5] of a simple satisficing, decision model. The process begins with the perception of a need for action and moves to the diagnosis stage. One action is devised and its outcome predicted and valued. If the expected outcome values satisfy the objectives, the action is adopted and the decision is completed. If the action is not satisfactory, another action is devised and the process is reiterated until an acceptable action is discovered. As shown in Figure 4–1, the mode is open loop, single stage. There is one recursive path through which the search for additional actions is made, if necessary.

Addition of a Feedback Loop

The model shown in Figure 4–2 is similar to that of Figure 4–1 except for the addition of a feedback loop. The loop permits the decision maker to test the consequences of the action adopted. If there are no undesirable consequences, the process is ended. If there are undesirable consequences, additional actions are devised until the undesirable effects are reduced to a tolerable level.

In spite of their apparent simplicity, the models shown in Figures 4–1 and 4–2 are widely used in making organizational and personal decisions and are especially popular with action-oriented people who are impatient with analysis and deliberation.

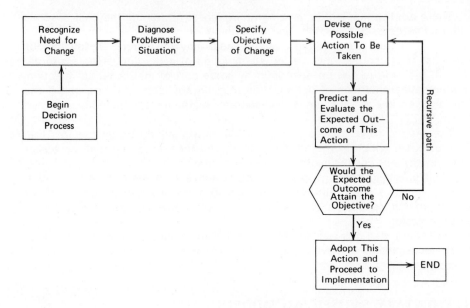

FIGURE 4–1. Flowchart diagram of a simple, single-stage, open-loop, single objective, satisficing decision model with one recursive path.

If the decision involves an emergency for which the costs of inaction or delay are high, these two models are useful. This is mainly because an experienced decision maker can usually devise an action on the first try that will cause a degree of improvement. After the emergency is over, he could take additional action to bring the situation to its desired state.

Addition of Rediagnosis Option

The model shown in Figure 4–3 has one additional feature. If the initial action has not been successful, the decision maker is given the option of trying more actions, or he can admit the possibility of faulty diagnosis. If faulty, the rediagnosis is carried out, either after the first pass through the model, or after a number of actions have been tried without success.

Further Elaborations

A more elaborate model is shown in Figure 4–4 where three additional sequences have been added:

1. A subroutine for the relaxation of decision objectives that are found to be too stringent and therefore unattainable at reasonable cost.

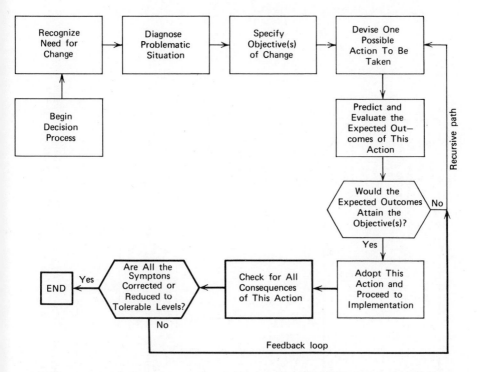

FIGURE 4–2. Flowchart diagram of a simple, single-stage, closed-loop, single objective, satisficing decision model with one recursive path and one feedback loop. This model differs from the one shown in Figure 4–1 in the possibility that the alternative chosen may not relieve the symptoms that gave rise to the decision process.

2. A subroutine that permits rescinding an action already adopted but which was subsequently found to be unsatisfactory.
3. A subroutine for additional steps to be taken for rediagnosis to prevent any possible recurrence of the problem.

Satisficing Evaluation Models

The basic evaluation model accepts a stream of subjects, measures the acceptability of each subject on one or more qualitative criteria, and classifies the subjects as either passed or failed.

The model shown in Figure 4–5 adds an additional subtlety because the criteria are divided into two groups: critical and noncritical. We would always prefer subjects to pass both the critical and noncritical criteria, but if the number of those which do is insufficient for our purpose, and addi-

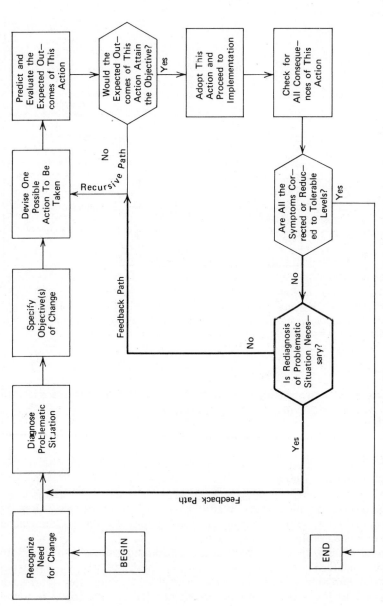

FIGURE 4–3. *Slightly more complicated flowchart diagram showing additional steps required by admission of the possibility of incorrect diagnosis. Model is single-stage, single objective, closed-loop, satisficing with recursive path and feedback.*

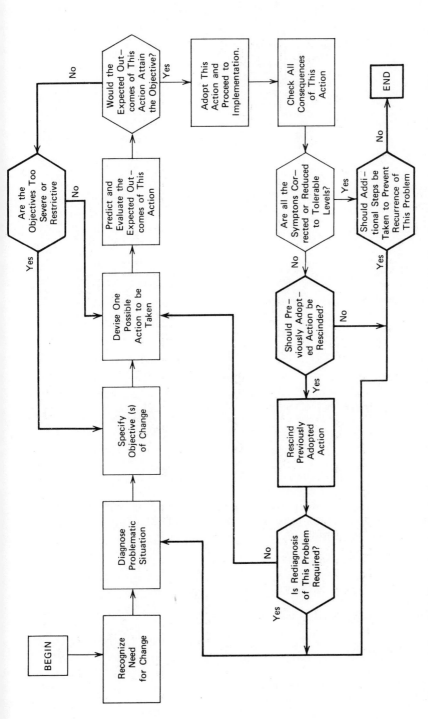

FIGURE 4-4. Flowchart diagram of a single-stage, closed-loop decision model with allowance for multiple objectives, relaxation of stringent objectives, rescission of previously implemented alternatives, possibility of long-term corrective action, and rediagnosis if required.

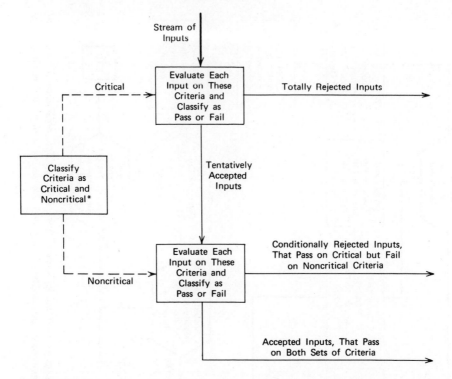

FIGURE 4–5. Basic model of satisficing evaluation process, in which criteria are graded as critical and noncritical and inputs are segregated into three categories: completely acceptable, completely unacceptable, and conditionally unacceptable.

tional subjects are not available, we may have to draw from those that failed only on one or more noncritical criteria.

The model in Figure 4–6 classifies the subjects that fail only on noncritical criteria by the number of criteria they pass and fail. Those that fail the least number are preferred.

BASIC OPTIMIZING MODEL

Basic Open-Loop Optimizing Model

A flowchart of an open-loop, single-stage, optimizing model is shown in Figure 4–7. This model consists of a number of discrete steps:[6]

1. Recognize the need for change.
2. Diagnose the problematic situation.

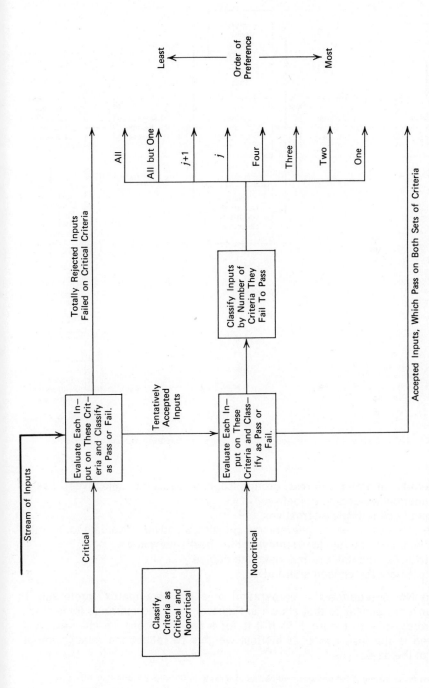

FIGURE 4-6. *Satisficing evaluation model in which inputs are tested for compliance with two sets of criteria: critical and noncritical. Those that fail on one or more critical criteria are unconditionally rejected. The remainder are classified by the number of noncritical criteria that they fail to meet.*

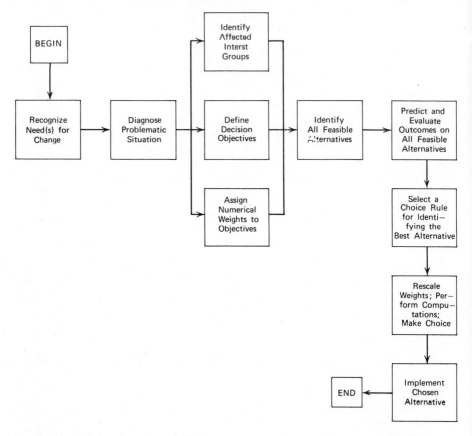

FIGURE 4–7. Generalized open-loop, single stage, optimizing decision model.

3.   Identify affected interest groups; define decision objectives; assign numerical weights to objectives.
4.   Identify all feasible alternatives.
5.   Predict outcomes of alternatives on all objectives; evaluate outcomes.
6.   Select a choice rule for identifying the "best" alternative.
7.   Perform computations and make the choice.
8.   Implement the chosen alternative.

Step No. 5 requires the preparation of a decision matrix (preferably in tabular form) similar to that shown in Figure 4–8a if the matrix is for a single time interval; or to Figure 4–8b if it is for a sequence of time intervals. Also required is the insertion of numerical weights to reflect the relative importance of the objectives.*

* Methods for preparing these decision matrices are discussed in Chapter 5 and in Part III.

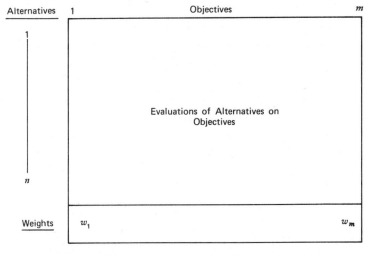

(a)

FIGURE 4–8a. Step 5 requires the preparation of a decision matrix in which the scores earned by each alternative of each objective are recorded in tabular form. Weights corresponding to each objective are also required. This single matrix will serve for any one time interval.

To complete Step No. 5, one must forecast the outcomes of the alternatives on every objective and then make a quantitative evaluation of the outcomes by means of an appropriate numerical scaling technique.

Step No. 6 requires that the decision maker devise a method for amalgamating the scores earned by the alternatives on the weighted objectives into an index by which alternatives can be compared for desirability. The method of amalgamation that is used may introduce quite definite biases into the process and in many closely balanced decisions problems may be the critical factor in the final ranking of alternatives.*

Evaluation Model with Optimizing Procedure

If the alternatives, objectives, and weights are predetermined, there only remains the task of performing the evaluations of the alternatives on the objectives, combining the partial scores into the figure-of-merit index, and ranking the alternatives in order of their desirability. This abbreviated process is shown in Figure 4–9.

Alternative Futures

In all of the decision models shown in this chapter and the next, the step "evaluation of alternatives" involved an assumption of a single, but unspeci-

---

* The procedure will be discussed in detail in Part IV.

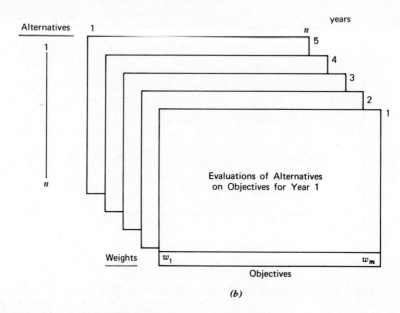

FIGURE 4–8b. This diagram contains five matrices similar to those in Figure 4–8a above. There is one matrix for each of five time intervals.

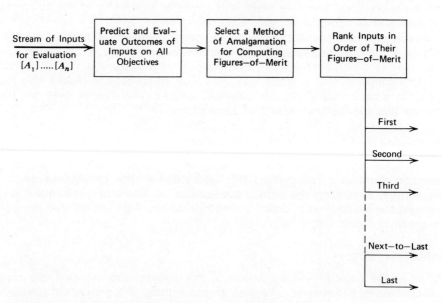

FIGURE 4–9. Evaluation model employing optimizing procedures.

fied state of the decision environment (see Chapter 2). If there are two or more alternative futures implied by the facts of the problem, it would become necessary to do a set of evaluations for each scenario about the future. Therefore, each model would have multiple branches at the "evaluation-of-alternatives step (as shown in Figure 2–1). These multiple branches are not shown on any of the decision model flowcharts because to show them would further complicate the diagrams. However, when tracing any of the flow-charts, one should always keep in mind the ever-present possibility that the problem may involve alternative futures and, therefore, multiple branches.

Notes and References

1. For several examples see Dale S. Beach, *Personnel: The Management of People at Work* (New York, The Macmillan Co., 1970) 2nd ed., pp. 308–341 and bibliography on p. 242.

2. See C. E. Lindbloom, "The Science of Muddling Through" *Public Administration Quarterly*, Spring 1959.

3. J. G. March and H. A. Simon, *Organizations* (New York, John Wiley and Sons, 1959) pp. 140–1.

4. For an extensive overview of mathematical optimization techniques see L. Cooper and D. Steinberg, *Introduction to Methods of Optimization* (Philadelphia, Penn., W. B. Saunders Co., 1970).

5. An excellent treatment of flowcharting in a somewhat different context than is shown in this chapter is contained in George A. Gliem, *Program Flowcharting* (New York, Holt, Rinehart and Winston, Inc. 1970).

6. Adapted from I. J. D. Bross, *Design for Decision* (New York, The Macmillan Co., 1953) pp. 18–32 and from William E. Newman, C. E. Summer, and E. K. Warren *The Process of Management* (Englewood Cliffs, New Jersey, Prentice-Hall, Inc., 1967) 2nd ed., pp. 310–405.

Important Words and Concepts

Choice
Evaluation
Single stage
Multistage sequence
Focused objective
Muddling through
Open-loop process

Closed-loop process
Satisficing
Optimizing
Feedback loop
Recursive loop
Rediagnosis
Subroutine
Critical criteria
Decision matrix
Weights
Amalgamating scores

Overview of Chapter 4

The term, decision, is used in two ways: to indicate a complex process, and synonymously with the word, choice. Evaluation refers to a stage in the decision process.

Decisions may come in single or multistage sequences, and they may be either of the focused objective or muddling-through types.

Closed-loop models involve feedback and are especially suited for trial-and-error experimentation processes. Open-loop methods involve more extensive analysis. Satisfying approaches involve finding a good-enough solution; optimizing involves finding the best.

Flowcharts are prepared for the basic satisficing model with variations for decision and evaluation. A basic optimizing model consisting of eight steps is shown. Alternative futures require multiple branches at the evaluation stage.

Questions for Review, Discussion, and Research

Review

1. Distinguish between *decison* and *choice.*

2. Distinguish beween *decision* and *evaluation.*

3. Distinguish between *single* and *multistage* processes.

4. What is the difference between *focused objective* and "muddling-through" decision types?

5. In what ways do "satisficing" and optimizing approaches differ?

6. Trace the steps in a simple satisficing model.

7. What is the effect of adding a recursive loop? A feedback path?

8. What additional options do the models contain?

9. Assuming three alternative scenarios about the future, sketch a flow-chart showing the multiple branches required.

10. What are the basic steps in the open-loop optimizing model?

Discussion

1. Under what circumstances would a muddling-through type of decision process be more appropriate than the focused objective type? (*Hint:* read the Lindbloom reference.)

2. Give the advantages and disadvantages of satisficing and optimizing procedures.

3. Give the advantages and disadvantages of open and closed-loop processes.

4. Why does the possible existence of alternative futures complicate decision making?

Research

1. Interview one or more decision makers and, for a particular decision they made, try to discover the degree of applicability of the decision models in this chapter to the real decision problem.

2. Reread the cases from Part I and try to identify and describe the decision processes by using the concepts and models developed in this chapter.

5. Decision Alternatives

The principal ideas developed in this chapter are:

1. *The quality of a decision cannot be better than the best alternative allows.*

2. *The scores earned by alternatives on multiple criteria can be expressed by means of outcome and valuation score-sets, and each of these sets can be combined into decision matrices.*

3. *The decision maker has a choice of representing the multiple criteria as variables, major or minor attributes, and a choice of measurement scales for scoring the criteria.*

When, in using one of the decision models shown in Chapter 4, the decision maker becomes convinced that the system undergoing critical scrutiny has an output that deviates intolerably from desired performance, he knows that he must take timely and appropriate corrective action to reduce the deviation to a tolerable level. He has studied the problematic situation and has arrived at a good understanding of the ways in which the system must be altered to achieve the desired state. He has ascertained who must be satisfied by the change, who will be affected, how they will be affected, and he has given thought to the criteria on which alternative courses of action will be rated. He knows that he must give proper weights to the interests of all affected parties so that the action program he finally adopts will simply not create new and perhaps more troublesome problems than the one that he initially set out to solve.

He is now ready to take the next step—to find a particular program of action which will, when adopted and implemented, very probably correct the excessive deviation. He has the option of searching for only one acceptable solution (satisficing) or searching for many from which he will choose one as the best (optimizing).

It would be a rare and happy coincidence if the first alternative thought of was the best. More than likely, he will conceive of several ways for dealing with the problem, each of which has its strong and weak points; each of which will favor one combination of interests and will disfavor others. He must, therefore, evaluate all alternative solutions on each of the relevant criteria as the first step toward arriving at a merit-ordering. He may find that there are many types of alternatives.

TYPES OF ALTERNATIVES

Disparate alternatives are those that are members of a *heterogeneous* class, that is, they differ in kind not in degree. For example, when John Jones, age 18, was graduated from high school and pondered his next move, he identi-fied the following disparate alternatives.

1. To go on to college.
2. To go into his father's business.
3. To get married immediately.
4. To find a job.
5. To become a beachcomber or a ski-bum.
6. To enlist in one of the armed services.
7. To join the Peace Corps.
8. To stay home and loaf.

These eight alternatives are members of the heterogeneous class "things for John Jones to do after graduation from high school."

Discrete alternatives are those that correspond to subjects, persons, objects, actions, or other members of a *homogeneous* class. Examples are the floors in a multistory building, the shares of common stock of a corpora-tion, and the keys of a typewriter. A share of common stock and a share of preferred stock would be a pair of discrete and disparate objects.

Alternatives are *continuous* if they are homogeneous, can be infinitely subdivided, and differ from each other in degree, not kind. As a practical matter, alternatives that are technically discrete may be deemed continuous if the differences between adjacent alternatives are negligibly small. For example, amounts of money make up a set of continuous alternatives; there is very little difference between $1,000,000 and $1,000,001 for most situations. But alternatives made up of integral multiples of $10,000 (for example, $10,000, $20,000, $30,000, and so forth) would be better characterized as discrete.

Alternatives are *mutually exclusive* if adopting one implies rejection of all others; mutually exclusive alternatives cannot be combined into programs. For example, if John Jones chooses to join the United States Army, he could not join the United States Navy or the Marine Corps at the same time. He could, however, join the United States Army *and* get married because these alternatives are not mutually exclusive.

Alternatives are either *simple* or *compound.* They are simple if they involve single, nondivisible or nonseparable actions. Thus all of John Jones' alternatives listed above are simple. If, however, he considers (*a*) going to the local community college *and* getting married *and* going into his father's business part-time, he will have adopted a compound alternative. Compound alternatives are combinations of nonmutually exclusive alternatives.

If a decision problem involves a multiplicity of symptoms underlying more than one dysfunctional condition, the alternatives may consist of bundles or programs made up of simple or compound alternatives. Some programs may consist of action sequences in which some parts of the program are implemented before others.

DEVELOPING WORKABLE ALTERNATIVES

The preferred alternative is the best (or least bad) of the set undergoing evaluation. But even the very best may not be good enough. If only poor alternatives are conceived, the one found to be best will not transcend the inherent shortcomings of the lot. For example, if the candidates for the job of bank cashier were drawn from a random sample of inmates from the state penitentiary who had been convicted at least twice of fraud and embezzlement, even the best of that lot might not make good bank cashier material. Finding good alternatives is an essential part of making good decisions because the quality of the ultimate decision cannot be better than the best alternative allows.[1]

There are many ways for devising suitable alternatives. Some techniques used by experienced people are:

1. Drawing on one's own past experience and making comparisons between the current problem and previous problems successfully resolved.
2. Drawing on the advice and recommendations of outside qualified experts who have dealt with similar problems for their clients.
3. Drawing on the experience of colleagues, or other administrators and executives either through face-to-face meetings or through library research.
4. Drawing on the collective creativity and expertise of special internal committees or task forces set up for the purpose of dealing with the current problem.
5. Drawing on the responses of representatives of the interest groups that would be affected by the decision.

THE ALTERNATIVES' SCORE MATRIX

The rating scores of the alternatives for the multiple criteria should be neatly arranged and displayed in tabular form. One preferred arrangement is the matrix shown in Figure 4–8a. The rows of this tableau contain the scores for each alternative on all criteria. The columns hold the scores for each criterion on all alternatives.

If the satisficing models shown in Figures 4–5 and 4–6 are combined with the optimizing model of Figure 4–7, a model combining both optimizing and satisficing procedures will result, as shown in Figures 5–1 and 5–2.

This combination model involves criteria expressed in three forms: (a) *variables,* (b) *major attributes,* and (c) *minor attributes* in a tableau similar to that in Figure 5–3.

Variables and Attributes

Criteria are expressed as *variables* when outcomes or valuations can be expressed on a multi-interval scale. They are expressed as *attributes* when only two states are possible: go, no-go; or pass-fail; or good-bad; and so forth. Variables are usually represented on a numerical scale; attributes by "one" (pass) or "zero" (fail).

Attributes may be subdivided into *major* and *minor* (synonyms: critical and noncritical). A critical attribute is one so important that failure to earn the "one" score would disqualify the alternative from further consideration regardless of the scores on other criteria. Major attributes are used for pre-screening alternatives for feasibility or admissability in a particular decision problem solution. For example, a patently unlawful action, although otherwise attractive, would be rejected out of hand.

A minor attribute is one that is less important and, therefore, failure to earn the "one" score would not necessarily disqualify the alternative.

Outcome Score-Sets

Associated with each alternative is an outcome score-set that expresses through a set of numbers the scores assigned to the alternative on each criterion. In symbolic form, the outcome score-set for the i_{th} alternative in a set of *n* alternatives is

$$[A_i]_{\text{outcome}} = [O_{i1}, O_{i2}, O_{i3}, \ldots O_{ij}, \ldots O_{im}] \tag{5-1}$$

where O_{ij} = the *number* representing the outcome for the ith alternative on the jth criterion.

When the outcome score-sets for all alternatives on the multiple criteria

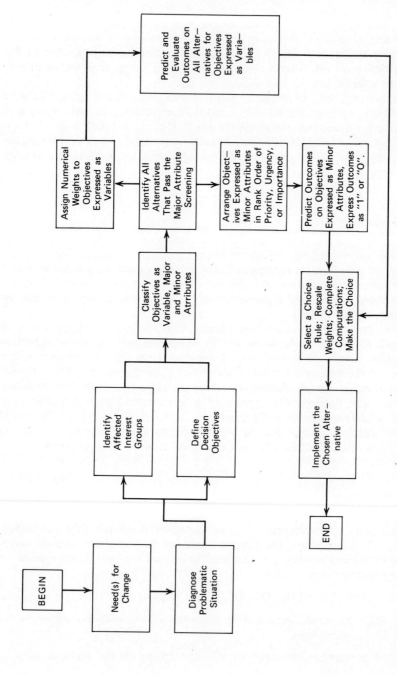

FIGURE 5–1. *Decision model that combines optimizing procedures for objectives expressed as variables and satisficing procedures for objectives expressed as major and minor attributes.*

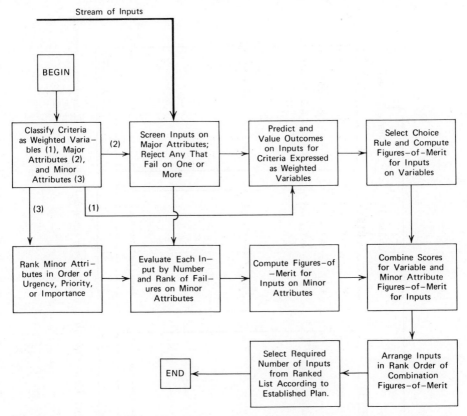

FIGURE 5–2. *Evaluation model that combines optimizing procedure for criteria expressed as variables and satisficing procedure for criteria expressed as major and minor attributes.*

are arranged in tabular form, they constitute the alternatives' outcome-matrix. For example, if there are three alternatives and five criteria, the outcome matrix is

Criterion Number

Alternative Number	1	2	3	4	5	
1	O_{11}	O_{12}	O_{13}	O_{14}	O_{15}	
2	O_{21}	O_{22}	O_{23}	O_{24}	O_{25}	(5-2)
3	O_{31}	O_{32}	O_{33}	O_{34}	O_{35}	

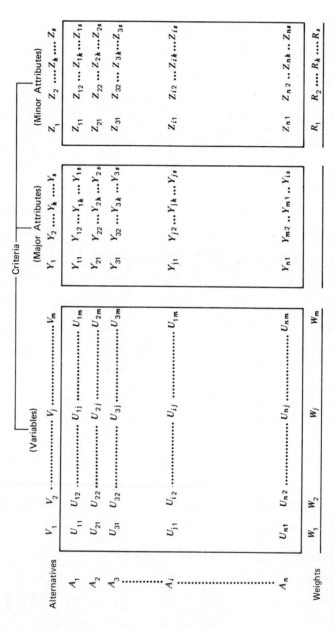

FIGURE 5–3. *Triple decision matrix showing scores for n alternatives on m criteria expressed as variables, and others expressed as major and minor attributes.*

Valuation Score-Sets

Corresponding to each outcome score-set is a valuation score-set. Each element in the latter corresponds to an element in the former. Each element in the valuation score-set represents a valuation of an outcome. In symbolic form the valuation score-set for the i_{th} alternative is

$$[A_i]_{\text{value}} = [u_{i1}, u_{i2}, u_{i3}, \ldots u_{ij}, \ldots u_{im}] \tag{5-3}$$

where u_{ij} equals the valuation attached to the O_{ij} s of expression (5–1).

And the alternatives' valuation score-matrix is

	Criterion Number					
Alternative Number	1	2	3	4	5	
1	u_{11}	u_{12}	u_{13}	u_{14}	u_{15}	
2	u_{21}	u_{22}	u_{23}	u_{24}	u_{25}	(5-4)
3	u_{31}	u_{32}	u_{33}	u_{34}	u_{35}	

The work involved in assigning numerical values to the cell entries of the outcome matrix (the O_{ij} s) and to the valuation matrix (the u_{ij} s) is explored in Part III. The rationale and methodology for amalgamating the elements of the valuation score-sets into indexes or figures-of-merit for the purpose of merit-ordering decision alternatives is developed in Part IV.

MEASUREMENT SCALES

Measurement of Common Properties

In the foregoing paragraphs, we mentioned the elements of the outcome score-set for an alternative on multiple criteria with elements represented by the symbol, O_{ij}, posited as being numbers on some sort of measurement scale. Using scales in this manner is analogous to their use in measurement practice in the physical or social sciences. A set of objects (or phenomena) is perceived by an observer as possessing one or more common properties on which they differ in degree. We use the particular measurement scheme to express these differences in terms of a position on a number or a language scale.

For example, a number of women are waiting in the outer office of a theatrical producer who is casting for a new play. Each woman has been given a form that is to be used for prescreening. The form contains a list of descriptive categories that include:

a.   Name and address.

b.   Age.

c.   Height.

d.   Weight.

e.   Physical measurements.

f.   Years of acting experience.

g.   List of acting credits.

h.   Marital status.

i.   State of health.

j.   Clothing sizes.

k.   Beauty.

l.   Voice quality.

m.   Facial type.

n.   Carriage.

o.   Charisma.

Obviously, some of these answers would be easier to express as numbers than others.

We could not tell how these outcome scores would be valued by the producer without first knowing more about the specific parts that he is trying to cast. If he is casting for the three witches in *Hamlet*, youth, physical beauty, and marital status might not be given much weight. But if he is casting for the romantic lead in *Wuthering Heights*, age, beauty, voice quality, and charisma may be given high priority.

Types of Scales[2]

Six scales often encountered in the literature of the social and physical sciences are:

1.   Nominal—language or numeric.
2.   Positional—language or numeric.
3.   Ordinal—language or numeric.
4.   Arbitrary—language or numeric.
5.   Relative—equal interval numeric.
6.   Absolute—equal interval numeric.

NOMINAL SCALES.   The most elementary scale of the six is the nominal, language or numeric, primarily intended for identification or coding purposes. For example, a firm prepares a list of employee names with their time clock, payroll, or social security identification numbers. Nominal scales do not ordinarily contain ordering or positional information, although they can be modified to contain both (for example, by assigning payroll numbers according to date of hire by department or work space assignment).

POSITIONAL SCALES.   This scale can be thought of as a refinement over the nominal scale. It provides locational or positional information without necessarily implying ordering. Examples of such scales are: home addresses, coordinates of an airplane's position (latitude, longitude, altitude), colors of the spectrum, and names of tones on the musical scale.

ORDINAL SCALES.   The simplest way of ordering is by language, as in expressing the temperature of water: boiling, very hot, hot, warm, tepid, cool, cold, very cold, or freezing. This language order can be converted into a numerical order by assigning an order number to each word as follows:

(hottest first) boiling (1), very hot (2), et cetera
(coldest first) freezing (1), very cold (2), et cetera

Ordinal scales are useful for ranking items by the magnitude of a measurement. Investment projects can be ranked by return on investment; golf contestants can be ranked by their game scores. The ordinal scale does not necessarily imply valuational judgment; but, of course, valuations can easily be attached to the rankings. We might, for example, arrange all large industrial firms in rank order of their liquidity, but we could not be certain that one liquidity score was any better than another.

The ordering of items contains no information about the relative spacing of adjacent items. For example,

Item No.	Weight (in lbs.)	Ranking	Difference (in lbs.)
4	5000	1st	—
2	4800	2nd	200
7	1000	3rd	3800
1	999	4th	1
3	998	5th	1
6	1	6th	997
5	⅛	7th	⅞

This example reveals the futility of attempting to infer the spacing of adjacent items from ranking scores. It is also evident that if the true measurements are known, placing the items in rank order causes the loss of much information. Conversely, less information is needed to place items in rank order than on a true measurement scale.

ARBITRARY SCALES. These scales are used for coding responses from a set of forced choices. For example, in conducting a public opinion poll, an interviewer asked a sample of Americans this question: "United States Senator Fullbright recently stated that he favors immediate and unconditional withdrawal of all American troops from Vietnam. What do you think of this? Answer: strongly agree (5), agree (4), don't know or don't care (3), disagree (2), strongly disagree (1)."

Arbitrary scales may be either unipolar (example: 1, 2, 3, 4, 5, 6, 7) or bipolar (example −3, −2, −1, 0, +1, +2, +3).

RELATIVE-EQUAL INTERVAL SCALES. This scale is one with uniform intervals but with no absolute zero point. The zero point must be established arbitrarily and all measurements must be related to the reference. For example, the distances from headquarters to all district offices of a firm would be measured (air miles or speedometer mileage) and placed on a relative scale.

If the location of the headquarters was changed, all office distances would have to be changed.

Depending on the physical meaning, this type of scale can have both positive and negative numbers. Negative distances from headquarters might have no physical meaning, but below zero temperature on a centigrade or Fahrenheit scale would be meaningful.

ABSOLUTE-EQUAL INTERVAL SCALES. This scale also has uniform intervals and in addition has an absolute zero. It is used when the measured quantity can be absent altogether or present in varying amounts. For example, the contents of a money box can be truly zero when it is empty.

Depending on the physical meaning, this scale, too, can have negative values. If one's bank account is overdrawn, it will require varying amounts of money to return it to zero. These amounts can be assigned negative signs.

Common Scales

The special computational requirements of an alternative ordering procedure may make it necessary to transform all scales (some of which have incommensurate units) into a common scale with commensurate units.[3] For example: man-hours, product shipments, returns and allowances, and the like, may be transformed into dollar equivalents for financial analysis.

For some transformations into common units, no difficulty is experienced because the relationship between the original scale and the transformed scale is linear. In other cases, the linearity condition may not hold true. For example; the relationship between man-hours worked per week and dollars of payroll cost may not be linear because of overtime premiums after eight hours per day of working time. The relationship between sound pressure and loudness sensation is not linear. The nonlinearity between physical measurements and utility scales is widely recognized.

An example of both a linear and nonlinear relationship between an original measurement scale and a transformed scale is given in the two tabulations below.

Alternative Number	Profit ($000)	Relative Attractiveness	Liquidity Ratio	Relative Attractiveness
a	100	10	0.500	20
b	200	20	0.800	40
c	300	30	1.000	50
d	400	40	1.500	75
e	500	50	2.000	100
f	600	60	3.000	75
g	700	70	4.000	50
h	800	80	5.000	20

Scale Conversion Constants

The units of a measurement scale may be changed by altering the size of the intervals. For example, a distance scale may have intervals of microns, inches, miles, or light-years, without changing the basic fact that the measurement is one of length or distance. The conversion of one scale to another, when only the interval size is changed, is accomplished by multiplication by a constant (feet are converted to inches by multiplying the number of feet by 12 inches per foot).

Reasonable caution is required to avoid errors in performing arithmetic operations with data derived from scales having different sized intervals. For example, if the scores on three criteria for three alternatives are:

Alternative Number	Criterion No 1 (Dollars)	Criterion No. 2 ($000)	Criterion No. 3 ($000,000)
1	100.00	2.000	0.500
2	720.00	2.300	0.800
3	350.00	1.800	0.200

Addition across the rows for alternative No. 1 (100 + 2.000 + 0.500) would clearly be nonsensical, whereas (100 + 2000 + 50,000) would be correct.

Notes and References

1. M. O. Edwards, op. cit., and A. F. Osborne, op. cit.

2. For a rigorous treatment of measurement scales in the social sciences see Johann Pfanzagl, *Theory of Measurement* (New York, John Wiley and Sons, 1968) and Clyde H. Coombs, *A Theory of Data* (New York, John Wiley and Sons, 1964).

3. For a general discussion of units and dimensions in measurement scales see P. W. Bridgman, *Dimensional Analysis* (New Haven, Yale University Press, 1931) and A. Porter, "Units and Dimensions," *Encyclopaedia Brittanica,* xiii edition and others.

Important Words and Concepts

Merit-ordering
Disparate
Discrete

Continuous
Mutually exclusive
SImple, compound
Programs
Variables
Minor attributes
Major attributes
Outcome score-set
Outcome matrix
Valuation score-set
Valuation matrix
Nominal scale
Positional scale
Ordinal scale
Arbitrary scale
Relative scale
Absolute scale
Conversion constants
Incommensurate units

Overview of Chapter 5

After working through the preliminary steps discussed in Chapters 4 and 5, the decision maker must develop a set of workable alternatives. He must find good alternatives because the quality of the ultimate decision cannot transcend the best alternative of the set.

The scores for an alternative on all criteria make up the outcome score-set which in combination make up the outcome matrix. The valuation score-sets and the valuation matrix correspond to the outcome sets.

A number of different kinds of measurement scales are available for measuring outcomes of alternatives including: (1) nominal, (2) positional, (3) ordinal, (4) arbitrary, (5) relative, and (6) absolute. Special computational requirements may dictate the need for common scales with commensurate units. Caution must be observed in the proper application of scale conversion constants.

Questions for Review, Discussion, and Research

Review

1. Review the steps in the decision process up to the preparation of the outcome and valuation matrices.

2. Distinguish between disparate and discrete alternatives.

3. Distinguish between discrete and continuous alternatives.

4. Why can't mutually exclusive alternatives be combined into programs or compound alternatives?

5. Why may finding the best alternative in the set presented for evaluation not be good enough?

6. Distinguish between variables and attributes.

7. Distinguish between minor and major attributes.

8. Distinguish between the outcome and valuation score-sets.

9. What are the six types of measurement scales and how do they differ in application?

10. Do the outcome and the valuation scales necessarily have a one-to-one correspondence?

11. Why is it incorrect to add $100.00 to 0.001 million of dollars to get the sum $100.001.

Discussion

1. How could a decision maker be more certain that he had the best possible alternatives in the set presented for evaluation?

2. Identify a set of criteria for a particular decision problem and discuss the pros and cons of representing them as variables, major or minor attributes.

3. The more precise the measurement scale that is used for developing outcome scores for alternatives, the greater the cost of obtaining reliable data. Discuss the validity of this proposition.

Research

1. Interview an executive who has made or is just making a complex decision involving multiple objectives. Try to identify the decision elements and to identify the alternatives that he has examined. Were any alternatives rejected in advance because they failed to pass muster on one or more major attributes?

2. For the decision found in No. 1 above or in any other you can find, identify the criteria used to gauge goal attainment. Are they valid criteria? On what kinds of scales are they measured?

CASES *for part two*

APPENDIX *to part two*

Additional Problems Involving Multiple Objectives

1. A company is contemplating the introduction of a new line of passenger automobiles into the United States market. They recognize that a new name is required for this line. What purposes do product names serve and what are the criteria on which proposed names should be evaluated?

2. A profitable firm with a tangible net worth of more than $10 million and no long-term debt is seeking to raise $2 million to finance a new product venture. What alternatives are available for raising these funds and what are the criteria that should be used for selecting the best method?

3. A firm that formerly concentrated on the sale of industrial goods has decided to undertake the marketing of a new consumer product. They are looking for an advertising agency to assist in the promotion of the new line. What criteria should they use for the selection of an agency?

4. A firm with a policy of intensive distribution of its line of proprietary medicines has decided to switch over to selling through exclusive wholesalers in each major trading area. What criteria should they establish for the selection of wholesalers to approach about taking on their line?

5. A United States Senate committee is considering legislation on revenue sharing. What purposes could such a plan serve and what bases for allocation of funds among the states should be used?

6. A medium-sized company in the automobile replacement parts field is approached by a large mail-order house about the possibility of manufacturing and packaging parts under the private label of the mail-order house. The proposed product mix would require allocation of more than 60 percent of the firm's present productive capacity. What are the principal factors that should be considered before coming to a firm decision on a reply to this inquiry?

7. A firm has developed a new product that involves special know-how. They are told by a marketing consultant that the products should have a sales potential in other countries besides the United States. They become interested in this potential market and wonder how they could reach foreign customers. Their marketing manager suggests these alternatives:
   (a) Sell to exporters as orders are received.
   (b) Set up an export division and appoint sales agents in several foreign countries.
   (c) Set up a company-owned sales subsidiary in each country in which sales potential exists and import from the United States parent.

(d) Enter in one or more joint ventures with foreign nationals for manu-
     facturing abroad.

(e) Sell know-how to foreign firms for a royalty.

(f) Set up wholly-owned manufacturing and sales subsidiaries in sev-
     eral countries.

How would you suggest they go about identifying the best alternative?
What criteria would you suggest that they use for making this determination?

CASE II-I
Manson Film Corp. Handles a Customer Complaint

SUMMARY: A complaint concerning fogged film is received from a customer in Florida, triggering an investigation. Bob Faye, Manson's photographic film engineer, makes a painstaking and successful diagnosis.

Manson Film Corp. is a supplier of large-area photographic film for specialized industrial processes. The product line consists of standard and specially sized sheets of high-definition, supersensitive photographic color film. The film sheets are prepared under closely controlled conditions, and the number of customer complaints about film quality has been virtually nil for the past five years.

On the 15th of August, Mr. James Robinson, sales manager for Manson Film, received a telephone call from Al Tysen, Manson's sales representative in the Florida territory. Tysen reported that three plants of the FWC company were complaining about receiving fogged film from Manson. The plants involved were located in Tampa, St. Petersburg, and Sarasota, Florida. Tysen also noted that the west coast of Florida was experiencing a spell of abnormally high temperatures and humidity and, perhaps, this was the cause of the trouble. He asked Robinson to replace the defective film immediately and to investigate the problem because he was afraid of losing the FWC account to a competitor. Robinson agreed that an immediate inquiry was necessary.

Bob Faye, Manson's photographic film sales engineer was assigned to the problem. His initial findings were as follows:

1. The complaint about fogged film represented a potential hazard and the cause must be found before a single case grew into an epidemic.
2. An examination of the in-plant processing, packaging, and handling revealed no unusual factors. There had been no increase in film defects, and quality standards and procedures had not been changed in any material way.
3. The only material changes made recently was in the kind of paper used to separate film sheets. The new paper had been carefully tested before adoption. The changeover had been made in February of that year.
4. The FWC complaints were the only ones received to date for film fogging. An investigation revealed that the film was shipped from stock and was from the first batch packed with the new paper separators. The film had been shipped to FWC's main office in Tampa and was stored in the Tampa stockroom until released to the three plants on August 1.

5. All of the film sent to FWC was reported as defective by each of FWC's three plant foremen.
6. One hundred percent of a second shipment made from Manson stock to replace the initial quantity was also reported fogged.
7. Testing of the film in Manson's stock revealed zero percent defective in all test samples.

Faye offered the following hypotheses:

1. The Manson film or its packaging contained a latent defect that only became apparent after prolonged exposure to abnormally high temperature and humidity. Since regular film stock was impervious to ordinary conditions that might be encountered throughout the United States, the new paper must be suspect.
2. The Manson film is not defective in any way, but the damage occurred somehow in transportation.
3. The film arrives in Tampa in perfect condition but something in the local environment on the Gulf coast produces the fogging; that is, radioactivity, atmospheric pollution, or the like.
4. The film arrives at the using plant in perfect condition but the subsequent processing is faulty, and the good film is spoiled by the customer's handling in the plants.

Faye then decided to test each hypothesis in order. He found:

1. A film sample manufactured at the same time as that shipped to FWC and similarly packaged was subjected to elevated temperature and humidity. *Results:* no substantial deterioration in film quality. Reject hypothesis no. 1.
2. Film samples from the same batch were shipped to Tampa by the same carrier used previously and marked "DO NOT OPEN—HOLD FOR ARRIVAL OF MANSON REPRESENTATIVE." Tests found this sample to be satisfactory. *Conclusion:* shipping was not at fault, except for a theoretical possibility of exceptional circumstances. Since two separate shipments had been defective, the probability of encountering identical exceptional circumstances in two consecutive shipments was small. Reject hypothesis no. 2.
3. FWC's Tampa stockroom was tested for radioactivity with a Geiger counter and for air pollution, temperature, and humidity. *Results:* no evidence of abnormal condition. Reject hypothesis no. 3.
4. Hand-carried samples of film delivered in person by Faye himself and processed routinely in the three FWC plants revealed no defects. Reject hypothesis no. 4.

Faye reported to Robinson, "Either I have missed something, or the two incidents of fogged film were a coincidence. Let's try a third shipment and see what happens." This was done and in due time Tysen telephoned that the third shipment was defective in the same manner as the other two.

Faye decided that he would follow a film shipment from the carrier's loading dock in Tampa until it reached each of the three plants. This is what he found:

1. The carrier drove around town for a few hours with the film in his truck before delivering it to FWC's receiving department.
2. The receiving clerk picked up the film package after signing the shipping document and carried it to the inspection department.
3. The inspector opened the package of film and counted the number of sheets to be certain that the number conformed to the quantity ordered. Then he restored the film to the package and placed it on his shelves for later delivery to the plants.

Faye approached the chief inspector and said:

"I noticed that you opened the packages of film and counted the number of sheets. Don't you know that photographic film is ruined if it is exposed to light? Can't you see the large red warning label on the box?"

The inspector became angry. "The hell with labels. My orders are to verify the count on every shipment and to notify the accounting and purchasing departments if there are any shortages. That's what I'm ordered to do and that's what I do until my boss tells me something different. Now get out of my shop before I have you thrown out on your ear!"

1. What should Bob Faye do now?
2. Review the diagnostic procedure used in this investigation and relate it to the eleven steps of a diagnosis in Box 3–1.
3. If you were in Bob Faye's shoes, would you have done anything differently? Would you have used a different sequence in testing the hypotheses. Why or why not?

CASE II-II
Holden Enterprise's Credit Problem

SUMMARY: The Capacitor Division's sales to industrial distributors are declining when they should be increasing. The sales manager's investigation reveals that Holden's credit department has been refusing to release deliveries to many distributors although they are not past due on their payments for capacitor deliveries. The sales manager discovers the reasons for the difficulty, but he is temporarily blocked by the controller's office; and he fears sales will continue to deteriorate unless a prompt corrective action can be taken.

Background

In the year 1964, the Holden Capacitor Division of Holden Enterprises, a broadly diversified manufacturer of electrical goods, was experiencing a puzzling decline in sales of its electrical capacitors to industrial distributors.

Holden manufactures a full line of electrical capacitors used in aircraft, automotive, home appliance, and electronics applications. Ninety percent of the division's sales are to original equipment manufacturers (OEM's), and the balance is to industrial distributors who, in turn, sell both to OEM's and to other small users.

Holden has a semi-exclusive distributor policy. In small cities one major distributor is designated as the exclusive, authorized Holden Capacitor outlet; in larger cities, for example, New York, Los Angeles, Chicago, Boston, two or three of the larger distributors are appointed. Authorized distributors are expected to carry reasonable inventories of Holden capacitors and, to encourage this practice, are given price protection up to 1000 pieces of a capacitor type.

The Capacitor Division has been very satisfied with the industrial program because of its effect in expanding the sales exposure of Holden capacitors and in keeping down the expense of handling small orders from the factory (all orders for under 1000 pieces of a type are referred to an industrial distributor who sells these quantities at the factory list price).

In May of 1964, Arnold Brewer, Holden Capacitor's distributor sales manager, noticed two disturbing things happening with his distributor customers: (a) an increasing frequency of complaints about delayed deliveries on distributor's orders, and (b) a reduction in new business. These phenomena were especially disturbing because of the following. (1) Capacitor sales were in a rising trend and the factory was not having any delivery problems with its OEM customers. (2) There was no change in the policy relative to the desirability of full use of the industrial distributor channel. (3) None of Holden's competitors were known to have mounted any new promotions to industrial distributors. Holden's sales were declining just at the time that they should have been rising.

Holden Capacitors did not employ factory-paid salesmen to call on distributor accounts but, instead, relied on manufactures' representatives. Thus the channels of communication between Holden and its industrial distributors were variable. Some distributors' purchasing agents telephoned their orders directly to the factory, some sent their orders by mail, and some sent them to the agent's offices for transmission to the factory. Thus Brewer knew only a few of the distributor buyers well, at least from telephone conversations, and some he knew not at all.

Brewer's Initial Investigation

The disturbing symptoms continued throughout May, June, and July, and Brewer knew that he would have to take some definite action. He began by making telephone calls to a number of industrial distributors' buyers whose orders had declined the most. One of his telephone conversations went like this:

BREWER: *Hello, Joe Pines? This is Arnold Brewer of Holden Capacitors. How are things with you? How's the wife and kids?*

PINES: Not bad, Arnold. Business is pretty good, Mary and the kids are doing fine. What can I do for you today?

BREWER: *Joe, I notice that you haven't been ordering capacitors from us recently. What's wrong, are capacitor sales falling off?*

PINES: Not at all Arnold. In fact, they are increasing every month. We haven't been ordering from you because we've had so much trouble with deliveries on our orders. You know we have plenty of capacitor suppliers dying to do business with us, so who needs a supplier that doesn't deliver on time?

BREWER: *I can't understand why there should be any trouble with deliveries, Joe. We have adequate stocks of the types you have been buying in our distributor inventory. Are you sure that's the reason? There are no quality problems, are there?*

PINES: None that I know of. It's just lousy delivery. Listen to this. I ordered 1000 pieces of the 9700 electolytics on May 10 and here it is August 20 and I still haven't gotten delivery. I had to order the units from someone else and had a devil of a time switching my customer to another brand. I'm sorry about the brand switching, I know that must hurt, but we all have to make a living.

BREWER: *That's terrible, Joe. I can't understand why your deliveries have been delayed. Why didn't you call me about it?*

PINES: Listen, Arnold. I buy thousands of items every day. I just don't have the time for that sort of thing. What I need most of all is a reliable supplier who never lets me down. You know—three strikes and you are out. Holden is on its fifth strikeout.

BREWER: *Thank's for being so frank with me, Joe. I'll look into the matter and will get back to you in a few days. OK?*

PINES: Fine, Arnold. Take your time. We have plenty of capacitor suppliers. So long.

Brewer's conversations with buyers from other distributors struck the same theme. He checked his outstanding orders and confirmed that there was an abnormal number of undelivered orders for items that were in plentiful supply.

Holden Procedures

In 1964 Holden Capacitor Division's distributor sales people had no pro-cedure for follow-up of order delivery because most orders were shipped from inventory the same day that they were received. If items were tem-porarily out of stock, the stockroom back-ordered them and shipped the missing items as soon as they became available. The distributor sales depart-ment received shipping notifications but because of the large volume of orders and the good experience, no procedure existed for checking the status and aging of distributor orders.

On receipt of an order for capacitors from an authorized distributor, the sales clerk checks the stock list for availability and the credit list for credit "holds." If the goods are in stock and there is no "hold," all orders for amounts under $500 are released to the shipping department. Special credit approval is required for orders over $500 in valuation. Withdrawals and additions to stock are posted on an inventory card file and, when inventory levels on items drop below a predetermined figure, replenishment orders are placed with the factory. Periodically, Arnold Brewer reviews the order back-log and the recent sales experience and prepares a sales forecast by capaci-tor type for the factory. This enables the factory to schedule distributor quantities as overruns on regular OEM production whenever possible. This combining of stock orders with regular production results in overall savings.

Further Investigation

Brewer checked the credit "hold" list and confirmed that many but not all of his best distributors were listed as past due or delinquent. He found this surprising because he had not heard that any distributors were in financial difficulty. He placed another long-distance call to Joe Pines.

BREWER: *Joe, this is Arnold Brewer. How are you?*

PINES: Not bad, Arnold. What's up?

BREWER: *Joe, I checked out your delivery complaints. I noticed that from time to time your deliveries were held up by our credit department. Is your company slowing up in payments of payables?*

PINES: Not that I know of Arnold. We aren't having any trouble with any of our other suppliers. As far as I know we are discounting all bills. I'm reasonably certain we pay all bills in ten to fifteen days from date of invoice.

BREWER: *Well that is queer. Why should we place a credit hold on your account if you are discounting?*

PINES: Search me, Arnold. Anything else?

BREWER: *No, thank you Joe. Regards to the missus. Good-bye.*

Brewer placed his next telephone call to Holden's central credit department in New York and spoke briefly to the credit manager. He found that, indeed, several of his largest distributors were on a delinquency list and for each there was a substantial past-due balance on the ledgers. Brewer asked for a list of invoice numbers, dates, and past-due balances for his accounts and received the list in the mail a few days later. The list confirmed the past-due amounts.

Consultation

Brewer then consulted with his boss, Walter Calkins, sales manager for Holden Capacitors, and outlined the general problem and the results of his preliminary investigation. Calkins instructed Brewer to fly to New York to personally inspect the company accounts receivable records to try to get more information about what was happening. This Brewer agreed to do.

Visit to the Credit Department

In his direct examination of customer invoices, Brewer observed that some of the past-due invoices were for capacitors and some were for an item called "UHF converters." The converter invoices were quite large and had dates in March of that year; all were past due by at least four months. Brewer went over to the credit manager's office with his findings.

BREWER: *I've been checking on those past-due invoices and I see that some of my customers have been billed for an item called "converter." Do you know anything about that?*

CREDIT MANAGER: Yes, those refer to UHF converters made by the tuner division. Certain distributors were sold these converters in March and most of the invoices remain unpaid.

BREWER: *My distributors have been paying for the capacitors they buy, haven't they?*

CREDIT MANAGER: I suppose so, but we can't always tell. If they send in a check with identifying invoice numbers we credit their accounts accordingly. But if the checks do not contain invoice number identification we credit the payments to the old unpaid amounts.

BREWER: *Could that account of the credit holds on some of my capacitor customers?*

CREDIT MANAGER: I can't help that. To us a customer is a customer, no matter what we sell him. If a distributor buys an item from any of our divisions, he is billed centrally and we monitor credit here. It doesn't matter to us what the customer buys, only what he pays against the unpaid balances. That is company policy.

BREWER: *Thanks, I guess I'll have to take a trip to Springfield and have a talk with the tuner people.*

The Springfield Visit

Arnold Brewer met with Kenneth Coster, UHF tuner and converter, distributor sales manager at the Springfield plant.

BREWER: *Ken, we are having problems with credit holds with some of our distributors and I have noticed that you are also having the same trouble.*

COSTER: Yes, that is true. Some distributors haven't been paying for the UHF converters we sent them in March.

BREWER: *How come? Most of these distributors are pretty big and are well financed?*

COSTER: Oh you know distributors. If you ship them something that doesn't sell right away, they won't pay.

BREWER: *Is that what happened with your converters?*

COSTER: Yes. Let me fill you in on what happened. As you may have heard there are new UHF television stations opening up in several parts of the country. Many of the older television sets can't get the new stations without some kind of a converter. We make a great tuner which we sell to OEM's, and our engineers figured that they would also make an equally good converter. They asked me about it and I agreed that there might be a market, but we would have to sell them through distributors.

BREWER: *Through industrial distributors?*

COSTER: Some industrial, some mail-order, and some appliance distributors.

BREWER: *How did it work out?*

COSTER: Well I thought that before we went all out on an expensive program, it might be a good idea to make a test. Instead of signing up a lot of strange distributors, I thought I'd look around for some distributors who were already good Holden customers. In that way I figured we'd meet less sales resistance.

BREWER: *And what happened?*

COSTER: I went out personally and sold the converters to as many Holden distributors as I could. I was fairly successful in placing inventory with several.

BREWER: *Were they on consignment?*

COSTER: No. On open account, but we gave them 30–60–90 day deferred billing.

BREWER: *Did any reorder?*

COSTER: A few, but most could not sell many converters. Part of the poor results was due to our name being unknown to the consumer, part to excessive competition, and part to delays in station openings.

BREWER: *Are you going to take the unsold units back for credit?*

COSTER: Not if we can help it. They will probably sell out in time. My boss gets a bonus on sales volume and the division manager has a profit incentive. If we have to take all the converters back at one time, the bonuses and incentive payments will suffer. They won't listen to any talk about returns of converters.

BREWER: *You know, don't you that when a customer doesn't pay, all shipments are blocked. My customers can't buy capacitors from me, which they would pay for promptly, because they are loaded up with unsalable UHF converters.*

COSTER: Yes, I suppose you're right about that; I hadn't thought of that angle. But that's outside of my bailiwick. I'd help you if I could, but there is nothing I can do. Take it up with the controller's office.

Brewer returned to his home base and reported to Walter Calkins. Calkins telephoned the Holden corporate controller who had jurisdiction over the centralized credit department. Calkins related Brewer's findings. The controller promised an investigation and a reply in a few days.

Interoffice Memorandum

HOLDEN ENTERPRISES

From: Office of the Corporate Controller
To: Walter Calkins, Arnold Brewer

Subject: Credit Policy for Industrial Distributors Selling
                Holden Products

1.   It is Holden's policy to combine all purchases from a customer

under one ledger account regardless of which division makes the sales.

2. It is Holden's policy to closely monitor customer receivable balances and aging. Late payments will automatically cause lowering of credit limts, and excessive delay in reducing past-due balances will result in blocking all shipments.

3. The size of the credit limit is determined by the credit worthiness of the customer and the payment experience.

4. Increases in credit limits or special extended terms for stocking inventories can be arranged, but each case is judged on its own merits. Recommendations from the cognizant sales department and credit worthiness of customers are taken into consideration.

5. With reference to individual distributors who have past-due balances because of unpaid invoices for UHF converters, unless these past-due balances are paid up or the merchandise is returned for credit, the accounts must continue to be blocked and further shipments to delinquent accounts must be withheld except on a "cash in advance" basis.

6. Return of merchandise for credit is subject to issuance of a return goods authorization by the cognizant sales organization, to inspection of the returned goods, and to Holden's customary restocking charges.

1. *What do you think Brewer should do?*
2. *Review the steps in Brewer's diagnosis and relate them to the eleven diagnostic steps in Box 3–1.*
3. *What interests are affected by this decision problem and what are their relative urgencies?*
4. *Identify the interested parties and try to infer their objectives in this particular problem.*
5. *Can you think of any way that this problem could have been avoided or how to change things so that it cannot happen again?*

CASE II-III
Alpha Industries' Budget Hassle*

SUMMARY: The marketing manager's request for funding of the next year's marketing program is slashed by 22 percent, but the president insists on retaining higher sales goals regardless of the cut. He accuses the marketing manager of taking a defeatist position when he protests against the cuts and retention of the higher goal.

The operating executives of the Alpha Industries division were seated around the long, rectangular directors' table waiting for Clarence Penny, Alpha's executive vice-president and general manager, to arrive for the first day of the annual budget meeting sequence. The teak-paneled room was noisy with conversation and laughter; the air was hazy from tobacco smoke. The mood of the assemblage was deceptively lighthearted; but for Joe Harris, Alpha's director of marketing, the atmosphere was reminiscent of those mornings in Korea when he and his fellow pilots had waited to be briefed for their next bombing mission. There had been humor and horseplay there too, but also the unmistakable undercurrent of tension and anxiety.

Clarence Penny entered the room and walked around the table chatting amiably and shaking hands with each of his executives. He exuded good humor and fellowship. He took his place at the head of the table and called the meeting to order. He began by saying:

"Gentlemen, please forgive me for being late. I had an important long-distance call from corporate headquarters about this meeting and that held me up longer than I expected. Suppose we begin today with Joe Harris. We need the sales forecast to begin to make sense of our budget. You all have the documents, do you not? Good. Now Joe, you start please."

Joe Harris walked to the lectern, paused a moment, then began:

"Gentlemen, at the top of your data pack you have our next year's sales forecast by product line and a comparison with this and last year's results. Notice that for this current year we show a 7 percent increase in sales income but this required a 10 percent increase in units shipped. The effect of industry-wide price-cutting and the new Japanese competition is only too apparent. We are forecasting the same percentage gains for next year. This should enable the Alpha Industries division to break the fifty-million dollar barrier for the first time in its history.

"Now on the next page, I have recorded our budgetary needs. Last year

* The text of this case is adapted (with permission) from the first half of the screenplay of a business educational film entitled *Presenting the Marketing Budget—A Time of Tension*, produced by Roundtable Films, Inc., Beverly Hills, California. The author created the original story and provided technical advice in the preparation of the screenplay.

our marketing expense, exclusive of salesmen's commissions, was equal to 8 percent of sales income. This year we will finish with an expense figure closer to 8½ percent. For the next year, we estimate a marketing cost close to 9 percent, or a total expenditure of $4,500,000. The rise in expenditures actually involves a reduction in marketing expense per unit of product, but a small rise in outlay per dollar of sales income. We have been able to hold the line and even make some gains in the face of worsening price competition and spiraling costs, but some increases in expense will be unavoidable. Are there any questions before I go into further detail?"

Clarence Penny spoke before anyone else could reply:

"Joe, thank you for a splendidly lucid presentation. I know and appreciate how hard you and your people have been working to raise our sales and market share. I'm delighted also that we will finally break through the fifty-million barrier. Headquarters will be pleased when I tell them the good news."

Penny hesitated, then continued:

"I have been studying your figures and I frankly can't see how we can allow you that much money for marketing next year. The economy is in a precarious state; the unions are making ridiculous wage demands; and costs are going up and up across the board. In spite of all these cost increases, our selling prices continue to be eroded. I'm afraid your department will have to tighten its belt along with all the others."

Penny glanced quickly around the table to be certain that everyone took in the import of those last words.

"But Clarence," Joe Harris protested. "I don't see how we can achieve our target growth without a much more vigorous marketing effort. And that costs money; lots of it."

"That's defeatist talk, Joe. We can't tolerate a defeatist attitude in our top people at Alpha Industries. That was the trouble with your ex-boss, Arnold Parkinson. He always took a defeatist position at our budget meetings . . . Joe, my boy, I have confidence in you and your staff—although I can think of one or two that could use a little jazzing up. I know you won't let us down, Joe. That's why I had you promoted into Parkinson's slot. Because of my confidence in your ability, I was able to convince headquarters that you were the best man for the job."

Penny continued, "Joe, I suggest you call another meeting of your crew and really sharpen your pencils. See if you can't shave at least . . . let me see." He paused and gazed at the ceiling as if performing a difficult mental calculation, "one million dollars off your expense budget."

"A million dollars?" Joe gasped in surprise and dismay. "Why . . . why. . . ." Penny's homilies about defeatism in high places and the pointed reference to the cause of Arnold Parkinson's recent departure from Alpha Industries reached Joe Harris's consciousness in time to forestall any further verbal protest. With a calm that concealed his inner turmoil and dismay, he replied:

"Of course, Clarence. I'll have a modified report ready for the next meeting."

Harris returned to his chair and sat there in a state of semishock. He and the other executives listened patiently to Clarence Penny's exhortations against the twin vices of defeatism and negative thinking. As the seemingly interminable meeting ground to an end, Penny made certain to have the last word. Still exuding optimism, he said:

"Gentlemen, that was a fine meeting. We accomplished a good amount of useful work. I'm sure now that Joe Harris's slightly conservative estimate of fifty millions in sales can be reached and probably exceeded. I'm depending on all of you to do your utmost to push us over the top. With a topnotch team like ours and a little extra effort, it should be a snap. I know none of you will let Alpha Industries down. OK? Good . . . We'll meet again two weeks from today to discuss the revisions to the budget. Have a pleasant day, fellows."

As he unlocked and opened the entrance door to his apartment, Joe Harris was greeted by his wife Martha, who said:

"Hi, Joe darling, I'll be with you in a second. I just have to adjust the flame in the oven. There's a shaker-full of martinis on the dining-room table."

When she returned, she noticed Joe Harris' grim facial expression. She said:

"I can see that today was one of the tough ones. I guessed that would happen. Dorothy used to tell me how tense Arnold was on the first day of the annual budget meeting. How did it go for you?"

"Awful, Martha. That louse Penny was giving us our lumps again. He's got me boxed into a corner and I don't know how to work myself out."

"Well, Joe, let's forget about business for a while. Let's have another cocktail and some dinner. Then we can talk some more about it if you want to. Maybe something will come to you."

After dinner and the wash-up chores were over, Joe Harris lost some of his tension and found himself more ready to talk with Martha about the meeting. She asked:

"What happened at the meeting, Joe?"

"Penny asked me to cut at least one million dollars out of a tight, four and a half million dollar budget estimate."

"Did he cut your sales objectives too?"

"Hell no. He expects me to meet the increased sales goal with 22 percent less money. That man is out of his mind."

"What will you do?"

"I haven't the faintest idea. I just know that I'll have to give him some kind of satisfactory answer if I want to keep my job, but I can't think of one right now."

"Can you agree to the smaller budget?"

"I don't think so. If I did that, he'd tell me that I was really only padding my request. He'd say that he could no longer have confidence in my forecasts. He'd accuse me of not having enough gumption to stand up for my figures when I believe them to be correct and fully justified. That's just what he said to Arnold when, two years ago, he naively and obediently went along with Penny's budget-cut directives."

"Can't you take a firm stand? No, I guess not. Dorothy told me that was what caused Arnold's downfall. Is that what happened to Arnold?"

"Yes. Arnold was so angered by Penny's needling him about his spinelessness—gutlessness, Penny called it—for going along with the cuts, that last year he flatly refused to accept any cuts. He accused Penny of being a "knee-jerk" budget-cutter. Arnold put his job on the line and demanded a vote of confidence in his judgment and integrity. He threatened to resign on the spot rather than to accept a substantial cut in funds without a corresponding drop in sales goals. Penny called Arnold's bluff, and he had no choice but to quit right at the meeting. That's how the vacancy was created and I got the promotion into Arnold's job."

"What can you do then, Joe? You can't accept the cut and you can't offer any outright resistance," Martha commented.

"I certainly don't want any confrontation with Penny on this issue at my first budget meeting, and I just can't see myself backing down. I'll think of something . . . I hope."

"What are the other executives going to do?"

"I don't know yet. I think they are waiting for me to take the lead. Everything depends on my sales forecast. No one has come to me yet with any helpful suggestions. Larry thought I should give in to Penny without making waves. Pete thought I should take a firm stand and go over Penny's head to headquarters if I'm convinced of the correctness of my estimates. I have an idea that they are more interested in seeing how I squirm out of this mess than they are in their own budgets. Hell, Martha, I'm tired of talking about it. Let's watch some television."

Later that evening Martha returned to the topic that dominated both their thoughts. She said:

"Joe, dear. I have a thought . . . Are you absolutely certain that you won't be able to meet the sales goal with Penny's amount?"

"Umm. . . . No, Martha. To be perfectly honest, I guess I'm not really that positive. It's theoretically possible if everything went my way and there were no unpleasant surprises. But that almost never happens; you know that."

"Yes, Joe, of course. Now, how about if you get the full amount you asked for; would you be absolutely certain of success?"

"No, I guess not. It's possible that I might fall short of the target if I got more than the usual number of bad breaks. But I'd be much more likely to succeed with the full amount because I have more margin for error."

"So what it boils down to is a matter of your confidence in your ability to meet the sales goal. If you get less money, you are less confident; more money raises your confidence."

"Mmmm. . . . I suppose that's true, Martha."

"Well, if that's the way it is, why don't you tell that to Penny. Maybe you can make him understand that argument."

Joe Harris mused a while over Martha's analysis of his problem; then he replied:

"I'll think about that, Martha. That's not a bad approach. . . . And I think I'll give Arnold a call in the morning. He may have some ideas on how to handle Penny.

1. *If you were Joe Harris, what would be your objectives in this situation?*
2. *What do you think Mr. Penny was trying to accomplish in his handling of Harris' budget request?*
3. *What alternatives are available to Joe Harris for coping with the situation?*

CASE II-IV
Who Will Get the Two Giant Pandas?

SUMMARY: On behalf of the People's Republic of China, Chou En-lai presents the visiting American President with two giant pandas. A controversy arises in the United States about which zoo will house the rare animals.

During President Richard M. Nixon's historic visit to mainland China in February of 1972, he presented the People's Republic of China with two musk oxen, Milton and Matilda, to be delivered at a later date by the director of the San Francisco zoo. In response to this goodwill gesture, Chou En-lai reciprocated with the gift of two giant pandas for the American people.

From the moment the news of Chou En-lai's gift appeared in the American press, a controversy arose concerning the place of residence of the pandas. Zoos in San Francisco, San Diego, St. Louis, Chicago, Washington, D.C., and New York all put claims. But on March 14, 1972 Mr. Nixon announced his decision to place the pandas in the National Zoo of the Smithsonian Institution in Washington, D.C. The rationale behind the choice was that the pandas were a gift to the American people and, therefore, a zoo financed by federal funds would be most appropriate.

In the ordinary course of events, the announcement would be sufficient to quiet the controversy, but critics of the decision pointed out that the giant pandas are very rare and that not many people could see them at the Washington zoo. The only other places in the world that have pandas, aside from the Peking zoo, are Moscow and London with one each. The critics said a more central location would be better.

Several of the disappointed zoo directors discussed the possibility of requesting Peking to send more pandas, but here, too, a controversy arose. The animals are very scarce, are an endangered species, and do not breed well in captivity.

1. *Assume that instead of making the decision he did, Mr. Nixon had appointed a commission to advise him on the best place to house the giant pandas. Assume also that you are a member of that commission. What would you do?*
2. *What objectives would such a decision serve and what are the relative urgencies?*
3. *Is the National Zoo in Washington the best place for the pandas?*

CASE II-V
Laundromatic Corp. Has a Nepotism Problem

SUMMARY: The president of Laundromatic Corp. is being pressured to hire an incompetent relative in a highly paid position and he resists. But he knows that he must do something constructive or his own security may be jeopardized.

(From a magnetic tape dictated by Robert Maughn, President of Laundromatic Corp.)

Hello Walt, old pal. It was good to hear from you after all these years. I remember those good old days when I used to come to you with all my problems. I'm glad to hear that you are well and enjoying your retirement in the Virgin Islands. Maybe I can impose on you once more because I have a nasty situation here that should be familiar to you. Maybe you can advise me how to proceed. But before I go into the gruesome details allow me to give you some of the background. As you may recall from your investment activities, Laundromatic Corp. is a publicly-owned company which designs, manufactures, assembles, leases, and services automatic, coin-operated washing, drying, and dry-cleaning machines for coin-operated laundries and apartment house laundries. When I say publicly owned, actually the public only owns 40 percent of the shares. The balance is owned by my wife Dolores' family. Dolores' father was the founder of the business and when he died, his 60 percent was divided equally among his heirs: Dolores; Mrs. Franklin, my mother-in-law; and Mrs. Veronica Hartmann, Dolores's sister. The family has complete control of the board of directors. I, myself own just a few thousand shares which I bought for investment at the time of the first public offering, before I married Dolores. I joined the company after my marriage to Dolores. It represented a financial sacrifice at the time because I had a big job with the Whirlaway Corp., the biggest outfit in the home-laundry business. But old Mr. Franklin had his heart set on keeping the business in the family, so I made the temporary sacrifice. It was worth it because now I'm in a pretty good position. I'm president and have the confidence of the board and the family. Up to now they've been willing to leave everything to me as long as the profits are good and the dividends are paid regularly. But now there's a fly in the ointment. The fly is Veronica's husband, Chauncey . . . I received a call from Mrs. Franklin about six weeks ago and she told me that darling Chauncey had just been fired from his job and that, after a short European vacation, he would start looking for another position. This was no surprise to me because my brother-in-law has changed jobs involuntarily at least once a year for the last ten years. I, myself think he's unemployable, but he is such a charming fellow, so well mannered and handsome, that prospective employers are dazzled by his surface charisma. But when it comes to doing a day's work or making a decision, Chauncey cops-out completely. What's worse, he doesn't even realize what's happening. I think there's something wrong with him psychologically, but the family refuses to face that possibility, particularly Veronica . . . Chauncey and Veronica have a large home and a high standard of living. The dividend income from Veronica's stock alone is hardly enough to meet the house payments, let alone their other extravagences. Without a regular source of employment income, the Hartmann's would have to cut their standard of living or, horrors, sell their Laundromatic shares. This last no one wants, least of all me, at least until I can place their shares in friendly hands . . . When Mrs. Franklin called she asked me if I could find a job for Chauncey somewhere, perhaps in the company. I said I'd think about it and call her back. I called Chauncey and had him come in to meet my division heads to see if any of them could use him. They all turned him down saying that they had no openings for such a high-salaried man. What they really meant was that they didn't want a member of the family working for them, especially a boob like Chauncey. So I had to call Mother Franklin back and tell her what had happened and that I'd try to look elsewhere. I did and failed. Chauncey has used up this generation of gullible employers . . . Meanwhile, my sister-in-law has been calling my wife and having tearful sessions about their increasing indebtedness and telling Dolores how cruel and heartless I am for refusing to help her husband and give him a top-level job in the company that he so obviously deserves because of their stock ownership. My mother-in-law is getting more demanding too . . . I'm determined that this issue is one on which I must be firm. If I give Chauncey a top job with the company, not only will he waste the salary and expenses (you know, an office staff and other perquisites due his exalted rank), but he'll cause untold damage within the firm and with our accounts. The man has no judgment whatsoever. I just can't have him in my hair. My job is complicated enough now. And if I hire him, there are lots of other Franklin kin that would like to get aboard too. Hiring Chauncey would set a poor precedent . . . Still, I must do something to get my mother-in-law and sister-in-law off my back. I don't want either of them to sell their shares right now and, between mother and daughter, their 40 percent could outvote me, even assuming that I could count on Dolores to back me up. She's totally unsophisticated when it comes to business matters and she loves her little sister Veronica. If it came to a showdown, I very much doubt that Dolores would side with me on this issue . . . So, Walt, I'm in a bind. I can't put my incompetent brother-in-law on the payroll because, if I did, he wouldn't have enough sense to stay away and leave things to me. He'd insist on having a say in the management. He feels so self-important that he'd meddle in everything. I can't let him get further into debt, because that would jeopardize the stock. I'm unwilling to add his household expenses to mine. They already owe me and Dolores more than $50,000. And I'm so damned busy with our new line that I can't waste any more energy thinking about it . . . Walt, do you have any suggestions on how I can resolve this matter? Oh, damnit!, I have to leave now. Could you drop me a letter with a few words of wisdom like in the old days? I have another nasty problem on my hands, but this is one I can handle myself. I need a new sheet metal supplier, one large enough and well enough equipped to handle our stamping, forming, plating, and enameling needs. My regular supplier was just acquired in a stock deal by my most active competitor, and they gave me notice that they will not be able to take care of all our needs in the future. Finding a new sheet metal house will keep me busy for the next few months . . . But I hope you'll be able to make some constructive suggestions, Walt. At least, give me the benefit of your wisdom; give me a rundown on your ideas. If you can't find a good idea, tell me the least bad. . . . Hey, I wonder if Maury Metals has a sales rep. Maybe I can swindle them into hiring Chauncey to handle our account . . . Strike that Miss Summers. Make me a blue draft of this memo. I'll go over it when I get back.

1. Identify the steps in this decision problem using one of the models from Chapter 5.
2. What are the interests that are affected by this situation and what are their relative urgencies?
3. What do you think Mr. Maughn's objectives are (or should be) and what criteria should be used to gauge goal attainment?
4. What would you advise Mr. Maughn to do about Chauncey?

APPENDIX TO PART II
A Note on Cost-Effectiveness and Cost-Benefit Studies

There is a good deal of overlap in the rationale and methodologies of cost-effectiveness studies, cost-benefit analysis, and complex decision making involving multiple objectives. Because many writers define each one of the three in quite different ways, it is virtually impossible to make a clear distinction among them. Some of the definitions are so broad and imperialistic that each could be used to encompass all three of the techniques. In actual use, however, the differences become more apparent, and they can be more easily understood if we deal with them according to the narrowest meanings, recognizing that each technique, theoretically, could be expanded to encompass the other two.

Cost Benefit Studies

Cost-benefit studies or analysis (hereafter abbreviated CBA) is a practical way for assessing the worth of projects where it is important to take the long view (in the sense of looking for repercussions) and the broad view (in the sense of looking for the effects on persons, groups, organizations, industries, and regions).[1] This form of analysis involves: (1) the enumeration and evaluation of all costs and benefits expected from a project, and (2) a comparison of the costs and benefits. Since the costs and benefits normally take a number of different forms, it is customary to try to make them commensurate by reducing them to common—usually money—values.[2]

Every project incurs costs and yields benefits at more than one point in time, and these must be translated into a common point in time, usually the present. Typically, an interest rate is used to discount costs and benefits to present values.[3]

Complex projects will usually produce costs and benefits for many interests both internal and external to the entity or jurisdiction executing the project. To do a thoroughly complete CBA, the analyst must identify every party at interest and must perform a CBA from each viewpoint.

Typically, cost-benefit studies focus on the effects on all readily identifiable parties, and the alternative is sought that could either maximize the money value-equivalents at a given level of cost, or minimize the cost for a

---

[1] A. R. Prest and R. Turvey, "Cost Benefit Analysis: A Survey," *The Economic Journal,* Vol. LXXV, No. 300 (December 1955), pp. 683–735. Definition adapted from page 683.

[2] W. D. Wood and H. F. Campbell, *Cost-Benefit Analysis and the Economics of Investment in Human Resources* (Kingston, Ontario; Industrial Relations Center, Queens University, 1970), page V. This source contains an extensive bibliography on cost-benefit analysis and many of its applications.

[3] Ibid.

given level of benefits. Since this form of analysis relies heavily on the quantification of both costs and benefits, it loses power when important costs and benefits cannot be expressed in money terms. In such cases, it becomes necessary to leave the unquantifiable factors out of the computations and account for them by narrative.

Lichfield uses a balance sheet of costs and benefits for all identifiable interests, quantifies those he can, and treats the others as contributory to the end evaluation.[4]

There are many practical difficulties in preparing such balance sheets in CBA. One especially frustrating factor is the collective effects that are so diffuse that they affect the well-being of entire populations. The United States landing on the moon was hailed as a boon to all humanity. The efforts of a municipality to eliminate air pollution involve collective costs and collective benefits, although not in the same proportion to all parties. The city that builds a highway span to bypass the business section incurs a collective cost to produce benefits to two segments of the population: (1) city residents who benefit from the reduced traffic flow, and (2) nonresidents who benefit from speedier passage around the congested city. The people who reside near the building site may suffer displacement, inconvenience, and other negative benefits during construction and further disadvantage after the ugly structure runs through their neighborhoods.

A cost-benefit study is one of the best ways to pinpoint potential trouble spots that become inevitable when one group receives the benefits and another pays the costs. Real or perceived inequities in the cost-benefit distribution can be expected to cause trouble for the project sponsors unless some equalization can be achieved by other means.

Another difficulty arises from the presence of noncompensable effects. A compensable effect is one for which there is a satisfactory equivalent, for example, a money payment, another place of residence or business, another piece of land, and the like. A noncompensable effect is one that involves the loss of an irreplacable value, for example, the loss of life, the loss of a friendly, happy neighborhood, the loss of personal liberty, and so on.

Cost-benefit studies can uncover such situations, but ordinary monetary equivalents cannot adequately reflect the disutilities associated with noncompensable effects. And since these effects do not lend themselves to quantification, thre is a danger that they will be given insufficient weight in the formation of the cost-benefit ratio or cost-benefit balance.

Cost-benefit studies have been used mainly in the public sector for evaluation of military,[5] highway,[6] waterway projects,[7] for urban planning,[8] health

---

[4] Nathaniel Lichfield, *Cost-Benefit Analysis in Urban Redevelopment* (Berkeley, Real Estate Research Project, University of California, 1962).

[5] C. J. Hitch and R. N. McKean, *The Economics of Defense in the Nuclear Age* (Cambridge, The Harvard University Press, 1963).

[6] *Road User Benefit Analysis for Highway Improvement* (Washington, D.C.; American Association of State Highway Officials, 1960).

[7] Otto Eckstein, *Water Resources Development* (Cambridge, The Harvard University Press, 1958).

[8] N. Lichfield, op. cit.

services delivery;[9] and for a large variety of governmental programs.[10]

Considering the many complications and subtleties involved in CBA, one should not be surprised that very few studies can be carried through to completion taking into account all of the possible effects on all parties. It is difficult enough to do one reliable CBA from the sole viewpoint of the primary beneficiaries of a project without becoming entangled with the unpredictable ideosyncracies of the too-often tendentious spokesmen of external interests.

Cost-Effectiveness Analysis

A cost-effectiveness analysis (hereafter abbreviated CEA) is a procedure by which alternatives for achieving specified objectives are compared. The purpose of CEA is to find the alternative that will attain the objective at least cost, or conversely, that will maximize the performance at a given level of cost.[11]

For example, a marketer with a fixed number of dollars to spend on advertising may wish to find the best combination of media, frequency, and timing of message insertion to maximize the potential audience's exposure to his advertising message. For a given level of cost he seeks to maximize the "reach" or, conversely, for a given target reach, he seeks to minimize the cost.[12]

A military commander may wish to find the most parsimonious combination of manpower and material to achieve a particular military objective.[13] An engineer seeks to find the most economical plant configuration to produce a given quantity of product at a set rate and quality level.[14]

In CEA there is usually an attempt to express the cost in current dollars (present worth of a time stream) to achieve an objective scaled on a numerical performance measure. The end result may be the ratio of units of performance per dollar of outlay. The marketer may compare media, timing, and frequency mixes by the number of target audience members reached per dollar of advertising outlay.

There is nothing in cost-effectiveness theory that prevents the analyst from taking both the long and broad views of his problem, although this is not

---

[9] H. E. Klarman, *The Economics of Health* (New York, Columbia University Press, 1965).

[10] R. N. McKean, *Efficiency in Government Through Systems Analysis* (New York: John Wiley and Sons, 1958).

[11] Karl Seiler, III, *Introduction to System Cost Effectiveness* (New York, Wiley Interscience, 1969).

[12] Edward J. Steadman, "Advertising Media Selection Via Linear Programming" in Allan Easton (ed.)," *Community Support for the Performing Arts;* Hofstra Yearbook of Business, Vol. 7, No. 5, 1970.

[13] For applications of CEA to defense see *(a)* B. S. Albert, "Cost-Effectiveness Evaluation of Mixes of Naval Air Weapons Systems" *Journal of the ORSA,* Vol. 11, 1963, and *(b)* R. Blum, "A Measure of Effectiveness For a Barrier Type of Surface-to-Air Defense," *Journal of the ORSA,* Vol. 9, No. 3 (May-June 1961).

[14] See D. Wilde and C. S. Beightler, *Foundations of Optimization* (Englewood Cliffs, New Jersey, Prentice-Hall, Inc. 1967), plant design example beginning on page 11 and continuing.

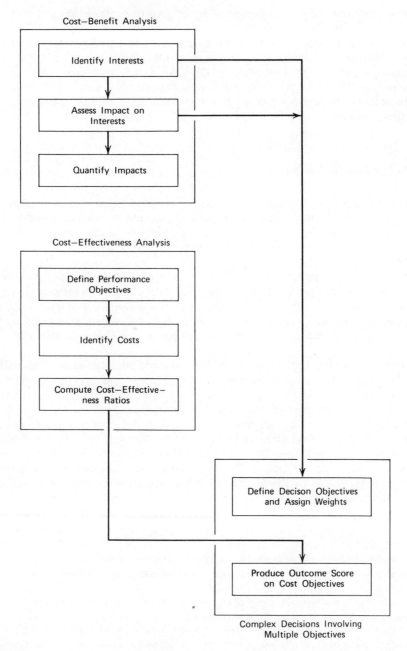

Cost–Benefit Analysis

Identify Interests

Assess Impact on
Interests

Quantify Impacts

Cost–Effectiveness Analysis

Define Performance
Objectives

Identify Costs

Compute Cost–Effective-
ness Ratios

Define Decison Objectives
and Assign Weights

Produce Outcome Score
on Cost Objectives

Complex Decisions Involving
Multiple Objectives

FIGURE A–1.   *Integration of CBA and CEA into complex decisions involving multiple objectives.*

usually the way these studies are performed. When the analyst expands his scope to encompass multiple objectives and the impacts on all affected parties, CEA and CBA overlap to the degree that they become virtually indistinguishable.

Integration of CBA and CEA into Multiple Objective Decision-Making

The methods described in this book for making complex managerial decisions involving multiple objectives use substantial parts of the CBA and CEA methodology, although the end result is a figure-of-merit based on utility determinations rather than on money equivalents. The early stages of a CBA are used to identify the parties at interest and to assess the impacts of the decision on their well-being. The enumeration of interests is used differently, however, to aid in the formulation of decision objectives. These objectives are intended to achieve a reasonable compromise of the interests of the affected parties. No attempt is made to directly quantify the "goods" and "bads" of the alternatives undergoing evaluation for the parties, as is done in CBA.

CEA is used directly for obtaining outcome scores on alternatives. Many complex decisions have, at least, one cost objective, and CEA can be used to provide numbers for the columns of the outcome matrix. A chart showing the uses of CBA and CEA for multiple-objective decision making is shown in Figure A–1.

Additional Appendix References

Harry P. Hatry, "Measuring the Effectiveness of Nondefense Public Programs," *JORSA*, Vol. 18, No. 5 (September–October 1970) pp. 772–784.

A. H. Packer, "Applying Cost-Effectiveness Concepts to the Community Health System," *JORSA*, Vol. 16, No. 2 (March–April 1968), pp. 227–253, plus bibliography on pp. 252–253.

III. TREATMENT OF DECISION ALTERNATIVES (A)

6.   Estimating Outcomes

The main ideas developed in this chapter are:

1. *Estimating outcomes for producing cell entries in the outcome matrix involves methods for dealing with certainty, risk, and uncertainty depending on the state of the decision environment.*

2. *Outcome estimates for an alternative on a criterion may result in either a single number or a time series. The multi-time approach requires a multiple-time matrix set in place of the ordinary single-time outcome matrix.*

CERTAINTY, RISK AND UNCERTAINTY[1]

When the decision maker produces a number for insertion into an outcome-matrix cell, he has acted on one of three assumptions, that

1. He can predict the outcome with complete certainty.
2. Although he cannot predict the outcome with complete certainty, he knows the probability distribution of different outcomes.
3. Although he has no knowledge of the probability distributions, he has devised a strategy for coping with the uncertainty which permits him to arrive at a numerical value for the outcome.

In the vocabulary of decision theory, these three assumptions correspond to (1) certainty, (2) risk, and (3) uncertainty.

The fact that the decision maker acts out one of these three assumptions and produces a number does not mean that he is correct. He may assume that he knows what is going to happen and be quite wrong. The probability distribution he carries around in his head may be completely erroneous. The alternative states of nature that he assumes in formulating his uncertainty strategies may not be the ones that will actually occur. In short, there are many ways to be wrong about the future.

Certainty

If he is reasonably correct in his methods and has a good understanding of the factual situation and of the underlying system functioning, the decision maker can make reliable estimates of the numbers to insert in the outcome score-set. Answers are not always easy to find because of system complexity, but he can have confidence that the answer will be good if his techniques are sound. There is a very substantial inventory of computational techniques for making estimates under conditions of certainty. The reader is referred to any good text on the subject for an explanation of these methods.[2]

Risk

There will be occasions when the decision maker cannot be certain about the outcome, but has—in his head—a probability distribution of possible outcomes. He can use this subjective probability distribution to arrive at some sort of estimate.[3] This probability distribution may be based on detailed observations of past happenings, or it may merely express a degree of confidence in a particular set of outcomes. Three examples of how subjective probabilities can be used in estimating outcomes are shown in Boxes 6–1, 6–2, and 6–3.

Box 6–1   Robert Sommers' Parking Problem

Mr. Robert Sommers lives and works in a suburb of New York City and is dissatisfied with his present position as an outside salesman for an industrial hardware firm. He has an interview concerning a new job for Monday at 10:30 A.M. Because he would like to call on one of his customers after the job interview, he decides to drive his car into the city that Monday so as to arrive at 10:00 A.M.

He arrives at the building that houses the firm granting the interview and looks for a place to park his car. About one block away, he notices a public garage that has space and also notices that the parking fee is $3. Before going into the garage, Sommers decides to look around on the street for a free space. He finds several empty spaces but notices also that there is a sign that reads, "No Parking Mon.-Wed.-Fri. 8:00 A.M. to 11:00 A.M." Sommers knows from past experience that the fine for illegal parking in this part of the city is $15. He wonders: should he park on the street and risk the 15 dollar fine, or should he pay the $3 and be safe?

To solve this problem, Sommers makes a probability estimate for receiving a summons for illegal parking. If he left the car at 10:25 A.M., he could be at his appointment on time and only be exposed to the risk of a fine for 35 minutes. If he deals solely with the cost minimization criterion and not with the morality goal, the expected value (EV) of parking illegally is:

$$EV = \$15.00 \text{ (probability of summons) } +$$
$$\$0.00 \text{ (probably of no summons)}$$

For EV to equal $3, the probability of receiving a summons must equal 0.20. Any higher probability would make the expected cost higher than the legal parking fee; a lower probability would make the expected cost lower than the legal fee.

When asked to give the rationale for his final choice of legal versus illegal parking, Sommers gave this probability distribution:

Number of minutes Illegal Parking	Probability of Summons	Probability of No Summons
90	0.80	0.20
45	0.50	0.50
35	0.40	0.60
15	0.20	0.80
10	0.10	0.90

If the weather was bad, the probabilities of receiving a summons would be somewhat less for each time because the police do not like standing out in the rain to write a summons.

On the basis of this probability distribution, the expected cost of 35 minutes of illegal parking would be $6 in nice weather and less for bad weather.

If cost minimization were the only criterion to be considered, Sommers would be better off parking in the garage for $3.

Box 6–2   ABC Corp.'s Accounts Receivable Problem

The ABC Corp. has an outstanding account receivable from Debtor Corp. in the amount of $100,000, but Debtor is in default. ABC's credit manager attended a creditors' meeting to ascertain the outlook for receiving payment. He discovered that most of Debtor's assets were of a nonliquid nature (production equipment, work-in-process, and doubtful receivables). The likelihood of ever receiving full payment was small, but there was a reasonable possibility of partial recovery. The credit manager was asked to prepare an estimate of the worth of this debt and to submit the computational details to the company's auditors. In response to this request, he presented these data:

Amount of payment (Q)	Probability (p_s)	Expected Value ($Q \times p_s$)
$90,000 to $100,000	0.00	$00,000.00
80,000 to 89,999	0.01	850.00
70,000 to 79,999	0.09	6,750.00
60,000 to 69,999	0.15	9,750.00
50,000 to 59,999	0.20	11,000.00
40,000 to 49,999	0.20	9,000.00
30,000 to 39,999	0.15	5,250.00
20,000 to 29,999	0.10	2,500.00
10,000 to 19,999	0.06	900.00
000 to 9,999	0.04	200.00
	1.00	$46,200.00

For purposes of valuation, this doubtful account could be said to be worth $46,200.

Box 6–3 Hiring the Creative Scientist

A firm is looking for a physicist for a top-secret defense project and must select a candidate who is both qualified professionally and who is likely to obtain top-secret security clearance. A young man highly recommended for his scientific creativity presents himself for the job. The interviewer is dismayed to see that the candidate is dressed in torn blue jeans and a ragged, flowered blouse; has unkempt, shoulder-length hair, and a ragged beard. The interviewer reasons as follows.

1. Hippie-like characters are likely to have unacceptable political and social orientation [probability of this being true (p_t) = 0.8; probability of it being false (p_f) = 0.2].

2. Persons of unacceptable political and social views are unlikely to obtain top-secret security clearance from the Department of Defense (p_t = 0.6; p_f = 0.4).

3. Four possibilities and their associated probabilities are:
   (a) The candidate is one of the hippie types, has unacceptable views, *and* he *can* get clearance.
   $$(0.8 \times 0.4 = 0.32)$$
   (b) The candidate is one of the hippie types, has unacceptable views, and he *cannot* get clearance.
   $$(0.8 \times 0.6 = 0.48)$$
   (c) The candidate has acceptable views in spite of his appearance, *and* he *can* get clearance.
   $$(0.2 \times 0.4 = 0.08)$$

(d)   The candidate has acceptable views in spite of his appearance, *and* he *can not* get clearance.

$$(0.2 \times 0.6 = 0.12)$$

The sum of all of these probabilities equals 1.00.

$$(0.32 + 0.48 + 0.08 + 0.12 = 1.00)$$

And so the interviewer who used these subjective probabilities and performed these mental calculations might reason: "the probability that this candidate can get security clearance is $0.32 + 0.08 = 0.40$; the probability that he cannot get security clearance is $0.48 + 0.12 = 0.60$. This fellow looks like a bad risk to me. The chances of his getting security clearance if we hired him are 40 percent yes, 60 percent no. If the odds were reversed, I might be willing to take a chance on this fellow; but with these probabilities, the answer must be negative."

Robert Sommers must make an estimate of the expected value of parking his car illegally and receiving a summons against the certainty of paying $3 or parking in a garage. (See Box 6–1 and Figure 6–1). The ABC Corp. tries to estimate the expected value of an outstanding account with an insolvent debtor (see Box 6–2). A firm looking for a physicist tries to estimate the

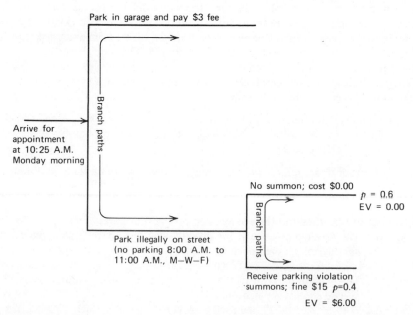

FIGURE 6–1. Graphical representation of Robert Sommers' parking problem (Box 6–1) involving a decision of whether or not to park illegally in order to avoid paying a $3 parking fee and to risk a $15 fine for illegal parking.

risk of a candidate for the position's failing to receive security clearance (see Box 6–3).

Uncertainty

Under conditions of certainty, the decision maker acts as if he knew which state of nature will occur. Under conditions of risk, he acts as if he knew the probability distribution of alternative futures. Under *uncertainty*, he acts as if the probability distributions of future states were either unknown or without meaning. Probabilities may be unknown in a stable environment because data and past experience are lacking; they may also be unknown because the environment is unstable, indeterminate, and therefore unknowable.

A method for estimating the outcomes of alternatives on one criterion at a time under conditions of true uncertainty requires that the decision maker do three things:

1. Guess what the possible states of nature will be.
2. Under each conceivable state of nature, forecast the outcomes as if these states were certain.
3. Choose one estimate based on his psychological predisposition or on organizational policy at the particular time.

For one particular decision criterion (the jth) on n alternatives and v states of nature, the uncertainty submatrix is as follows:

Alternative Number	States of Nature for the jth Criterion				
	E_1	E_2	E_3	E_q	E_v
1	O_{1j1}	O_{1j2}	$O_{1j3}\ldots\ldots\ldots$	O_{1jq}	O_{1jv}
2	O_{2j1}	O_{2j2}	$O_{2j3}\ldots\ldots\ldots$	O_{2jq}	O_{2jv}
3	O_{3j1}	O_{3j2}	$O_{3j3}\ldots\ldots\ldots$	O_{3jq}	O_{3jv}
.	. .	. .	$\ldots\ldots\ldots\ldots\ldots\ldots\ldots$		
i	O_{ij1}	O_{ij2}	$O_{ij3}\ldots\ldots\ldots$	O_{ijq}	O_{ijv}
.	. .	. .	$\ldots\ldots\ldots\ldots\ldots\ldots\ldots$		
n	O_{nj1}	O_{nj2}	$O_{nj3}\ldots\ldots\ldots$	O_{njq}	O_{njv}

(6-1)

where O_{ijq} equals the outcome of the ith alternative on the jth objective under the qth assumed state of nature.

In the special case when the decision maker is willing or able to assign numerical probabilities (whether they be in discrete or continuous distributions matrix 6–1 becomes a *risk* submatrix.

The relationship between matrix 6–1 and the complete outcome matrix is shown in Figure 6–2. For a particular outcome matrix there would be an intersecting uncertainty (or risk) submatrix for each criterion that was subject to the uncertainty (or risk) condition.

By assigning real meanings to the E_1 to E_v symbols (the states of nature)

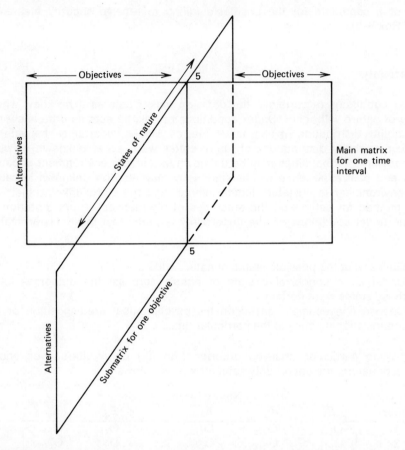

FIGURE 6–2. Schematic representation of intersecting matrices. The matrix in the plane of the page is the main decision matrix containing cell entries for alternatives of objectives for a time interval. The intersecting submatrix contains the various set of cell entries for a particular objective assuming several states of nature (or combination) resulting from conditions of risk or uncertainty. Some of the objectives in the main matrix may be operating under certainty, some under risk, some under uncertainty. Only those under uncertainty would require the intersecting submatrix.

and arriving at estimates of the cell entries (the o_{ijq}'s) in the uncertainty submatrix, we can move to the third step referred to in the preceding paragraphs. There are several well-known methods for making the choice of one or a combination of submatrix columns for insertion into the outcome matrix cells for the criterion under consideration.[4]

THE PESSIMISM RULE. Suggested by Abraham Wald, also called the *maximin* rule, it requires that the decision maker assume that the worst state of nature will prevail, for example E_w. All entries in the E_w column of the submatrix are inserted into the outcome matrix. If this had been a single-objective decision problem, the alternative with the "best" score on the worst state of nature would be chosen for adoption; but because the problem involves multiple objectives all alternative scores for that objective and state of nature are used. Under this rule, we can be assured that nothing worse than this could happen.

THE OPTIMISM RULE. Suggested by Leonid Hurwicz, also called the *maximax* rule, it is used when the decision maker feels lucky, that everything will go right for him. He finds the most favorable state of nature, for example E_f, and inserts the entries of the E_f column of the uncertainty submatrix into the outcome matrix. If this had been a single-objective decision problem, the alternative with the best score on the most favorable state of nature would have been chosen for adoption.

Perhaps the decision maker is neither completely optimistic nor pessimistic but is somewhere in between these two states. To reflect this intermediate condition, he could use a combination of the best and worst outcomes. He could assign probabilities to each and could compute the expected values of the combination by use of the following:

$$O_{ijw-f} = p_w O_{ijw} + p_f O_{ijf} \qquad (6\text{-}2)$$

where O_{ijw-f} = the probable outcome of the ith alternative on the jth objective under the indicated combination of the best and worst states of nature.

p_w = the subjective probability of the worst state of nature happening.

p_f = the subjective probability of the most favorable state of nature occurring, and $p_w + p_f = 1$.

This computation would be carried out for each alternative and the values resulting would be inserted into the outcome matrix in the appropriate column.

THE RATIONALITY RULE. Also known as the Bayes or Laplace rule. It is based on the assumption that in the absence of any real knowledge of the probabilities of the various possible states of nature, in the absence of any knowledge that one state is more probable than another, they all are assumed equiprobable. If they are v states of nature, each state is assigned the probability $1/v$. The probable outcome, according to this rule would be

$$\sum_{q=1}^{v} (1/v)(O_{ijq}) \qquad (6\text{-}3)$$

A numerical illustration of the application of the uncertainty rules is shown in Box 6–4.

Box 6–4   Mr. Grant Buys a Personal Residence

Mr. and Mrs. Joel Grant have been married for three years and have been living during this time in Mr. Grant's former bachelor apartment. They have deferred having children because they wanted to save enough money to buy a house in the suburbs. Mr. Grant is a registered representative for a small broker-dealer-underwriter and has been enjoying steadily rising earnings and a growing clientele.

One day Mrs. Grant told her husband that he was about to become a father and that the doctor had predicted a multiple birth. It suddenly became obvious that their present apartment was wholly inadequate for a family of four or more; some action on the purchase of a house was necessary.

After spending some time with real estate agents and answering newspaper advertisements, they realized that they were not certain about the kind of house or neighborhood that they preferred. As a result of much thought and discussion, five essential criteria for judging the suitability of a house emerged:

1. The quality of the neighborhood must be satisfactory for raising small children, and the threat of deterioriation must be minimal.

2. The school system must be of excellent quality.

3. The distance from the city and the cost of transportation must be reasonable.

4. The cash down-payment must be within their ability to pay, and still must leave enough for moving expenses and the cost of new furnishings.

5. The monthly upkeep must be within their ability to pay based on Mr. Grant's earning expectations.

Of these five criteria, all except the fifth were easy to handle. Mr. Grant was convinced that his earnings would increase with time providing that there was no severe economic downturn in the national economy or no serious stock market crash. If this were the case, why should they limit themselves to a small house that they would grow to dislike? But, on the other hand, if they really extended themselves by buying the size house that they would ultimately like to own, the risks would rise alarmingly if there was a severe economic downturn in the securities business.

As an aid to making his decision, Mr. Grant prepared a decision matrix for each alternative on the five criteria. In addition he prepared an uncertainty submatrix for criterion five.

The three alternatives were:

1. A modest house costing $30,000.

2. A nice new house for $45,000.

3. A luxurious house for $65,000.

Grant foresaw three possible states of nature that might have a bearing on his choice:

E_1 a severe economic downturn
E_2 a continuation of moderate economic growth
E_3 a burst of greater prosperity, a boom

The score matrix which best expressed his feelings was:

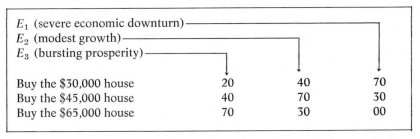

E_1 (severe economic downturn)			
E_2 (modest growth)			
E_3 (bursting prosperity)			
Buy the $30,000 house	20	40	70
Buy the $45,000 house	40	70	30
Buy the $65,000 house	70	30	00

where a score of 100 represents their bliss point and a score of zero, absolute disaster.

If Mr. Grant knew certain which of the three states would prevail, he could insert the proper scores into the main decision matrix. If he did not know for certain but were willing to assume probabilities, he could calculate expected values as follows (the risk condition):

$$p \text{ of } E_1 = 0.25$$
$$p \text{ of } E_2 = 0.50$$
$$p \text{ of } E_3 = 0.25$$

then

$$(A_1) - (0.25 \times 20) + (0.50 \times 40) + (0.25 \times 70) = 42.5$$
$$(A_2) - (0.25 \times 40) + (0.50 \times 70) + (0.25 \times 30) = 52.5$$
$$(A_3) - (0.25 \times 70) + (0.50 \times 30) + (0.25 \times 00) = 32.5$$

These values would then be entered into the main matrix in the column for criterion no. 5.

If instead of knowing the probabilities of the various states of nature, Mr. Grant had no idea which state would eventually occur, but he felt he must assume the worst (E_1) he would get

$$A_1 - 70; \ A_2 - 30; \ A_3 - 0 \text{ (pessimism rule)}$$

Or if he was a total optimist and assumed the most favorable state of nature, he would get E_3 on criterion no. 5

$$A_1 - 20; \ A_2 - 40; \ A_3 - 70 \text{ (optimism)}$$

Assuming a mildly optimistic outlook $[p(E_1) = 0.25 \ p(E_2) = 0.75]$ he would get

$$A_1 - 32.5; \ A_2 - 37.5; \ A_3 - 52.5$$

But if he assumed that all states were equally probable [that is, $p(E_1) = p(E_2) = p(E_3) = \frac{1}{3}$], he would get

$$A_1—43.3; A_2—46.7; A_3—33.3$$

Recapitulating the various rules

For	Insert for Each Alternative in Column Corresponding to Criterion no. 5		
	A_1	A_2	A_3
Risk	42.5	52.5	32.5
Pessimism	70.0	30.0	0.00
Optimism	20.0	40.0	70.0
Qualified-optimism	32.5	37.5	52.5
Equiprobable	43.3	46.7	33.3

SINGLE NUMBERS VERSUS TIME SERIES

For many decision problems, the elements of an alternative's outcome score-set are numbers that refer to an outcome without reference to a time dimension. This happens even if the alternatives under consideration have consequences that are spread out over a long time. In these cases, the cell entry may be thought of as a kind of "present value," average, or amalgamation of a time stream of outcome estimates.

There is room for doubt that any single number can adequately express the characteristics of a time-varying outcome stream. Should there not be, instead of a single number, a time series? One such possible arrangement is shown in Figure 6–3. There is one complete outcome matrix for each time interval; in this example, one for each of eight years. Each alternative is to be scored on each criterion for each of the eight years. Although the alternatives and objectives do not change from year to year, both the cell entries and the weights might change.

The cell entry for the ith alternative on the jth criterion for the tth year is O_{ijt}. The triple-subscript notation is used to distinguish the present value (the O_{ij}) from the partial score for the specific time. Double-subscript notation is used for the criterion weights. The first corresponds to the criterion number; the second to the time interval.

The idea of amalgamating a series of time-dependent numbers into a single number is not new. The present-value concept[5] from financial mathematics is one of the commonest examples of amalgamation through time. The concept is based on the time preferences for money. A dollar today is worth more than the same dollar received later. A premium is demanded to compensate for waiting for payment. For example, a corporate bond with a ten-year maturity, a face-value of $1000, and a 6 percent coupon ($30 every

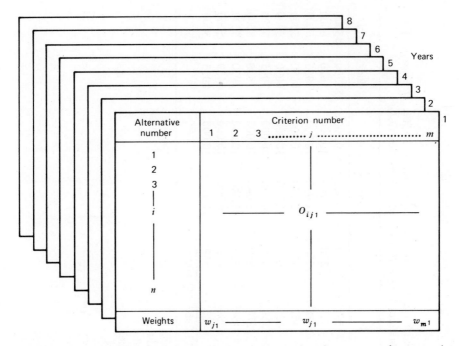

FIGURE 6–3. *Multiple-time matrix. Front matrix is for first year, others are for succeeding years. Alternatives and objectives do not change from year to year. Weights do not necessarily remain constant. First subscript of cell entry corresponds to alternative number; second, to objective number; third, to year number.*

six months) will command a market price that is an amalgamation of the present worths of a stream of twenty $30-payments along with the expectation of receiving a lump sum payment of $1000 ten years hence. The total payments would equal $1600, but the bond might actually command a market price of $700. The premium paid for deferring the payments in this case would be $900.

The conventional present-worth formula translated into the symbols used in Figure 6–3 for an interest rate r is

$$O_{ij} = \sum_{t=1}^{8} \frac{1}{(1+r)^t} (O_{ijt}) \tag{6-4}$$

Although this formula for combining the cell entries in the eight matrices seems quite straightforward, there is a very serious difficulty concealed in it. There is the implicit assumption that all combination of o_{ijt}'s which pro-

TABLE 6-1 *Alternative Payment Schedules, Any One of Which Has a Present Value Equal to 10,000. If Present Worth Were the Only Factor To Be Considered, Any of the Above Schedules Would Be as Desirable as Any Other*

Year	d_k^a	1a	1b	2a	2b	3a	3b	4a	4b	5a	5b
1	.9434	$1359	$1282	$1060	$1000	$1537	$1450	$10,600	$10,000	$5300	$5000
2	.8900	1359	1210	1124	1000	1517	1350	11,240	10,000	5620	5000
3	.8396	1359	1141	1191	1000	1488	1250	11,910	10,000	5955	5000
4	.7921	1359	1076	1263	1000	1452	1150	12,630	10,000	6380	5000
5	.7473	1359	1016	1338	1000	1405	1050	13,380	10,000	6690	5000
6	.7050	1359	958	1419	1000	1339	950	14,190	10,000	7095	5000
7	.6651	1359	904	1504	1000	1278	850	15,040	10,000	7520	5000
8	.6274	1359	853	1594	1000	1196	750	15,940	10,000	7970	5000
9	.5919	1359	804	1690	1000	1099	650	16,900	10,000	8450	5000
10	.5584	1359	759	1791	1000	985	550	17,910	10,000	8955	5000
		$13,590	$10,003^b	$13,974	$10,000	$13,296	$10,000				

Column 1a: constant payment schedule; column 1b: present values.
Column 2a: increasing payment schedule; column 2b: present values.
Column 3a: decreasing payment schedule; column 3b: present values.
Column 4a: single payment alternatives; column 4b: present values.
Column 5a: two payment alternatives; column 5b: present values.

^{a} d_k is the discount factor based on an annual rate of interest of 6 percent $d_k = \dfrac{1}{(1+r)^k}$

^{b} Rounding error.

duced the same numerical value of present-worth would be equally valued. Some investigation of this assumption is required.

The columns of Table 6–1 show a number of alternative payment streams all of which have identical present worths, in this case, $10,000. Column 1a shows a stream of constant payments of $1359 each; column 2a shows an increasing stream, beginning with $1060 and ending with $1791; column 3a shows a decreasing stream, beginning with $1537 and ending with $985. Column 4a shows the sizes of a single payment during any one year that would have a present worth of $10,000. These payments range in size from $10,600 for one year to $17,910 for ten years. Column 5a shows how a two-payment plan might work. Each item has a worth of $5000 so any two together have a combined worth of $10,000. For example $6380 (year 4) plus $8450 (year 9) together are worth $10,000.

If present worth, as computed by the conventional compound discount formulas and tables, was the only consideration, an investor might be just as happy with $10,600 a year from now as he would be with $17,910 ten years hence. But suppose this particular investor were planning to pay part of his living expenses with the payments received from his $10,000 capital. By the time he was ready to receive the $17,910 payment he might be dead from starvation. This deferred single payment would be less worthwhile for him than a smaller, but more regular stream. In such cases, the present-worth method does not give good results when it is used alone. Much better would be a multiple-objective method that took into consideration factors other than present worth.

Whether a single-time outcome matrix or a multiple-time matrix set, as shown in Figure 6–3, should be used depends very much on the particular set of facts in the problematic situation. In making planning decisions that involve a discrete time sequence of decisions, it may be preferable to deal with each year as a separate entity and to prepare outcome matrices for each interval.*

In either case, whether we use the single or multiple matrix, it is important to recognize the main point made in this section. Every cell entry of the outcome matrix has within itself the compression of a time sequence.

Notes and References

1. A simple but highly competent treatment of these concepts is contained in D. W. Miller and M. K. Starr, *The Structure of Human Decisions* (Englewood Cliffs, New Jersey, Prentice-Hall, Inc., 1967) pp. 106–134. Also see Daniel Bell, "Twelve Modes of Prediction—A Preliminary Sort-

* Case IV-II is an example of a situation that can be handled by either single or multiple-time matrices.

ing of Approaches in the Social Sciences" *Daedalus* Vol. XCIII, No. 3 (1964), pp. 845–873.

2. Decision making under certainty is covered in standard works in managerial economics, operations research, production management, and others in specialized fields.

3. For a more thorough development of subjective probability than is possible here see Robert Schlaifer, *Probability and Statistics for Business Decisions* (New York, McGraw-Hill Book Co., 1959); Robert Schlaifer, *Introduction to Statistics for Business Decisions* (New York, McGraw-Hill Book Co., 1961); and H. Raiffa and R. Schlaifer, *Applied Statistical Decision Theory* (Boston, Division of Research, Harvard Business School, 1961). A more elementary treatment can be found in D. W. Miller and M. K. Starr op. cit.

4. See Howard Raiffa, *Decision Analysis—Introductory Lectures on Choices under Uncertainty* (Reading, Massachusetts, Addison-Wesley, 1968).

5. A complete treatment of the present worth concept can be found in Eugene L. Grant and W. Grant Ireson, *Principles of Engineering Economy* (New York, The Roland Press, 1960), 4th ed. See also James G. Abert, "Structuring Cost-Effectiveness Analyses," *The Logistics Review and Military Logistics Journal,* Vol. II, No. 7 (March–April 1966), pp. 19–31. See also Chapter 11 "Decision Making over an Unbounded Horizon," in Harvey M. Wagner, *Principles of Operations Research* (Englewood Cliffs, New Jersey, Prentice-Hall, Inc., 1969).

Important Words and Concepts

Certainty
Risk
Uncertainty
Probability distribution
Expected value
State of nature
Uncertainty submatrix
Pessimism rule
Maximin
Optimism rule
Maximax
Rationality rule
Time series
Multiple-time matrix
Present worth

Overview of Chapter 6

Outcomes of alternatives on criteria may be estimated in an environment known to be certain, risky, or uncertain. Risk involves probability calculations. Uncertainty rules depend mainly on the psychological state of the decision maker or on organization policy. Rules for uncertainty conditions are pessimism (Wald), optimism (Hurwicz), and rationality (Bayes, LaPlace). An uncertainty submatrix can be used as an adjunct to the usual outcome matrix.

The cell of the outcome matrix can be viewed as a composite of a time series. A particular decision problem involving a time sequence can result in a single- or multiple-time matrix.

Questions for Review, Discussion, and Research

Review

1. Distinguish between risk and certainty.

2. Distinguish between risk and uncertainty.

3. What is a subjective probability distribution and how is one used in decision making?

4. What is an uncertainty sub-matrix and how does it relate to the ordinary outcome matrix?

5. How is the pessimism rule applied?

6. How is the optimism rule applied? The qualified optimism variation?

7. How is the rationality rule applied?

8. How can a single number be made to represent a time series?

9. What are multiple-time matrices and how do they relate to the ordinary outcome matrix?

10. What kinds of information are lost in the usual present-worth calculations?

Discussion

1. In many problems the uncertainty rules each give quite different choices (see Box 6–4, for example). Of what use are these rules and how does one know which to use?

2. All of the methods of estimating outcomes shown in Chapter 6 depend

on assumptions about the decision environment (states of nature). Once assumptions are made, all the methods reduce to "certainty." Discuss the validity of the foregoing statements.

3. Relate the concept "states of nature" to the discussion of "assumptions about the nature of the decision environment" in Box 2–1.

4. Discuss the gains and losses associated with the use of a single number to represent a time series, as for example in a present-worth computation.

5. Present-worth methods are applicable to time streams of money. Are they equally applicable to other kinds of time streams?

Research

1. Interview one or or more decision makers and try to discover how they actually deal with situations involving certainty, risk, and uncertainty.

2. How do cost-benefit and cost-effectiveness methods relate to the discussion in this chapter on multiple-time matrices?

3. By using the data in Table 6–1, construct a number of alternative packages all of identical present worth, and conduct a preference survey among your acquaintances. Can you draw any inferences about their preferences?

7. Valuing Outcomes — Utility Estimation

The main ideas introduced in this chapter are:

1. *Objects or collections have utility if they are capable of satisfying human needs or aiding goal attainment.*

2. *All persons make utility judgments routinely.*

3. *Utility functions may exhibit nonlinearities.*

4. *The outcomes of alternatives on criteria can be valued by use of a utility chart or a quality-point table.*

UTILITY

After estimating outcomes on all decision criteria, the result is an outcome score-set similar to formula 5–1. The elements of these score-sets are measurements on a variety of scales. Usually, but not always, the elements are numbers, and often the units of measurement are incommensurate. Taken together, the outcome score-sets make up the outcome matrix.

It is further necessary to transform the outcome score-sets into valuation score-sets as shown in formula 5–3. Taken together, these transformed score-sets make up the valuation matrix. In most instances a simple transformation will not suffice because the relationship between *quantities* and *utilities* is not linear.

An object, action, collection, event, or stimulus has *utility* if it has the capability, directly or indirectly, immediately or ultimately, of (a) satisfying one or more human needs, or (b) contributing to the attainment of an individual, group or organizational goal.

Utilities may be either positive or negative; negative utility is called *disutility*. Utilities are disutilities if they directly or indirectly, immediately or ultimately, tend to cause injury or frustration of need satisfaction or goal attainment and, thereby, cause a reduction of well-being.

Synonyms for utility are desirability, attractiveness, worth, and positive valuation. Synonyms for disutility are undesirability, unattractiveness, repulsiveness, lack of merit, and negative valuation.

Utilities cannot be measured with accuracy. Yet, every person who has ever made a choice among alternatives has made some very complex utility judgments, although he may have been unaware that he did so. Making such judgments is an unavoidable part of all decision processes. The proper question is not whether one *should* or *can* make these judgments; one *must* do so if he expects to make even the simplest choices among alternatives.

The fact that efficient, explicit, precise, or easily understood methods for measuring utility are not yet available for guiding the decision maker in this task may be temporarily distressing, particularly if he has a passion for rationality and for orderly, logical thought. But, in the absence of good and rigorous methods, he must make do with whatever methods can be devised, however imperfect they may be.[1]

UTILITY FUNCTIONS

Shapes of Utility Functions

When one thinks about utility, it is not always necessary to define units. It may be useful to visualize the shapes of utility functions and not be unduly concerned about the actual range of values. Figures 7–1 to 7–6 contain sketches of several common utility functions, but the extent and range of the horizontal (quantity, q) and vertical (utility, U) axes are left undefined. These are examples of utility relationships in an unbounded space. Figure 7–1 contains five differently shaped functions:

1. Curve *A* represents *linear utility* and *constant marginal utility.** Each increment of quantity is equally valued.
2. Curve *B* represents utility that does not increase proportionately with increments of q. This shape represents *declining marginal utility*. A person with this kind of utility function might react toward increases in q by saying, "The more of q I get, the less I want further increases, but I'll be glad to take all there is available."
3. Curve *C* represents utility that continues to accelerate as q increases (*increasing marginal utility*). A person with this kind of utility function might react by saying, "The more of q I get, the more I like additional increments. Keep it coming." This shape reflects a rising appetite or aspiration.
4. Curve *D* contains an S-shaped function that is a combination of curves *B* and *C*. First marginal utility increases. Then as q increases further, the marginal utility drops off.

---

* The marginal utility is the rate of change of utility with quantity; it is defined as the limit as Δq approaches zero of $\Delta U/\Delta q$ or as dU/dq. The symbol used is M.

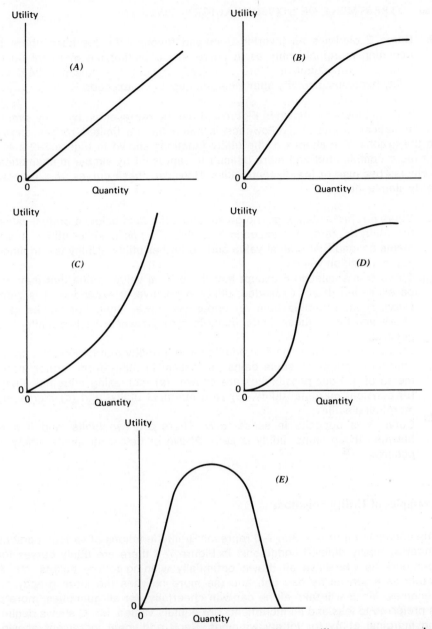

FIGURE 7–1. *Five different utility functions:* (A) *linear utility; constant marginal utility;* (B) *nonlinear utility, declining marginal utility;* (C) *nonlinear utility, increasing marginal utility;* (D) *nonlinear utility, increasing then decreasing marginal utility;* (E) *U-shaped utility, decreasing marginal utility. These five functions are continuous and can be represented by a simple mathematical function. (Note: All curves are for an instant of time.)*

5. Curve *E* contains an inverted-U-shaped function. In this case, there is declining marginal utility as in curve *A* except that the marginal utility actually turns negative. More *q* actually becomes a nuisance because utility becomes disutility after a certain quantity is exceeded.

All of the functions shown in Figure 7–1 can be represented by fairly simple mathematical formulas, if allowance is made for the limited ranges shown in the graphs. The shapes of the utility functions shown in Figure 7–2 are a bit more complicated and more difficult to represent by simple mathematical formulas because of the discontinuities. However, these curves, too, express fairly simple ideas:

1. Curve *F* represents the go, no-go situation. If *q* falls below a critical value, the utility is zero; if it exceeds that value, it has positive utility. Increments beyond that critical value add no further utility. (Utility is undefined at the transition values.)
2. Curve *G* is similar to *F* except that the critical value is one that may not be exceeded. If not exceeded, utility is positive; if exceeded, it is zero.
3. Curve *H* incorporates both an upper and lower limit. For values of *q* above and below these limits, utility is zero. Between the two limits, it is positive.
4. Curve *J* is a variation on *F*. It admits the possibility that beyond the upper limit there might be some gains (or losses) in utility from further increments of *q*. Four possibilities are shown: (*a*) increasing marginal utility, (*b*) constant marginal utility, (*c*) zero marginal utility, and (*d*) increasing marginal disutility.
5. Curve *K* is opposite in sense to *H*. There are two limits, and if *q* is between these limits, utility is zero. Above or below the limits, utility is positive.

Examples of Utility Functions

The curves in Figures 7–3 to 7–6 represent utility functions of various persons under specially defined conditions. In Figure 7–3 there are utility curves for four persons who have all drawn potentially winning lottery tickets. Mr. A wants as much as he can get, and the more he wins the more greedy he becomes. Mr. B will take all he can win cheerfully; for all quantities, more *q* is preferred to less and all increments are equally valued. Mr. C shows declining marginal utility for lottery winnings. Each additional increment of winnings is valued less than the preceding, although all are positively valued. Mr. D is actually worried that the prize might be too big and, therefore, might cause him trouble. He views too large a prize as a nuisance.

Figure 7–4 shows how a hypothetical salesman might feel if he was working for a sales organization that used a sales incentive plan. If his sales are

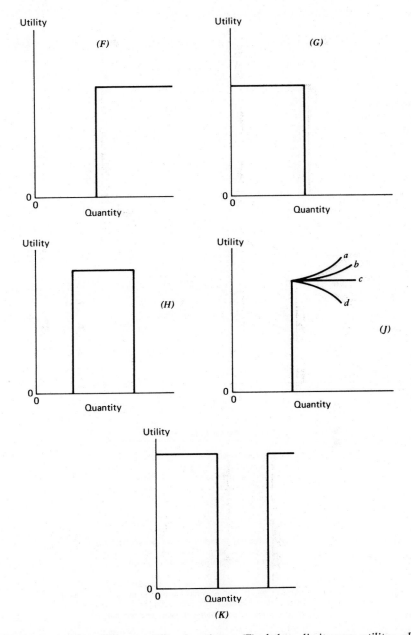

FIGURE 7–2. *Five different utility functions:* (F) *below limit zero utility; above limit, constant;* (G) *below limit constant utility; above limit, zero;* (H) *zero utility above and below limits; constant at and between limits;* (J) *zero utility below limit; increasing, constant, or declining above limit;* (K) *constant utility above and below limits; zero between limits. These five functions are discontinuous and cannot be represented by a single, simple mathematical function. (Note: All curves are for an instant of time; the utility is undefined at the transition values.)*

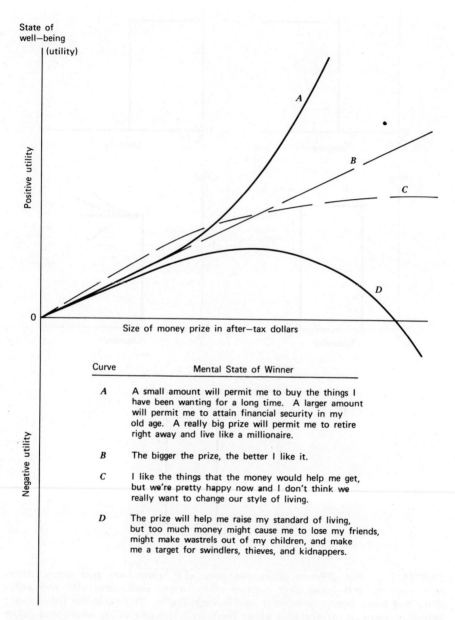

Curve	Mental State of Winner
A	A small amount will permit me to buy the things I have been wanting for a long time. A larger amount will permit me to attain financial security in my old age. A really big prize will permit me to retire right away and live like a millionaire.
B	The bigger the prize, the better I like it.
C	I like the things that the money would help me get, but we're pretty happy now and I don't think we really want to change our style of living.
D	The prize will help me raise my standard of living, but too much money might cause me to lose my friends, might make wastrels out of my children, and make me a target for swindlers, thieves, and kidnappers.

FIGURE 7–3. States of mind produced in four potential winners in a lottery at an instant of time.

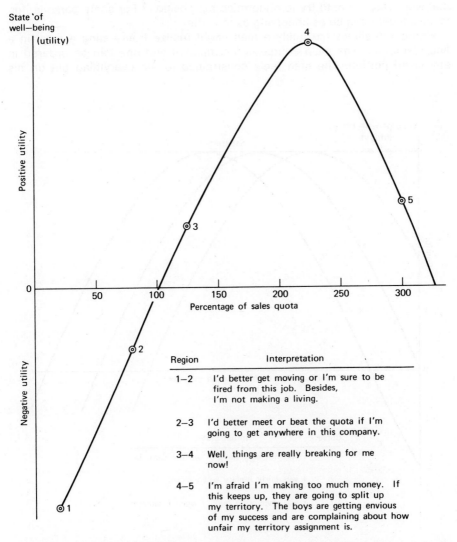

FIGURE 7–4. *The state of well-being produced by a salesman's earnings on a companywide sales incentive program for several time intervals.*

below quota (points 1-2), he is worried because he is not making enough money and he feels insecure. As he meets and exceeds the quota (points 2-3), his aspirations rise. With great success (points 3–4), he is exuberant. But after a while as his sales increase further he becomes worried (points 4–5), but for a different reason. He wonders: is he making too much money? Is he proving that his territory was too lucrative and should now be split up between two salesmen? Are there jealousies among the less successful men that will cause them to try to undermine his position? For some persons, too much success can be as unnerving as too little.

Figure 7–5 shows the utility a man might realize from eating a meal in a fine restaurant. The main course is filet mignon and one can be ordered in any sized portion. The man feels constrained to eat everything put on his

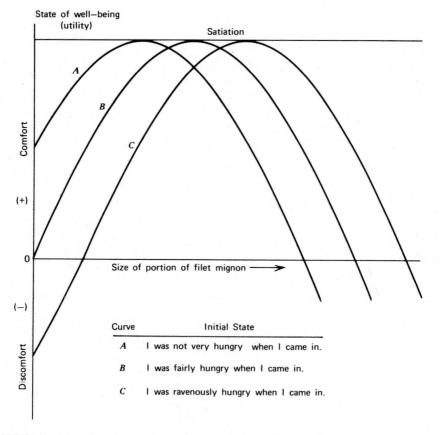

FIGURE 7–5. *The utility of various size portions of filet mignon served at a restaurant to a man who will eat everything put on his plate.*

plate. Depending on how hungry he was at the time that he entered the restaurant, the satisfaction possible from different sized portions would vary.

Figure 7–6 illustrates a variation on the go, no-go situation shown in Figure 7–2, curve *J*. Honesty in employees is positively valued, but gradations are hard to distinguish. The utility might rise slightly for greater honesty if it were possible to measure gradations, but the utility increases would probably be small. Dishonesty has disutility, and the disutility increases rapidly with the seriousness of the dishonesty. Dishonesty can be measured in terms of the money equivalents of the resulting losses or in terms of legal gradations (petty larceny, grand larceny, and the like).

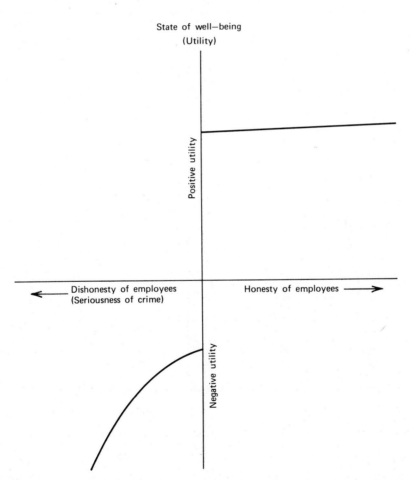

FIGURE 7–6. State of well-being associated with the honesty and dishonesty of employees at a firm.

Bounded Utility Spaces

All of the foregoing utility functions were drawn in an unbounded space. The curves in Figure 7–7 are drawn in a space with defined boundaries. The utility axis has a maximum range of 100 units with equal gradations between zero and 100. The horizontal quantity axis is shown with a range from zero to 1000, but any other linear scale could be substituted.

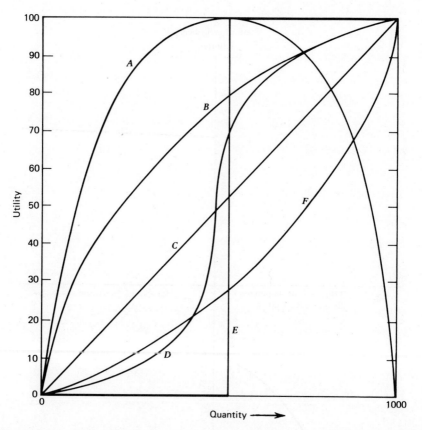

FIGURE 7–7.   *Utility functions in a bounded space; utility ranges from zero to 100.* (A) *U-shaped utility function (declining marginal utility);* (B) *nonlinear utility (declining marginal utility);* (C) *linear utility function (constant marginal utility);* (D) *S-shaped utility function (increasing then decreasing marginal utility);* (E) *step-shaped utility function (constant utility below and above limit value);* and (F) *nonlinear utility (increasing marginal utility).*

Utility Scales

A graph similar to that shown in Figure 7–7 can be used to transform outcomes into numerical utility estimates. Suppose, in a particular problem, there are a number of alternatives whose outcomes are dollar profits ranging from zero to $1,000,0000. If we knew the utility function for money in this situation, it would be possible to find a utility estimate for each outcome from one of the graphs.

UTILITY ESTIMATION

A Chart for Utility Scaling

If the outcomes can be measured or otherwise expressed on a multi-interval scale, the utility of each can be estimated by the use of one of the utility scales shown in Table 7–1. This table contains twenty-two different utility scales. Columns 1 to 10 show varying degrees of increasing marginal utility. Column 11 contains a scale for constant marginal utility. Columns 12 to 21 have scales for varying degrees of diminishing marginal utility, and column 22 has a scale for a U-shaped utility function. These scales are shown in graphical form in Figures 7–8 and 7–9.

A Quality-Point Table

If the outcomes cannot be expressed as numbers on a multi-interval scale, or if they are nonquantifiable and are expressed on a language scale, a quality-point scale like that shown in Box 7–1 can be used to assign utility

---

Box 7–1 Direct Estimation of Utility on a Quality-Point Scale

Valuation of Outcome of Alternative on One Specific Objective or Criterion	Quality-Point Scores	
	Unipolar Scale	Bipolar Scale
Superb, terrific, exquisite, irresistable	87.5 to 100	75 to 100
Exceptionally good, exceptionally beneficial	75 to 87.5	50 to 75
Very good, very desirable, or beneficial	62.5 to 75	25 to 50
Good, moderately beneficial, or desirable	50 to 62.5	0 to 25
Neutral	50	0
Mediocre, passable, very little merit	37.5 to 50	−25 to 0
Very poor, much lacking in merit, harmful	25 to 37.5	−25 to −50
Exceptionally poor, very harmful, very unattractive	12.5 to 25	−50 to −75
Absolutely repulsive, terribly harmful, awfully bad	0 to 12.5	−75 to −100

TABLE 7–1   A Set of Data for Curves Having Marginal Utilities That Are Increasing (Columns 1–10), Constant (Column 11), Declining (Columns 12–21) and U-shaped (Column 22). Envelope of Curves for Columns 1–21 Are Shown in Figure 7–8; for Column 22, in Figure 7–9. To Use This Table, Select a Utility Curve That Is the Best Fit for Your Utility Function for the Particular Criterion under Examination. Transform the Outcome Scales into a 0–100 Scale for the Quantity Variable.

Quantity	1	2	3	4	5	6	7	8	9	10	11
0	0	0	0	0	0	0	0	0	0	0	0
10	1.0	1.9	2.8	3.7	4.6	5.5	6.4	7.3	8.2	9.1	10.0
20	4.0	5.6	7.2	8.8	10.4	12.0	13.6	15.2	16.8	18.4	20.0
30	9.0	11.1	13.2	15.3	17.4	19.5	21.6	23.7	25.8	27.9	30.0
40	16.0	18.4	20.8	23.2	25.6	28.0	30.4	32.8	35.2	37.6	40.0
50	25.0	27.5	30.0	32.5	35.0	37.5	40.0	42.5	45.0	47.5	50.0
60	36.0	38.4	40.8	43.2	45.6	48.0	50.0	52.8	55.2	57.6	60.0
70	49.0	51.1	53.2	55.3	57.4	59.9	61.6	63.7	65.8	67.9	70.0
80	64.0	65.6	67.2	68.8	70.4	72.0	73.6	75.2	76.8	78.4	80.0
90	81.0	81.9	82.8	83.7	84.6	85.5	86.4	87.3	88.2	89.1	90.0
100	100	100	100	100	100	100	100	100	100	100	100

Quantity	12	13	14	15	16	17	18	19	20	21	22
0	0	0	0	0	0	0	0	0	0	0	0
10	10.9	11.8	12.7	13.6	14.5	15.4	16.3	17.2	18.1	19.0	36
20	21.6	23.2	24.8	26.4	28.0	29.6	31.2	32.8	34.4	36.0	64
30	32.1	34.2	36.3	38.4	40.5	42.6	44.7	46.8	48.9	51.0	90
40	42.4	44.8	47.2	49.6	52.0	54.4	56.8	59.2	61.6	64.0	96
50	52.5	55.0	57.3	60.0	62.5	65.0	67.5	70.0	72.5	75.0	100
60	62.4	64.8	67.2	69.6	72.0	74.4	76.8	79.2	81.6	84.0	96
70	72.1	74.2	76.3	78.4	80.5	82.6	84.7	86.8	88.9	91.0	90
80	81.6	83.2	84.8	86.4	88.0	89.6	91.2	92.8	94.4	96.0	64
90	90.9	91.8	92.7	93.6	94.5	93.4	95.3	96.2	97.1	98.0	36
100	100	100	100	100	100	100	100	100	100	100	0

scores. Of course, even quantifiable data can be scored on this chart if desired, although the discipline involved in choosing a scale from Table 7–1 may prove more beneficial.

WORKED-OUT PROBLEM IN UTILITY ESTIMATION

Dr. Kent Seeks a New Position

Phillip Kent, M.D., Ph.D. in pharmacology, is employed as director of pharmacology in a large hospital in a small city thirty miles away from a large

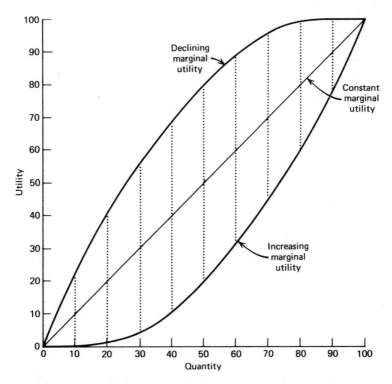

FIGURE 7–8. Family of parabolic curves representing the range from declining to constant to increasing marginal utility (data from Table 7–1).

metropolis. He has become dissatisfied with his position and has made a number of confidential inquiries about other positions. Because of his excellent reputation in clinical and research pharmacology, Kent is seen as an attractive candidate and a number of positions are offered to him by institutions that employ pharmacologists. Because these institutions vary so widely in their facilities, reputation, and offerings, Dr. Kent decides to examine the criteria on which he will evaluate the competing offers. He identifies the following ten factors as important in his choice process:

1. Salary (in dollars per annum).
2. Fringe benefit package (annual dollar equivalent).
3. Opportunity for advancement in field (qualitative).
4. Prestige of institution (directory ranking on several subfactors).
5. Amount of away-from-home travel (days per year).
6. Distance away from hometown, relatives, parents, and old friends (miles).

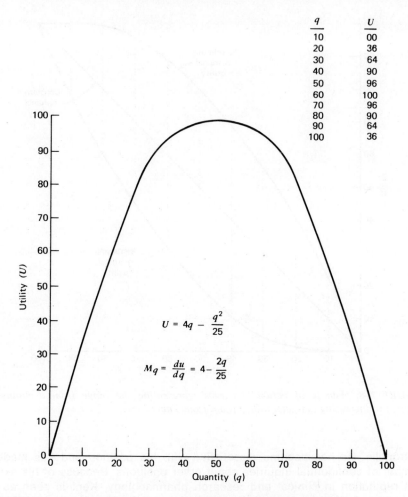

q	U
10	00
20	36
30	64
40	90
50	96
60	100
70	96
80	90
90	64
100	36

$$U = 4q - \frac{q^2}{25}$$

$$M_q = \frac{du}{dq} = 4 - \frac{2q}{25}$$

FIGURE 7–9. *A U-shaped utility function and the table of values.*

7. Availability of good housing, neighborhoods, schools, and cultural activities that make up the quality of life in the locality (qualitative).
8. Availability of good medical school or affiliation with good school (qualitative).
9. Quality of research done by staff (qualitative).
10. Level of technology and equipment available at the institution (qualitative).

Kent narrowed the field down to six alternative job offers that seemed to him to be reasonably satisfactory. He then proceeded to record the scores of each institution on each criterion as shown in Tables 7–2 to 7–11.

TABLE 7–2   Criterion No. 1—Salary

Alternative	Amount	Equivalent Q[a]	Utility Curve[b]	Utility Score
1	$17,500	70	1	49.0
2	20,000	80	1	64.0
3	15,000	60	1	36.0
4	25,000	100	1	100
5	22,500	90	1	81.0
6	19,500	78	1	78.2

[a] Multiply each dollar amount by 4/1000 to convert to a 0–100 scale.
[b] Kent exhibits increasing marginal utility for salary increments.

TABLE 7–3   Criterion No. 2—Fringe-Benefit Package

Alternative	Amount	Equivalent Q[a]	Utility Curve[b]	Utility Score[c]
1	$1750	58.3	8	50.0
2	2200	73.3	8	67.5
3	2800	93.3	8	91.5
4	3000	100	8	100
5	2000	66.6	8	60.0
6	1800	60.0	8	52.8

[a] Multiply each dollar amount by 1/30 to convert to a 0–100 scale.
[b] Increasing marginal utility but not as pronounced as for salary.
[c] In between values by linear interpolation.

TABLE 7–4   Criterion No. 3—Opportunity for Advancement in Field

Alternative	Valuation	Quality Points
1	Good	55
2	Good, but not as good as 1	50
3	Exceptionally good	80
4	Very good, not as good as 3	70
5	Exceptionally poor	20
6	Very good, better than 4	75

TABLE 7–5   *Criterion No. 4—Prestige of Institution*

Alternative	Directory Rank	Equivalent Q[a]	Utility Curve[b]	Utility Score
1	337	66.3	15	75.0
2	210	79.0	15	85.6
3	10	99.0	15	99.4
4	500	50.0	15	60.0
5	180	82.0	15	87.6
6	425	57.5	15	67.1

[a] Formula for conversion to 0–100 scale: $(1000–R)/10$.
[b] Diminishing marginal utility.

TABLE 7–6   *Criterion No. 5—Amount of Away-From-Home Travel*

Alternative	Expected Number of days	Equivalent Q[a]	Utility Curve[b]	Utility Score[c]
1	100	100	22	5
2	10	10	22	38
3	90	90	22	36
4	30	30	22	90
5	60	60	22	96
6	5	5	22	18

[a] Values used as is.
[b] U-shaped utility curve. Kent likes to travel some of the time.
[c] Where a zero value would be called for a "5" is used in its place because zeros produce difficulties in some choice rules that are applied in a later chapter.

TABLE 7–7   *Criterion No. 6—Distance Away from Hometown*

Alternative	Distance in Miles	Equivalent Q[a]	Utility Curve[b]	Utility Score
1	1200	60	1	36.0
2	500	83.3	1	69.0
3	2	99.3	1	99.4
4	2000	33.3	1	11.3
5	100	96.7	1	93.7
6	1500	50.0	1	25.0

[a] Computing formula: $100\,(1\text{-}d/3000)$.
[b] Increasing marginal utility for closeness to hometown.

TABLE 7–8 Criterion No. 7—Availability of Good Housing, Neighborhoods, Schools, and Cultural Activities

Alternative	Valuation	Quality Points
1	Very good	70
2	Mediocre	40
3	Exceptionally good	80
4	Neutral (better than 2)	50
5	Exceptionally poor	20
6	Very good (better than 1)	75

TABLE 7–9 Criterion No. 8—Availability of Affiliation with Good Medical School

Alternative	Valuation	Quality Points
1	None available (unacceptable)	5
2	Fair school (affiliated)	70
3	Superb school (affiliated)	100
4	Good school, not affiliated, far	40
5	None available	5
6	Good school (affiliated)	90

TABLE 7–10 Criterion No. 9—Quality of Research Done by Staff

Alternative	Valuation	Quality Points
1	Small amount, low quality	30
2	Small amount but very high quality	70
3	Large amount and very high quality	100
4	Large amount but low quality	40
5	None	5
6	Large amount and good quality but not as good as 3	90

TABLE 7–11   Criterion No. 10—Level of Technology

Alternative	Valuation	Quality Points
1	Poorly equipped	30
2	Small quantity, good equipment	50
3	Large amount, completely modern	100
4	Large amount, some very old	40
5	Small amount, up to date	65
6	Small amount, up to date, better than alternative no. 5	70

Dr. Kent's utility estimates can be summarized in the following valuation matrix (see Table 7–12):

TABLE 7–12   Summary Table of Valuations

Alternative	Criterion Number[a]									
	1	2	3	4	5	6	7	8	9	10
1	49.0	50.0	55	75.0	5	36.0	70	5	30	30
2	64.0	67.5	50	85.6	38	69.0	40	70	70	50
3	36.0	91.5	80	99.4	36	99.4	80	100	100	100
4	100	100	70	60.0	90	11.3	50	40	40	40
5	81.0	60.0	20	87.6	96	93.7	20	5	5	65
6	78.2	52.8	75	67.1	18	25.0	75	90	90	70

[a] Utility numbers are shown to one decimal place for those that are derived from Table 7–1 to help the reader with this distinction, and not to indicate any specific degree of precision of measurement.

Which alternative should Dr. Kent accept? This question cannot be answered at this point because a number of other items are still unknown: criterion weights and the method Kent will use for identifying the best alternative. Kent's tradeoffs of salary against other factors is unknown thus far. A number of possible solutions to this problem will be found in later chapters.

Notes and References

1. The reader who wishes to become acquainted with some of the extensive literature on utility estimation and measurement should see the following.

(a)   E. H. Galenter, "The Direct Measurement of Utility and Subjective Probability," *American Journal of Psychology,* Vol. 75, 1962.

(b)   H. Gullison, "Measurement of Subjective Values," *Psychometrica,* Vol. 21, 1956.

(c)   F. Mosteller and R. Gonzales, "An Experimental Measure of Utility," *Journal of Political Economy,* Vol. 59, 1951.

(d)   J. Sayer Minas and Russel L. Ackoff, "Individual and Collective Value Judgments," in M. W. Shelly, II, and G. L. Bryan (eds.), *Human Judgments and Optimality* (New York, John Wiley and Sons, 1964), pp. 351–359.

(e)   G. M. Becker, H. M. DeGroot, and J. Marshak, "Measuring Utility by a Single Response Method," *Behavioral Science,* Vol. 9, 1964.

(f)   K. R. MacCrimmon and M. Toda, "Utility Measurement" (working paper, Graduate School of Industrial Administration, Carnegie-Mellon University), 1969.

(g)   Ward Edwards and Amos Tversky, *Decision Making* (London, Penguin Books), 1967.

(h)   J. R. Miller, III, *Professional Decision Making* (New York, Praeger Publishers, 1970).

(i)   Erik Johnson, *Studies in Multiobjective Decision Models* (in English) (Lund, Denmark, Economic Research Center in Lund, 1968).

(j)   Ralph L. Keeney, "Utility Independence and Preferences for Multi-attributed Consequences," *JORSA,* Vol. 19, No. 4, (July–August 1971), pp. 875–893 and bibliography on pp. 892–893.

Important Words and Concepts

Utility
Disutility
Incommensurate
Marginal utility
Increasing marginal utility
Diminishing marginal utility
U-shaped utility function
Bounded space
Unbounded space
Quality points

Overview of Chapter 7

An object, event, collection, action, or stimulus has utility if it has the capability of satisfying human needs or can contribute to the attainment of an individual, group, or organizational goal. Negative utility, disutility, acts to frustrate need satisfaction or goal attainment.

Although the measurement of utility is difficult and imprecise, all living things must make utility judgments if they are to make choices among alternatives.

Utility functions may exhibit constant, increasing, or diminishing marginal utility. Utility functions may have the form of simple mathematical functions or more complex discontinuous functions.

Utility can be estimated by use of a utility chart or by a quality-point estimation procedure. A worked-out example of how to estimate utility with either variously shaped utility schedules or a quality-point chart is presented.

Questions for Review, Discussion, and Research

Review

1. Define utility and disutility.

2. Why is it always necessary for people to make utility judgments?

3. Sketch a utility function that has diminishing marginal utility. Do the same for other shapes.

4. What is the difference between a bounded and unbounded space as it is used in this chapter?

5. How does the utility scale from Table 7–1, which has diminishing marginal utility, differ from one with increasing marginal utility?

6. What is a quality-point scale and how is it used?

7. What is meant by a go, no-go or limit utility function?

8. What kind of a utility function has a U-shape?

Discussion

1. Analyze a number of choices that you have observed people making and try to identify the utility judgments that they made.

2. Can you think of any decisions that do not involve utility judgments?

3. What are some applications of U-shaped and limit utility functions?

4. What justification can you offer for the use of a bounded utility scale?

5. Under what circumstances would a bipolar scale be preferred to a unipolar scale?

6. Why do you think people have nonlinear utility functions?

Research

1. Collect several useful obects of approximately the same money value and ask a number of people to rank them by preference. Do they all show the same preferences? Discuss the nature of their utility judgments.

2. Design a test instrument that will enable you to test the shape of a person's utility function for various quantities of different kinds of things. (Hint: See Ralph O. Swalm, "Utility Theory—Insights into Risk Taking," *Harvard Business Review*, Vol. 44, No. 6 (November–December 1966), pp. 123–136 and James S. Dyer, "An Empirical Investigation of a Man-Machine Interactive Approach to the Solution of the Multiple Criteria Problem," working paper—Western Management Science Institute—U. of California. Los Angeles, Oct. 1972.)

3. Using this instrument, conduct a survey among your associates and try to sketch their utility functions. Are there some classes of items for which there are diminishing marginal utility and others that have different utility functions?

8. Ordering Multivalued Alternatives

The main ideas developed in this chapter are:

1. Alternatives can be put in merit order by employing the dominance and equality relation or by a vector-to-scalar transformation.

2. It is better to use valuation scores than to use outcome scores directly.

3. Different merit-ordering methods may produce different orders of alternatives.

4. Criterion weights, too, affect the merit order.

INTRODUCTION

The procedure described in Chapter 7 for estimating utility is used to transform outcome scores into valuation scores. The end result of these transformations is a valuation matrix with numerical cell entries as shown in Figure 8–1.

$$
\begin{pmatrix}
u_{11} & u_{12} & u_{13} \ldots\ldots\ldots\ldots u_{1j} \ldots\ldots\ldots\ldots u_{1m} \\
u_{21} & u_{22} & u_{23} \ldots\ldots\ldots\ldots u_{2j} \ldots\ldots\ldots\ldots u_{2m} \\
u_{31} & u_{32} & u_{33} \ldots\ldots\ldots\ldots u_{3j} \ldots\ldots\ldots\ldots u_{3m} \\
\cdots & \cdots & \ldots\ldots\ldots\ldots\ldots\ldots\ldots\ldots\ldots\ldots\ldots\ldots \\
\cdots & \cdots & \ldots\ldots\ldots\ldots\ldots\ldots\ldots\ldots\ldots\ldots\ldots\ldots \\
u_{i1} & u_{i2} & u_{i3} \ldots\ldots\ldots\ldots u_{ij} \ldots\ldots\ldots\ldots u_{im} \\
\cdots & \cdots & \ldots\ldots\ldots\ldots\ldots\ldots\ldots\ldots\ldots\ldots\ldots\ldots \\
\cdots & \cdots & \ldots\ldots\ldots\ldots\ldots\ldots\ldots\ldots\ldots\ldots\ldots\ldots \\
u_{n1} & u_{n2} & u_{n3} \ldots\ldots\ldots\ldots u_{nj} \ldots\ldots\ldots\ldots u_{nm}
\end{pmatrix}
\quad (8\text{-}1)
$$

FIGURE 8–1. *The valuation matrix formed after the outcome score-sets have been assigned utility scores. There are* n *alternatives and* m *criteria in this symbolic matrix.*

The next phase in the decision problem, in the general case, is to arrive at a *merit ordering* of the alternatives. In special cases, the procedure can be abridged either by looking for the one "best" alternative, or by classifying the alternatives into categories such as: accept-reject, good-better-best, first prize-second prize-third prize-honorable mention, and the like. Even though these shortcuts may be perfectly satisfactory for many problem situations, it is worthwhile to study the more general approach before dealing with the abridgements.

Order Relations

In some rare decision problems one alternative will emerge as being so obviously superior to all others that finding the one for first place is trivially simple. This will happen when the superior alternative is *dominant*. For example in a six-criterion matrix with scales of 0–100, an alternative with scores 100,100,100,100,100,100 could only be equaled, never topped. Or, if a number of factory workers were being considered for promotion to the rank of foreman and the criteria for consideration were (a) seniority, (b) know-how, and (c) getting along with people, clearly a candidate who surpassed on all three of these traits would be obviously the best. *Truly dominant alternatives are superior to all others in the set no matter what system of ordering is used, or what criterion weights are assigned.*

By similar reasoning, an alternative could be *contra-dominant,* if criterion by criterion, each of its scores were lower than for any other alternative in the set. For example, an alternative with the scores 0,0,0,0,0,0 is clearly contra-dominant. In the foreman promotion example, a candidate with (a) the least seniority, (b) the least know-how, and (c) the poorest in getting along with people, would be contra-dominant.

Stated symbolically, alternative $[A_a]$ is the dominant member of the *entire set* of n alternatives on m critera if

$$u_{aj} > u_{ij}$$

for all values of i and j (except $i=a$) where i runs from l to n and j from l to m.

Or in a more limited sense, for a *pair* of alternatives, $[A_a]$ dominates $[A_b]$ if

$$u_{aj} > u_{bj}$$

for all values of j.

By like reasoning alternative $[A_c]$ is contra-dominant with respect to members of the set if

$$u_{cj} < u_{ij}$$

for all values of i and j except $i=c$.

For a pair of alternatives, alternative $[A_c]$ is contra-dominant with respect to $[A_d]$ if

$$u_{cj} < u_{dj}$$

for all values of j.

Thus, it is theoretically possible to accomplish the merit ordering of alternatives by use of the dominance relation alone, although cases so delightfully simple are disappointingly rare.

For example, for

$$[A_1] \equiv [100, 90, 80, 90, 100]$$
$$[A_2] \equiv [\ 60, 65, 55, 60, 70\ ]$$
$$[A_3] \equiv [\ 70, 75, 60, 70, 80\ ]$$
$$[A_4] \equiv [\ 90, 80, 70, 80, 90\ ]$$

Clearly $[A_1]$ is dominant and $[A_2]$ contra-dominant. $[A_1]$ dominates $[A_4]$; $[A_4]$ dominates $[A_3]$; $[A_3]$ dominates $[A_2]$, and the rank order is

$$[A_1], [A_4], [A_3], [A_2]$$

and this rank order would remain invariant regardless of the method that was used for combining the numbers into an index or figure-of-merit,* or of the weights assigned to the criteria.

Equality is another possible relation. Two alternatives, $[A_a]$ and $[A_b]$ are equal if, and only if,

$$u_{aj} = u_{bj}$$

for all values of j. The equality relation is unaffected by the weights assigned to the criteria and by the method used for combining the elements of the score-sets into indexes of figures-of-merit. Equal alternatives are given tied ranks.

Vector-to-Scalar Transformation

One very common method for comparing alternatives on multiple criteria is to convert the vector

$$[A_i] \equiv [u_{ij}]$$

into a scalar quantity, $\mathring{A}_i$. This is what we would be doing if we compared alternatives by the lengths of their vectors in a geometric space. For example, Figure 8–2 shows two alternatives scaled on three criteria as vectors in a 3-space. The lengths of the vectors can be computed by application of the Pythagorean theorem

---

* There is one exception to this rule. If we took the reciprocals of the valuation scores, the ranking of the alternatives would be reversed because the dominant alternative would have been transformed into the contra-dominant, and vice versa.

$$\mathring{A}_1 = \sqrt{u_{11}{}^2 + u_{12}{}^2 + u_{13}{}^2}$$

$$\mathring{A}_2 = \sqrt{u_{21}{}^2 + u_{22}{}^2 + u_{23}{}^2}$$

and thereafter it would be obvious if $\mathring{A}_1$ was equal to, greater than, or smaller than $\mathring{A}_2$.

Procedures of this sort, where multivalued alternatives are transformed into single-valued items, are called by Coombs[1] "collapsing" or "compressing a natural partial order into a simple order," or "comparing incomparables." The collapsing operation is necessary because we do not know how to compare multivalued alternatives directly unless, accidentally, they appear in a dominance, contra-dominance, or equality relationship.

Real-life decisions do not often present such transparent choices. More usually, an alternative with high scores on some criteria will have low scores on others. High seniority foreman candidates may have low know-how or poor skill with people. Candidates with good know-how may have low

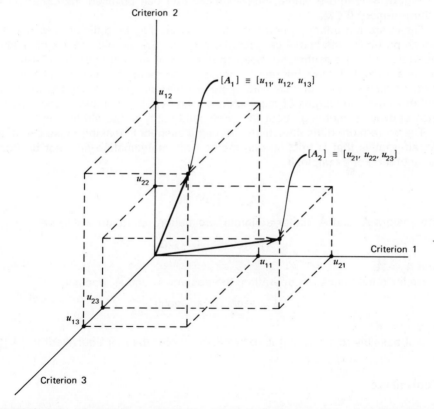

FIGURE 8–2. Geometric representation of two alternatives in a three-dimensional space. The alternative valuation vectors are shown as line vectors in the space.

seniority, and so forth. This is the case, also, in the Dr. Kent valuation matrix (Chapter 7) where there are no dominant, no contra-dominant, and no equal alternatives. In such cases it is not possible to tell by simple inspection which alternative is better than another. More refined methods must be used for merit ordering such alternatives.

THE AMALGAMATION PROBLEM

A Glimpse at the Problem

If alternatives cannot be ranked or otherwise compared by taking advantage of the dominance or equality relation, all that remains is the vector-to-scalar transformation. This operation involves the amalgamation of the elements of each alternative's valuation score-set (the row vectors of the valuation matrix of Figure 8–1) into a single index-number that can be used thereafter as a figure-of-merit (FOM).[2]

These are not difficult operations to do. What may be difficult is to decide which particular mathematical operation to use. Should we use a summation operation like the arithmetic mean that will give an average utility? Should we use a multiplicative operation similar to the geometric mean that gives a kind of mean, too, but one with quite a different gestalt? Or would it be better to use the lengths of the vectors in the hypothetical hyperspace which also conveys something about the composite utility of the alternative?

There are more difficulties than one might suspect in making those choices. An alternative that is best on one method of amalgamation may not be best on another. For example, if

$$[A_1] \equiv [50 \quad 50]$$
$$[A_2] \equiv [100 \quad 20]$$

the scalars $\mathring{A}_1$ and $\mathring{A}_2$ under a simple summation operation would be

$$\mathring{A}_1 = 100 \qquad \mathring{A}_2 = 120$$

and $\mathring{A}_2 > \mathring{A}_1$

Under a multiplication operation, the scalars A_1 and A_2 become

$$\mathring{A}_1 = 2500 \qquad \mathring{A}_2 = 2000$$

and $\mathring{A}_2 < \mathring{A}_1$

Is it possible to say if $[A_1]$ is better than, poorer than, or equivalent to $[A_2]$?

Equivalence

It is possible for two alternatives to have equal scalars even though the corresponding valuation score-sets are quite different. For example, under addition

$$[A_3] \equiv [50 \ 50]$$
$$[A_4] \equiv [80 \ 20]$$

the scalars $\mathring{A}_3$ and $\mathring{A}_4$ would both be equal to .100. But under a multiplication operation, $\mathring{A}_3$ would be equal to 2500 and A_4 would be equal to 1600—definitely not the same as for addition. Thus, two alternatives might have equal scalars under one mathematical operation and unequal scalars under others.

When two alternatives have equal scalars, that is equal index-numbers or equal figures-of-merit, they are defined as *equivalent under an operation* or just *equivalent* if the words *under an operation* are understood.*

If the index-number or figure-of-merit is assumed to be representative of the goodness of the alternative, that is, we accept it as representative of the relative merit, worth, attractiveness, or desirability, then equivalent alternatives are equally meritorious. If one dominates another, the dominant one will always be more worthwhile than the contra-dominant one. But, whether or not two nonidentical alternatives are equally meritorious depends very much on the method used for combining valuation scores into the FOM.

Equivalence, however measured, is a transitory phenomenon because the partial utilities (valuation scores) may be changing with time. Thus alternative X may be judged better than alternative Y today; tomorrow Y may be better than X; the next day they may be equivalent; the day after, both may be judged repulsive because their partial utilities may have changed into disutilities.

An interesting conclusion can be drawn for the foregoing material in this chapter. *We cannot properly state that one of a pair of unequal, nondominant alternatives is superior, inferior, or equivalent to a second unless we first specify the method for transforming the vector score-set into a scalar (method of amalgamation), because under one mathematical ordering system, a particular alternative may be superior while under another system, it may prove inferior.*

Why Not Amalgamate Outcome Scores Directly?

The reader may be wondering why it is necessary to perform the transformation of outcome scores into valuation scores. Why is it not just as good to amalgamate outcome scores? If this were done, the labor involved in estimating utility would be avoided along with the unsettling matter of making utility judgments.

Although there will be exceptions, in general, the outcome scores will not have commensurate units. For example, in a hypothetical problem the units may be for

---

* Two theorems become immediately apparent: (1) all equal alternatives are equivalent (but equivalent alternatives are not necessarily equal); and (2) If one alternative dominates a second, the pair can never be equivalent.

O_{11},   hours
O_{12},   tons
O_{13},   feet per second
O_{14},   dollars
O_{15},   man-days

Operations with incommensurate units are much more limited than with commensurate units. Addition and the allied operations are not defined for incommensurate units, although multiplication and its allied operations are. Being confined only to multiplication, division, powers, and roots may be a disabling limitation. For example, it is not possible to compute the length of a vector in a space using these operations. A simple example may help illuminate this difficulty. It would make no sense at all to compute the value of X in this expression

$$X = \sqrt{Y^2 + T^2 + R^2}$$

where Y = cost in dollars
T = time in days
R = number of people

But, although the units are incommensurate, this operation makes perfectly good sense:

$$X = (RT)/Y$$

X would have the units man-days per-dollar of cost.

If outcome scores only were used, the dominance and equality relation would be defined, but equivalence and ordering relations would be defined only on multiplication and its allied operations: division, roots, and powers. There would be only these limited ways of transforming the vector into a scalar.

To allow additive operations to be used, we must first transform the units from the outcome scores into a homogeneous set. For example, all units would have to be expressed in money equivalents, by places on a rank order, or by utilities.

To use the outcome scores directly involves a hidden assumption that the underlying values are expressible by means of an increasing function. Clearly, a U-shaped utility function for one or more criteria would wreak havoc with the accuracy of any figures-of-merit derived directly from outcome scores.

Transforming outcome scores into money equivalents, as is done in many cost-benefit[3] studies, may work in some situations, but some criteria do not lend themselves to money values; utilities are easier to estimate than money equivalents.

A simple merit-ranking of outcome scores, column by column, criterion by criterion, would also work, but the ranking scale is much weaker than the utility scales shown in Chapter 7. These utility scales fall somewhere between the domains of ordinal and cardinal utility. No attempt is made to measure utility in absolute units (utils), nor has utility been treated as merely a preference ordering of unmeasurable quantities. The utility scales are weaker than equal-interval cardinal scales, but stronger than simple ranking scales. This means that the decision maker must locate his zero and ecstasy points and from these interpolate the intermediate values. This procedure does not prove difficult for most individuals. Reasonably introspective people can make quite good guesses about the shapes of their utility functions if they understand something about utility theory and if they ask themselves properly framed questions. They can tell if they have constant, diminishing, or increasing marginal utility or if their utilities can be better expressed by means of some sort of discontinuous function.

Specific Choice Rules and Merit-Ordering Techniques

The decision maker has a very large number of choice rules for finding the best alternative for merit ordering and for classifying alternatives. Some are simple; some are not. The next two chapters present several of these methods along with variations that lend themselves to translation into simple English sentences easily comprehended by persons with little or no advanced mathematical training. All involve elementary algebraic operations.

The foregoing discussion shows that different mathematical methods could possibly produce different merit ordering of alternatives. Therefore, it is a matter of considerable moment which particular operation is chosen for use. We may be concerned with how and why the various methods differ in their treatment of alternatives.

The decision maker may be fortunate enough to have absolute discretion in choosing a particular amalgamation rule, and he may be accountable to no one for his choice. But if affected parties who have the power and knowledge to do so find out that the decision has an unfavorable effect on their welfare, they may challenge the decision. Such protests will be much more likely if it appears that another method of amalgamation than the one used would have produced startlingly different results.

It is possible to imagine that, in a few special circumstances, the choice of an amalgamation rule may be the subject of interparty bargaining as, for example, in a labor negotiation where numerical rating schemes are used for merit-rating, awarding merit raises or promotions. There may be debates and prolonged negotiations by the advocates of parties who argue that the rule used systematically discriminates against their clients' interests. They may argue that if another rule had been used, their clients would not be so disfavored. Conceivably, someday, in the not-too-distant future, the selection of a choice rule might become a proper matter for legal challenge, for court decision, or for a congressional investigation.*

---

* For an inkling how such a challenge might be made and countered, see Case A-III entitled, "Attacking and/or Defending the Executive Decision." Criteria useful in selecting a choice rule are discussed in Chapter 16.

Part IV of this book deals exhaustively with the characteristics and individual differences of the various amalgamation techniques. Its analysis reveals which rules express what kinds of attitudes, and which may introduce systematic patterns of discrimination into the merit ordering of alternatives.

Effects of Criterion Weights

The merit order of nondominant, nonequal alternatives can be drastically altered by the weights assigned to the decision criteria.* For example, if

Alternative	Criterion	Scores
	1	2
$[A_1]$	30	70
$[A_2]$	70	30
Weights	w_1	w_2

Under summation we would be indifferent between $[A_1]$ and $[A_2]$ if, and only if, w_1 were equal to w_2. If w_1 were larger than w_2, we would prefer $[A_1]$ to $[A_2]$; if w_2 were larger than w_1, we would prefer $[A_2]$ to $[A_1]$. It can be seen from this little example that $[A_1]$ and $[A_2]$ are equivalent if, and only if, the criterion weights are equal. Nothing we do with criterion weights affects the merit ordering of equal or dominant alternatives. (The proof of this statement is left to the reader as an exercise.)

* Multiple-criterion weighing is discussed in Chapters 14 and 15.

APPENDIX TO CHAPTER 8

A NOTE ON VECTOR SPACES[4]

An incommensurate vector space is a set of axes (or sheets) each of which is associated with one element of a set on incommensurate units. These units may be *simple* or *compound.* Examples of simple units are: length in feet (L), time in seconds (T), weight in pounds (M). Examples of compound units are: feet per second (LT^{-1}), pounds per cubic foot (ML^{-3}), and foot-pounds per second (LMT^{-1}).

It may be helpful to think of a unit axis on an incommensurate vector space as a page in a ledger. All permissible operations on an axis can be contained on the page assigned to the axis. Other operations across axes require moving to another page. Thus the operation $5 \times j$ and the operation $3j + 5j$ can be done on the "*j* page," but the operation $j \times j$ cannot and must be moved to the j^2 page. Whenever an operation produces a change in units, the result must be moved to the page that has those units.

The permissible operations *on* a unit axis of an incommensurate space are: addition and subtraction, plus multiplication or division by a pure number. Ordinary multiplication, division, and derived operations are not defined because these operations produce compound units. For example, multiplying five feet by six feet requires a move to the square-foot axis. Exceptions to this rule are such self-rectifying operations as $(j \times j)^{1/2}$ or $(j^3)^{1/3}$. These operations require a temporary move to another page but an immediate return to home base.

Operations *across* incommensurate axes are limited to multiplication and its allied operations. But if compound units are formed, those products must be moved to the new axis. For example, if the operation on three axes (*a*) number of people R, (*b*) number of days T, and (*c*) cost in dollars Y was

$$X = RTY^{-1}$$

X would have the units man-days per dollar of cost and all operations with this formula would fall on the RTY^{-1} axis.

Figure 8–3 shows how the physical meanings associated with an incommensurate axis differ from those on a commensurate axis. Figure 8–3*a* shows the familiar diagram vector depicting the addition of two force vectors. The addition is defined on this commensurate axis. The vector sum V_r has meaning as does the angle θ. In contrast, Figure 8–3*b* shows two incommensurate axes. The units are gallons of white paint and pounds of nails. The vector sum is undefined; the lengths of the lines from P_1 and P_2 to the origin are without physical meaning; the angles, too, are without

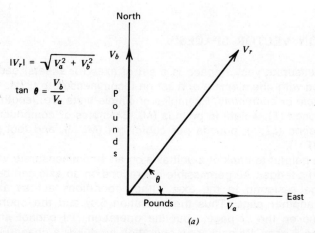

FIGURE 8–3a. Vector representation of two forces applied to a body and the resultant force V_r having both magnitude and direction. Both vector axes have the same units (pounds of force).

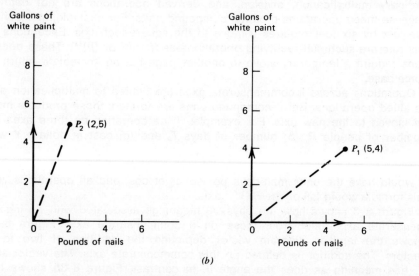

FIGURE 8–3b. Vector representation of two purchase orders for quantities of white paint and nails. The points P_1 and P_2 represent the two orders (combinations of paint and nails). Contrary to 8–3a, there is no meaning attached to the distance from P_1 or P_2 to the origin nor to their angular position.

physical meaning. The Point P_1 can only be interpreted as "five pounds of nails and four gallons of white paint."

There is one way to transform a vector in an incommensurate space into a scalar, that is to collapse the space onto a line. That involves one of the multiplicative operations. By multiplying all the elements of a score-set together, we have a number with compound units. This permits us to say if $[A_a]$ is better than, poorer than, or equivalent to $[A_b]$.

There are a number of limitations to the usefulness of the multiplication operation, the most important of which are:

1. A zero in one score makes the scalar zero. This makes it impossible to compare two alternatives both of which have a zero in their sets. For example, if

$$[A_1] \equiv [100, 100, 100, 100, 100, 0]$$
$$[A_2] \equiv [\ \ 0, \ \ 0, \ \ 0, \ \ 0, \ \ 0, 0]$$

we would find that both $\mathring{A}_1$ and $\mathring{A}_2 = 0$ and we would be unable to discriminate between the two.

2. Bipolar scales cannot be used with multiplicative operations. If there were any number of negative scores in the set, the knowledge of their negativity would be lost, and they would be treated as if they were positive. It makes a great deal of difference whether a score is $+100$ or -100. The multiplicative model cannot preserve this essential distinction. If there was an even number of negatives, the scalar would be positive (good); if there was an odd number, the scalar would be negative (bad). Obviously, whether the number of negative scores is odd or even has no physical meaning in this context, and certainly not the meaning that would necessarily be attached.

Notes and References

1. Clyde H. Coombs, "Comparing Incomparables: Compressing Partial Orders to Form Decisions," in *A Theory of Data* (New York, John Wiley and Sons, 1964), pp. 284–291.

2. See Leo Goodman, "On Methods of Amalgamation" in R. M. Thrall et al., *Decision Processes* (New York, John Wiley and Sons, 1954), pp. 39–48.

3. A. R. Prest and R. Turvey, "Cost-Benefit Analysis: A Survey," *The Economic Journal,* Vol. LXXV, No. 300 (December 1965), pp. 683–735 and bibliography.

4. For a full and rigorous treatment of this subject see Paul McDougle, *Vector Algebra* (Belmont, California, Wadsworth Publishing Co., Inc. 1971).

Important Words and Concepts

Merit ordering
Order relations
Dominance
Contra-dominance
Valuation matrix
Index number
Figure-of-merit
Equality
Vector-to-scalar transformation
Amalgamation
Hyperspace
Equivalence under an operation
Incommensurate units
Commensurate units
Additive operations
Multiplicative operations
Money equivalents
Cost-benefit studies
Ordinal utility
Cardinal utility
Criterion weights
Indifferent
Vector space

Overview of Chapter 8

The next phase after preparing the valuation matrix is to do a merit ordering of the alternatives. This can be done by employing the dominance and equality relations, or by transforming the matrix row vector into a scalar. It is better to use valuation scores for this purpose than to use outcome scores.

There are many ways for doing the transformation, and they do not all produce the same ordering. The choice of a particular method may be the subject of debate or negotiation. Criterion weights, too, are influential in the merit ordering of alternatives.

Questions for Review, Discussion, and Research

Review

1. How is the valuation matrix constructed? Identify the components: the row vectors, the column vectors, the valuation score-sets, and the cell entries for alternatives on criteria.

2. Define dominance, contra-dominance, and equality. Give numerical examples.

3. Test the validity of the assertion that a dominant alternative will remain dominant regardless of the method for computing the scalar or the weights assigned.

4. What is to be done with the valuation matrix after it is constructed?

5. For a pair of alternatives, one of which dominates the other, take the reciprocals of the cell elements and see if their dominant positions are interchanged.

6. How do the concepts "vector-to-scalar transformation" and "compressing a natural order into a simple order" relate?

7. Define equivalence under an operation and prepare an example to illustrate the concept. Why may equivalence be transitory?

8. Test the two theorems in the footnote on page 173.

9. Discuss the physical meanings of the measurements in Figure 8–3.

10. Why is it preferable to amalgamate valuation scores rather than to operate on the outcome scores directly?

11. What transformations of outcome scores can be used for amalgamation other than utility scores? What are the pros and cons of each?

12. What is a "strong" or a "weak" scale, and how do they differ?

13. How can criterion weight affect the merit ordering of a set of alternatives? Prepare a simple numerical example to test this statement.

Discussion

1. Why do you think different amalgamation techniques produce a different merit order?

2. Do you think a decision maker should consult with anyone else before selecting an amalgamation method? If yes, when? If no, why not?

3. How can a decision maker avoid the ambiguity associated with the merit ordering of alternatives?

4. Debate the various advantages and disadvantages of using utility, money equivalents, or simple ranking scores for the valuation matrix?

Research

Search through the literature or through a company's files for a selection or evaluation decision such as a plant location problem, a vendor choice problem, or an executive hiring problem. Try to discover if a change in the amalgamation technique of criterion weights would have produced a different decision or recommendation. If so, why? If not, why not?

9. Techniques for Merit Ordering (I)

The principal objective of this chapter is to present a number of choice rules that can be used for (a) merit-ordering alternatives, (b) finding the best, or (c) classifying alternatives into merit categories.

A GO, NO-GO RULE

Choice Rule No. 1. Establish a standard of acceptability for every decision criterion. Reject any alternative with scores that fail to meet or exceed standards.

The standards may be minimum limits, maximum limits, or a combination of the two. And it is not necessary that all criteria have identical standards; one can have a minimum limit; a second can have a maximum limit, and a third, a combination of the two, and so forth.

Finding the "Best"

There are three possible outcomes when using this rule for finding the "best" alternative in the set (see Figure 9–1):

1. One alternative will survive the test.
2. No alternatives will survive.
3. Two or more may survive.

If only one survives, that one is the best of the lot and the problem is over. If none survives, there are two possibilities: (a) to continue the search for more alternatives until one that passes is found, or (b) to progressively relax the standards by small increments (for example, in 5 percent steps) until one alternative falls into the modified acceptance region. If the latter course is chosen, limits should be adjusted to reflect the relative urgencies of the criteria. The standards for the less important criteria should be relaxed more rapidly than for those having greater weight.

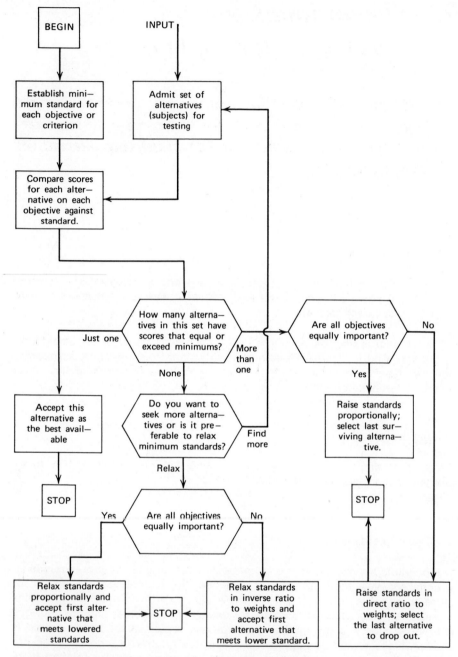

FIGURE 9–1. *Flowchart of procedure for selection of a single best alternative. If two or more alternatives are required, the procedure can be repeated.*

If two or more alternatives survive the test, the standards are raised progressively in small increments until only one alternative survives. Here, too, recognition can be given to criterion weights. The standards for the more important criteria should be raised more rapidly than for the lesser weighted criteria.

With slight modification, this procedure can be used to merit order the alternatives. The best alternative is removed from consideration and the process is repeated to find the best of the remaining alternatives. When the second-best is found, the process is repeated once more to find the third-best, and so forth, until just one remains. Ties can be broken by making slight adjustments in standards to favor the more important criteria.

Satisficing Applications of Rule No. 1

If the population of alternatives is very large, it might not be worthwhile to search for the "best"; a "good-enough" alternative might have to suffice. Standards would be established, and the first alternative that had scores within the acceptance regions would be adopted and further testing would be stopped.

Conditions may be such that an alternative remains available for a limited time only. If it is not accepted on the spot, it may not be available later. There is a definite risk that the one that might have been found best could have disappeared by the time the remainder of the population was tested. In those cases, too, the "good enough" alternative will have to do.

Choice Rule No. 1 may be used to prescreen alternatives that will be subjected to further evaluation by other means.

If Choice Rule No. 1 is aimed at finding just one or just a few good-enough alternatives, the order in which they are tested may be important to someone. For example, it may be of no importance to an employer which of a stream of acceptable applicants for jobs are ultimately selected, but it might be terribly important to the applicants. Thoroughly acceptable applicants may fail to obtain badly needed positions simply because their applications are close to the bottom of the pile and the openings are filled before their applications are reached.

Figure 9–2 shows the procedure that a purchasing agent might use for finding a vendor with which to place a purchase order. There are a number of possibilities as to how the buyer might decide whom to call first. He might arrange the potential vendors according to the following:

1. Order of distance from supply house to firm.
2. Order of probability of finding the needed items in stock.
3. Order of alphabetical listing in the classified telephone directory.
4. Preference based on buyer's previous experience.
5. A purely random process.

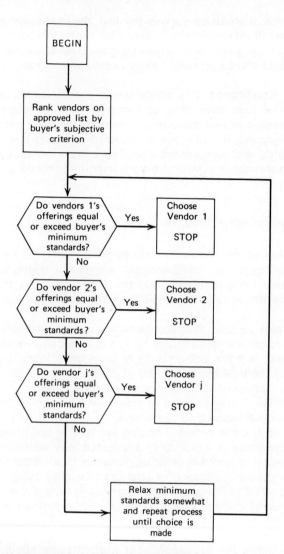

FIGURE 9–2. Schematic flow diagram of vendor choice.

If the seller had some knowledge of the buyer's decision-making procedures, he might be able to do something to raise the probability of being called first.

This example illustrates an important and often overlooked point. Most of the material on decision making treats the alternatives undergoing evaluation as passive. The foregoing purchasing example indicates that the passivity notion may be inaccurate. Alternatives may not be lying there submissively waiting to be judged; they may, if they are people, use their knowledge of the process to influence the outcome in ways that are not apparent to the person who is making the decision or evaluation.

Units for Choice Rule No. 1

Choice Rule No. 1 has one very important advantage that other rules do not have. Almost any kind of units can be accommodated and, therefore, transformation of outcome scores into valuation scores may not be necessary. The rule can be applied to outcome scores even if the units are incommensurate. However, this advantage has an offsetting disadvantage for some applications. The process does not produce figures-of-merit on which alternatives can be compared. Merit ordering can be done with this rule, but it is a nonmetric ordering that is weaker than metric ordering.

Application of Rule No. 1 to Dr. Kent's Choice Problem

Table 9–1 is a reproduction of Dr. Kent's evaluation matrix introduced in

TABLE 9–1   Dr. Kent's Evaluation Matrix

	Decision Criteria									
Alternatives	1	2	3	4	5	6	7	8	9	10
1	49	50	55	75	5	36	70	5	30	30
2	64	68	50	86	38	69	40	70	70	50 ←
3	36	92	80	99	36	99	80	100	100	100
4	100	100	70	60	90	11	50	40	40	40
5	81	60	20	88	96	94	20	5	5	65
6	78	53	75	67	18	25	75	90	90	70

Note: all numbers rounded to two figures. (*Source.* Dr. Kent's matrix, Chapter 7.) Arrow indicates "best" alternative by using Choice Rule No. 1.

Chapter 7, except that the values have all been rounded to two figures. Assume that Dr. Kent has assigned the minimum limits of 50,50,50, and so forth, to all criteria. In that case all six alternatives would be rejected because every one has at least one score that falls below 50. If we remember that a score of 50 stands for a mediocre evaluation, this outcome is not surprising. Dr. Kent might want to reject all of these job offers and remain in his present position until he can find a job offer that has no mediocre features. On the other hand, he might decide that perhaps he has been too severe in his standards and that some relaxation can be tolerated. If he progressively relaxes all criterion limits by small increments, the first alternative whose scores fall into the acceptance region is no. 2. Its smallest score is 38 on criterion no. 5 and is the "best worst."

COMBINATION GO, NO-GO AND OPTIMIZING RULE

> **Choice Rule No. 2.   Establish standards of acceptability for every criterion except the one judged most important. Reject every alternative with scores on the nonreserved criteria that fail to meet or exceed standards. For those alternatives not so rejected, select the one with the best score on the reserved criterion.**

If a utility scale is used for the reserved criterion, the rule will give a "weak" figure-of-merit for the alternative chosen as "best."

Application

This combination rule is used by the industrial purchasing agent. He has a list of approved suppliers for each item he buys routinely. He may say to himself, "Among the suppliers who meet my standards for delivery, service, and quality, I will place the order with the one who quotes the lowest price." In a shortage emergency, the reserved criterion might be the delivery date. If all suppliers' offerings, including price, are the same, the buyer may think to himself, "Among all suppliers who meet my standards for delivery, price, and quality, I will place the order with the one whose salesman I like best" or, "with the one that gave me the best gift last Christmas." The application of Choice Rule No. 2 to such situations is diagrammed in Figure 9–3.

Application to Dr. Kent's Matrix

If Dr. Kent established salary (criterion no. 1) as the reserved criterion and 30,30,30,30, and so forth, as the lower limits on all others, alternatives nos. 2 and 3 would fall into the acceptance region. However, alternative no. 2 would be preferred to no. 3 (salary score for no. 2 is 64; for no. 3, 32). If, on the other hand, opportunity for advancement (criterion no. 3) was reserved, alternative no. 3 (score 80) would be preferred to no. 2 (score 50).

WEIGHTED SUM OF THE POINTS RULE

> **Choice Rule No. 3.   Multiply each cell entry in the valuation matrix by the corresponding weight and add the weighted cell entries for each alternative (cross the matrix row). The alternative with the largest score is the best, the next largest, second best; and so forth.**

For ranking purposes, the raw sums may be perfectly acceptable. If a figure-of-merit is desired that has the same range as the criterion scores, the arithmetic mean may be used.

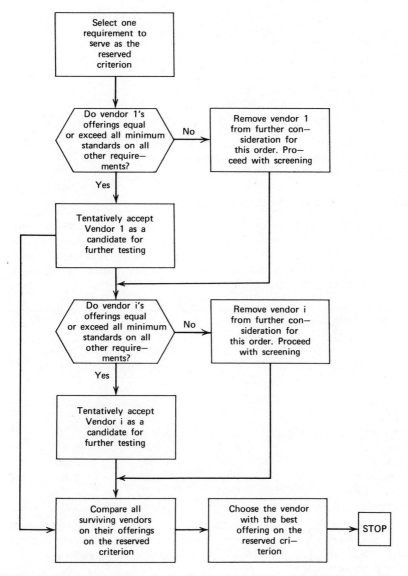

FIGURE 9–3. Schematic flow diagram of the application of Choice Rule No. 2 to industrial purchasing routines.

The computing formula for Rule No. 3 is

$$S_i = \sum_{j=1}^{m} w_j\, u_{ij} \qquad (9\text{-}1)$$

and for the figure-of-merit

$$\text{FOM}_i = \frac{1}{\Sigma w_j} \sum_{j=1}^{m} w_j\, u_{ij} \qquad (9\text{-}2)$$

where

S_i = the weighted sum for the ith alternative of the set of n alternatives.
FOM_i = the figure-of-merit for the ith alternative.
w_j = the numerical weight assigned to the ith criterion.
u_{ij} = the valuation score for the ith alternative on the jth criterion. j runs from 1 to m.

A simple computing chart for formula 9–2 is shown in Figure 9–4. One such chart is required for each alternative.

Examples of the Use of Choice Rule No. 3

This is a widely used method for dealing with alternatives scaled on multiple criteria.[1] It is used for computing grades in schools, for computing cumulative grade-point scores in colleges, and for computing a suitability index for evaluating investment opportunities.[2] An example of its use for measurement of product fit is shown in Box 9–1.[3]

Box 9–1   Measuring the Product Fit

Performance Criteria	Relative Weight	Score for this Product	Score for this Criterion
Company personality and good will	0.20	0.60	0.120
Marketing	0.20	0.90	0.180
Research and development	0.20	0.70	0.140
Personnel	0.15	0.60	0.090
Finance	0.10	0.90	0.090
Production	0.05	0.80	0.040
Location and facilities	0.05	0.30	0.015
Purchasing and supply	0.05	0.90	0.045
	1.00		0.720 (accept)

Rating scales: 0–.40 poor; .41–.75 fair; .76–1.0 good. Minimum performance overall for acceptance 0.70.
Source. Barry M. Richman, "A Rating Scale for Product Innovation" in T. L. Berg and A. Suchman (eds.), *Product Strategy and Management* (New York: Holt, Rinehart and Winston, Inc., 1963), pp. 434–442.

Row	Description of operation	Subject name or number (Alternative)										
		Decision objectives (performance criteria)										
		I	II	III	IV	V	VI	VII	VIII	IX	X	RESULT
1	Enter performance (or utility) scores for this subject											
2	Enter numerical weights for each criterion (or objective)											
3	Multiply row 1 entries by row 2 entries											
4	Compute sum across row 3 entries											
5	Compute sum across row 2 entries											
6	Divide row 4 sum by row 5 sum THIS IS THE FIGURE–OF–MERIT FOR THIS SUBJECT											

FIGURE 9–4. *Computing chart for weighted sum of the points rule (Choice Rule No. 3) based on figure-of-merit formula 9–2. Chart has places for ten objectives but can easily be expanded to include any number. One such computation is required for each alternative.*

Application to Dr. Kent's Matrix

Using the chart in Figure 9–4 on the data in Dr. Kent's matrix with equal weights for all criteria gives:

Alternative	FOM
1	40.5
2	60.5
3	82.2
4	60.1
5	53.4
6	64.1

From this tabulation alternative no. 3 is the best with a score of 82.2. However, if Dr. Kent decided that salary was very important to him, so important that he wished to give it the weight, 10, the tabulation of scores would become:

Alternative	FOM
1	45.5
2	62.2
3	60.2
4	79.0
5	66.5
6	70.8

It should not be surprising to find that with salary given so much weight, alternative no. 4 which paid the highest salary moves to first place and no. 3, formerly first, is now next to last.

WEIGHTED PRODUCT OF THE POINTS RULE

Choice Rule No. 4 (Exponential Form). Compute the weighted product of the cell entries of the valuation matrix by the formula

$$P_i = \left[\prod_{j=1}^{m} (u_{ij})^{w_j} \right] \tag{9-3a}$$

Choice Rule No. 4 (Logarithmic Form). Compute the weighted produce of the cell entries of the valuation matrix by the formula

$$P_i = \text{antilog} \left[\sum_{j=1}^{m} w_j \log u_{ij} \right] \tag{9-3b}$$

The alternative with the largest P_i is the best; the alternative with the next highest, next best, and so forth.

If the situation would be better served by a figure-of-merit score, the formulas can be modified to become

$$\text{FOM}_1 = \left[\prod_{j=1}^{m} (u_{ij})^{w_j} \right]^{\frac{1}{\Sigma w_j}} \qquad (9\text{-}4a)$$

And the logarithmic form:

$$\text{FOM}_i = \text{antilog} \left[\frac{1}{\Sigma w_j} \sum_{j=1}^{m} w_j \log u_{ij} \right] \qquad (9\text{-}4b)$$

A computing table for the figure-of-merit using Choice Rule No. 4 is shown in Figure 9–5.

Box 9–2 contains an illustration of the application of this rule. Eleven

---

Box 9–2   RSM Office Products Company Interviews Receptionists

The RSM Office Products Company employed a large number of secretaries who were also required to do double duty as receptionists and sales clerks. The company found that two characteristics were important for these positions: (a) secretarial ability, and (b) beauty. On a particular day, the personnel department interviewed a number of candidates and prepared a rating chart as follows (data fictitious):

Applicant's Name	(1) Ability Score	(2) Beauty Score	Product[a]
Adele Borden	00	100	0000
Betty Darin	10	90	900
Clara Roberts	20	80	1600
Doris Schuh	30	70	2100
Ethel Walter	40	60	2400
Frances Haber	50	50	2500 Best ←
Gerta Morris	60	40	2400
Helen Wales	70	30	2100
Irene Busch	80	20	1600
Jane Peters	90	10	900
Kate Parker	100	00	000

Formula 9–3a with $w_1 = w_2 = 1.00$.

	Subject name or number (Alternative)	Decision objectives (Performance criteria)										
		I	II	III	IV	V	VI	VII	VIII	IX	X	RESULT
Row	Description of operation											
1	Entrance performance (or utility) scores for this subject											
2	Enter logarithms for row 1 entries											
3	Enter weights for each criterion (or objective)											
4	Multiply rwo 2 entries by row 3 entries											
5	Compute sum across row 2											
6	Compute sum across row 3											
7	Divide row 5 sum by row 6 sum											
8	Get antilogarithm of row 7 result THIS IS THE FIGURE–OF–MERIT FOR THIS SUBJECT (ALTERNATIVE)											

FIGURE 9–5. Computing chart for figure-of-merit for weighted product of the points rule based on formula 9–4b. One such computation is required for each alternative.

candidates for the position, receptionist, are tested on two characteristics, ability and beauty. The product of the points rule is used to find the best candidate.

Formulas 9–4a and 9–4b can be interpreted as the geometric mean of the elements of the valuation score set. If outcome scores with incommensurate units are used, the geometric mean interpretation is not applicable.

THE "FURTHEST FROM THE WORST" RULE

> **Choice Rule No. 5.** Establish a dummy alternative with the scores 0,0,0,0, and so forth as the worst possible alternative (absolutely repulsive on all counts) in a 0–100 space. Compute the deviation of all real alternatives in the valuation matrix from the worst case. The alternative furthest from the worst is the best; furthest is the next best, and so on.

The distance of the point corresponding to the valuation score set to the dummy point (actually the origin) is

$$D_i = \left[\sum_{j=1}^{m} (w_j \, u_{ij})^2 \right]^{1/2} \tag{9-5}$$

And in figure-of-merit form:

$$\text{FOM}_i = \left[\frac{1}{\Sigma w_j^2} \sum_{j=1}^{m} (w_j \, u_{ij})^2 \right]^{1/2} \tag{9-6}$$

Formula 9–5 can be interpreted also as the length of the vector in the m-space. Formula 9–6 can be interpreted as the weighted quadratic mean of the valuation scores. The alternative with the longest vector or largest quadratic mean is the best. A computing chart for formula 9–6 is shown in Figure 9–6.

If this choice rule was applied to the secretary-receptionist data from Box 9–2, the results would be:

> If $w_1 = w_2$, Kate and Adele earn scores of 100 and would be the best of the lot.
> If $w_1 > w_2$, Adele would be preferred to Kate.
> If $w_1 < w_2$, Kate would be preferred to Adele.

In either case, this rule selects candidates at the extreme ends of the chart (Kate 100,0; Adele 0,100) rather than at the middle (Frances 50,50) as chosen by Rule No. 4, the product rule.

THE "DISTANCE FROM PERFECTION" RULE

> **Choice Rule No. 6.** Establish a dummy alternative that represents the perfect alternative (for example, 100,100,100, . . . 100 in a 0–100

	Decision objectives (Performance criteria)										
Subject name or number (Alternative)	I	II	III	IV	V	VI	VII	VIII	IX	X	RESULT
Row	Description of operation										
1	Enter performance (or utility) scores for this subject										
2	Enter numerical weights for each objective										
3	Multiply each row 1 cell entry by corresponding row 2 entry										
4	Square each row 3 entry										
5	Square each row 2 entry										
6	Compute sum across row 4										
7	Compute sum across row 5										
8	Divide row 6 sum by row 7 sum										
9	Take square root of row 8 result THIS IS THE FIGURE-OF-MERIT FOR THIS SUBJECT										

FIGURE 9–6. Computing chart for figure-of-merit for "distance from the worst" choice rule based on formula 9–6. One such computation is required for each alternative.

space). Compute the deviation of each real alternative from this perfect case. **Select the alternative that is closest to perfection as the best; next closest, second best, and so on.**

The deviation of the ith alternative from the perfection point is

$$d_i = \left[\sum_{j=1}^{m} (100-u_{ij})^2 \right]^{1/2} \tag{9-7a}$$

If weights are used:

$$d_i = \left[\sum_{j=1}^{m} w_j^2 (100-u_{ij})^2 \right]^{1/2} \tag{9-7b}$$

and the corresponding figure-of-merit:

$$\text{FOM}_i = 100 - \left[\frac{1}{\Sigma w_j^2} \sum_{j=1}^{m} w_j^2 (100-u_{ij})^2 \right]^{1/2} \tag{9-8}$$

A computing chart for this rule is shown in Figure 9–7. An application of the distance from perfection rule to the problem of selecting an advertising agency is shown in Box 9–3.[4] The results are shown for two sets of criterion weights. If this rule had been applied to the RSM problem of Box 9–2, Frances would have been chosen as the best candidate.

Box 9–3   ABC Corp. Hires an Advertising Agency[4]

The ABC Corp. was seeking to retain an advertising agency to assist the firm in marketing a radically new product line to the industrial market. The staff assistant to the sales executive had been instructed to examine the offerings and capabilities of several advertising agencies in the light of the firm's requirements and marketing objectives. He was requested to devise a rational scheme for the evaluation of each candidate agency's qualifications and then to make a specific recommendation based on the rational selection plan.

Four agencies were found that could survive the initial coarse screening process, and each was invited to make a formal presentation to the executives of the firm. During the evaluation, the staff assistant personally interviewed several clients of each agency. After much thought and discussion, six criteria were judged to be relevant and important in the choice of an agency (order not significant).

1. Quality and quantity of service given to clients.

2. Detailed knowledge of client's industry.

3. Originality and creativity of agency output.

4. Quality and extent of in-house facilities.

5. General reputation of the agency.

Row	Description of operation	Performance criteria						RESULT
	Subject name or number	I	II	III	IV	V	VI	
1	Enter performance scores for this subject							
2	Enter coordinates of the perfection point							
3	Enter weights for each criterion							
4	Multiply row 2 entries by row 3 entries							
5	Multiply row 1 entries by row 3 entries							
6	Subtract row 5 entries from row 4 entries							
7	Square each row 6 entry							
8	Square each row 3 entry							
9	Compute sum across row 7							
10	Compute sum across row 8							
11	Divide row 9 entry by row 10 entry							
12	Enter perfection score							
13	Compute square root of row 11 entry							
14	Subtract row 13 entry from row 12 entry THIS IS THE FIGURE–OF–MERIT SCORE FOR THIS SUBJECT							

FIGURE 9–7. Figure-of-merit computing chart.

6. Annual service fee.

The evaluation judgments of the four agencies based on scales of 0–100 were:

Agency	Criterion Number					
	1	2	3	4	5	6
A	10	90	20	90	20	90
B	50	.50	60	50	60	50
C	70	30	30	30	80	80
D	30	70	40	70	40	70

Using equal weights for the six criteria, the figures-of-merit for the four agencies were (Rule No. 6):

Agency	FOM	Preference Order
A	40.4	4th
B	53.0	1st
C	47.0	3rd
D	50.4	2nd

However with different weights $(w_1 = 2; w_2 = 1; w_3 = 3; w_4 = 1; w_5 = 2; w_6 = 1$, the results were:

Agency	FOM	Preference Order
A	23.9	4th
B	56.2	1st
C	45.5	2nd
D	41.2	3rd

Notes and References

1. See for example these two references: Robert Kalich, *The Baseball Rating Handbook* (New York, A. S. Barnes and Co. 1969) and "Evaluation of Supplier Performance" (New York, National Association of Purchasing Agents, 1963).

2. See as two examples: Arnold Bernhard, *The Evaluation of Common Stocks* (New York, Simon and Schuster, 1959) and any monthly issue of *The Value Line Investment Survey*.

3. Barry M. Richman, "A Rating Scale for Product Innovation," in T. L. Berg and A. Schuchman (eds.), *Product Strategy and Management* (New York, Holt, Rinehart and Winston, 1963), pp. 434–442.

4. Adapted from Allan Easton, "Advertising Decision Involving Multiple Criteria" (New York, The Advertising Research Foundation), *Proceedings of the 11th Annual Conference, October 5, 1965.*

Important Words and Concepts

Choice rule
Go, No-Go rule
Standards
Minimum limits
Maximum limits
Acceptance region
Passivity notion
Weak figure-of-merit
Nonmetric ordering
Weighted sum of the points rule
Computing chart
Weighted product of the points rule
Logarithmic form
Exponential form
Furthest from the worst rule
Dummy alternative
Distance from perfection rule
Perfection point

Overview of Chapter 9

Choice rules are needed to enable the decision maker to arrive at a merit-ordering of alternatives or to permit him to find the best of a set. There are many possible rules that can be used for this purpose, among which are the following:

1. Go, no-go rules for satisficing or nonmetric ordering.
2. Go, no-go plus optimizing procedures.
3. The weighted sum of the quality-points rule.
4. The weighted product of the quality-points rule.
5. The "furthest from the worst" rule.
6. The "distance from perfection" rule.

Examples of the applications of these rules are given.

Questions for Review, Discussion, and Research

Review

1. State Choice Rule No. 1.

2. How is it used for finding a satisfactory alternative?

3. How is it used for finding the best?

4. How can it be used for nonmetric ordering?

5. What kinds of units can be used for Rule No. 1?

6. State Rule No. 2 and answer questions 2, 3, 4, and 5 concerning this rule.

7. How can Rule No. 2 be used for developing "weak" figures-of-merit?

8. State Rule No. 3. How does it relate to the arithmetic mean? What units are used for this rule?

9. State Rule No. 4. How does it relate to the geometric mear? What units can be used? How does this rule treat alternatives with zeros in the score set? Can bipolar scales be used? (*Hint:* review Chapter 8.)

10. State Rule No. 5. How does it relate to the quadratic mean and to the vector distance in the vector space?

11. State Rule No. 6. What is meant by the perfect specimen?

12. In Rule No. 5, what is meant by the worst possible case?

Discussion

1. What would you recommend the people at ABC Corp. do about picking an agency? Do you think a score of less than 60 is good enough for this purpose? If you used Rule No. 5 instead of Rule No. 6, would your opinion be altered?

2. What is the difference between nonmetric ordering, ordering by "weak" figures-of-merit, and metric ordering by Rules Nos. 4, 5, or 6?

3. Which, if any, of the six job offers should Dr. Kent take? Why?

4. How could a vendor or job applicant raise the probability of his case being taken up earlier than others?

5. Can you think of any reasons why different choice rules produce different merit orders or different choices of the best?

6. In the RSM case, which girl do you think is best? Why?

7. In your own personal life, do you try to make your behavior the "furthest

from the worst" or the "closest to perfection"? Would your behavior be different with one or the other criterion?

Research

1. Retrospectively examine a number of decisions or evaluations you or your associates have made. These could be business, social, political, or other judgments. Can you detect any parallel between your judgments and those that would be made by choice rules in this chapter?

2. Develop a hypothesis on why Rules Nos. 3, 4, 5, and 6 give different choices in the RSM case. Try different weights for beauty and ability and compare the merit ordering of the candidates by the different choice rules. Does the strong preference for one criterion over another cause the choices to converge?

10. Techniques for Merit Ordering (II)

The main ideas developed in this chapter are:

1. *Profiles can be matched by a point distance computation.*

2. *Alternatives can be compared pair-by-pair.*

3. *Rules can be devised for accommodating criteria expressed as variables, minor and major attributes.*

4. *A set of synthetic rules will give a large variety of rules for computing figures-of-merit and statistical means.*

PROFILE MATCHING RULES

> **Choice Rule No. 7. Establish a standard or target score profile. Compute the deviation of all alternatives' score profiles from the standard. The alternative with scores that are the closest match is the best; the next closest, second-best; and so on.**

If the score-set for an alternative is viewed as a point in an *m*-dimensional hyperspace (where *m* is the number of criteria or the number of columns in the outcome matrix), then the set of alternatives can be viewed as a swarm of points in the space, one of which is the point representing the standard score profile.[1]

The coordinates of the target point can be expressed as

$$[T_a] \equiv [t_{a1}\, t_{a2}\, t_{a3}\, \ldots\, t_{aj}\, \ldots\ldots\, t_{am}]$$

and those for the *i*th alternative as

$$[A_1] \equiv [u_{i1}\, u_{i2}\, u_{i3}\, \ldots\, u_{ij}\, \ldots\, u_{im}]$$

Then the Euclidian distance between the *i*th point and the target point is

$$d_{i-a} = \left[\sum_{j=1}^{m} (u_{ij} - t_{aj})^2 \right]^{1/2} \tag{10-1}$$

If criterion weights are to be incorporated,

$$d_{i-a} = \left[\sum_{j=1}^{m} w_j^2 (u_{ij} - t_{aj})^2 \right]^{1/2} \tag{10-2}$$

With formulas 10–1 and 10–2, alternatives that match the target more closely will have smaller scores. Perfectly identical pairs would have zero for their scores. Formula 10–2 can be converted into a similarity index or figure-of-merit for which more similar pairs would earn higher scores than less similar pairs:

$$[S.I.]_i = FOM_i = 100 - \left[\frac{1}{\Sigma w_j^2} \sum_{j=1}^{m} w_j^2 (u_{ij} - t_{aj})^2 \right]^{1/2} \tag{10-3}$$

A computing chart for formula 10–3 is shown in Figure 10–1.

Applications of Rule No. 7

For some problems, the scales used for scoring alternatives on the criteria may not be quality points in the sense that a higher score is better than a lower score. They may, instead, be based on a position in a distribution. No valuations can be inferred from these scores until the target score-profile is established.

For example, one well-known psychological test, the 16 PF test of personality[2] has scales on sixteen personality factors. The scores for any one individual represent his position on a distribution of scores for the entire adult population. An example of one such distribution scales is given in Box 10–1.

Box 10–1   Interpretation of the Sten Scale

Sten Score (Range 1 to 10)	Percentage of Adults Earning This Score
1	2.3
2	4.4
3	9.2
4	15.0
5	19.1
6	19.1
7	15.0
8	9.2
9	4.4
10	2.3

Source. See Reference 3.

Row	Description of operation	I	II	III	IV	V	VI	VII	VIII	IX	X	RESULT
						Decision objectives (Performance criteria)						
1	Enter performance (or utility) scores for this subject											
2	Enter numerical weights for each factor (criterion)											
3	Enter target profile scores											
4	Subtract row 1 entries from row 3 entries											
5	Square row 4 entries											
6	Square row 2 entries											
7	Multiply row 5 entries by row 6 entries											
8	Compute the sum across row 7											
9	Compute the sum across row 6											
10	Divide row 8 sum by row 9 sum											
11	Take square root of row 10 result											
12	Subtract row 11 result from 100 THIS IS THE FIGURE-OF-MERIT FOR THIS SUBJECT											

Subject name or number (Alternative)

FIGURE 10-1. Similarity index or figure-of-merit computing chart for Choice Rule No. 7.

In such applications, the matrix cell entries convey no valuations but only the standing of the test subject in relation to a large number of test subjects. How these scores are used depends on the specifics of the problematic situation.

An application of Choice Rule No. 7 and the Sten Scale in Box 10–1 is shown in Box 10–2. In this case example, the surviving partners of a man-

---

Box 10–2   Jones, Doe, and McPherson Set Out to Replace Doe

Jones, Doe, and McPherson (name fictitious) is an old-established management consulting firm. Mr. Jones and Mr. McPherson are still active in the firm as managing partners, but Mr. Doe is in poor health and wishes to decrease his participation in the day-to-day activities of the firm. From the first year that they entered into their business partnership, the three men recognized that they were very different individuals with contrasting personalities, but somehow they were able to work together exceptionally well. At a banquet given to celebrate their twenty-fifth anniversary as partners, Judge Goldstein, a close friend of the three, made a speech in which he likened the three partners to three tennis champions. One was the most creative, another was the most diligent and enduring, and the third was the most crafty. Each man was, in his own way, a champion, but each had a personal style that differed from the other two.

Naturally both Jones and McPherson were unhappy with Doe's decision to disengage himself from the firm, but they recognized that the burden was becoming too great for Doe's delicate health. If they wanted to help prolong his life, they would have to do something to replace him and relieve him of some of the load. Neither Jones nor McPherson believed that they could add Doe's duties to theirs, since they, too, were getting along in years.

After giving the matter of a replacement for Doe some thought, McPherson had a suggestion. There were many good management consultants of partnership caliber in the country who would be delighted to join Jones, Doe, and McPherson if the terms of partnership were attractive enough. But introducing a new personality into the firm at partnership level might be likely to upset the very fine working relationship that they had up to this time. Why not try to find a competent man with a personality configuration just like Doe's? In that way the risk of introducing a discordant element into the firm would be reduced. The partners agreed to explore this idea with one of their staff psychometricians.

The upshot of the investigation was the decision to go ahead and develop a pool of qualified candidates for the partnership and then to give each candidate a personality test. The test profiles so obtained would be compared with Doe's, and the candidate with the closest match would be given an offer of a probationary partnership.

The test to be used was the I.P.A.T. 16 PF Test Profile. Doe's scores on this test were as follows:

Factor A   B   C   E   F   G   H   I   L   M   N   O Q_1 Q_2 Q_3 Q_4

Score   7   9   9   7   4   6   7   3   5   6   3   3   7   9   5   3

The meanings of the test factors are (see Reference 3):

Factor	A Person with a Low Score on this Factor Is Described as	A Person with a High Score on this Factor Is Described as
A	Reserved, detached, critical, cool	Outgoing, warmhearted, easy-going, participating.
B	Less intelligent, concrete thinking	More intelligent, abstract-thinking, bright.
C	Affected by feelings, emotionally less stable, easily upset	Emotionally stable, faces reality, calm
E	Humble, mild, obedient, conforming	Assertive, independent, aggressive, stubborn
F	Sober, prudent, serious, taciturn	Happy-go-lucky, heedless, gay, enthusiastic
G	Expedient, a law to himself, bypasses obligations	Conscientious, persevering, staid, rule-bound
H	Shy, restrained, diffident, timid	Venturesome, socially bold, uninhibited, spontaneous
I	Tough-minded, self-reliant, no-nonsense	Tender-minded, dependent, overprotected, sensitive
L	Trusting, adaptable, free of jealousy, easy to get along with	Suspicious, self-opinionated, hard to fool
M	Practical, careful, conventional, regulated by external realities, proper	Imaginative, wrapped up in inner urgencies, careless of practical matters, bohemian
N	Forthright, natural, artless, sentimental	Shrewd, calculating, worldly, penetrating
O	Placid, self-assured, confident, serene	Apprehensive, worrying, depressive, troubled
Q_1	Conservative, respecting established ideas, tolerant of traditional difficulties	Experimenting, critical, liberal, analytical, free-thinking
Q_2	Group-dependent, a joiner and a sound follower	Self-sufficient, prefers own decisions, resourceful
Q_3	Casual, careless of protocol, untidy, follows own urges	Controlled, socially-precise, self-disciplined, compulsive
Q_4	Relaxed, tranquil, torpid, unfrustrated	Tense, driven, overwrought, fretful

Two of these factors were judged to be very important by both Jones and McPherson because they both lacked these characteristics (Factors C and Q_2); so they decided to give these additional weight in making profile comparisons.

agement consulting firm set out to find a replacement for a retiring partner and decide to look for a man with a very similar personality profile as measured by the 16 PF test.

RULE FOR CRITERIA EXPRESSED AS VARIABLES AND ATTRIBUTES

The comparison of alternatives with scores on criteria expressed as both attributes and variables (matrix in Figure 5–3) will usually involve different rules for each submatrix.

MAJOR-ATTRIBUTE SUBMATRIX.   The scores are, by definition, pass, one; fail, zero. These are combined by the product rule (Choice Rule No. 4). According to this rule, if an alternative has one or more zero scores, the product of the row entries will be zero. If the scores are all ones, the product will be one. One means accept; zero means reject the alternative. For this submatrix, weights have no meaning.

This part of the triple decision-matrix is used to prescreen alternatives for compliance with indispensable criteria. Failure of an alternative to meet every one of these prerequisites is enough to eliminate it from further consideration.

MINOR-ATTRIBUTE SUBMATRIX.   The scores are by definition, one or zero, but for this part of the triple matrix, the accept-reject meanings are not applicable. These criteria, too, are not quantifiable on a multi-interval scale, but they are not nearly as indispensable as the major attributes. Weights can be applied to the minor attributes, and the scores can be combined by the weighted-sum-of-the-points rule (Choice Rule No. 3) into a partial figure-of-merit. Box 10–3 shows how alternatives can be rated on weighted minor-attribute scores. In this example, minor attributes are ranked in importance (best=1) and inverse rank numbers are used as criterion weights (the most important has the greatest weight).

This example can be generalized as follows: for an alternative being evaluated on minor attributes $Z_1, Z_2, \ldots, Z_s$, which can have cell entries of either one or zero, the partial figure of merit for the ith alternative is

$$\text{FOM}_{(\text{partial})} = \frac{1}{\sum\limits_{1}^{s} k} \sum_{k=1}^{s} R_k \, z_{ik} \tag{10-4}$$

where $s=$ the number of minor attributes in the submatrix.

$k=$ the general minor attribute (k goes from 1 to s).

$R_k=$ the inverse rank number used to weight the kth minor attribute.

$z_{ik}=$ the score (1 or 0) assigned to be the ith alternative on the kth minor attribute.

Box 10–3   Example of FOM computation for Minor Attributes Using Formula 10–4

Minor Attribute Number (k)	Rank Number $(7-R_k)$	Pass (1) or Fail (0) (z_{ik})		Rank Number Weight (R_k)		Score $(R_k z_{ik})$
1	1	0	×	6	=	0
2	6	1	×	1	=	1
3	2	0	×	5	=	0
4	5	1	×	2	=	2
5	3	1	×	4	=	4
6	4	1	×	3	=	3
$\Sigma k = 21$				Total score $\Sigma (R_k z_{ik}) =$		10

If alternative failed on no minor attributes perfect score $= \Sigma k = 21$.

Figure-of-merit for this alternative $= \left[\dfrac{\Sigma R_k z_{ik}}{\Sigma k} \right] = \dfrac{10}{21} = 0.47$

This partial figure-of-merit has little value until it is combined with the figure-of-merit of the variable submatrix. Just how this is done depends on the relative importance of the minor attributes relative to the variables.

The attribute FOM may be used for breaking ties, or it may be combined arithmetically with the variable FOM. An example of how this can be done is shown in Box 10–4. The formula used in this example is

$$\text{FOM}_{(\text{combined})} = \text{FOM}_{(\text{minor attributes})} \times \text{FOM}_{(\text{variables})} \qquad (10\text{-}5)$$

Box 10–4   Computing a Figure-of-merit from Formula 10–4*

Alternative Number	FOM Variable Submatrix		FOM Attribute Submatrix		FOM Overall
1	75.8	×	1.00	=	75.8
2	60.5	×	0.70	=	42.4
3	43.2	×	0.90	=	38.9
4	80.6	×	0.30	=	24.2

* Fictitious data.

RULES FOR PAIR-BY-PAIR COMPARISONS

The Elimination Procedure

Instead of computing figure-of-merit scores for each alternative and then identifying the alternative with the largest figure-of-merit as the best, it may be possible to find the "best" in a more economical way by using pair-by-pair comparisons. With this method it is not necessary to know *how much* better one alternative is than another, only that it is better. A procedure of this type is shown in Figure 10–2.

The initial comparison is made between alternative $[A_0]$ (do nothing) and any other alternative, $[A_1]$. This is phase one. The better of the two is called the survivor, $[S_1]$, and this survivor alternative is compared with the next, $[A_2]$. This is phase two. The survivor of phase two is $[S_2]$. This procedure is continued through *n* phases until only one alternative survives. The method is similar to the elimination tournaments used in athletic competitions.

The special case of tied alternatives is not shown in the diagram. In instances of this kind either both alternatives are carried along to the next phase, one of the pair is dropped as redundant, or some tie-breaking technique is applied, perhaps, by introducing one or more additional criteria not included in the original set.

The elimination method can be used for merit-ordering alternatives. To accomplish this it is only necessary to repeat the procedure after the best is removed from the set. The best from the second pass is the second-best, and so forth.

Pair-by-Pair Rules

POINTS OF SUPERIORITY—EQUAL WEIGHTS. For a pair of alternatives $[A_a]$ and $[A_b]$ with score sets

$$[A_a] \equiv [u_{a1}\, u_{a2}\, u_{a3} \ldots \ldots u_{ij} \ldots \ldots u_{am}] \quad \text{and}$$
$$[A_b] \equiv [u_{b1}\, u_{b2}\, u_{b3} \ldots \ldots u_{bj} \ldots \ldots u_{bm}]$$

if $u_{a1} > u_{b1}$ replace u_{a1} with one and u_{b1} with zero;

if $u_{a1} < u_{b1}$ replace u_{a1} with zero and u_{b1} with one.

Repeat this procedure with all column pairs. Count the number of nonzero entries for each alternative. The one with the largest number of nonzeros is the better of the pair.

POINTS OF SUPERIORITY RULE—UNEQUAL WEIGHTS. Do the score-by-score comparisons as described above giving a one to the alternative with the higher criterion score and a zero to the lower score. Multiply each

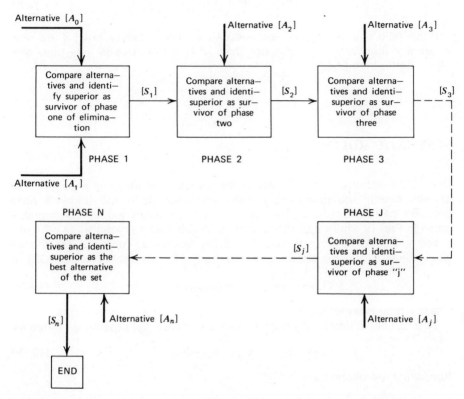

FIGURE 10–2. Model of a pair-by-pair comparison of alternatives. The survivor of the first comparison is used for the next phase; the inferior of the two is rejected. The process is repeated with the survivor being compared with the next alternative until there is only one survivor; that one is the best of the set.

criterion score (the one or zero) by the corresponding criterion weight and add the weighted scores. The one with the greatest weighted score is the better of the pair.

THE RATIO RULE.[4]   For a pair of alternatives $[A_a]$ and $[A_b]$ set up the ratio

$$R_{a/b} = \left(\frac{u_{a1}}{u_{b1}}\right)^{w_1} \times \left(\frac{u_{a2}}{u_{b2}}\right)^{w_2} \times \left(\frac{u_{a3}}{u_{b3}}\right)^{w_3} \cdots \left(\frac{u_{am}}{u_{bm}}\right)^{w_m} \qquad (10\text{-}6a)$$

or, more generally,

$$R_{a/b} = \prod_{j=1}^{m} \left(\frac{u_{aj}}{u_{bj}}\right)^{w_j}$$

(10-6b)

If the ratio equals one, the two alternatives are equally valued; if the ratio is greater than one, $[A_a]$ is better than $[A_b]$; if the ratio is less than one, $[A_b]$ is better than $[A_a]$.

SYNTHETIC RULES[5]

One of the important ways in which the various choice rules shown in this chapter and in the preceding chapter can differ is in the trade-off rates between pairs of criteria. This subject will be examined in considerable detail in Part IV where it is shown that every rule has a unique trade-off logic.

For a pair of criteria, X and Y, having scores u_{ix} and u_{iy} (for the ith alternative) it can be shown that the trade-off rate (abbreviated TOR) is

$$\text{TOR} = -du_{iy}/du_{ix} = (u_{iy}/u_{ix})^{\eta}$$

(10-7a)

where η (eta) is a parameter.

This simple differential equation can be solved by separating variables:

$$\int (1/u_{iy})^{\eta}\, du_{iy} = -\int (1/u_{ix})^{\eta}\, du_{ix}$$

(10-7b)

from which we obtain for $\eta \neq 1$

$$(u_{ix})^{(1-\eta)} + (u_{iy})^{(1-\eta)} = a \text{ constant}$$

(10-8a)

and for the special case when $\eta = 1$

$$\ln u_{ix} + \ln u_{iy} = a \text{ constant}$$

(10-8b)

And if we wish the constant of integration to be our FOM,

$$\text{FOM} = \text{either } u_{ix} \text{ or } u_{iy} \text{ when } u_{ix} = u_{iy}$$

When we apply this new condition to equations 10–8a and 10–8b, it gives (for $\eta \neq 1$):

$$\text{FOM}_i = \left[\frac{(u_{iy})^{(1-\eta)} + (u_{ix})^{(1-\eta)}}{2}\right]^{1/(1-\eta)}$$

(10-9a)

and for $\eta = 1$

$$\text{FOM}_i = [(u_{ix})(u_{iy})]^{\frac{1}{2}}$$

(10-9b)

Notice that for $\eta = 1$ we get a geometric mean; for $n = 0$, an arithmetic mean.

Although in the foregoing, only two criteria were used, the reasoning applies, by analogy, with equal force to m criteria. In such a case, equation 10–9a becomes

$$FOM_i = \left[\frac{1}{m} \sum_{j=1}^{m} (u_{ij})^{(1-\eta)} \right]^{1/(1-\eta)} \tag{10-10a}$$

and if criterion weights are intended

$$FOM_i = \left[\frac{1}{\sum w_j^{(1-\eta)}} \sum_{j=1}^{m} (w_j u_{ij})^{(1-\eta)} \right]^{1/(1-\eta)} \tag{10-10b}$$

And equation 10–9b becomes

$$FOM_i = \left[\prod_{j=1}^{m} (u_{ij}) \right]^{1/m} \tag{10-11a}$$

and with criterion weights

$$FOM_i = \left[\prod_{j=1}^{m} (u_{ij})^{wj} \right]^{1/\Sigma wj} \tag{10-11b}$$

The Discriminator Parameter, Eta

There is no limitation to the values that can be assigned to the parameter, eta. Either fractions or integers, positive or negative may be assigned. Thus it becomes evident that an almost infinite variety of choice rules can be created simply by choosing different values for eta. Box 10–5 contains the solutions for equations 10–10 and 10–11 for several values of eta. Notice that for

eta = -1, we have the "furthest from the worst rule."
eta = 0, we have the "weighted sum of the quality points" rule.
eta = $+1$, we have the "product of the points" rule.

Apparently equations 10–10b and 10–11b can be used to generate a number of familiar rules along with some new ones.

An examination of Box 10–5 reveals some interesting facts:

eta = 0 gives the arithmetic mean
eta = $+1$ gives the geometric mean
eta = -1 gives the quadratic mean
eta = $+2$ gives the harmonic mean

and, of course, other values of eta will produce other new statistical means.

Box 10–5   Weighted and Unweighted Statistical Means and Figures of Merit for Nine Values of eta

Eta	Unweighted Mean (FOM)	Weighted Mean (FOM)
-3	$\left[\dfrac{1}{m}\sum_{j=1}^{m}(u_{ij})^4\right]^{1/4}$ (quartic)	$\left[\dfrac{1}{\Sigma w_j^{4}}\sum_{1}^{m}(w_j u_{ij})^4\right]^{1/4}$
-2	$\left[\dfrac{1}{m}\sum_{j=1}^{m}(u_{ij})^3\right]^{1/3}$ (cubical)	$\left[\dfrac{1}{\Sigma w_j^{3}}\sum_{j=1}^{m}(w_j u_{ij})^3\right]^{1/3}$
-1	$\left[\dfrac{1}{m}\sum_{j=1}^{m}(u_{ij})^2\right]^{1/2}$ (quadratic)	$\left[\dfrac{1}{\Sigma w_j^{2}}\sum_{j=1}^{m}(w_j u_{ij})^2\right]^{1/2}$
$-\tfrac{1}{2}$	$\left[\dfrac{1}{m}\sum_{j=1}^{m}(u_{ij})^{3/2}\right]^{2/3}$ (semicubical)	$\left[\dfrac{1}{\Sigma w_j^{3/2}}\sum_{j=1}^{m}(w_j u_{ij})^{3/2}\right]^{2/3}$
0	$\dfrac{1}{m}\sum_{j=1}^{m}u_{ij}$ (arithmetic)	$\dfrac{1}{\Sigma w_j}\sum_{j=1}^{m}w_j u_{ij}$
$+\tfrac{1}{2}$	$\left[\dfrac{1}{m}\sum_{j=1}^{m}(u_{ij})^{2/3}\right]^{2}$ (square-rooted)	$\left[\dfrac{1}{\Sigma w_j^{1/2}}\sum_{j=1}^{m}(w_j u_{ij})^{1/2}\right]^{2}$
$+1$	$\left[\prod_{j=1}^{m}u_{ij}\right]^{1/m}$ (geometric)	$\left[\prod_{j=1}^{m}(u_{ij})^{wj}\right]^{\frac{1}{\Sigma w_j}}$
$+2$	$\left[\dfrac{1}{m}\sum_{j=1}^{m}(u_{ij})^{-1}\right]^{-1}$ (harmonic)	$\left[\dfrac{1}{\Sigma w_j^{-1}}\sum_{j=1}^{m}(w_j u_{ij})^{-1}\right]^{-1}$
$+3$	$\left[\dfrac{1}{m}\sum_{j=1}^{m}(u_{ij})^{-2}\right]^{-1/2}$ (harmonic squared)	$\left[\dfrac{1}{\Sigma w_j^{-2}}\sum_{j=1}^{m}(w_j u_{ij})^{-2}\right]^{-1/2}$

Thus equations 10–10b and 10–11b may be thought of as generating functions for an infinite number of choice rules and statistical means of which the arithmetic, quadratic, geometric, and harmonic are but special cases.

Some Useful Relations Among the Means and FOMs

For a given score set

$$[A_i] \equiv [u_{i1}, u_{i2}, u_{i3} \ldots u_{ij} \ldots u_{im}]$$

(and all u_{ij}'s are equal to or greater than zero)

$$\left.\text{FOM}\right]_{\eta>0} \leq \left.\text{FOM}\right]_{\eta=0} \tag{10-12a}$$

The equality will hold true when all the u_{ij}'s are equal; when they are unequal, the inequality holds true. Since, when eta is greater than zero, the means and FOMs will be equal to or less than the arithmetic mean, it follows that the particular subset of means have their maximum values when all the u_{ij}'s are equal. They become progressively smaller than the arithmetic mean as the inequality among the u_{ij}'s becomes greater.

On the other hand, when eta is less than zero

$$\left.\text{FOM}\right]_{\eta<0} \geq \left.\text{FOM}\right]_{\eta=0} \tag{10-12b}$$

Again the equality holds true if all the u_{ij}'s are equal. When they are not equal, the means (FOMs) will be larger than the arithmetic mean. This means that the FOMs generated from formulas for which $\eta < 0$ have their minimum values when all the u_{ij}'s are equal and become progressively larger as the degree of inequality among the u_{ij}'s becomes greater.

Another interesting observation is that when the u_{ij}'s are identical, all means and FOMs from the generating equations are equal. This relationship holds true for weighted means as well as for unweighted means.

Box 10–6 contains a set of data that illustrates the relationships among

---

Box 10–6   Figures of Merit for Four Alternatives on Eleven Criteria with Seven Different Rules*

Criterion Number	Alternative Number			
	1	2	3	4
1	11.0	12.0	16.0	18.0
2	12.0	14.0	18.0	19.0
3	10.5	11.0	12.0	13.0
4	11.0	12.0	15.0	16.0
5	10.5	11.0	12.0	13.0
6	10.0	10.0	10.0	10.0
7	9.5	9.0	8.0	7.0
8	9.0	8.0	5.0	4.0
9	9.5	9.0	8.0	7.0
10	8.0	6.0	2.0	1.0
11	9.0	8.0	4.0	2.0
Average deviation[a]	0.91	1.82	4.17	5.09

Value for	Figures of Merit for Alternatives Numbered[b]			
Eta	1	2	3	4
+3	9.85	9.22	5.14	2.63
+2	9.88	9.49	6.66	4.48
+1	9.94	9.55	8.46	7.40
0	10.00	10.00	10.00	10.00
−1	10.05	10.20	11.20	11.70
−2	10.13	10.45	11.77	12.78
−3	10.17	10.59	12.65	13.46

[a] Average deviation $= \dfrac{1}{11} \sum_{1}^{11}(|u_{ij} - U_j|)$

[b] Formulas from Box 10–5.

* Fictitious data.

the means for different values of eta and for different degrees of profile scatter in the u_{ij}'s. Evidently, the greater the magnitude of eta, the greater the disparity of the resulting FOMs from the FOM for eta equals zero, but the degree of disparity is also a function of the extent of inequality of the scores.

Notes and References

1. See L. J. Cronbach and G. C. Gleser, "Assessing Profile Similarity," *Psychological Bulletin* Vol. 50 (November 1953), pp. 456–473.

2. See Raymond B. Cattell, *The Scientific Analysis of Personality* (Baltimore, Maryland, Penguin Books, Inc., 1965).

3. I.P.A.T. 16 PF Test Profile (worksheet) (Institute for Personality and Ability Testing, Champaign, Illinois, no date).

4. The material in this section is based on a series of unpublished lectures by Allan Easton entitled "Index-Construction for Multi-Dimensional Scaling," "Generating Statistical Means," and "Combining Effectiveness Scores," 1969–1973.

Important Words and Concepts

Score profile
Target point
Similarity index

Distribution scales
Sten score
Inverse rank number
Partial figure-of-merit
Elimination procedure
Pair-by-pair comparison
Ratio rule
Synthetic rule
Trade-off ratio
Parameter
Generating function
Statistical mean
Profile scatter

Overview of Chapter 10

This chapter gives some additional choice rules for ranking alternatives or finding the best of a set. The new rules are:

1. Profile matching rule.
2. Rules for problems involving criteria expressed as variables, minor and major attributes.
3. Elimination rules for pair-by-pair matching.
4. A set of synthetic rules based on a generating function that produces several of the rules from Chapter 9 plus a large variety of others. These rules can also produce a large number of statistical means of which the well-known means are but special cases.

Figures-of-merit based on values of the parameter, eta, greater than zero will be smaller than those based on eta equals zero (the arithmetic mean or the sum-of-the-points rule). Those based on values smaller than zero, are larger than the zero, eta rule.

Questions for Review, Discussion, and Research

Review

1. Restate the profile matching rule.

2. What is meant by the target point?

3. What is a similarity index?

4. How can the similarity index be used in personnel work?

5. Are variables and attributes treated differently in developing figures-of-merit? If so, how?

6. What practical differences are there between minor and major attributes?

7. What is meant by pair-by-pair comparisons of alternatives? What are the advantages and disadvantages of this method of merit ordering?

8. What is an elimination process and how does it work?

9. What are some of the pair-by-pair comparison rules?

10. What is a synthetic rule or a synthetic mean?

11. What is the parameter, eta? What is the effect of assigning different numbers to it?

12. What is the relationship between a figure-of-merit and a statistical mean?

13. For a given score set, rank the following by the size of the resulting FOM: arithmetic mean, quadratic mean, geometric mean, and harmonic mean.

14. For a given score-set what is the effect of profile scatter on the FOM?

Discussion

1. Under what circumstances would Rule No. 7 be preferred to all other rules?

2. Why use Euclidean distances between the target point and the test point? Why not use the sums or products of the coordinate differences?

3. How would you decide between an attribute and a variable; between a major and a minor attribute?

4. Discuss the concept of nonmetric scaling with reference to pair-by-pair comparisons.

5. What possible difference could it make to a decision maker that different values of eta produce different rules?

6. Develop a definition of a statistical mean or figure-of-merit based on the insights gained from this chapter.

7. How could you decide in a particular problem which value of eta to use in constructing a choice rule?

Research

1. Make a literature search on the subject of profile matching. What other methods other than Rule No. 7 are used?

2. What are some of the practical applications of profile matching and of similarity indexes?

3. Using the methodology and reasoning developed in this chapter, develop a set of synthetic rules (or means) derived from Rule Nos. 6 and 7.

   Hint:

   $$\text{TOR} = -du_{iy}/du_{ix} = \left(\frac{100 - u_{iy}}{100 - u_{ix}}\right)^{\eta}$$

   $$\text{TOR} = -du_{iy}/du_{ix} = \left(\frac{T_{ay} - u_{iy}}{T_{ax} - u_{ix}}\right)^{\eta}$$

CASES *for part three**

* Cases for Part IV may also be used with Part III.

CASE III-I
Miracle-Skin Cosmetics Plans a Christmas Bonus

SUMMARY: The factory personnel benefits committee meets to discuss the Christmas bonus for factory employees but cannot agree on any one plan.

MIRACLE-SKIN COSMETICS CORP.

Minutes of the Dec. 1, 197.. meeting of the Factory
Personnel Benefits Committee

Those present: Harvey Walker (for personnel)
Marion Persky (for payroll)
Sophie Burke (for accounting)
Vincent Conte (for production)
Amy Lufkin (for executive staff)

Mr. Walker called the meeting to order and announced that he was authorized to spend up to $50 per person for the 250-female-factory employees in the bargaining unit or a total of $12,500, for some sort of Christmas bonus or gift. He asked for suggestions.

Miss Persky suggested that the same present as last year be given: a large basket of food containing a turkey or a ham plus an assortment of gourmet delicacies.

Mr. Conte pointed out that they had had many complaints last year because some of the girls were Jewish and couldn't use nonkosher foods; some didn't like the assortment of gourmet delicacies; some complained that they couldn't get the large package home on the bus so that they had had to spend money for taxicab fare. Mr. Conte asked why the company couldn't just give the employees $50 in cash.

Miss Burke explained that to give a girl $50 would cost the company much more because of the withholding taxes, social security deduction, and other payroll costs. To give a cash gift that would cost the company $50 would net the employee less than $38. Also there would be an extra set of payroll administration costs.

Mr. Walker suggested that the company give each girl two extra days off before Christmas. Very little useful work is done in the week before Christmas anyhow. Since the girls average $25 a day, this would just come to $50.

Mr. Conte objected because he thought the union would use this as a precedent to get two more paid holidays in the contract. They would demand this as a regular benefit.

Mr. Walker said that the annual Christmas bonus was a regular benefit too.

Mr. Conte pointed out that the contract allows for a discretionary Christmas bonus if company profits permitted. This option was reserved to the company, and the contract stipulated that the size of the bonus or gift could fluctuate from year to year. It was recognized in the contract as an expression of gratitude or good will and not as a part of the compensation package. Mr. Conte cautioned that the manner of payment or offering of the gift should preserve this distinction.

Miss Lufkin suggested a gift certificate from a large department store or nationally known mail-order house. A fifty-dollar gift certificate could be bought for $45 in lots of 200 or more. This could save the company at least $1250.

Miss Persky objected because she thought a gift certificate would be considered as the equivalent of cash, taxwise.

Miss Burke said that although, technically, Miss Persky was right, noncash gifts, had an ambiguous tax treatment. The company would probably not be required to withhold on a noncash gift, and the employees should report it as income in their annual tax returns and pay a tax at that time.

Mr. Conte suggested that the company give each girl a gift box of Miracle-Skin cosmetics. If they didn't like the particular shades and styles in the package, they could use the items as gifts to others. This would save them money. A fifty-dollar box at retail would cost the company less than $20.

Miss Lufkin objected that the girls were already stealing all the cosmetics they could use, and this would not be considered a gift. And a fifty-dollar box at retail price would be considered as being too cheap. This would defeat the purpose of the company's offering. And to give a box that had a wholesale value of $50 would create the danger that the local market would be disrupted. Already dealers were complaining that too many of the company's products were being sold out of regular channels.

Miss Persky suggested that the company give each girl a batch of trading stamps worth $50. Stamps cost about $3 per thousand and for $50 they could give 16,666 stamps per girl. This would come to about sixty-six books (assuming 2500 stamps per book). Nice gifts could be obtained for that many books of stamps.

Miss Burke objected because she had heard that different stamp companies use different stamp values, and it would take weeks of research to find the value equivalents and there wasn't enough time left. Also there were several supermarkets operating in the area all using different stamps. The employees might complain if the company gave them stamps different from the ones that they regularly collected.

Mr. Walker asked for more suggestions but no more were forthcoming. He then called for discussion and a vote on each proposal. No proposal could muster the required majority of three votes.

Mr. Walker suggested that Miss Lufkin prepare a recapitulation of the proposals and that Miss Burke prepare cost estimates for each. He offered to prepare a list of advantages and disadvantages for each proposal. He would combine these three contributions into a final report for Mr. Farrington. Mr. Walker will advise Mr. Farrington that the committee could not agree on any one proposal.

There being no further business, the meeting was adjourned.

1. *Prepare an analysis of this decision using one of the models in Chapter 5.*
2. *What are the objectives of the decision and what are the relevant criteria for gauging goal attainment?*
3. *Prepare an outcome and valuation matrix for the set of alternative gift proposals presented in the body of the case plus for any additional alternatives you might like to suggest.*
4. *How would you go about merit ordering these alternatives?*
5. *Which alternative do you think is best? How did you come to that conclusion?*

CASE III-II
Computer Dating

COMPUTER DATING QUESTIONNAIRE*

INSTRUCTIONS TO RESPONDENTS: *The accuracy with which the computer will select your dates depends entirely on how truthfully you answer each of the questions.* Mark all of your answers directly on the form. Answer questions 1 to 4 by printing in the required information. Answer the remaining questions by placing an "X" mark within the box that immediately precedes the best answer. Mark only one answer for each question except where you are instructed otherwise. If none of the multiple-choice answers following any particular question is the exact answer that you wish to give, then mark the answer that comes closest.

1. Your age: _____ years
2. Your occupation: _____
3. Your height: _____ ft _____ in.
4. Your weight: _____ lbs
5. Your sex:
   ( ) male   ( ) female
6. Your race:
   ( ) white   ( ) oriental
   ( ) negro   ( ) other
7. Your religion:
   ( ) Protestant   ( ) other
   ( ) Catholic   ( ) none
   ( ) Jewish
8. Your religious convictions:
   ( ) strong   ( ) mild
   ( ) average   ( ) none
9. Do you date members of other religions?
   ( ) yes   ( ) never
   ( ) occasionally
10. Your birthplace:
    ( ) United States   ( ) Spanish-speaking country
    ( ) other English-speaking country ( ) other country
11. Your health:
    ( ) excellent   ( ) often poor
    ( ) usually good   ( ) poor

* Reproduced with permission of Selectra-Date Corp., 13–22 Jackson Ave., L.I. City, New York 11101.

12. Your political leanings:
    ( ) liberal   ( ) middle-of-the-road
    ( ) conservative   ( ) none
13. Your political convictions:
    ( ) strong   ( ) mild
    ( ) average   ( ) none
14. Years of high school completed:
    ( ) 1 ( ) 2 ( ) 3 ( ) 4
15. What was your favorite subject:
    ( ) math/science   ( ) phys. ed.
    ( ) English   ( ) none
    ( ) history
16. Years of college completed:
    ( ) 0 ( ) 1 ( ) 2 ( ) 3 ( ) 4
17. Years of other secondary schooling:
    ( ) 0 ( ) 1 ( ) 2 ( ) 3 ( ) 4
18. How many more years will you go to school?
    ( ) 0 ( ) 1 ( ) 2 ( ) 3 ( ) more than 3
19. Your high school class rank:
    ( ) upper ¼   ( ) upper ¾
    ( ) upper ½   ( ) other
20. Do you watch television?
    ( ) often   ( ) seldom
    ( ) sometimes   ( ) never
21. Do you read books?
    ( ) often   ( ) seldom
    ( ) sometimes   ( ) never
22. How often do you read newspapers?
    ( ) everyday   ( ) seldom
    ( ) several times a week
23. What are your favorite kinds of movies? (Check all that apply.)
    ( ) westerns   ( ) foreign
    ( ) adventure   ( ) travel
    ( ) comedies   ( ) war
    ( ) horror   ( ) cartoons
    ( ) musicals   ( ) documentaries
    ( ) dramas   ( ) none
24. What kind of magazines do you read regularly? (Check all that apply.)
    ( ) news   ( ) special interest
    ( ) movie   ( ) literary
    ( ) sport   ( ) comics
    ( ) fashion   ( ) none
    ( ) general interest
25. What languages do you speak fluently? (Check all that apply.)
    ( ) English   ( ) French
    ( ) Spanish   ( ) other
    ( ) German

26. Which of the following activities do you enjoy? (Check all that apply.)

( ) reading
( ) driving
( ) cards
( ) household chores
( ) bowling
( ) puttering
( ) dancing
( ) talking
( ) drinking
( ) fishing
( ) camping
( ) working
( ) loafing around
( ) thinking
( ) gardening
( ) necking
( ) chess
( ) partying
( ) writing

( ) flying
( ) traveling
( ) studying
( ) attending meetings
( ) shopping
( ) playing music
( ) listening to music
( ) collecting
( ) gambling
( ) walking
( ) building things
( ) fixing things
( ) creating art
( ) outdoor sports
( ) watching sports events
( ) indoor sports
( ) eating
( ) competing in sports

27. Where do you like to go when you date? (Check all that apply.)

( ) movies
( ) dances
( ) lunch
( ) dinner
( ) driving around
( ) cocktail lounges

( ) concerts and plays
( ) group activities
( ) weekend trips
( ) sports events
( ) each other's homes
( ) outdoor activities

28. Which qualities do you look for in a date? (Check all that apply.)

( ) physique
( ) intelligence
( ) kindness
( ) looks
( ) money
(·) popularity
( ) patience
( ) honesty
( ) loyalty
( ) sensitivity
( ) ambition
( ) virtue

( ) mystery
( ) decisiveness
( ) passion
( ) daring
( ) compliance
( ) sense of humor
( ) social standing
( ) sophistication
( ) excitement
( ) self-assurance
( ) punctuality
( ) understanding

29. What sort of people do you feel most at home with? (Check all that apply.)

( ) outdoorsmen
( ) artistic
( ) average folks
( ) intellectuals
( ) working people

( ) professionals
( ) hippies
( ) cultured
( ) none

30. What type of music do you like? (Check all that apply.)
   ( ) folk   ( ) light classics
   ( ) country and western   ( ) religious
   ( ) Latin American   ( ) classics
   ( ) popular   ( ) none
   ( ) jazz
31. What size community were you brought up in?
   ( ) small town   ( ) medium city
   ( ) small city   ( ) large city
32. How many brothers and sisters do you have?
   ( ) 3 or more   ( ) none
   ( ) 1 or 2
33. How would you describe your upbringing?
   ( ) strict   ( ) indifferent
   ( ) liberal
34. Do you feel that premarital sex can be justified?
   ( ) yes   ( ) it depends
   ( ) no
35. Do you like going steady?
   ( ) yes   ( ) it depends
   ( ) no
36. Have you been engaged?
   ( ) yes, several times   ( ) no
   ( ) yes, once
37. Have you ever been married?
   ( ) no   ( ) yes (have children)
   ( ) yes (childless)
38. How often do you date?
   ( ) almost every night   ( ) a few times a month
   ( ) a few times a week   ( ) irregularly
   ( ) once a week   ( ) seldom
39. How often do you like to date?
   ( ) more often than now   ( ) less often than now
   ( ) the same as now   ( ) it depends
40. How do you feel about "dutch" dating?
   ( ) good idea
   ( ) don't mind occasionally   ( ) don't like it
41. When would you like to get married?
   ( ) soon   ( ) not for a long time
   ( ) in a few years
42. Are you considered attractive?
   ( ) yes, very   ( ) sometimes
   ( ) usually   ( ) no
43. Are most of your dates considered attractive?
   ( ) yes   ( ) no
   ( ) usually

44. How much is usually spent when you date?
   ( ) less than $5   ( ) $10 to $20
   ( ) $5 to $10   ( ) more than $20
45. Do you like children?
   ( ) yes   ( ) it depends
   ( ) no
46. What age group do you usually date?
   ( ) my own   ( ) somewhat younger
   ( ) somewhat older   ( ) a lot younger
   ( ) a lot older   ( ) it varies
47. How well do you dance?
   ( ) very well   ( ) fair
   ( ) average   ( ) not at all
48. How much do you drink?
   ( ) a lot   ( ) very little
   ( ) moderately   ( ) not at all
49. How much do you smoke?
   ( ) a lot   ( ) not at all
   ( ) occasionally
50. How close to your house do you like your dates to live?
   ( ) closer than 15 minutes   ( ) closer than 60 minutes
   ( ) closer than 30 minutes   ( ) it doesn't matter

How Computer Dating Systems Work

A respondent who sends in a completed questionnaire expects to receive a list of names and addresses of members of the opposite sex whose age, general background, and interests are similar to his. The hypothesis implicit in computer dating systems is that the more similar the pairs are, the more likely it is that they will find themselves compatible. Thus, if a sufficiently large pool of respondents is available, a number of persons who would make good matches for the respondent can be found.

When a questionnaire is received from a new respondent, it is coded and the data recorded on a punched card. A comparison check is run with all cards in the opposite-sex file. Cards for earlier respondents that exhibit a predetermined degree of similarity (or the ten most similar) are pulled out and selected as matches for the new respondent. Then the new respondent's card is placed in the file.

A new respondent, therefore, has a chance of receiving a list of well-matching person's names and addresses within a few days of sending in the questionnaire, and then his name can be pulled out of the file at any time in the future if his profile matches with that of a future respondent.

1. *Prepare a coding system that will enable respondents with similar profiles to be identified.*

2. *Prepare a coding system that lends itself to the computation of an index so that each matching operation produces a numerical similarity index on a 0–100 scale. Hint: classify items as variables, minor and major attributes and use the sequence major attributes, minor attributes, and variables for arriving at the similarity index.*

3. *If the score 100 on the similarity index corresponds to identical profiles and lesser scores to lesser matches, what score will you establish as an acceptable match; what score will you establish as a borderline match; what scores, an unacceptable match?*

CASE III-III
Hometown National Bank's Consumer Loan Campaign

SUMMARY: The Hometown National Bank and Trust Company plans to mount a drive to expand their consumer loan business and they are trying a new type of loan application.

Martin Paulsen waited patiently on the soft leather chair outside Mr. George Wilson's office. Paulsen was Hometown's director of marketing activities and his appointment with Mr. Wilson, the bank's executive vice-president, was related to the drive to increase the bank's consumer loan business. After a short wait, Paulsen was admitted into Wilson's office and their conference began. Wilson said:

"Marty, I'm looking for a fresh idea on how to promote the consumer loan part of our business. I wrote you a memo about it last week. Did you come up with anything?"

"Yes, sir. I have," Paulsen replied. "I have just finished reading a working paper prepared by the Banking and Marketing departments of the School of Business at State University which gave me a good idea. The report showed that a large percentage of potential loan applicants hesitate to go to a commercial bank for a loan because they think that the banks will be too tough and their loan applications will be rejected. Since very few people like to be rejected for anything, this anxiety prevents them from applying."

"That's very true, Marty." Wilson said. "I know that the small loan companies have been working very hard to present a friendly, helpful image. They have done it so successfully, that they have cornered the small loan business in this country. We make equivalent loans at much lower rates of interest, but we don't get a crack at the customer."

"The fear of rejection is very powerful," Paulsen observed.

"I know. But what can we do about it?"

"I have an idea about that too. One of the big city banks ran an ad in *The New York Times* with the lead, 'The Score Yourself Bank Loan.' Look, I have a clipping here."*

"Yes, I see," Wilson said. "That's very interesting. It says, 'Take this simple test and discover how easy it is to get a loan from North America.' And here it says, 'It's simple. Just get a pen and write the number on each line that applies to you. Then add up your points. If you score 17 points or more, send it in,' and so on. That's pretty clever, Marty. If an applicant scores that much he's not likely to be turned down for the loan."

"That's the idea. And if he scores high enough on the test, he is less afraid

---

* *The New York Times*, January 23, 1969.

of being rejected. It takes most of the suspense, uncertainty, and anxiety out of applying for a loan. It serves to screen out the unsuitable applicants. They eliminate themselves so we would never have to say 'no' to them."

"That's a great idea, Marty. Why don't you prepare something like that for us. We run full-page ads in the *Hometown Record* three times a week, so the ads will cost us nothing extra. Let's try it and see how it works."

"OK, George, but one thing. Do you want to do it exactly like the *Times* ad?"

"No, I don't think so. Our clientele is different from the kind the big city banks serve. Let's tailor the thing to our conditions. I think in the beginning we should be more restrictive so we don't make any more enemies for the bank than is absolutely necessary while we are getting experience. Later, if our experience is good, we can relax the standards a bit until we find just the right level for our purposes. Can you work that out, Marty?"

"Sure thing, George. I'll have a self-rating system worked out in about two weeks. Is that soon enough?"

"That's fine. I'd like to see it before you release it to the advertising agency. Maybe, our esteemed leader would like to pass on it too."

1. Obtain one or more consumer loan applications from local banks and prepare a list of the criteria that they use for evaluating loan applicants.
2. Classify the criteria as major or minor attributes, and variables.
3. Prepare a self-rating chart that is suitable for Hometown's purpose.
4. Which rule for computing a self-rating score (the applicant's figure-of-merit) do you think would be best for this purpose? Why?

CASE III-IV
University Applied Research Corp.'s Model-Shop Problem

SUMMARY: University Applied Research Corp. wishes to act on a management consultant's recommendations regarding the reorganization of their model-making facilities.

University Applied Research Corp. (UARC) is a nonprofit research and development organization specializing in the translation of new discoveries in the physical sciences into commercial products and processes. The company has a loose affiliation with several universities and often undertakes projects for the United States DOD, AEC, CAA, and NASA as well as for private industry. UARC has a permanent staff of scientists, engineers, technicians, and nonscientific personnel. In addition, UARC draws on the university communities for special expertise.

Any excess of income over expense is used to finance additional unpaid scientific work or accrues to the treasury of the UARC Foundation. In addition to direct reimbursement for research and development work from its client organizations, UARC has a substantial income from patent royalties and sales of licenses to domestic and foreign industry.

UARC does no manufacturing but has a small pilot plant that is used for short runs on new products so that it can deliver both preproduction samples of new products and design drawings to its clients. The pilot plant is supported by a complete machine, metal-forming, woodworking, foundry, and engineering model shop. In addition to this large model-making facility, each project has similar facilities, but on a smaller scale.

Research Funding Declines

After the presidential election in 1968, the new Republican administration sought to curtail government spending, and the money available for applied research in the physical sciences was diminished. UARC found itself temporarily overstaffed and very short of new contracts. For the first time since its founding in 1950, UARC was faced with an unmanageable budget deficit and some belt-tightening appeared inevitable.

UARC's president, Dr. Louis A. Ogden, retained a consulting firm and asked them to review the UARC organization to see where economies could be made without reducing their basic capability for doing high-quality applied research. The consulting firm made a number of worthwhile recommendations, some of which dealt with the model-making facilities, the drafting function, and the duplication of technical manual preparation groups. Because the model shops involved much greater amounts of investment and expense, it was studied in greater detail.

The Model-Making Function

UARC was organized along project lines with each project functioning as an autonomous entity. The project manager drew his staff from a common pool, but once established, the project functioned as an independent entity until it was disbanded. Except for services such as payroll, wage and salary administration, report production, printing, central filing, and a typing pool, each project had its own services. Among these services were drafting, model-making, and technical manual preparation.

The consultant who was assigned to the study of the model-making facilities reported that he found a great deal of duplication of machinery and skilled manpower among the projects. Each project manager insisted that his own model shop be capable of satisfying peak demand. As a result, machine utilization was less than 10 percent on the average. Skilled machinists, sheet-metal workers, pattern makers, and model makers were often idle and were required to keep themselves occupied with work involving lesser skills. This was wasteful and contributed to much grumbling and to poor morale.

On occasion, a project manager would requisition a high-priced machine or other equipment even though three identical machines might be working a less than 10 percent capacity in other project's shops. No workable method was used to avoid this wasteful duplication of costly facilities or manpower.

After a thorough study of the inventory of machines, manpower, work loads, and machine utilization, the consultant became convinced that consolidation and centralization of the machine, metal forming, woodworking, and model-making functions of all projects should be undertaken as one of the first economy measures. The consultant's proposal was presented at a special meeting of the professional staff. It met with unanimous disapproval. Only after Dr. Ogden stated that the alternatives would be worse, that a substantial reduction in the professional staff might be needed to help UARC weather the hiatus in research funding, was the proposal given grudging acceptance. Faced with nothing but bleak alternatives, the professional staff voted to permit the consultants to formulate several proposals for the consolidation and centralization of the model-making functions. If the plan worked, similar reasoning would be applied to the drafting and technical manual services.

The Consultant's Proposals

The major proposal to bring all model-making services under one roof under the direction of a general manager was taken as the basis for future action, but a number of policy variations were offered for discussion and debate:

To whom Should the General Manager Report?
1. To one or more of the project managers.
2. To the controller's office.
3. To Dr. Ogden either directly or through his assistant.
4. To the trustees.
5. To no one at UARC.

How Shall Work Be Assigned and Charges Assembled?
1. It should be set up as a cost center with a cost-reduction incentive for the general manager who accepts only UARC work.
2. It should be as a profit center with a profit incentive for the general manager who may, if he elects, take in outside work in addition to handling UARC work.

How Shall Services Be Priced?
1. Prices set solely by the shop manager.
2. Prices set by the controller's department.
3. Prices set by negotiation between shop manager and project manager for each job order.

What Are the Project Manager's Options?
1. He must get all of his work done in the central shop.
2. He can, if he wishes, go outside the company to buy his services if he is not satisfied with the central shop.
3. He can begin again to accumulate machinery as is necessary in emergencies or when he cannot get good service.

Who Will Evaluate the Shop Manager's Performance?
1. The shop manager's superior advised by the project managers.
2. Dr. Ogden on the advice of the project managers.
3. Solely by the project managers.

On What Basis Should the Project Managers Do the Evaluation?
1. A merit score

$$\overline{G} = \left[\prod_{j=1}^{m} (P_j)^{wj} \right]$$

where P_j is the merit score assigned by the j_{th} project manager (0–100 scale).
w_j is the proportion of the total work done by the shop for the j_{th} manager.
n is the total number of project managers involved in the evaluation procedure.

2. Merit score

$$\overline{X} = \sum_{j=1}^{m} (w_j P_j)$$

3.   Merit score

$$\frac{\overline{G} + \overline{X}}{2}$$

1.   *Assuming that the model shop consolidation will go through:*
      (a)   To whom should the model shop manager report?
      (b)   How should the work assignment be handled?
      (c)   How should prices be set?
      (d)   Who should evaluate the shop manager's performance?
      (e)   Which formula should be used to evaluate the shop manager?
2.   *For each of the foregoing questions, prepare a reasoned explication of your choice of alternatives based on one of the decision models from Chapter 5 and one or more of the merit-ordering rules from Chapters 9 and 10.*

IV. TREATMENT OF DECISION ALTERNATIVES (B)

11. Utility Surfaces and Indifference Maps

The main ideas developed in this chapter relate the usefulness of the tools of indifference analysis to the study of the characteristics of the various choice rules and statistical means developed in Chapters 9 and 10.

FROM UTILITY SURFACES TO INDIFFERENCE MAP

Utility concepts were introduced in Part II as aids in valuing the outcomes of alternatives on multiple criteria. Utility functions were then introduced to show that there might be nonlinear relationships between the quantities of things and their utilities. The curves in Figure 7–1 and Figures 7–3 to 7–9 contain two-dimensional representations of several of these relationships.

A general expression for the utility of a set of criterion scores (for example, for criterion x) is

$$U_x = f(x) \tag{11-1}$$

and for criterion y

$$U_y = f(y) \tag{11-2}$$

These two expressions can be combined into

$$U_{x,y} = f(x,y) \tag{11-3}$$

A graphical representation of equation 11–3 requires three dimensions. Showing

$$U_{x,y,z} = f(x,y,z) \tag{11-4}$$

graphically would require four dimensions.

Those individuals fortunate enough to have the gift of good space visualization have no difficulty in coping with three-dimensional diagrams, but figures requiring four and more dimensions are impossible to visualize unless some reduction technique is used.

If, for example, there was a problem involving four dimensions, the four-space could be reduced to four three-dimensional subspaces:

$$I, II, III$$
$$I, III, IV$$
$$I, II, IV$$
$$II, III, IV$$

or to six two-dimensional subspaces:

$$I, II$$
$$I, III$$
$$I, IV$$
$$II, III$$
$$II, IV$$
$$III, IV$$

By this means, it becomes possible to reduce any multidimensional hyperspace into two- or three-dimensional subspaces, and although it is not possible to directly visualize spaces with more than three dimensions, it becomes possible to do so indirectly. As the number of dimensions gets larger, the required number of auxiliary views becomes cumbersome, but there should be no real conceptual difficulty in spite of the large amount of labor involved in the preparation of the partial views.[1]

Persons who have learned to read blueprints and engineering design drawings usually acquire a knowledge of orthographic projection. This is a technique used by engineers for reducing three-dimensional figures to a set of three two-dimensional views. With practice it becomes possible mentally to reconstitute the partial views into the original surface.[2]

Figure 11–1 is a three-dimensional rendering of the function

$$U_{x,y} = f(x,y) \tag{11-3}$$

where

$$U_x = k_1 x$$
$$U_y = k_2 y \tag{11-5}$$

and k_1 and k_2 are constants determined by the dimensions of the bounded space. Both U_x and U_y exhibit constant marginal utility. The corners of the figures are marked to aid identification.

The actual utility surface representing equation 11–3 is the tilted plane (0-4-2) which cuts the U_x plane at (0-2) and the U_y plane at (0-4) The horizontal plane (0-5-7-1) which is also the X-Y plane corresponds to the zero utility level. The horizontal plane (6-4-3-2) corresponds to a higher level of utility. All points on this plane have the same utility.

The line (4-2), which is the intersection of the plane, $U_{x,y}$ with the constant utility plane (6-4-3-2) is an indifference line. It represents all possible combinations of criteria X and Y scores that have the same utility. All points on

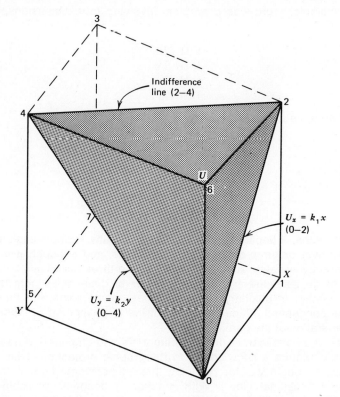

FIGURE 11-1. Three-dimensional rendering of the utility surface $U_{x,y}$ *(0-4-2). The* U_x *plane (0-1-2-6) and the* U_y *plane (0-5-4-6) are mutually perpendicular to the XY plane (0-5-7-1). The line formed by the cutting of the* $U_{x,y}$ *plane with the constant utility plane (2-6-4-3) is an indifference line.*

this line, all combinations of *X* and *Y* scores that fell on this line, would be equally valued.

Figure 11-2 is the orthographic projection of Figure 11-1. The corners are numbered for easy identification.

If a number of parallel, horizontal, constant-utility planes were passed through the solid Figure 11-1 (for example, at intervals: 10, 20, 30, 40, 50, 60, 70, 80, 90) the orthographic projection would change to that shown in Figure 11-3. Since these planes are surfaces of constant utility, the intersections with the U_{xy} plane must all have constant utility. These lines of equal utility are additional indifference lines, and the array of lines is called an indifference map.

If there had been 99 or 999 parallel planes, instead of 9, passed through the $U_{x,y}$ plane, the indifference lines would be more densely packed. Only a

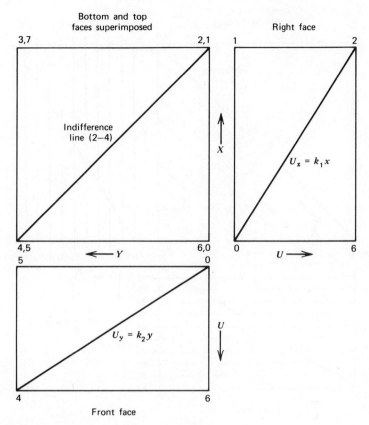

FIGURE 11–2. *Orthographic projection of solid in Figure 11–1. Three faces are laid flat. Numbers correspond to numbers on Figure 11–1.*

few are needed, however, to illustrate the method by which they are generated.

Figure 11–4 contains sketches of three other three-dimensional utility functions. Surface *a* is a right circular cone with utility defined only over points that fall within the limits of the conic volume. The utility reaches its maximum value at the cone's apex. An orthographic projection of this surface is shown in Figure 11–5. The indifference map produced by the constant utility cutting planes is a set of concentric circles.

Curve *b* of Figure 11–4 is a section of a paraboloid with utility increasing as either *x* or *y* increase, but at a diminishing rate. An orthographic projection of this surface is shown in Figure 11–6. The indifference map produced by the constant utility cutting planes is a set of curves that bend away from the origin.

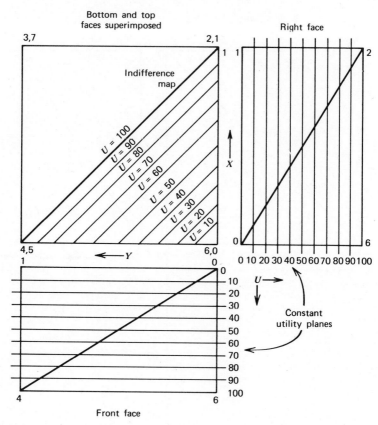

FIGURE 11–3. Orthographic projection similar to that shown in Figure 5–13 except that nine constant utility planes are shown along with the resulting indifference map in the X-Y plane.

Curve c is a section of a hemisphere. Utility increases with increases of either x or y, but at an increasing rate. An orthographic projection is shown in Figure 11–7. The indifference map consists of a set of circular arcs bending toward the origin.

The indifference map is uniquely determined by passing constant-utility cutting planes through the utility surface, but the converse does not necessarily hold true. It may not be possible to infer the shape of the utility surface from the shapes of the indifference curves. For example, cones, spheres, paraboloids, ellipsoids of circular cross section can all have indifference maps made up of sets of concentric circles. This would be true for any surface of circular cross section, and the same kind of ambiguity exists for indifference maps of other shapes.

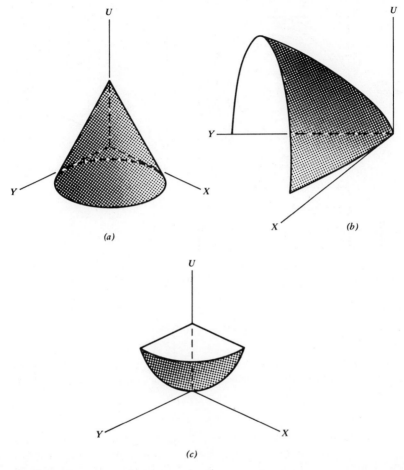

FIGURE 11-4. Three utility surfaces: (a) *right circular cone;* (b) *parabolic section;* (c) *quarter section of a hemisphere.*

When the decision problem involves more than the two criteria, x and y, the indifference maps exist in sets, one map for every criterion pair. Thus if there are "m" decision criteria, there would be

$$\frac{m(m-1)}{2} \tag{11-4}$$

maps in the set.

The shape of the indifference curves in a particular map set depends very much on the shapes of the utility functions for the criterion pairs. The utility

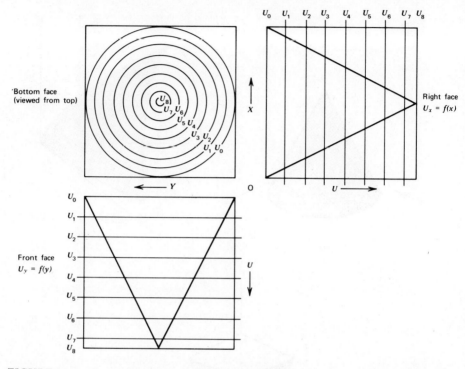

FIGURE 11–5. *An orthographic projection of the right circular conic surface of Figure 11–4a. The utility surface is cut by constant-utility planes and the resulting indifference map is a set of concentric circles.*

surfaces sketched in Figure 11–4 have U_x and U_y similarly shaped, but this was done for convenience, not because it is more realistic. In real problems, the utility functions, U_1, U_2, U_3, . . . , U_m could have a variety of shapes. For all to be similarly shaped would be rare. However, there are three good reasons for treating all criteria similarly:

1. To economize on computational expense.
2. Because there may be no way of knowing the true shapes.
3. Because the differences that do exist may not be important enough.

HOW TO READ AN INDIFFERENCE MAP

Figure 11–8 contains a hypothetical indifference map for two criteria, X and Y, having oddly shaped curves. Each indifference curve has six segments:

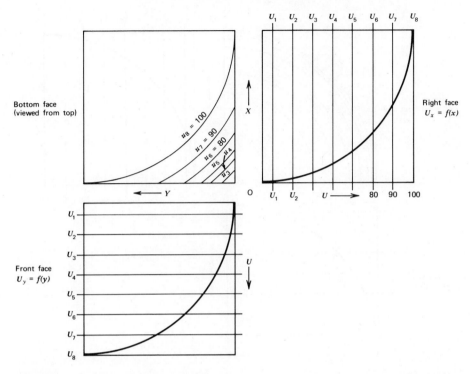

FIGURE 11–6. Orthographic projection of a utility surface, $U_{x,y}=f\ (x,y)$ (shown in Figure 11–4b).

one vertical, two negatively sloped, one horizontal, and two positively sloped. The inner curve (marked with primed numbers) represents a higher level of utility than the outer. Therefore, movement from the inner to the outer curves represents a loss in utility; movement from outer toward inner, a gain in utility.

The vertical line segment 1–2 represents a region of satiety for quantities of Y. If we increase the amount of Y by a small amount, we get no gain in utility because we find that we are on the same utility level. The same is true for a small decrease in Y. This is not true for X, however. An increase in the quantity of X moves us up to a higher utility level; a decrease, to a lower level. For this part of the surface, increments of Y are without value, whereas increments in X are positively valued.

The line segment 2–3 conveys a different meaning. An increase of either X or Y would move us to a higher utility level; a decrease in either would move us to a lower level. This means that quantities of both X and Y are positively valued at this part of the curve.

The line segment 3–4 is similar in meaning to line segment 1–2 except

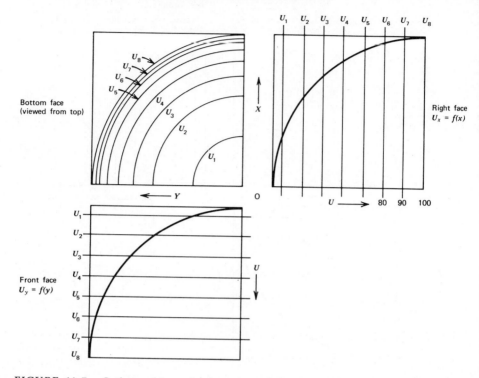

FIGURE 11–7. Orthographic projection of a utility surface $U_{x,y} = f(x,y)$ (shown in Figure 11–4c).

that it is X we are satiated with, not Y. Small changes in X leave us on the same utility level, but changes in Y give us more or less utility.

The line segment 4–5 represents a condition where X is really a nuisance. More of X would leave us less well off; less of X, better off. Y is still positively valued on this segment.

The line segment 5–6 represents a condition in which both X and Y are nuisances because we would have to reduce both to move to a higher level of utility.

The line segment 6–7 is similar to line segment 4–5 except that it is Y that is the nuisance not X; an increment of X would move us to a higher level of utility, but it would take a reduction in Y to do the same thing.

The technique in this hypothetical example can be used to ascertain whether quantities of X and Y are positively or negatively valued. If an increment moves us to a higher utility level, the criterion is positively valued at that point on the indifference curve. The example also shows that the valuations can change with changes in quantity; at one point a quantity of X could be highly valued, at another it would be a nuisance.

Figure 11–9 contains an indifference map with rather special properties.

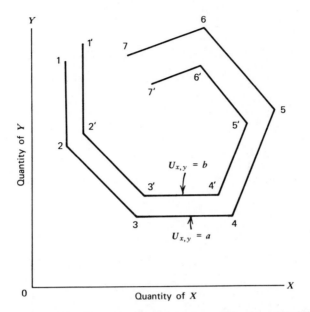

FIGURE 11–8. An indifference map consisting of specially shaped indifference curves. The line 1'–7' has higher utility than the line 1–7 because the constant-utility cutting plane had higher utility for this cut than for the other. Movement from the nonprimed line to the primed line causes an increase in utility. Movement from the nonprimed line away from the primed line causes reduction in utility.

One end of the indifference curve cuts the X axis, the other end is asymptotic to a value of X equal to X_{min}. If an indifference curve cuts the X axis it means that Y is not indispensable. We could get along with zero Y as long as we could get enough of X to offset the loss in Y. At the other end, the matter is a little more complicated. If the amount of X goes lower than X_{min}, there is no utility at all; we have fallen off the lowest indifference curve. At the asymptote, we are satiated with Y, and it takes just a small change in X to move us from a high to a low level of utility.

When an indifference curve cuts an axis, we know that the criterion is not-indispensable and that we can always make up for its absence or low scores if enough of others are available. If the indifference curve is asymptotic to an axis or to another line, it means that there is some minimum score for the criterion for there to be any utility.

Figure 11–10 shows three indifference maps that represent extreme cases. In curve set *a*, neither X nor Y are indispensable. If quantities of X and Y involve costs, we would be better off with only one of the two, not both.

Curve *b* shows a situation where X and Y are required in fixed proportions. If both X and Y have cost, the best quantities would occur at the corners.

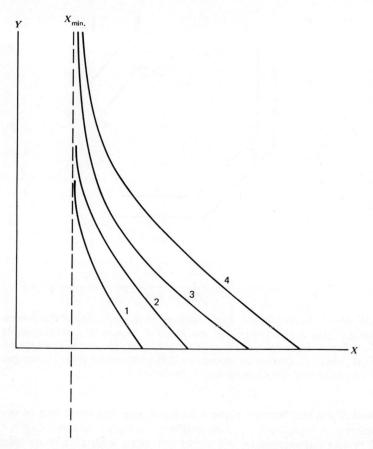

FIGURE 11–9. An indifference map consisting of curves that cut the X axis and are asymptotic to the value of X equal to X_{min}. The utility of line 4 is greater than that of 3, 3 greater than 2, 2 greater than 1.

Curvo c chowo tho caee of perfect substitutability. Neither is indispensable, there are many combinations of X and Y that could produce the same level of utility.

Thus in curve a we must have one or the other, not both. In curve b, we must have both in fixed proportions. In curve c we could have many combinations of X and Y and be equally pleased.

TRADE-OFF RATES

Another important property can be inferred from the study of the shapes of indifference curves; the trade-off rates between criterion pairs (also called

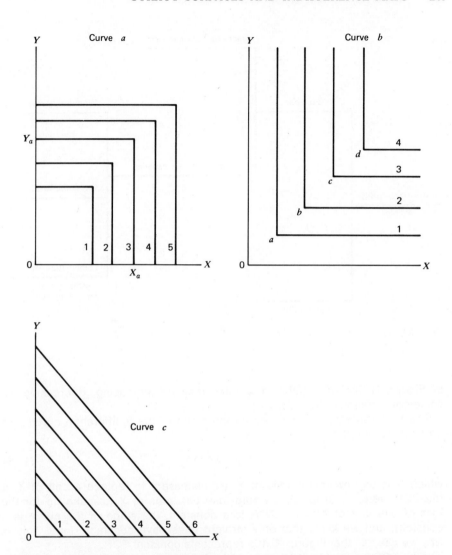

FIGURE 11–10.   Curve a, *one or the other not both; neither is indispensable; curve* b, *both are required on fixed proportions; curve* c, *neither is indispensable, many combinations of* X *and* Y *would be equally pleasing.*

by economists, the marginal-rate-of-substitution). The possibilities are charted in Figure 11–11.

In some instances, trade-offs are not possible as is illustrated in Figure 11–10b. More often, trade-offs are possible, and if so, the rates may be either constant or variable. The case of constant trade-off rate is illustrated

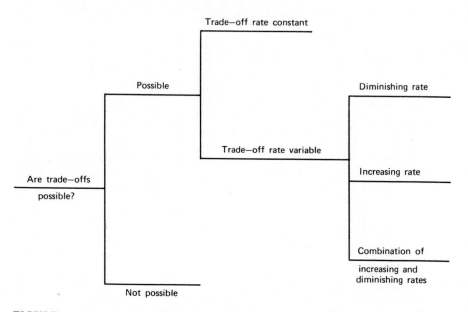

FIGURE 11–11. *Some possibilities for trade-off rates between criteria.*

in Figure 11–10c. If variable, the rates may be increasing, decreasing, or some combination of the two.

The trade-off rate is measured by the slope of the indifference curve at a particular point, that is

$$TOR = \Delta Y / \Delta X \tag{11-5}$$

which tells us how many units of Y are necessary to replace a unit of X. If the TOR were equal to 10, it would take ten units of Y to make up for the loss of one unit of X. If the TOR is a constant, the slope of the curve is a constant; and we know that only straight lines have constant slope. This is why we can say that Figure 11–10c represents constant TOR.

If the TOR is variable, it could have the form:

$$TOR = k_1 X \tag{11-6}$$

which says that the trade-off rate varies directly with the size of X. Or it might have the form:

$$TOR = k_1 / X \tag{11-7}$$

This says that the TOR diminishes as X increases.

Possibly the TOR could have the form:

$$TOR = k_1 + k_2X - k_3X^2 \qquad (11\text{-}8)$$

which would tell us that the TOR might first rise and then decline as X varied from zero to some positive number.

The indifference curves in Figure 11–6 exhibit diminishing trade-off rates for Y and X as X increases. In the general case, curves that bend away (convex) from the origin will show the diminishing TOR property.

The curves in Figure 11–7 exhibit the increasing TOR. Curves that bend toward the origin (concave) show the increasing trade-off-rate property. The curves in Figure 11–5 exhibit both increasing and decreasing TORs depending on which quadrants of the circular indifference curves are considered.

It can be shown that for every indifference curve set there is a corresponding unique TOR formula. A simple statement of this relationship (for the two-dimensional case) is

$$TOR = -dy/dx = M_x/M_y \qquad (11\text{-}9)$$

where M_x = marginal utility of x
M_y = marginal utility of y

INDIFFERENCE MAPS AND EQUIVALENCE

The term equivalence was introduced in Chapter 8 to define a useful property of pairs of valuation score-sets (the matrix row vectors). Two such vectors are equivalent under an operation when their scalars (figures-of-merit) are equal. It follows, therefore, that two alternatives with equal figures-of-merit are equivalent because they have equal scalars.

An indifference curve, defined by its own construction formula, contains points of equal utility. It is, therefore, the locus of all equivalent alternatives having that level of utility, under that specific operation.

For each operation there is a corresponding indifference map. For each indifference map, there is a corresponding trade-off function. These correspondences are diagramed in Figure 11–12.

These correspondences are very useful because they allow us to analyze the properties of the various choice rules by using the tools and concepts of indifference analysis. Simply by sketching the indifference map for a choice rule, we have the tools to infer many of that rule's subtle properties. We have the means to identify and distinguish the individual differences among the various rules.

Chapters 12 and 13 are devoted to a detailed examination of the inner logics of the various rules and means discussed in Chapters 9 and 10, using the tools of indifference analysis developed in this chapter.

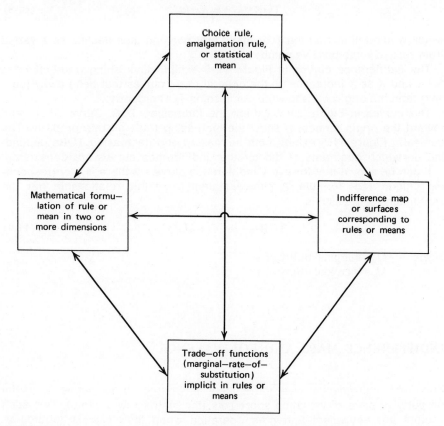

FIGURE 11–12. *The four-way correspondence between choice rules (or means) and mathematical formulas, indifference maps, and trade-off functions.*

Notes and References

1. For a work dealing with multidimensional geometry see, Henry Parker Manning, *Geometry of Four Dimensions* (New York, The Macmillan Co., 1914) and also Paul McDougle, *Vector Algebra* (Belmont, California, Wadsworth Publishing Co. Inc., 1971).

2. Almost any good work of engineering drawing will contain a treatment of orthographic projection. See, for example, any edition of T. E. French, *Engineering Drawing* (New York, The McGraw-Hill Book Co., many dates).

Important Words and Concepts

Utility surface
Reduction to a subspace
Orthographic projection
Constant utility plane
Indifference curve
Indifference map
Positively or negatively valued
Indispensable
Asymptote
Trade-off rate
Marginal-rate-of-substitution
Diminishing TOR
Increasing TOR
Convex with respect to the origin
Concave with respect to the origin
Locus (loci)

Overview of Chapter 11

Utility functions can be combined to give multidimensional utility surfaces. It is not possible to visualize multidimensional surfaces unless a reduction technique such as orthographic projection is used.

An indifference curve is formed from the cutting of the utility surface by a constant utility plane. A set of indifference curves is obtained when several such cutting planes are used. The shapes of the indifference curves are derived from the shapes of the indifference surfaces.

There is an indifference map for each pair of criteria. In most cases it is reasonable to assume that all are derived from similarly shaped utility surfaces.

From a close reading of the indifference map it is possible to infer the following:

1. Whether a decision criterion is positively or negatively valued at all places on the curve.
2. Whether satiation with a criterion can exist.
3. If a criterion is indispensable or nonindispensable.
4. Whether trade-offs are possible between criterion pairs and if so what kinds.

Indifference curves are the loci of equivalent alternatives. For each curve there is a mathematical formula, a trade-off function, and a corresponding choice rule or statistical mean.

Questions for Review, Discussion, and Research

Review

1. What are some of the shapes utility functions can have?

2. How is the utility surface related to the utility function?

3. How can the reduction of multidimensional utility surfaces be accomplished?

4. What is orthographic projection and how is it used here?

5. How is the indifference curve related to the utility surface?

6. Can a utility surface be inferred from the indifference curves? Why or why not?

7. How do indifference curves derived from planar, conical, parabolic, and spherical surfaces differ?

8. If there was a twelve-criterion problem, how many indifference maps would there be in the complete set?

9. How can one tell if criteria are positively or negatively valued? If they are indispensable or nonindispensable?

10. How is satiation with a criterion indicated on an indifference curve?

11. What interpretation is given to a curve that cuts an axis? That is asymptotic to an axis?

12. How could you tell if a pair of criteria were perfectly substitutable or if they must be present in fixed proportions?

Discussion

1. Why is it not possible to infer a utility surface from the shapes of the indifference curves? Is this also true for inferring the underlying utility functions from the indifference curves?

2. How could one tell from the indifference curves if the trade-off rates were constant, diminishing, increasing, or were a combination of these?

3. Of what value is indifference analysis in the study of the properties of choice rules and statistical means developed in Chapters 9 and 10?

Research

1. Search the economics and decision theory literature for various illustrations of indifference curves and analyze them, basing your analysis on the tools developed in this chapter.

2. What other uses are there for indifference analysis? How does indifference analysis relate to such things as isoquants, isogonal lines, and the like?

3. How does indifference analysis relate to the entire body of utility theory?

12. Indifference Analysis of Merit Ordering Techniques (I)

In this chapter the indifference maps (in two dimensions) associated with Choice Rules Nos. 1 to 7 are presented and interpreted.

INDIFFERENCE ANALYSIS OF RULE NO. 1*

> **Restatement of Rule No. 1. Establish a standard of acceptability (a maximum, minimum, or combination) for every decision criterion. Reject any alternative with scores that fail to meet or surpass standards.**

Indifference maps for Choice Rule No. 1 are shown in Figures 12–1 and 12–2 for the two criterion case. The unshaded area in Figure 12–1 bounded by the lines *AB* and *BC* is an indifference region. All alternatives with scores that fell wholly in this region would be deemed equivalent. Further increases in either *X* or *Y* scores might add cost but would add no utility. Line *AB* is horizontal and represents satiation with criterion *X*. Line *BC* is vertical and represents satiation with criterion *Y*. Both *X* and *Y* are indispensable criteria with no trade-off possible when the criterion scores fall below the minimum standards. At or above the standard, *X* and *Y* are substitutable in any combination with no gains or losses in utility. If both *X* and *Y* involve costs, the most economical combination of their scores occurs at the point *B*.

Figure 12–2 shows a variation of Rule No. 1 in which the criteria have both upper and lower limits. The acceptance region is bounded by the lines *AB*, *BD*, *DC*, and *AC*. Only those alternatives with every score within the region *A B C D* would be accepted.

Although Figures 12–1 and 12–2 are drawn in two dimensions, the reasoning can be extended by analogy to three or more.

The effects of criterion weights cannot be shown in these figures because the effect of the weights is to alter the rates of change in the movement of the minimum and maximum levels.

---

* The Go, No-Go Rule of Chapter 9, page 183.

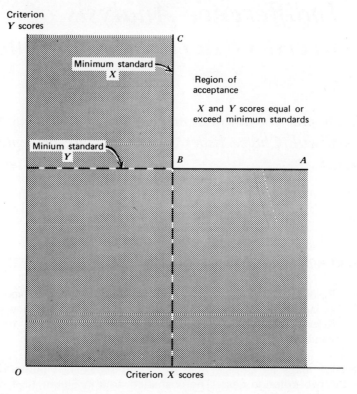

FIGURE 12–1. *Indifference map for Choice Rule No. 1. The shaded areas represent regions of rejection. Area bounded by lines* AB *and* BC *encloses region of acceptance for which* X ≥ *(minimum standard)* x *and* Y ≥ *(minimum standard)* y.

INDIFFERENCE ANALYSIS OF RULE NO. 2*

Restatement of Rule No. 2. Establish standards of acceptability for every criterion except the one judged most important. Reject every alternative with scores on the nonreserved criteria that fail to meet or surpass the standards. For those alternatives not so rejected, select the one with the best score on the reserved criterion.

The indifference map for Rule No. 2 is shown in Figure 12–3. The shaded area is the rejection region for alternatives with scores on the X criterion that fall below X_{min}. Within the acceptance region, the map consists of a set

---

* The combination go, no-go and optimizing rule of Chapter 9, page 188.

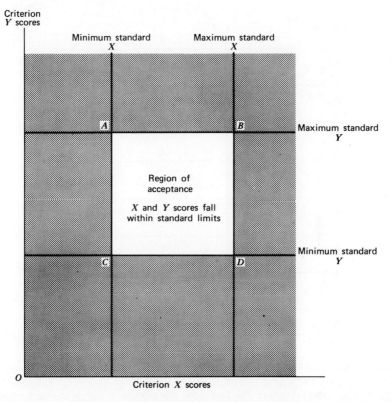

FIGURE 12–2. Indifference map for Choice Rule No. 1 when upper and lower limits for X and Y are specified. Shaded areas represent regions of rejection. The area enclosed by the lines AB,.BD, DC, and AC represents the region of acceptance.

of horizontal lines, one for every value of Y. All alternatives with identical Y scores (and X scores equal to or greater than X_{min}) would be deemed equivalent. Alternatives with higher Y scores would be preferred to those that fell on lower indifference lines.

The horizontal lines in the acceptance region represent satiation with criterion X. Scores larger than X_{min} produce no gains in utility. If increments of X have cost, the most economical combinations of X and Y would fall on the vertical line $X = X_{min}$.

The indifference curves A B C and A' B' C' show that for each level of utility no trade-offs between X and Y scores are possible. The level of utility is determined uniquely by the quantity of Y; less Y means less utility; more Y means more utility. No amount of X beyond X_{min} can affect the level of utility.

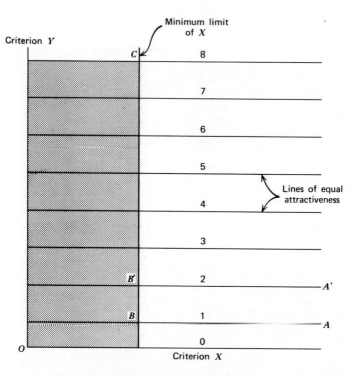

FIGURE 12–3. Indifference map for Choice Rule No. 2. The shaded area represents the rejection region. All alternatives with scores that fall on or above the minimum X limit are potentially acceptable, but the one with the highest Y value would be preferred above all others.

INDIFFERENCE ANALYSIS OF RULE NO. 3*

> **Restatement of Rule No. 3.   Multiply each cell entry in the valuation matrix by the corresponding weight and add the weighted cell entries for each alternative (across the matrix row). The alternative with the largest score is the best, the next largest is the second best, and so forth.**

An indifference map in two dimensions is shown in Figure 12–4. The map consists of a set of negatively sloped straight lines that cut both the X and Y axes. These indifference lines can be interpreted as follows:

1.   All alternatives with weighted sums that fall on the same indifference

---

* The weighted sum of the points rule of Chapter 9, page 188.

line are equivalent. Alternatives with combined scores that fall on a higher utility line are preferred to those that fall on a lower line. All combinations of X and Y scores that fall on the same line are equally desirable;

2. Since all lines cut both the X and Y axes, neither criterion is indispensable. We could be equally happy with no X or no Y if one was present in sufficient quantity to offset the lack of the other.
3. The fact that the lines are perfectly straight means that the trade-off rates between X and Y, Y and X are constants.
4. Negatively sloped lines indicate that both criteria are positively valued (are not nuisances). An increase in the size of either X or Y scores would move us up to a higher utility level.
5. The slope of the indifference lines is equal to $-w_x/w_y$. This tells us that the slope of the lines is affected by the criterion weights. The trade-off rate is equal to the slope of the lines.

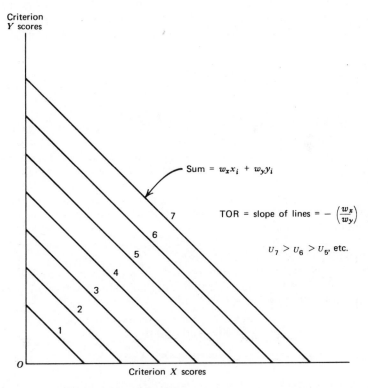

FIGURE 12–4.   *Indifference map for weighted sum of quality points (Choice Rule No. 3). Numbers 1 to 7 represent gradations in overall desirability. All alternatives whose sums fall on a line would be equally desirable.*

The above reasoning can be extended by analogy to more than two dimensions. For a three-criterion case, the lines would be replaced by negatively sloped planes. All points in a plane would correspond to equivalent alternatives.

INDIFFERENCE ANALYSIS OF RULE NO. 4*

Restatement of Rule No. 4. Compute the weighted product of the cell entries of the score matrix (either the outcome or valuation scores) by using the exponential or logarithmic form of the computing formula. The alternative with the largest weighted product is the best, the next largest is the second best, and so forth.

The indifference maps for Rule No. 4 are shown in Figures 12–5 and 12–6. In Figure 12–5, the curves are shown as rectangular hyperbolas asymptotic to the X and Y axes. In Figure 12–6, the curves are transformed into negatively sloped straight lines on logarithmic axes. Figure 12–4 can be interpreted as follows:

1. Both X and Y are indispensable criteria for near-zero values since none of the curves cuts an axis. However, for criterion scores not close to zero, X and Y are substitutable, one for the other.
2. The trade-off rate between X and Y scores is variable and approaches extreme values near the asymptotes.
3. For small Y values the curves are nearly horizontal, which indicates near-satiation with X. Large increments of X are required to move us up to a higher utility level.
4. For small values of X the curves are nearly vertical, indicating near-satiation with Y. Large increments of Y are needed to move us up to a higher utility level.
5. Both X and Y are positively valued criteria; an increase in either will move us up to a higher utility level.
6. The curves are convex with respect to the origin (bend away), which means that there is a diminishing marginal rate of substitution, that is, a diminishing trade-off rate.

The trade-off rate for unweighted criteria is

$$\text{TOR} = \text{slope} = -Y/X \tag{12-1}$$

---

* The weighted product of the points rule of Chapter 9, page 192.

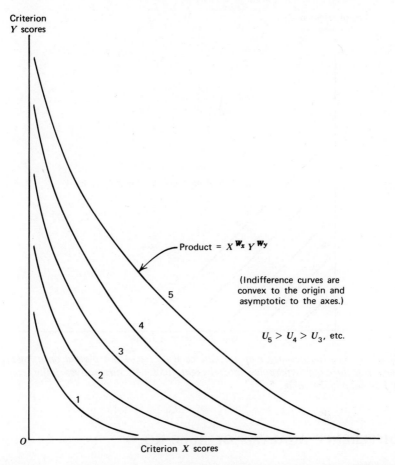

FIGURE 12–5. Indifference map for weighted product of quality points (Choice Rule No. 4). Numbers 1 to 5 represent gradations of overall desirability. Curves are rectangular hyperbolas and are convex to the origin. All alternatives falling on a given curve are equally desirable.

For weighted criteria

$$TOR = slope = -(w_x/w_y)(Y/X) \qquad (12\text{-}2)$$

which is consistent with the earlier statement that the trade-off rates between criteria X and Y are variable. Notice that the effect of the criterion weights is to alter the shapes of the indifference curves in the sense that their slopes at any point are modified by the quantity (w_x/w_y).

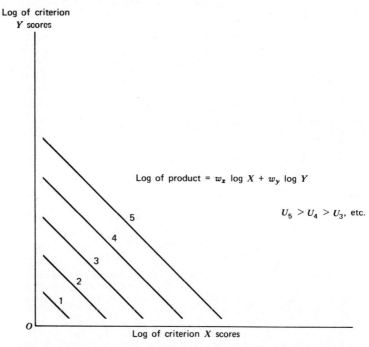

FIGURE 12–6. *Indifference map for Choice Rule No. 4 but plotted on a log-log scale thereby transforming hyperbolas into straight lines. All alternatives falling on a line would be equally desirable.*

INDIFFERENCE ANALYSIS OF RULE NO. 5[*]

Restatement of Rule No. 5. Establish a dummy alternative with the scores 0,0,0, and so forth as the worst possible alternative (absolutely repulsive) in a 0–100 space. Compute the deviation of all real alternatives in the valuation matrix from the worst case. The alternative furthest from the worst is the best, the next furthest is the next best, and so on.

The indifference map for this rule is shown in Figure 12–7 for two criteria, X and Y, for the worst case at the origin, and for equal criterion weights. If the criterion weights were not equal, the curves would be quarter arcs of ellipses instead of quarter arcs of circles.

[*] The furthest from the worst rule of Chapter 9, page 195.

Criterion Y scores

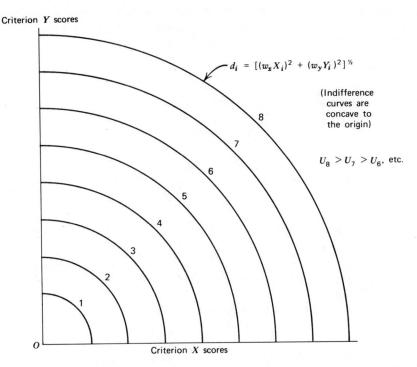

$d_i = [(w_x X_i)^2 + (w_y Y_i)^2]^{1/2}$

(Indifference
curves are
concave to
the origin)

$U_8 > U_7 > U_6$, etc.

Criterion X scores

FIGURE 12–7.   *Indifference curves for Choice Rule No. 5. Curves further from the origin represent more desirable sets of alternatives. All alternative scores on a particular line would be equally attractive. Curves are concave to the origin. If weights w_x and w_y were unequal, curves would be arcs of ellipses instead of circles.*

These indifference curves can be interpreted as follows:

1. All alternatives with deviation scores that fall on the same quarter arc are equivalent. Those falling on a quarter arc of greater radius are preferred to those that fall on arcs of lesser radius. All combinations of X and Y scores that fall on the same curve are equally desirable.
2. Since the curves intercept both axes, neither criterion is indispensable. We could be equally happy with no Y or no X if one was present in sufficient quantity to offset the loss of the other.
3. The fact that the curves are vertical at the X axis and horizontal at the Y axis indicates satiation with Y as Y diminishes and with X as X diminishes. This implies that as X or Y get smaller, they are more easily dispensed with altogether.
4. The fact that the indifference curves are not straight implies that the trade-off rate is variable. Since the curves are concave with respect (bend toward) the origin, this suggests that the trade-off rate is opposite

in sense to the TOR for Rule No. 4, where the curves were convex; that there is an increasing rather than a diminishing trade-off rate.

5. The fact that the curves have negative slope means that both X and Y are positively valued criteria. More of either would move us up to a higher utility level.

The trade-off rate for this rule is

$$TOR = slope = -(w_x/w_y)^2 (X/Y) \qquad (12\text{-}3)$$

which is consistent with the statement contained in item no. 4 above. A comparison of formulas 12–3 and 12–2 reveals that for Rule No. 5 the TOR varies with X/Y whereas for Rule No. 4 it varies with Y/X.

INDIFFERENCE ANALYSIS OF RULE NO. 6*

Restatement of Rule No. 6. **Establish a dummy alternative that represents the perfect alternative (for example, 100,100 100,100, and the like in a 0–100 space. Compute the deviation of each real alternative from this perfect case. Select the alternative that is closest to perfection as the best, the second closest as the second best, and so forth.**

The indifference map for Rule No. 6 is shown in Figure 12–8 for two criteria, X and Y, and equal weights. The map consists of a set of quarter-arcs of circles with center at the perfection point. If the weights were not equal, the curves would be quarter-arcs of ellipses.

The curves in this map can be interpreted as follows:

1. All alternatives with distance from perfection scores that fall on the same indifference curve are equivalent. Those falling on a quarter-arc of *lesser* radius are preferred to those on greater radii. All combinations of X and Y that fall on the same curve are equally desirable.
2. Whether or not X and Y are indispensable depends on the radius of the indifference curve. If the radius is equal to or greater than 100, the curves will cut both axes and, therefore, X and Y will be nonindispensable. For curves with radii less than 100, the criteria become partly indispensable. For example, if the radius equals 50, the least X or Y we could accept and still not fall to a lower level of utility is 50. If we have more than 50 of one we could give up some of the other, but less than 50 of X or Y must throw us to a loss of utility.
3. The fact that the curves are vertical or horizontal implies that we have satiation with X or Y for some values of the criteria.
4. The fact that the indifference curves are not straight implies that the

---

* The distance from perfection rule of Chapter 9, page 195.

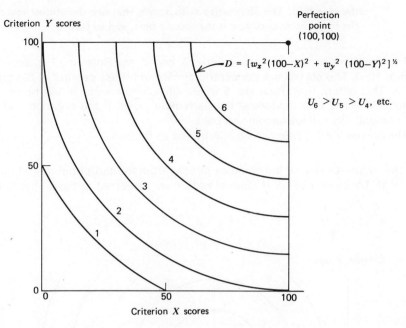

Criterion Y scores

Perfection point (100,100)

$D = [w_x{}^2(100-X)^2 + w_y{}^2 (100-Y)^2]^{1/2}$

$U_6 > U_5 > U_4$, etc.

Criterion X scores

FIGURE 12–8.   *Indifference map for Choice Rule No. 6. Curves further from the origin contain sets of alternatives that are preferred to those closer to the origin. All alternatives whose point scores fall on a particular curve would be equally attractive. This curve set* is convex *to the origin. If w_x were unequal to w_y, the curves would be quarter-arcs of ellipses.*

trade-off rate is variable. The curves are convex with respect to the origin so that there will be a diminishing rate of exchange between Y and X. In this respect Rule No. 6 is similar to Rule No. 4 and different from Rule No. 5.

5.   The negatively sloped curves indicate that both X and Y are positively valued. More of either will put us on a higher level of utility.

The trade-off rate for this rule is

$$\text{TOR} = \text{slope} = -(w_x/w_y)^2 \, (100-X)/(100-Y) \qquad (12\text{-}4)$$

which is consistent with item no. 4 above.

INDIFFERENCE ANALYSIS OF RULE NO. 7*

Restatement of Rule No. 7.   Establish a standard or target score profile. Compute the deviation of all alternatives' score profiles from

* The profile matching rule of Chapter 10, page 203.

the standard. The alternative with scores that are the closest match is the best, the next closest is the second best, and so forth.

The indifference map for two criteria, X and Y, for Rule No. 7 is shown in Figure 12–9. The curves are concentric circles with their centers at the target point. This differs from Rule No. 5 where the centers were at the origin and from Rule No. 6 with centers at the perfection point. If the criterion weights are unequal, the circles become ellipses.

The curves for this rule can be interpreted as follows:

1. All alternatives with the same deviations from the target point are equivalent. Those on circles of smaller radius are preferred to those that fall on

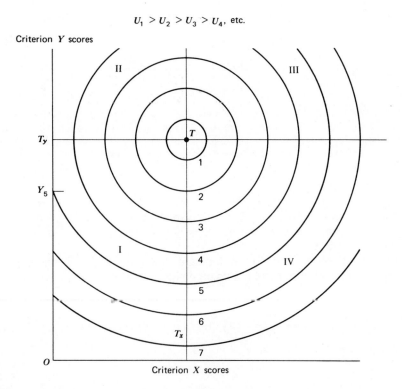

$$U_1 > U_2 > U_3 > U_4, \text{ etc.}$$

FIGURE 12–9. Indifference map for Choice Rule No. 7. Curves are circles having their centers at the target point T. The convexity or concavity of the curves changes with the quadrant in which they fall. In quadrant I, curves are positively sloped; in II, negatively; in III, negatively; in IV, positively sloped. If w_x and w_y were unequal, the circles would become ellipses.

larger circles. All combinations of X and Y scores that fall on the same circle are equally attractive.

2. Whether X and Y increments are positively or negatively valued depends on the quadrant into which the X and Y scores fall.

   (a) In the first quadrant $(X \leq T_x;\ Y \leq T_y)$ an increase in either X or Y moves us to a higher level of utility except as the curves approach T_x and T_y where satiation is indicated. In this quadrant, both X and Y are positively valued criteria.

   (b) In the second quadrant $(X \leq T_x);\ (Y \geq T_y)$ increments of Y are nuisances, but increments of X are still positively valued.

   (c) In the third quadrant $(X \geq T_x;\ Y \geq T_y)$ both X and Y are nuisances.

   (d) In the fourth quadrant $(X \geq T_x;\ Y \leq T_y)$ X is a nuisance and Y is positively valued.

According to this rule, it may be just as bad to miss the target by overshooting than by undershooting. It is how close to the target one gets that counts.

The trade-off rate is variable, but whether there is increasing or diminishing rate of exchange depends on the quadrant under consideration. In the I quadrant, the curves are convex; in the III quadrant, they are concave. The formula for the TOR is

$$\text{TOR} = \text{slope} = -(w_x/w_y)^2 (T_x - X) / (T_y - Y) \tag{12-5}$$

Important Words and Concepts

Indifference region
Satiation with a criterion
Region of acceptance
Region of rejection
Variable trade-off rates

Overview of Chapter 12

The indifference maps (with criteria taken two at a time) for the first seven choice rules are as follows:

Choice Rule No.	Shape of Map (two dimensions)
1	Region bounded by limit values of criteria X and Y
2	In region bounded by limit values of criterion X, a set of horizontal straight lines, one for each value of Y
3	A set of negatively-sloped straight lines
4	A set of rectangular hyperbolas (or negatively sloped straight lines on a log-log scale)
5	A set of quarter-arcs of circles (or ellipses if weights are unequal) with centers at the origin
6	A set of quarter-arcs of circles (or ellipses if weights are unequal) with centers at the perfection point
7	A set of concentric circles (or ellipses if weights are unequal) with centers at the target point

Although all maps are shown in two dimensions, representing criteria taken in pairs, the reasoning can be extended to three or more dimensions. In that case, the curves will be replaced by surfaces or hypersurfaces.

Questions for Review, Discussion, and Research

Review

1. By what reasoning is it possible to represent the various choice rules by indifference maps?

2. Interpret the following indifference curve properties for each choice rule:
    (a) Horizontal segment of curve.
    (b) Vertical segment of curve.
    (c) Cuts an axis.
    (d) Asymptotic to an axis.
    (e) Positively sloped segment.
    (f) Negatively sloped segment.
    (g) Curvature.
    (h) Concave to origin.
    (i) Convex to origin.
    (j) Degree of bending.
    (k) Distance of curve from origin.
    (l) Corners.
    (m) Regions.

3. What is the effect of unequal criterion weights on the curves for each choice rule?

4. Interpret the TORs for each rule in ordinary language.

Discussion

1. Under what circumstances would it be useful to draw indifference maps in more than two dimensions?

2. What significance for decision-making purposes do the various curve properties in question 2 above have?

3. What is the significance of unequal criterion weights for rules nos. 4 to 7?

4. What is the significance of nonconstant TORs for rules nos. 4 to 7?

Research

1. Sketch the maps for rules nos. 4 to 7, using unequal criterion weights and several values of w_x/w_y.

2. Sketch the maps for rules nos. 1 to 7 in three dimensions.

3. Sketch the TOR functions for rules nos. 4 to 7. What would be the effect of unequal criterion weights? Discuss the differences in the TORs for the various rules reasoning from the TOR curve shapes.

13. Indifference Analysis of
Merit Ordering Techniques (II)

This chapter contains the indifference analyses of four special cases: (a) combination rules (Nos. 1 and 3, 5 or 6), (b) uncertainty rules, (c) synthetic amalgamation rules with various values assigned to the parameter, eta, and (d) rules that involve unequal marginal utilities.

INDIFFERENCE ANALYSIS OF SOME COMBINATION RULES

It is possible to combine Rule No. 1 with several of the others. Figure 13–1 shows the indifference map for Rules Nos. 1 and 3 combined. The region of acceptance is to the right of X_a and above Y_a, the lower limits of X and Y, respectively.

All alternatives with criterion scores that equaled or exceeded the lower limits are tentatively admitted for further evaluation. Among these survivors, the best alternative would the one with the largest weighted sum. All alternatives with identical weighted sums and with scores that equaled or exceeded the minimums would be admissible and equivalent, and all would fall on a single indifference line.

With this combination of Rules Nos. 1 and 3, it is quite possible for a rejected alternative to have a larger weighted sum than one accepted. In Figure 13–1, the point labeled R represents a rejected alternative because its Y value is below minimum even though its weighted sum is greater than for the alternative represented by point S. Thus, using minimum limits enables us to add the indispensability condition for criteria over one portion of their range, and allows for trade-off over another part of their range of scores.

The special advantage of combining Rule No. 1 with another is that it can be done selectively. It is possible to assign special limits (minimum, maximum, or any combinations) to one or more of the decision criteria without affecting any of the others. Since the typical, simple amalgamation rule treats all criteria in the same way, the ability to exercise some selectivity in adding the indispensability condition can be especially useful in some decision problems.

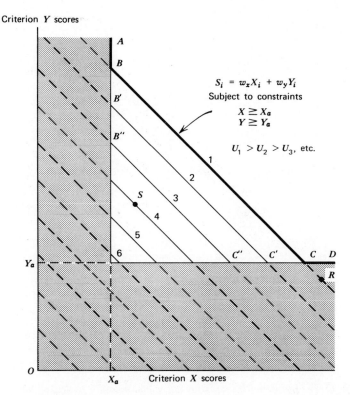

FIGURE 13–1. *Indifference map showing a combination of Choice Rules Nos. 1 and 3. The shaded area represents the region of unconditional rejection. For alternatives whose scores on* X *and* Y *exceed* X_a *and* Y_a, *respectively, the weighted sum of quality points is used. Indifference curve 1 extends from points marked ABCD; 2, AB'C'D; 3, AB''C''D; 4, AB'''C'''D, and so forth. This combination implies interchangeability over a limited range only.*

The effect of adding lower limits is to introduce convexity with respect to the origin in amalgamation rules that might not otherwise exhibit this property. Rule No. 3 in its pure form has indifference lines that are neither convex nor concave with respect to the origin. Notice in Figure 13–1 that the addition of the lower limits produces convex curves, for example *ABCD* and *A'B'C'D'*, and so forth. *ABCD*, the darkened curve is not smooth, but it does bend *away* from the origin.

Figure 13–2 contains a curve set for the combination of Rules Nos. 1 and 5, the "furthest from the worst" rule. Note how the combination produces a set of indifference curves that are both concave and convex with respect to the origin. The curve *ABCD* is convex around the corners, *B* and *C*, and concave between the points *B* and *C*.

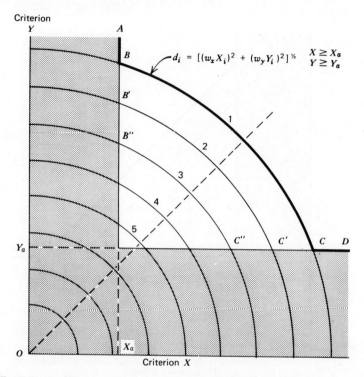

FIGURE 13–2. Indifference map showing a combination of Rules No. 1 and 5. The shaded area represents the region of unconditional rejection. For alternatives whose scores on X and Y exceed X_a and Y_a, respectively, the furthest from the worst rule is used. Indifference curves for curve 1 extend from ABCD; curve 2, AB'C'D; curve 3, AB"C"D, and so forth. Thus an indifference curve is partly concave and partly convex with respect to the origin.

Figure 13–3 contains the indifference curve set for the combination of Rules Nos. 1 and 6. For this pair of rules, the convexity may be altered by the addition of the lower limits.

We should expect that the process that converts the indifference map for a rule from concave to convex would affect the inner logic of the rule, and this is exactly what does happen. The addition of lower limits causes alternatives with below-limit scores to be cast out regardless of how high their scores on other criteria might be, and regardless of how high their merit scores on the simple rule alone might have been.

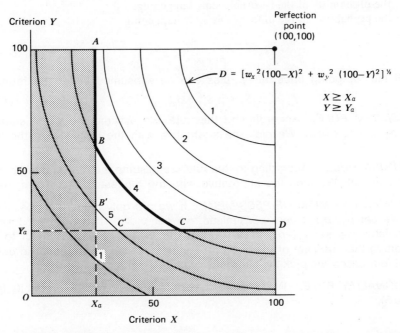

FIGURE 13–3. *Indifference map showing a combination of Rules No. 1 and 6. The shaded area represents the region of unconditional rejection. For alternatives whose scores on X and Y exceed X_a and Y_a, respectively, the distance from perfection rule is used. Indifference curves 4 and 5 show effects of Rule No. 1. For curve 4 the extent is ABCD; for curve 5, AB'C'D. The shapes of curves 1, 2, and 3 are unaffected by the use of lower limits for X and Y.*

INDIFFERENCE ANALYSIS OF UNCERTAINTY RULES

Several rules for rating alternatives on a single criterion under conditions of uncertainty were given in Chapter 6. They were:

1. Pessimism (Wald)
2. Optimism (Hurwicz) or modified optimism
3. Rationality (Bayes, LaPlace)

To proceed with the indifference analysis of these rules, we assume a set of n alternatives and m criteria and two possible states of nature (favorable and unfavorable). For the i_{th} alternative on the j_{th} criterion let:

S_{ij} = the valuation score that will be inserted in the valuation matrix.
S_{ijf} = the valuation score that would result under the favorable state of nature.
S_{ijg} = the valuation score that would result under the unfavorable state of nature.

p_f = the probability of the favorable state happening.
p_g = the probability of the unfavorable state happening.

and

$$p_f + p_g = 1$$

All the foregoing uncertainty rules can be subsumed under the formula:

$$S_{ij} = p_f S_{ijf} + p_g S_{ijg} \qquad (13\text{-}1)$$

PESSIMISM RULE.   According to this rule, we assume the worst state of nature ($p_g = 1$; $p_f = 0$). We pick the alternative with the highest S_{ij} (the best worst).

OPTIMISM RULE.   According to this rule, we assume the best state of nature ($p_f = 1$; $p_g = 0$). We pick the alternative with the highest S_{ij} (the best, best).

MODIFIED OPTIMISM OF PESSIMISM.   If we are only moderately pessimistic, we set $p_g > p_f$; if very pessimistic, we set $p_g \gg p_f$. If we are moderately optimistic, we set $p_f > p_g$; if very optimistic, $p_f \gg p_g$ (always subject to the condition that the sum of the two probabilities, p_f and p_g are equal to unity). In all four cases, we pick the alternative with the highest S_{ij}.

RATIONALITY RULE.   We assume that both states are equiprobable ($p_f = p_g = 0.5$).

Indifference Maps

The indifference map generating function for the various uncertainty rules is

$$S_{ijg} = -(p_f/p_g)S_{ijf} + (1/p_g)S_{ij} \qquad (13\text{-}2)$$

which clearly represents a set of straight lines of slope $-(p_f/p_g)$ which intersect the vertical axis at $(1/p_g)S_{ij}$.

Several possibilities are shown in Figure 13–4a to e. When $p_g = 0$ (unqualified optimism), the indifference map consists of a set of vertical lines with the highest s_{ij} furthest along the horizontal axis. When $p_f = 0$ (unqualified pessimism), the lines are all horizontal with the topmost representing the highest s_{ij}. For modified optimism ($p_f > p_g$) the map has a set of negatively sloped lines with slope greater than one. For modified optimism the lines also have negative slope, but with slopes less than 1. How much the last two tilt depends on the degrees of optimism or pessimism. For rationality, the lines have unity slope.

INDIFFERENCE ANALYSIS OF THE SYNTHETIC RULE

A visual comparison of the indifference maps for some of the synthetic rules derived from formula 10–7a of Chapter 10 reveals an interesting phenome-

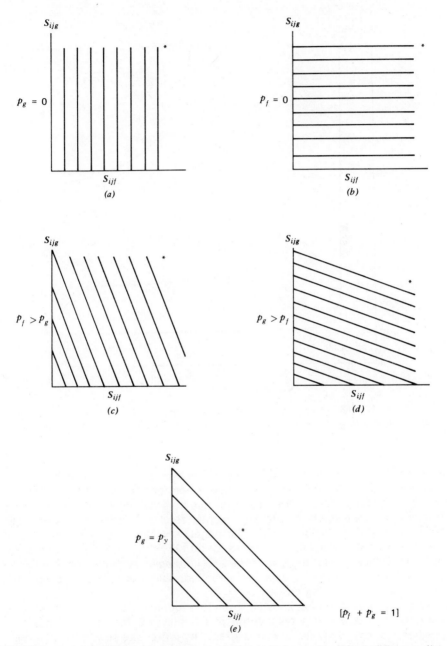

FIGURE 13–4.   *Indifference curves for several uncertainty rules. The indifference line representing the highest Sij is marked with an asterisk* (*). (a) *Unqualified optimism;* (b) *unqualified pessimism;* (c) *qualified optimism;* (d) *qualified pessimism; and* (e) *rationality.*

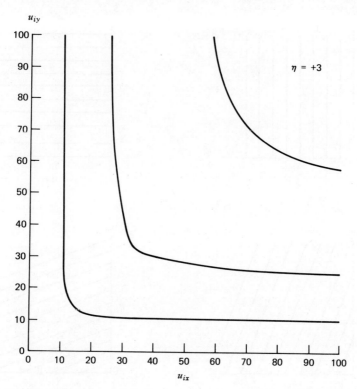

FIGURE 13–5. *Indifference map for a synthetic amalgamation rule with the parameter* η *assigned the value* +3.

non. The curvature of the map components varies in a systematic manner. Figures 13–5, 13–6, 13–7, and 13–8 show maps for eta equal to +3, +2, +1, and +½. A study of these four maps reveals that the degree of bending away from the origin lessens as eta approaches zero and increases as eta gets larger. Something similar happens for negative values of eta as is illustrated in Figures 13–9, 13–10, 13–11, and 13–12 (eta is −½, −1, −2, and zero). For negative values of eta, the curvature also increases as the absolute value of eta increases, but in the opposite direction. The curves bend toward the origin instead of bending away.

Thus, as could be anticipated from the generating formula, the value assigned to eta controls the degree of curvature of the map components: positive eta, convexity in varying degrees; negative eta, concavity in varying degrees. When eta is zero, the curves are midway between concave and convex; they are straight lines.

This relationship between curvature and eta can be made more explicit by

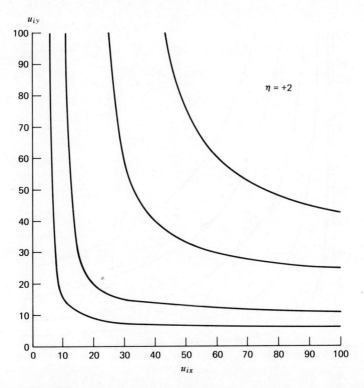

FIGURE 13–6. Indifference map for a synthetic choice rule with the paramter η assigned the value $+2$.

the following reasoning. The traditional formula found in calculus textbooks for degree of curvature is

$$K = \frac{d^2y/dx^2}{[1 + (dy/dx)^2]^{3/2}} \qquad (13\text{-}2)$$

Substituting equation 10–7a into equation 13–2 and performing the indicated operations gives

$$K = \frac{\eta[(u_{iy}^{2\eta-1} + u_{iy}^{\eta} u_{ix}^{\eta-1})/u_{ix}^{2\eta}]}{[1 + (u_{iy}/u_{ix})^{2\eta}]^{3/2}} \qquad (13\text{-}3)$$

If we confine our exploration to the place on the indifference curves where $u_{ix} = u_{iy}$, that is along the axis of symmetry of the indifference curves, formula 13–3 reduces to

$$K = \frac{\eta}{\sqrt{2}\, u_{ix}} \qquad (13\text{-}4)$$

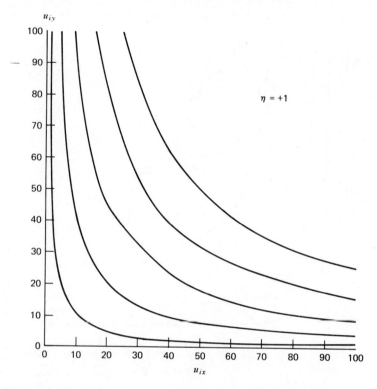

FIGURE 13–7. *Indifference map for synthetic amalgamation rule with the parameter* η *assigned the value +1.*

In words, K, the curvature of an indifference curve, is directly proportional to the value assigned to eta, and is inversely proportional to the distance of the curve from the origin. This relationship is consistent with the curves in Figures 13–5 to 13–12. As the magnitude (without regard to sign) of eta increases, the curvature of the map components increases but, on all maps, the curves closer to the origin have greater curvature than those located further from the origin (greater u_{ix}).

The curvature analysis has produced a very significant finding: **We can produce amalgamation rules that have indifference maps with any degree bending either toward or away from the origin simply by selecting the appropriate value for the parameter, eta.**

INDIFFERENCE ANALYSIS—UNEQUAL MARGINAL UTILITIES

Choice rules Nos. 1 to 7 and the synthetic rules derived from various values of the parameter, eta, have one important attribute in common. They all imply

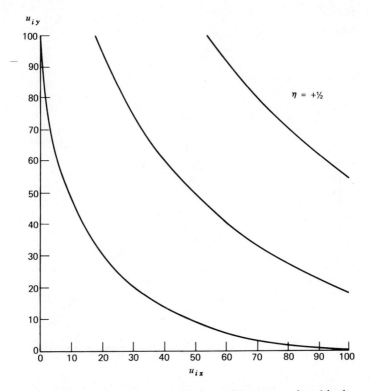

FIGURE 13-8. Indifference map for synthetic amalgamation rule with the parameter η assigned the value $+\frac{1}{2}$.

that the criteria involved have identical marginal utilities. We do not know for certain what the actual marginal utility functions are for each choice rule because marginal utilities cannot be uniquely determined from indifference maps.

Although no rules involving unequal marginal utilities have been given thus far in this book, it is possible, theoretically at least, to construct many such rules. For example, assume $M_x = X$ (the marginal utility of criterion X varies directly with the size of X) and $M_y = 1$, then

$$\text{MRS}^* = dy/dx = -M_x/M_y = -X \tag{13-5}$$

Solving this equation gives

$$2Y + X^2 = C \tag{13-6}$$

It is easily recognized that this equation is the formula for a set of parabolic arcs. When $X = 0$, $Y = C/2$. When $Y = 0$, $X = C^{1/2}$. From this we can infer that the indifference curves will be taller than they are wide. Unequal weights can alter the curve shapes in either direction.

* Marginal rate of substitution.

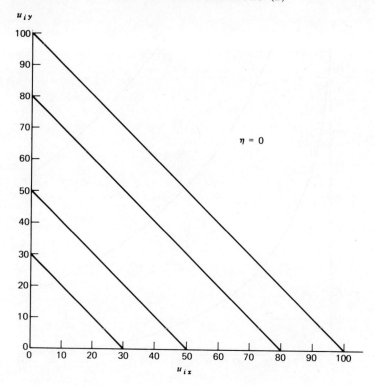

FIGURE 13-9. *Indifference map for synthetic amalgamation rule with parameter* η *assigned the value zero.*

Overview of Chapter 13

By combining Rule No. 1 (minimum, maximum or combinations of limits) with one of the others, for example, Nos. 3, 5, or 6, a composite amalgamation rule that will afford protection against low-valued criterion scores can be developed.

Uncertainty rules can be represented by indifference maps made up of straight lines, the slope of which depends on the degrees of optimism or pessimism concerning the states of nature.

A judicious selection of the value for the parameter, eta, will permit the development of an amalgamation rule with any desired degree of bending of indifference curves (either toward or away from the origin).

It is possible to develop special amalgamation rules in those cases where the details of the problematic situation call for unequal marginal utilities for the criteria. One such simple rule has indifference curves that are arcs of parabolas, taller than they are wide.

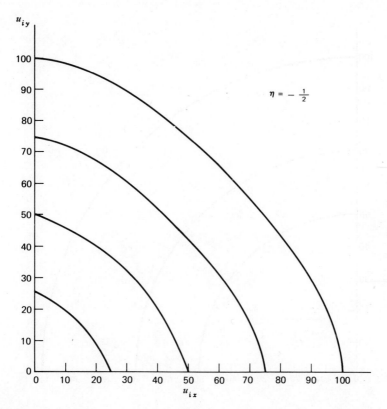

FIGURE 13–10.   Indifference map for synthetic amalgamation rule with parameter η assigned the value $-\frac{1}{2}$.

Questions for Review, Discussion, and Research

Review

1. What are the special benefits of combining Rule No. 1 with another rule?

2. Show how uncertainty rules can be represented by indifference lines of different slopes.

3. What would happen if eta was assigned decimal values or fractional values instead of integral values?

4. With unequal marginal utilities are the indifference curves symmetrical or unsymmetrical? Why?

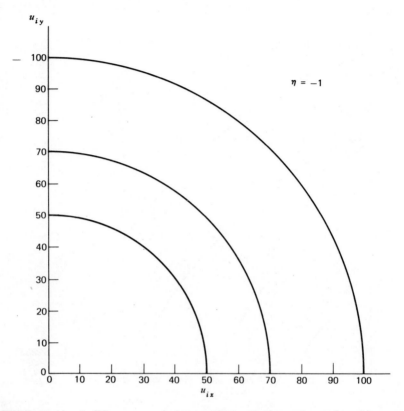

FIGURE 13–11. Indifference map for synthetic amalgamation rule with parameter η assigned the value -1.

Discussion

1. In what kinds of decision problems would Rule No. 1 be combined with another?

2. What would happen if Rule No. 1 was used with maximum limits or with a combination of upper and lower limits? What would the indifference curves look like? What would be the significance of using these limits?

3. Can you think of any situations that would justify the trouble of creating an amalgamation rule for unequal marginal utilities?

Research

1. Sketch a combination of Rule No. 1 (with various kinds of limits) with one or more of the other rules, in three dimensions. What happens if the

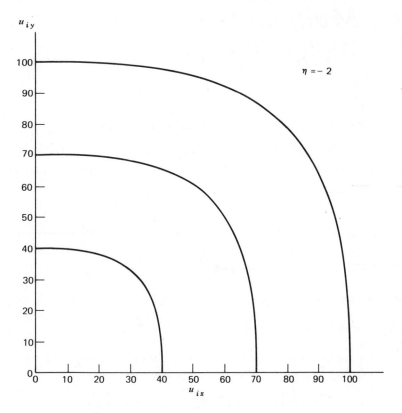

FIGURE 13–12. *Indifference map for synthetic amalgamation rule with parameter* η *assigned the value* -2.

limits are applied to one criterion only? To two only? If one was an upper limit and another a lower limit?

2. By using different marginal utility functions (increasing, diminishing, s-shaped, and the like) and by using unequal marginal utilities for criteria, construct synthetic amalgamation rules for a three-criterion problem.

3. Construct indifference maps for extreme values of eta; for example, $+10$ and -10. How high would you have to go with eta to make the indifference curves virtually rectangular? What is the significance of rectangular indifference curves?

4. Substitution elasticity or trade-off elasticity is defined as the percent change in criterion X produced by a percent change in criterion Y. Explore this idea and try to decide if it is more or less useful than TOR or MRS.

14. Multiple Criterion Weighting (I)

This chapter deals with the problem of weighting multiple criteria. Two methods of estimating criterion weights are presented along with a discussion of attendant difficulties.

CRITERION TRADE-OFF RATES

Virtually every multiple objective decision problem involves criteria of differing importance to the decision maker and to the parties affected. Some interests are more urgent than others; some objectives must be given priority over others.

How can the relative importance of one criterion compared to a second be conceptualized? There are several possibilities; it might be that:

1. Both criteria are indispensable and no trade-off is possible.
2. Both are indispensable up to some limiting value, but beyond that limit additional quantities are of little or no value.
3. Both are indispensable up to some limiting value, and beyond that value trade-off is possible, although the trade-off rate may be variable.
4. One of the criteria is indispensable, but the second can be traded-off without limitation.
5. Neither criterion is indispensable; either can be traded-off, although one may be more important than the other.

It is quite possible, in a particular decision problem that all five of the foregoing possibilities will be represented.

Possibility 1 involves critical criteria expressed as attributes (not variables) and does not allow for any trade-offs.

Possibility 2 is a restatement of Choice Rule No. 1. Trade-offs are not possible outside the limits, and are possible without restraint, within the limits.

Possibility 3 is a restatement of the combination of Choice Rule No. 1 with one of the others as was discussed in Chapter 13. Within the limits, possibility 3 merges into possibility 5.

Possibility 4 is a restatement of Choice Rule No. 2. For this rule, trade-off is an undefined concept.

Possibility 5 is the one for which multiple criterion weighting is a major concern.

EFFECTS OF CRITERION WEIGHTS

We have seen from the reasoning in Chapters 12 and 13 that for every amalgamation rule there is an implicit trade-off function (also called marginal rate of substitution) between pairs of criteria—as, for example, criterion X and criterion Y. Some rules imply constant exchange rates; some imply increasing or decreasing rates; some, both increasing and diminishing. We have also seen that the explicit numerical weights (w_x and w_y) act to modify the unweighted TOR or MRS.

The effect of unequal criterion weights is to alter the symmetry of the indifference curves for each amalgamation rule. One way to visualize the effect of unequal weights on an indifference map is to imagine that the map is drawn on a sheet of very stretchable rubber material. If the weight assigned to the X criterion is larger than that assigned to the Y criterion, stretch the sheet in the horizontal direction. This idea is shown in Figure 14–1. If Y's weight is greater than X's, stretch the sheet more in the vertical than the horizontal. This operation will destroy the symmetry of symmetrical curves. For example, if the curves are a set of concentric circles and a Y weight is greater than the X weight, the circles will be stretched so that they become ellipses with the longer (major) axis on the Y dimension.

EXPLICIT AND IMPLICIT CRITERION WEIGHTS

Definitions

An *explicit weight* is an externally applied factor, usually deliberately introduced, which is used to express the importance of each criterion relative to the others. Explicit weights are usually, but not always, constants.

An *implicit weight* is an internal factor, perhaps inadvertently introduced, which gives the affected criterion differential stress relative to others. Implicit weights may be either constants or variables, and they may depend on the relative magnitudes of the criterion scores. In practice, implicit weights may go unrecognized, may be imperfectly understood, and may inadvertently bias the results.

Examples of the use of explicit weights are shown in Boxes 14–1, 14–2, and 14–3. Box 14–4 is an example of one kind of implicit weight that can be

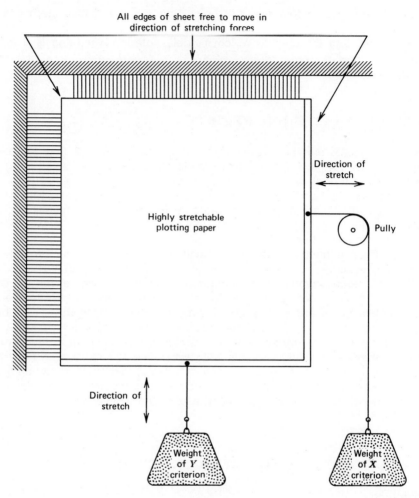

All edges of sheet free to move in
direction of stretching forces

Direction of
stretch

Highly stretchable
plotting paper

Pully

Direction of
stretch

Weight
of Y
criterion

Weight
of X
criterion

*FIGURE 14–1.   Mechanical analog of application of differential weights to stretch the
X or Y dimension in accordance with criterion weights.*

expressed as an equivalent explicit weight. Box 14–5 shows an example of
implicit weighting that can produce a double-counting bias.

Box 14–1   Combining Merit Rating Scores

The manager of a stenographic and typing pool renders services to four
departments in his company. He is rated on his ability to satisfy the
managers of each of the four departments, subject to his budgetary limitation.

In preparing his personal rating of the pool manager, each department head rates him on a 0–100 scale. These four ratings are turned in to the general manager who assigns an explicit weight to each department's rating score in proportion to the quantity of pool services charged to each department. The rating formula is

$$\text{Composite score} = w_1 R_1 + w_2 R_2 + w_3 R_3 + w_4 R_4$$

where w_1, w_2, w_3, $w_4 = $ the explicit weights assigned by the general manager in proportion to the amount of services rendered to the four departments.

R_1, R_2, R_3, $R_4 = $ the rating scores on a 0–100 scale prepared by each department head.

and

$$w_1 + w_2 + w_3 + w_4 = 1.00$$

Box 14–2   Preparing a Materials Cost Index

The purchased-materials analyst for a television receiver manufacturer prepares a materials cost index annually. As part of his task, he classifies materials into a number of categories:

1. Sheet-metal parts, internal.
2. Screw-machine parts.
3. Metal castings.
4. Plastic-molded parts.
5. Bright metal parts.
6. Electrical parts.
7. Vacuum tubes, transistors, diodes.
8. Picture tubes.
9. Cabinets, knobs.
10. Hardware.
11. Wire.
12. Paper and printed matter.
13. Cartons and shipping materials.
14. Miscellaneous materials and supplies.

He compares the prices within each category at two points in time by means of the ratio:

$$\frac{P_j}{P_j'} = \frac{\text{the price of the } j\text{th material at year's end}}{\text{the price of the } j\text{th material at year's start}}$$

Because some categories (for example, picture tubes) account for more of the total materials cost than others, he chooses to express the differential contributions as explicit weights. The material index is

Purchased material
Cost index
$$= \prod_{j=1}^{14} \left(\frac{P_j}{P_j'} \right)^{w_j}$$

where w_j is the proportion of the total materials cost contributed by the jth material category and $\Sigma w_j = 1.00$.

Box 14–3   A Plant Location Problem

A large nationally known manufacturing firm is contemplating opening a new factory somewhere in the United States to produce a new product for the automotive industry. The manufacturing process is mainly one of precision assembly of purchased components, and extensive electrical and mechanical testing follows assembly. The search committee is instructed to find a number of suitable sites, taking into account the following criteria (order not significant):

1. Availability of skilled labor.
2. Wage rates paid by similar producers.
3. Experience with organized labor in the locality.
4. Adequacy of housing, educational, and cultural facilities for managerial and professional personnel.
5. Adequacy of public utilities (clean water, clean air, power, and natural gas).
6. Adequacy of public transportation for people and materials (buses, rail, air, motor truck, and water).
7. Receptivity of local communities to construction of a new plant.
8. Nature and extent of tax and other financial inducements offered by state and municipal authorities.
9. Adequacy of medical and hospital facilities in the community.
10. Climate regarding racial conflict or integration of schools and housing.
11. Economic cost factors such as land, building, and transportation costs, insurance rates, and availability of reasonably priced expansion space.

A subcommittee of the site search committee was set up to develop a set of criterion scales and criterion weights to assist in the comparative evaluation of alternative plant sites. The weights were assigned as follows:

Factor	Weight	Factor	Weight	Factor	Weight
1*	3.0	5*	3.0	9*	1.5
2	1.0	6*	2.0	10*	2.0
3	1.0	7	2.0	11	5.0
4	2.0	8	1.0		

Items marked with an asterisk (*) must meet minimum standards before the site can be reconsidered for selection; beyond the minimum levels, weights are applied as indicated.

Box 14–4—Employee Merit Rating System

In an employee merit rating system, there are five criteria, and each is assigned a maximum number of points as follows:

Name of Criterion	Maximum Grade Points
1. Employee productivity	25
2. Employee reliability	20
3. Employee attitude toward company	15
4. Employee cooperation with others	10
5. Employee promotion potential	10

Interpretation of Grade Point Scores

	25	20	15	10
Outstanding	20-25	16-20	12-15	8-10
Very good	15-20	12-16	9-12	6-8
Meets minimum standards	10-15	8-12	6-9	4-6
Poor—improvement needed	5-10	4-8	3-6	2-4
Extremely unsatisfactory consider termination	0-5	0-4	0-3	0-2

Note. The implicit weighting of this rating system could be converted into explicit weighting by employing a uniform 0–10 scale and by using the following weights: $w_1 = 2.5; w_2 = 2.0; w_3 = 1.50; w_4 = 1.0; w_5 = 1.0$.

Box 14–5   Determination of Credit-Worthiness of Card Holders

A credit-card firm rates the credit worthiness of potential credit-card holders by the following criteria (all equally weighted):

1. Annual income from all sources.
2. Cost of residence (if owned) or monthly rental of apartment or house.
3. Experience with other creditors.
4. Number of dependents.
5. Amount of present indebtedness.
6. Number of years in present employment.
7. Number of years living in present residence.
8. Character references.

Note. Because annual income and cost (or rental) of residence are highly positively correlated, there is double counting of the income factor. Because length of employment and length of stay in residence are positively correlated, these two double count the stability factor. The double counting introduces bias in favor of some factors over others, perhaps, unintentionally.

When Explicit Weights Have No Meaning

When one alternative in a set completely dominates another, no combination of positive explicit weights can alter the dominance and, therefore, the weights are meaningless and irrelevant. It is self-evident that alternative

$$[A_1] \equiv [100, 100]$$

will always be preferred to

$$[A_2] \equiv [50, 50]$$

and that no method of weighting the criteria by positive numbers can alter the superiority of $[A_1]$ over $[A_2]$. It is only in the event that an alternative is not dominant (it has both high and low scores relative to others) that weights can make a difference.

For example if

$$[A_3] \equiv [100, 20]$$
and
$$[A_4] \equiv [\ 30, 80]$$

by the sum-of-the-points method, $sum_3 = 120$ and $sum_4 = 110$; $[A_3]$ would be preferred to $[A_4]$. However, if the first criterion was assigned the explicit weight 1.0; and the second criterion was assigned the explicit weight, 2.0, the preference order would change because

$$\text{weighted } sum_3 = 1 \times 100 + 2 \times 20 = 140$$
$$\text{weighted } sum_4 = 1 \times \ 30 + 2 \times 80 = 190$$

Should a particular problem have one alternative that dominates all others, but other alternatives have score-sets with both high and low scores, the assignment of explicit weights may not affect the first rank earned by the dominant alternative, but it may affect the ranking of the remaining non-dominant alternatives.

MUST EXPLICIT WEIGHTS BE CONSTANTS?

Explicit criterion weights are used to express, by means of a simple number, the importance of one criterion relative to others. Therefore, if the importance of a criterion changes for any reason whatsoever, its weight should be adjusted to reflect that change.

Often weight variations are systematic, that is, the change happens in some regular fashion. In these cases, the weight can be represented by some function of an exogenous variable. Examples of some sources of change are: secular trend, seasons of the year, employee seniority, geographical position, age, income level, and the like. We could expect the explicit weight assigned to the item-class "home heating fuel," used in the preparation of an index of consumers' prices, to vary with latitude (being lowest in the region closest to the equator and higher, according to season, in the colder northern regions). Also, the weight assigned to regular income relative to capital appreciation in personal investment programs for middle-income people can be expected to vary with the age of the investor.

Because explicit weights are reflections of human judgments, both person-to-person and firm-to-firm variations are to be expected. Thus, in a collective bargaining negotiation, the firm may place a fixed amount of money on the bargaining table with the statement (understood, if not explicitly stated), "Spend this money on increases in wages and fringe benefits in any combination, as long as the total package does not cost us more than the amount of our offer." The union may then decide to apportion the money package among:

1. Increases in hourly wage rates.
2. Increases in medical and life insurance benefits.
3. Increases in vacation days and paid holidays.
4. Supplemental unemployment benefits.
5. Increased pension benefits.

The union members will have differing views on how the benefit package should be put together. The high seniority workers, who have less fear of layoffs, will place lower emphasis on supplemental unemployment benefits than will the newly hired men. The older workers will place more emphasis on increased pension benefits than the younger people. Women workers with employed husbands may not care a bit about increased health insurance benefits because this protection is provided by the husband's employer. The single, widowed, or divorced woman employees, on the other hand, will find medical benefit increases highly attractive.

Special circumstances can produce shifting priorities. For a receptionist's job, pleasing personal appearance will be assigned greater weight than manual dexterity; for the factory operative, the emphasis would undoubtedly be reversed. In industrial purchasing practice, the weights assigned to the factors price, availability, delivery, quality, service, and terms of payment will be very much affected by whether the order is large or small, whether there is ample lead time, or if it is an emergency need.

Thus, explicit weights may be functions of one or more exogenous variables (for example, time or distance), they may be constants whose actual numerical values are subject to adjustment to fit specific conditions, or they may be invariant; which, depends on the nature of the decision-evaluation problem at hand.

TECHNIQUES FOR ESTIMATING EXPLICIT WEIGHTS

In some instances, the numbers to be used for explicit weights can be uniquely determined from the facts in the case, although judgment may still play a part. In the earlier example of the general manager's preparing the stenographic pool manager's merit-rating score, the proportion of services rendered to each of the four using departments could be readily obtained from company cost records (assuming that they exist). However, he could have decided to count each department manager's rating equally instead of proportionately if, in his judgment, this was a better way of assigning weights. With either alternative, the task of estimating the weights is simply defined and no conceptual difficulty is present.

In other, perhaps more typical, decision problems, the explicit weights cannot be uniquely determined from any simple rule because the weights must reflect individual, group, or organizational preferences of objectives. These preferences are difficult, if not impossible, to quantify with precision, and some method for eliciting information concerning the criterion preferences, to aid in arriving at estimates of explicit weights is sorely needed.

The material for preparing estimates of explicit weights is crude and imprecise, but until better methods become available, we shall have to make do with present techniques. The alternatives to using these crude methods are (a) outright guesses at weights, and (b) to ignore weights entirely; that is, assume they are all equal. The decision maker must decide for himself which is the best way of dealing with the criterion weighting problem.

Estimating Begins with Ranking of Criteria

The first step in the estimating process is to arrange the decision-evaluation-rating criteria (all of which are assumed to be unequally important) in rank order of importance giving due cognizance to tied ranks. In practice this is a rather easy task, although if more than one person is involved, their rankings may not agree perfectly. It is often convenient to prepare a dual ranking chart with straight ranking (best=1, next best=2, etc.) and an inverse ranking (worst=1, next worse=2, etc). For a six-criterion situation the chart might look something like Table 14–1.

TABLE 14–1

Criterion Number	Rank (Straight)	Rank (Inverse)
1	3	4
2	1 (best)	6 (best)
3	6 (worst)	1 (worst)
4	4	3
5	5	2
6	2	5

If the problem involves group preferences rather than an individual judgment, the ranking can be determined by either polling the group members and arriving at a consensus ranking or by taking the individual rankings and computing a simple average rank for each criterion.[2] Finding the average rank from two persons' preferences (Mr. Smith and Mr. Jones) can be accomplished as shown in Table 14–2.

TABLE 14–2

Criterion Number	Inverse Rank Smith	Inverse Rank Jones	Average Rank
1	4	5	4.5
2	6	6	6 (best)
3	1	1	1 (worst)
4	3	2	2.5
5	2	3	2.5
6	5	4	4.5

The problem may involve the interests of more than one faction in an organization or political entity, each of which has different preferences. One example of this was given earlier in the case of the assignment of portions of a company wage offer among several types of benefits. As when dealing with preferences of two or more persons, some averaging process is indicated, although with the case of factions it may be wise to give some recognition to the relative urgency, legitimacy, or trouble-making capability of each.

When factional rankings are to be averaged and there is a differential urgency to the criteria, the same logic as above can be applied but with urgency weights assigned (see "The Problem of Infinite Regress," in Chapter 16). An example is shown in Table 14–3.

TABLE 14–3

Criterion Number	Faction No. 1 Score ($w_1 = 3.0$)	Faction No. 2 Score ($w_2 = 2.0$)	Faction No. 3 Score ($w_3 = 1.0$)	Weighted Mean of 3 Faction Scores
1	4×3	5×2	6×1	4.33 [2]
2	6×3	6×2	4×1	5.66 [1]
3	1×3	1×2	3×1	1.33 [6]
4	3×3	2×2	1×1	2.33 [5]
5	2×3	3×2	4×1	2.66 [4]
6	5×3	4×2	2×1	4.17 [3]
	↑__ Inverse rank			Straight rank __↑
	↑__Weight			

Alternative Technique No. 1—Estimation from a Ratio Scale

The estimation of criterion weights from a ranking can be aided by use of a ratio scale similar to that shown in Figure 14–2. The criteria are placed along the scale on the basis of their relative importance to the individual or group. The procedure is as follows:

1. Arrange the criteria in rank order of importance.
2. Place a numbered arrow alongside the 100 mark of the scale and mark it with the number of the most important criterion.
3. For the second ranking criterion, place an arrow in a position on the ratio scale corresponding to its importance relative to the most important, and mark it with the number of the second most important criterion.
4. Repeat this process with every other criterion until all have been placed

TABLE 14–4

Criterion Number	Straight Rank	Place on Ratio Scale	Ratio of This Criterion to Lowest[a]
1	3	75	3.0
2	1	100	4.0
3	6	25	1.0
4	4	42	1.7
5	5	42	1.7
6	2	75	3.0

[a] The numbers in the last column can be used as explicit weights.

on the ratio scale in a position corresponding to their relative importance compared with all others.

5. Compute the ratio of each criterion's ratio score to the score for the least important criterion and place these ratios in a table like Table 14–4 (data from Figure 14–2).

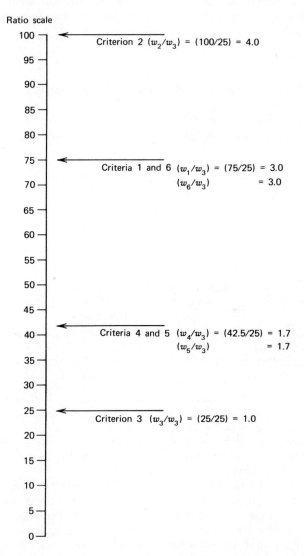

Ratio scale

Criterion 2 (w_2/w_3) = (100/25) = 4.0

Criteria 1 and 6 (w_1/w_3) = (75/25) = 3.0
(w_6/w_3) = 3.0

Criteria 4 and 5 (w_4/w_3) = (42.5/25) = 1.7
(w_5/w_3) = 1.7

Criterion 3 (w_3/w_3) = (25/25) = 1.0

FIGURE 14–2. Illustration of the use of a ratio chart for estimation of criterion weights. Criteria are placed on the scale in a position corresponding to their urgency relative to the most important.

A simple variation of the ratio rule is as follows:

1. Designate 100 points as the sum of all criterion weights.
2. Allocate the points among the criteria in proportion to the relative importance of each, being certain to use up all 100 points in the process.
3. Use the numbers so obtained directly as criterion weights, or divide every number by the same factor such that the smallest criterion weight equals unity.

Alternative Technique No. 2—Estimation From a Scaling Factor

This method depends on the ability to devise or conceive of a pair of equally attractive alternatives scored on two criteria, preferably the least and most important. If

$$[A] \equiv [X_a, Y_a] \text{ and } [B] \equiv [X_b, Y_b]$$

and [A] and [B] are equivalent, then

$$w_x X_a + w_y Y_a = w_x X_b + w_y Y_b$$

from which we get

$$w_x/w_y = Y_b - Y_a/X_a - X_b$$

where X_a = the score for alternative [A] on criterion X.
X_b = the score for alternative [B] on criterion X.
Y_a = the score for alternative [A] on criterion Y.
Y_b = the score for alternative [B] on criterion Y.
w_x = the explicit weight for criterion X.
w_y = the explicit weight for criterion Y; and criterion X is the most important of the set; Y, the least important.

We assume that the decision maker will be able to find values for X_a, X_b, Y_a, and Y_b in the usual manner. If, for purposes of illustration, [A] ≡ [20,90] and [B] ≡ [30,50], then (w_x/w_y) = 4.0.

What remains now is to replace the weight of the most important criterion by the number 4.0, to replace the least important by 1.0 and, by linear interpolation, to adjust the intermediate weights.

If the criteria used for devising the pair of equivalent alternatives were not the most and least important but, instead, were the second and least important, the results would be different in detail, but not in conception.

Although we now have some justification for establishing numerical values for the explicit weights corresponding to the most and least important criteria, the justification for the intermediate values is much less firm. This happens because the ranking procedure always causes some loss of information concerning the true spacing of numbers in a sequence. If, for example, the extremes of a three-number sequence are 2 and 10; when using inverse rank numbers, 2 has the rank 1, and 10, the rank 3; and any number greater than 2 and less than 10 could be legitimately assigned the rank number 2. The fact that the intermediate number may fall very close to either the top or bottom numbers in the sequence is obscured by the ranking process. Either 2.00001 or 9.9999 would be assigned the rank 2. This same loss of information occurs when criteria are ranked for preference; for this reason, it is often worthwhile to make a fine adjustment in the intermediate weights and not to rely on inverse rank numbers.

The fine adjustment of intermediate weights is accomplished by making comparisons of criteria of adjacent rank, for example, criteria no. 2, no. 1, and no. 6 in the *Faction Weight* sequence. This gives:

Most important	no. 2	$w_2 = 4.0$
Next in importance	no. 1	$w_1 = 3.5$
Next in importance	no. 6	$w_6 = 3.3$

Now we ask, "Is no. 1 closer in importance to no. 2 or to no. 6? If it is closer to no. 2, we adjust w_1 closer to 4.0; if closer to no. 6, we adjust it to approach 3.3; if it seems about right as it is, we leave it alone.

We repeat the procedure for the next triple:

Most important	no. 1	w_1 as adjusted
Next in importance	no. 6	$w_6 = 3.3$
Next in importance	no. 5	$w_5 = 2.1$

and make any indicated adjustment to w_6.

The process is repeated again for the next triple:

Most important	no. 6	w_6 as adjusted
Next in importance	no. 5	$w_5 = 2.1$
Next in importance	no. 4	$w_4 = 1.9$

until every intermediate weight has been tested for spacing between its superior and inferior. This procedure must be repeated a sufficient number of times until the fine adjustments of intermediate weights stabilize.

TENTATIVE WEIGHT SETS—SINGLE AND MULTIPLE

There will be occasions, particularly in large organizations with important, complex problems, when the responsibility for making estimates of criterion weights and for final choice among alternatives will be divided. For example, the chief of a firm, the government agency, and the large organization may rely on their staffs for identification of feasible alternatives, for establishing criteria, and for evaluation of the alternatives on the multiple criteria. But the staff may have only the vaguest notion of the weights that the chief will place on the criteria. And very often even the chief, himself, does not know what the relative urgencies of criteria are because interest-group pressures and factional divisions change with the passage of time. It is very possible that priorities that seemed just right at the time the problem study began are obsolete and irrelevant by the time the choice has to be made. In circumstances like these, the staff may have to present alternative weight sets, solve the matrix for each set of weights, and leave to the chief the choice of correct priorities.

One way to proceed under such fluid circumstances is to develop a set of weights for each interest group that has a legitimate stake in the decision outcome. This can be done by any one of the estimating methods described earlier in this chapter. By using these weights, one for each interest group, the alternatives are evaluated and placed in rank order of desirability according to each priority set. Then the staff reports as follows:

> We find that there are a number of interest groups that have a legitimate stake in the outcome of this decision. Each group has a different view of the priorities of the various criteria used in the evaluation of the ten alternatives under consideration. The Staff has identified the most probable criterion weights for each interest group and has proceeded to rank the alternatives for desirability as we think they would be if they were rated by each interest group. In summary:

Interest Group	Weight Set	Preference-Ordering for Alternatives Based on These Weights
A	1	10, 6, 5, 1, 4, 9, 8, 2, 7, 3
B	2	6, 10, 1, 5, 4, 9, 8, 2, 7, 3
C	3	5, 10, 6, 1, 4, 8, 9, 3, 7, 2
D	4	10, 5, 6, 1, 9, 8, 4, 3, 7, 2
E	5	2, 6, 5, 9, 10, 4, 3, 1, 8, 7

> Alternatives 10, 5, 6, and 1 seem to be near the top of most interest group rankings. The Staff recommends that the final choice be made from among these four alternatives.

As a matter of practical politics and psychology, this procedure of developing multiple sets of weights and multiple rankings has much appeal. The cost difference is small because the work, after the weights have been estimated, is primarily computational; this is usually not expensive to perform. The claims of competing interest groups will be carefully considered making the probability of encountering unpleasant, unanticipated consequences less, which is good political tactics. The chief will still have leeway in choosing among alternatives offered to him by the staff. Having options makes it much less likely that he will capriciously reject the staff's recommendations because their thoroughness makes him feel hemmed in, or because he feels that it is depriving him of the power to make decisions.

Notes and References

1. Several authors that deal with multiple criterion weighting are:
   (a) R. T. Eckenrode, "Weighting Multiple Criteria," *Management Science* (November 1965).
   (b) Paul G. Goodman, "A Method for Evaluation of Subsystem Alternate Designs," *I.E.E.E. Transactions on Engineering Management* (February 1972), pp. 12–21.
   (c) J. R. Miller, *Professional Decision Making* (New York, Praeger Publishers, 1970).
   (d) R. N. Shepherd, "On Subjectively Optimum Selection Among Multi-attribute Alternatives," in M. W. Shelly, II and G. L. Bryan, *Human Judgments and Optimality* (New York, John Wiley and Sons, Inc., 1964), pp. 257–281.

2. See P. G. Goodman, op. cit., for an example of the use of the polling method.

Important Words and Concepts

Symmetrical indifference curve
Explicit weight
Implicit weight
Exogenous variable
Ranking criteria by importance
Organizational faction
Differential urgency
Ratio scale
Scaling factor
Inverse rank
Linear interpolation
Fine adjustment
Tentative weight set

Overview of Chapter 14

Most multiple objective decision problems involve criteria of differing importance, and explicit numerical criterion weights can be used to express these differences. Implicit weights, inadvertently included, may cause unintentional bias.

Explicit weights have meaning only with nondominant alternatives. If an alternative is dominant, it will remain so regardless of the size of the weights assigned to the criteria. Explicit weights may either be constants or functions of exogenous variables. Weights may also vary from person to person, and from interest group to group.

Weight estimation begins with ranking decision criteria in order of importance. Thereafter, weights can be estimated from a ratio scale or a scaling factor. Fine adjustment of criterion weights should be made to overcome the loss of information from plain rankings.

In some problems, it is advisable to solve the matrix with alternative weight sets. This enables one to judge how different interests might view the relative desirability of decision alternatives.

Questions for Review, Discussion, and Research

Review

1. How can differential urgencies among multiple criteria be conceptualized?

2. What is the effect of assigning unequal criterion weights on the shapes of the indifference curves?

3. Distinguish between explicit and implicit weights.

4. What is the effect of criterion weighting on a dominant alternative? Demonstrate your conclusion with a numerical example.

5. Must explicit weights be constants?

6. What is an exogenous variable and how does it apply to multiple criterion weighting?

7. What causes criterion weights to differ from person to person?

8. How do straight and inverse rankings differ?

9. How can a compromise ranking of different persons or factions be accomplished?

10. How is the ratio scale used for estimation of criterion weights?

11. On what ability does the scaling factor method of weight estimation depend?

12. Why are fine adjustments of weights necessary after performing criterion ranking or other methods of estimation?

13. What are some of the advantages of solving the score matrix by using alternative sets of weights?

Discussion

1. Suppose that the decision maker found the weight estimation procedure too difficult, time consuming, or imprecise and as a result decided to ignore weights altogether. What would be the net effect?

2. What are some of the advantages and disadvantages of the polling method for estimating criterion rankings? (Hint: see reference 1b)

3. What theoretical objections are there to using raw, inverse, criterion rank numbers as criterion weights? Would you feel any differently if the number of criteria in a problem were very small? Very large?

4. What would be the effect of multiplying all criterion weights by the same constant?

5. What would be the effect of having one criterion weight very much larger than the others (say, 10:1)?

6. Under what circumstances would variable weights be appropriate?

Research

1. Search the literature for solved multiple criterion decision or evaluation procedures and try to identify the authors' ways for dealing with criterion weights.

2. Conceive of a simple, multiple-criterion decision or evaluation problem that will affect multiple interests. Conduct a poll of the different interest groups and try to find out how each ranks the criteria for importance. Can you find a satisfactory compromise ranking? If not, what would you do?

3. Develop a multi-alternative, multiple criterion score matrix having these characteristics:
   (a) 1 dominant alternative.
   (b) 1 contra-dominant alternative.
   (c) three or more nondominant alternatives made up of different scores but all with identical row sums.
   Can you find any criterion weights that will alter the rank order of the dominant and contra-dominant alternatives, using any amalgamation rule of your choice? Test the effect on the ranking of assigning a very high weight number to one of the criteria.

15. Multiple Criterion Weighting (II)

This chapter examines three additional topics in multiple criterion weighting:

1. *Sensitivity analysis.*
2. *Inferring criterion weights from rater's rankings.*
3. *Criterion impurity and multiple-counting bias.*

SENSITIVITY ANALYSIS

For problems of importance, a sensitivity analysis should be performed to discover just how sensitive is the ranking of alternatives to small changes in criterion weights. If the ranking remains unaffected as the weights are changed by modest increments, this can be accepted as evidence that small errors in the estimation or criterion weights are not material. The weights can be changed—one at a time, by small amounts—until a significant alteration in the ranking of alternatives is detected.

In actuality, a full sensitivity analysis requires the complete solution of the score matrix for each trial condition. The trials involve incremental changes in one or more criterion weights. With a large number of criteria, this process could involve hundreds or thousands of trials, and could be prohibitively expensive if manual methods were employed. But, if an electronic computer is available, thousands of computations can be done in a very short time.

What we are seeking is knowledge of how much a particular weight must be changed to produce a *significant* alteration in the initial ranking of alternatives. How much of a change in the ranking is significant depends on the details of the specific decision problem. Two possibilities for defining the standard are:

1. The coefficient of linear correlation between the original rank-order series and a trial ranking series drops from 1.00 to ____(perhaps, 0.8).
2. The FOM for the second ranking alternative (or any other in the set) rises to equal the FOM of the first-ranking alternative in the original series.

Having established a standard of significance, we vary one of the criterion weights—first increasing it, then decreasing it, until the standard is reached. Weights can be changed two at a time or three at a time if desired. If the range of variation is substantial, we can be confident that small errors in weight estimation will not have a material effect on the rank order of alternatives. If one or more of the weights proves to be very sensitive, the analysis will indicate how accurately they must be estimated and how stable is the ranking of alternatives.

INFERRING CRITERION WEIGHTS AND ETA
FROM RATER'S RANKINGS

Under favorable circumstances, it is possible to make reasonably good inferences of both criterion weights and eta* from a rater's merit-ordering of the alternatives in a set.[1] The rater is presented with a score matrix similar to that shown in Figure 5–3 (taking care to allow him to know nothing else about the alternatives but their criterion scores). He is asked to arrange the alternatives according to his preferences. He can do this by pair-by-pair comparison as was shown in Figure 10–1, or in any other way he likes. Pair-by-pair, although the most tedious and time consuming, gives the most accurate preference ordering.

The result of this preliminary procedure is a rank-order number for each alternative. Taken together they make up the *R series*. As a first approximation, a multiple, linear regression computation is performed using the *R* series as the criterion variable and the matrix scores (columns) as the predictor variables.[2] Admittedly, for a large multiple criterion decision matrix, this operation can be very difficult and time-consuming, but if it is done on a high-speed electronic computer, it takes very much less time.[3]

The result of the multiple regression analysis is an equation in the form:

$$K_i = w_1 u_{i1} + w_2 u_{i2} + \ldots w_j u_{ij}, \ldots + w_m u_{im}$$

where w_j is the desired criterion weight for the jth criterion.
K_i is a number corresponding to a figure-of-merit for the ith alternative.

Just how good this regression equation is and how accurate the weights are can be determined by correlating the *R* series with the K_i series. (The K_i series is obtained by multiplying the found weights by the corresponding cell entries and performing the summation across the matrix rows.) A coefficient of linear correlation near to one indicates that the rater's weighting logic has been captured.

Of course, there is no reason to believe that the rater necessarily uses a

---

* Eta is the discriminator parameter used also for the multiplicity of synthetic amalgamation rules described in Chapter 10.

linear-additive model for ranking alternatives; that is, an amalgamation method based on a value of eta equal to zero. He may have unknowingly used an amalgamation rule with an eta different from zero.

To explore this possibility, nonlinear, multiple regression analyses are performed by computer for a series of values of eta both positive and negative. Again the coefficients of linear correlation are computed from the resulting K series and the R series. The value of eta that gives the largest coefficient of correlation is the best estimate.

It is quite likely that the criterion weights that emerge from the nonlinear multiple regression computations will be different for each eta tried, and the more the trial etas deviate from zero, the greater will be the changes in the found weights.

It is difficult (for a procedure as complex as this) to know in advance just how many alternatives there must be in the set undergoing ranking for the end results to be reliable. If too few alternatives are used in the multiple regression computations, the reliability of the higher numbered weights will be doubtful, and the procedure will give unsatisfactory results. Also to produce a reliable estimate of the eta used by the rater, the procedure should not be attempted without many alternatives (perhaps 100) and several ranking trials.

This procedure can be repeated with different raters ranking the same alternatives. If successful, it can reveal the criterion weights and the values of eta used by each in forming his intuitive judgments. The other raters may be representatives of various interest groups who are known to have different weights and to use rules with different etas.

If the procedures outlined above are carried out by computer, the workload on the executive-rater will involve only the ranking step. This part can be tedious, but worthwhile if the rater is a highly placed executive whose decision-making logic we are trying to uncover. Obviously, this complex method for criterion and eta estimation cannot be used for trivial problems or insignificant decisions, but if the matter is of sufficient moment, the large outlays for manpower, programming, and computer time would be justifiable.

CRITERION IMPURITY AND WEIGHTING BIAS

The Nonredundancy Assumption

The construction logic and the indifference analyses of the various amalgamation rules discussed in the previous chapters were based, in part, on an unstated but very important assumption that the decision criteria are all nonredundant (synonyms: pure, independent). In the geometric analogy, the nonredundancy assumption implies that all the criterion axes are orthogonal (mutually perpendicular). This important assumption requires clarification.

Definitions

Two criteria are *redundant-synergistic* if they are identical in effect, if not in name. This condition causes the same criterion to appear more than once in the decision matrix under different names, and the result is multiple-counting bias. For example, if one criterion was "high before-tax profits" and the second, "high after-tax profits," it is quite evident that the two criteria are, at least, partially redundant. The effect of using these two criteria in this way is the equivalent to using one of them with a doubling of the weight. The redundant-synergistic condition is illustrated in Figure 15–1a.

If two equally weighted criteria are *redundant-antagonistic*, they act to cancel each other's contributions to the score matrix. The effect of using two criteria of this type is to wipe out their influence; it is the equivalent of using one of them with a zero weight. The redundant-antagonistic condition is illustrated in Figure 15–1b.

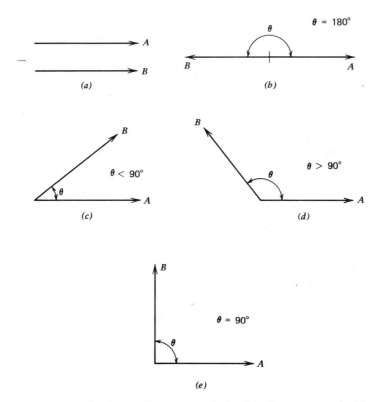

FIGURE 15–1.   *Graphical representation of relationships between two decision criteria,* A *and* B. (a) *Redundant-synergistic;* (b) *redundant-antagonistic;* (c) *overlapping-synergistic;* (d) *overlapping antagonistic; and* (e) *independent.*

Criteria that are only partly redundant may be called *overlapping*: *overlapping-synergistic* or *antagonistic*. Overlapping criteria are "impure" because they are really combinations of two or more criteria. The proportions of the mixture can be inferred from the angles between criterion pairs represented by their vectors. Overlapping criteria are illustrated in Figures 15–1c and 15–1d. A pair of pure criteria are shown in Figure 15–1e.

Multiple counting bias will be at its maximum when the criteria are perfectly redundant (their vectors are colinear). The bias will be minimum when the criteria are nonredundant (their vectors are orthogonal). Between orthogonality and colinearity, the bias will have intermediate effects.

Linear Correlation as a Test for Redundancy

One interpretation of a coefficient of linear correlation between two criterion series (column vectors) is that r is the *cosine of the angle between the vectors*. Then, r^2 is the proportion of shared variance between vectors; that is, the proportion of elements common to both vectors.

This interpretation of r provides a practical test for criterion redundancy or overlapping. All one need do is to compute the coefficient of linear correlation between pairs of score-matrix columns and perform a test of significance. An r significantly different from zero indicates that the criteria are not pure. An r significantly different from unity indicates that the criteria are overlapping. A positive coefficient means that the overlap is synergistic; a negative coefficient means that the overlap is antagonistic. Box 15–1 contains a tabular summary of the interpretations of r and r^2.

Box 15–1   Interpretation of Criterion Correlations

Condition	Angles between Vectors A and B	Cosine of Angle (r)	Statement of Commonality
Purity (independence)	±90°	0.00	No elements of A in B; none of B in A
Redundant synergistic	0° or 360°	1.00	100 percent of A in B
Redundant-antagonistic	±180°	−1.00	100 percent of A in B
Overlapping-synergistic	0°<θ<90° 360°>θ>270°	>0.00 <1.00	Some A in B, or Some B in A
Overlapping-antagonistic	90°<θ<180° 270°>θ>180°	>0.00 <−1.00	Some A in B; Some B in A

TABLE 15–1   Criterion Scores for a set of Hypothetical Alternatives. A *and* B *Are Redundant-Symergistic;* C *and* D *Are Redundant Antagonistic;* E *and* F *Are Overlapping-Synergistic;* G *and* H *Are Approximately Independent;* I *and* J *Are Overlapping-Antagonistic. All Are Significant to the 0.05 level.*

Alternative	Criteria									
	A	B	C	D	E	F	G	H	I	J
1	20	40	150	20	20	10	10	60	20	110
2	40	60	120	60	30	60	30	90	40	130
3	50	70	110	80	50	70	40	20	50	90
4	60	80	90	100	60	30	60	60	60	100
5	70	90	80	140	60	110	60	110	70	70
6	80	100	70	160	80	90	70	10	70	120
7	90	110	50	180	100	70	80	70	80	50
8	100	120	40	220	100	110	100	30	100	30
9	120	140	30	240	120	140	120	110	120	70
10	130	150	10	300	130	110	130	70	90	80
	$r=1.0$		$r=1.0$		$r=0.76$		$r=0.14$		$r=-0.69$	
	$\theta=0°$		$\theta=180°$		$\theta=40°$		$\theta=82°$		$\theta=133°$	

Table 15–1 shows a number of matrix columns that correspond to criteria exhibiting different degrees of redundancy. Criterion pair A and B are redundant-synergistic; C and D are redundant-antagonistic; E and F, overlaping-synergistic; I and J, overlapping-antagonistic; and G and F, close to being nonredundant.

The fact that we must apply a statistical test of significance to the correlations suggests that the reliability of the test for nonredundancy will improve as the number of alternatives in the matrix is increased. If the particular matrix has just a few alternatives, the test for criterion purity will not give useful results, but if it has many alternatives (for example, from 30 to 100 are included), the reliability of the test for nonredundancy will be satisfactory.

The test for criterion purity should be performed with every criterion pair. If they all prove to be pure, an extremely unlikely occurrence except in the most meticulously defined decision problem, we can be content that the multiple-counting bias has been expunged. If, on the other hand, some pairs of criteria prove to be redundant or substantially overlapping, some further steps are required. If highly redundant, one of the pair can be dropped from the matrix altogether; if substantially overlapping, some method of purification must be employed.

How to Purify Overlapping Criteria

The most direct method for purifying criteria is to factor-analyze the score matrix and to use the orthogonal factors as "new" criteria.[4] This method may present some conceptual difficulties if the factors are not readily interpretable in terms of the particular decision problem.

A less elegant, but easier to conceptualize, method involves finding a *surrogate* criterion to replace the overlapping pair, triple, or *n*-uple of criteria. This can be done by combining two or more criteria believed to be closely associated with the desired one. For example, if a sportswriter wished to rank all of the baseball players in major league baseball by *batting ability*, he could make his pure criterion series, batting ability, from an amalgamation of the following:

1. Batting average.
2. Number of home runs hit in season.
3. Number of 3-base hits made in season.
4. Number of 2-base hits made in season.
5. Number of one-base hits made in season.
6. Number of foul balls hit in season.
7. Number of times batter struck out in season.
8. Number of runs batted in during season.
9. Number of base-on-balls earned in season.

Each of the above will contain a high proportion of variance attributable to the factor, *batting ability,* but the correlations will not be perfect because each has other sources of variance. A surrogate variable that combined all nine would reinforce the batting ability factor and would swamp out the other less prominent sources of variation.[5] Box 15–2 contains another example of

---

Box 15–2   Purifying the Size Criterion

The Problem. To create a surrogate variable that corresponds to the pure criterion, *company size.*

Discussion. Business firms come in many sizes: small, medium, and large. But what is really meant when one refers to the size of a firm? Is size measured by the number of persons employed, its market share, the aggregate area of its physical plant, the amounts of invested capital, totals assets, or sales volume? Or is it some ad hoc combination of all of these measures? Is it meaningful to refer to the size of a business firm; or is the term so loosely used that it has no real meaning?

Yet, when we are confronted with gross differences in size, our common sense notion does not deceive us. When General Motors is compared with American Motors, General Motors is the larger of the two by almost any measure we can devise. But with firms for which the size disparity is not so great, we may encounter difficulty in deciding which is larger. A firm first on one set of measures that are believed to be indicative of size may not be first on other equally good measures. For the year 1961, General Motors Corp.

ranked first among industrials on sales income, net profit, and number of employees; but it ranked second on total assets and invested capital. For the same year, Standard Oil of New Jersey ranked first on total assets and invested capital, but *seventh* on number of employees and *second* on sales income. Which is larger, General Motors or Standard Oil?

Common sense reinforced by published financial data tells us that larger firms (however defined) tend—on the average—to have larger scores on the usual size-related variables than do smaller firms, but this is a tendency not a certainty. Usually the correlations among the size-indicative variables are less than unity; but the fact that they are highly correlated suggests that they do have something in common. Common sense tells us that the common element is the elusive size factor.

Methodology in Constructing Surrogate Variables. Find a number of variables believed to be high in *size* content. Ten such variables are:

1.   Stockholders' equity (net worth).

2.   Market value of outstanding common shares.

3.   Sales income for the year.

4.   Cost of plant and equipment.

5.   Total liabilities and reserves.

6.   Number of employees.

7.   Number of common shares outstanding.

8.   Cash dividends paid on common for the year.

9.   Before-tax cash flow.

10.   Year-end working capital.

For a sample of large industrial firms, values were obtained for these ten variables and the variable series were placed in rank-order form. For each of the 100 firms in the sample, an average rank was computed, and these average ranks were reranked to form the surrogate series. (If the method is correct, this series is a good surrogate for the pure series, company size.)

Testing the Series. A multiple factor analysis was performed on the ten size-related variables and the surrogate series. (If the communality of the surrogate series is cose to unity, it is a good stand-in for company size.) The communality was very close to 1.00 for the surrogate series.

Source. The material in this box is based on an unpublished doctoral dissertation by Allan Easton entitled, *Global Properties of Business Firms* (University Microfilms, No. 65-7490, 1964). Details of the computations can be found in this work.

how a number of variables can be combined to produce a surrogate variable that is a good replacement for the pure criterion, company size.[6]

The end result of this procedure applied to every pair of overlapping criteria should be a score matrix consisting of uncorrelated (orthogonal) criteria. Only in this way can we be certain that multiple-counting bias has been expunged from the score matrix.

Notes and References

1. The material in this section is adapted from ideas contained in a group of papers in the Summer 1966 *Journal of Experimental Education:*
   (a) R. E. Christal, "JAN: A Technique for Analyzing Group Judgment," JEE Vol. 36, No. 4, pp. 24–27.
   (b) R. A. Bottenberg and R. E. Christal, "Grouping Criteria—A Method which Retains Maximum Predictive Criteria," ibid., pp. 28–34.
   (c) R. E. Christal, "Selecting a Harem—and Other Applications of the Policy Capturing Model," ibid., pp. 35–41.

2. M. Ezekiel and K. A. Fox, *Methods of Correlation and Regression Analysis* (New York, John Wiley and Sons, 1959), and W. W. Cooley and P. R. Lohnes, *Multivariate Procedures for the Behavioral Sciences* (New York, John Wiley and Sons, Inc., 1962).

3. Most computer facilities have program libraries that contain programs for multiple regression analysis. One of these collections is published periodically as the BIMED program book (Biomedical Computer Programs; Health Services Computing Facility, Department of Preventive Medicine and Public Health School of Medicine; University of California, Los Angeles, California).

4. See any good work on multiple factor analysis. For example, B. Fruchter, *Introduction to Factor Analysis* (New York, D. Van Nostrand, Inc., 1954), and also Cooley and Lohnes, no. 2 above.

5. For details on the construction of a number of the composite criteria that the author calls "categoricals," see R. A. Kalich, *The Baseball Rating Handbook* (New York, A. and S. Barnes & Co., 1969).

6. The material in the box was drawn from Allan Easton, *Global Properties of Business Firms* (unpublished doctoral dissertation; Ann Arbor, Michigan; University Microfilms, Document No. 65-7490), and from _____ Corporate Image versus Corporate Style," *Journal of Marketing Research,* Vol. III (May 1966), pp. 168–74. The variables were renumbered for the purposes of the example.

Important Words and Concepts

Sensitivity analysis
Incremental change
Coefficient of linear correlation
Trial ranking series
Standard of significance
R series
K series
Criterion variable
Predictor variable
Multiple linear regression
Linear-additive model
Nonlinear multiple regression
Nonredundant
Independence
Orthogonal
Redundant-synergistic
Redundant-antagonistic
Overlapping criteria
Multiple-counting bias
Colinearity
Shared variance
Surrogate criterion

Overview of Chapter 15

A sensitivity analysis involves a full solution of the score matrix for each trial condition. A trial involves an incremental change on a criterion weight. The objective is to discover just how much each criterion weight can be changed before there is a significant change in the initial ranking of alternatives.

Under favorable circumstances it is possible to make a good inference of both criterion weights and eta from a rater's merit ordering of alternatives. Weights can be inferred from a linear multiple regression analysis; eta can be inferred from nonlinear multiple regression.

In setting up all amalgamation rules, there was the hidden assumption that all the criteria were nonredundant. Redundant or overlapping criteria introduce multiple-counting bias. When redundance is uncovered, one of the redundant criteria can be dropped altogether. Overlapping criteria should be purified by factor-analytic procedures or should be replaced by a pure, surrogate criterion.

Questions for Review, Discussion, and Research

Review

1. What is a sensitivity analysis and how is it used?

2. What are the two standards for significance of changes in the ranking of alternatives?

3. By what means is it possible to infer the weights intuitively used by a decision maker?

4. By what means is it possible to infer the value of the parameter, eta, intuitively used by a decision maker?

5. What is the difference between redundant and nonredundant criteria? Between redundant and overlapping? Between antagonistic and synergistic overlapping?

6. What happens when two or more criteria in the score matrix are redundant? If they are overlapping?

7. How can one tell if and how much criteria are overlapping; or if they are redundant; or if they are pure?

8. If the criteria are found to be redundant or overlapping what should be done to correct the situation?

Discussion

1. Under what circumstances should a sensitivity analysis be performed?

2. Under what circumstances would it be both feasible and worthwhile to infer the criterion weights and the eta used in a decision problem?

3. How much overlapping of criteria can be tolerated? Can a sensitivity analysis be used to answer this question? If not, why not? If so, how?

4. Under what circumstances is it advisable to test the decision criteria for overlap or purity?

5. What is the probable effect of using impure criteria with high weights?

6. In performing the test for criterion purity, what is the effect of using just a small number of alternatives' score sets?

Research

1. Prepare a sensitivity analysis for a score matrix developed for one of the cases in this volume.

2. For a set of empirical valuation scores on multiple criteria, for example,

in a beauty contest, or for the evaluation of investments or vendors, have a colleague merit order the subjects from their score profiles. Prepare an estimate of his criterion weights by using the method described in this chapter.

3. Search the literature for a multiple-criterion decision or evaluation problem and test the criteria there used for purity.

4. Can you devise a method for correcting the criterion weights for impurity other than the method described in this chapter?

5. Can the method of sensitivity analysis be used for changes in eta as well as for criterion weights? If so, what are the implications for selection of a choice rule? If not, why not?

CASES *for part four*

(Note: These cases may also be used for Part III.)

CASE IV-I
How To Exploit the New Invention

SUMMARY: A husband and wife team develop a new medical instrument and receive several propositions for the commercial exploitation of the
product.

SIMON ALBERT'S BACKGROUND

Simon Albert, age 35, is a sales engineer for the Medical Specialties Division
of Algernon Bates, Ltd. Simon is married and has small children; two boys,
age 2 and 10; two girls, age 4 and 7. Mrs. Adele Albert, the former Adele
Seymour, daughter of United States Congressman Seymour, is a graduate
electrical engineer. Simon has a B. S. and an M. S. in biochemistry, two years
of medical school, and an MBA from State University. He had had to leave
medical school when his mother's lingering illness exhausted the family's
ability to further subsidize an expensive medical education. Simon switched
his interest to business and, after dropping out of medical school, enrolled
at night for the MBA program, which he completed with honors. His first
position was with Medical Specialties Division as a junior sales engineer.
With the passage of time, he improved his standing in the company.
   As part of his regular duties, Simon calls on physicians, commercial medical laboratories, hospitals, and medical research institutions. He sells and
demonstrates biochemical assay equipment, but does no high-pressure
selling. He serves as a source of information and helps technicians or
researchers with their particular problems.
   Simon earns $14,000 per annum plus an annual cash bonus based on
shares in the profit contribution of his division. The size of the bonus varies
from year to year; it has been as high as 25 percent of salary and as low as
5 percent. Simon expects annual salary increments of at least 10 percent per
year and eventual designation as chief sales engineer, a position that does
not now exist, but one that will be created as the division's sales and market
penetration grow.

MR. ALGERNON BATES, JR.

Bates, Jr. is the scion of a wealthy Eastern family who inherited the majority
interest in Algernon Bates, Ltd., from his father. The company, in its early
life, had manufactured textile machinery, but that part of the operation had
been sold off years ago. At present, the parent company is engaged in the

so-called high-technology lines of business similar to Litton Industries and Teledyne, except that Bates, Jr. has no desire to emulate their growth. He prefers, instead, to keep the company small enough so that he can manage it personally with the aid of a full-time president and a small headquarters staff. He prides himself on his close contact with creative people and is constantly on the alert for bright new people from other companies or from the universities who can bring new, fascinating products to Bates.

Bates, Jr.'s formula is to set up a man with a worthwhile product idea as if he were in business for himself except that the parent provides all kinds of supporting services, such as drafting, model shop, sales, accounting, payroll, and advertising. In this way the inventor-manager can concentrate on his product without becoming distracted by irrelevancies. When a man produces something worthwhile, he is handsomely rewarded with substantial cash bonuses in addition to a good salary.

There was some unofficial talk about setting up a stock-option plan, but no action was taken because the company is privately owned, and Bates, Jr. will not agree to "going public." During the 1958 to 1961 period Bates lost some exceptionally creative men because of his inability to match the highly lucrative stock deals offered by other investment groups that were more public-ownership oriented. Several of those who left Bates did very well; they had substantial ownership positions and a few are now "paper millionaires."

SIMON'S AFTER-WORK ACTIVITY

Simon and Adele have an eight-room split-level home with a large dry basement that has been fitted out with a compact but efficient model shop and laboratory. A substantial portion of their assets has been invested in a lathe, a milling machine, and other tools and instruments. Because of his special expertise in biochemistry and medical technology and Adele's training in electrical engineering, they became fascinated with the problem of electro-stethoscopy. Physicians are still using the ancient stethoscope technique and improved methods are either not available or are too expensive. Simon had been thinking of a new approach to stethoscopy using a newly developed transducer and advanced microcircuitry. In his spare time, on weekends and vacations, he built a working model of the new instrument. He quietly asked some of his physician customers to test it for him. Their responses were uniformly favorable. He found that there was great interest in the device if it could be produced for a reasonable price. Moreover, if the instrument could be adapted for visual displays and to making high-fidelity recordings of heart and chest sounds, the market would be even larger.

After hearing several enthusiastic reports and after correcting a number of minor deficiencies in the device, Simon became convinced that he was ready to exploit this very saleable product. He invested his last thousand dollars of savings in patent applications that he assigned to the S & A Development Company, Inc., wholly owned by him and his wife. The way seemed clear for doing something constructive about the MicroSteth instrument.

RESULTS OF EARLY EXPLORATION

There was a major problem that required attention before moving forward to exploit the MicroSteth. Mr. Bates raised the question about his proprietary rights to the invention. This took some time to resolve. Every Bates creative employee was required to sign a patent assignment in favor of Bates as a condition of employment. Apparently, however, sales engineers had never been considered as being creative, because Simon had never been asked to sign such an assignment. Then Bates asked for shop rights, but after negotiation, he good naturedly admitted defeat, and Simon's way was cleared to proceed.

Bates, however, was determined not to lose the chance to add the MicroSteth to his line. He called Simon to his office and presented him with three alternative proposals:

1. Simon would continue in his present job and would sell 100 percent of the capital stock of S & A Development Company (along with all rights, patents, designs, and the like) for a $20,000 advance against a 2 percent royalty on factory selling price for ten years (with a guaranteed annual minimum after the first four years of $5000). This would provide a royalty income of $50,000 over a ten-year period with the possibility of even greater income should the product sell well. In addition, Simon would be eligible for early promotion to chief sales engineer.
2. Simon would leave his present assignment and would become general manager of a new Bates division, the MicroSteth Division. In consideration for assigning all the rights to the invention, Simon would get $20,000 in cash, a 10 percent salary increase plus 10 percent of the new division's profit contribution, payable annually for ten years.
3. Simon would leave his present assignment and would become president of a newly formed Bates subsidiary, the MicroSteth Corp. 85 percent owned by Bates and 15 percent by Simon. Bates, Jr. would advance the firm $150,000 in cash for working capital—$50,000 as permanent capital and $100,000 as a long-term, low-interest loan. Simon would have a salary of $15,000 per annum subject to upward revision later. Each party would sign a "buy-out" agreement that would give the other first call on the purchase of any shares offered for sale at a per-share price equal to

$$\frac{\text{(book value of assets)} + \text{(most recent six months' sales)}}{\text{(number of shares outstanding)}}$$

All three of the foregoing offers were subject to the outcomes of three things:

1. Patent searches.
2. A thorough market survey.
3. Product design review made by Bates engineeering people.

All of these would be started and carried out at Bates' expense after the signing of a letter of intent, and all would be finished in three months.

FURTHER DEVELOPMENTS

Although Simon was tempted to accept one of the three plans presented by Mr. Bates, his wife Adele urged him to take some time to think it over. Together they composed a letter to Mr. Bates.

Dear Mr. Bates,

In spite of much thought, I am still unable to decide which, if any, of your three proposals I should accept. I am undecided because the outcomes would depend very much on market factors that we cannot yet anticipate. Also, before deciding, I really must think through what I want out of life because each of your three offers implies a quite different personal commitment.

This morning I telephoned my father to tell him the wonderful news and to ask his advice. He, as you may recall, is Professor of Marketing at State University, and he had an interesting and worthwhile suggestion. His marketing research seminar is just beginning a new semester, and he thought one or more of his students might like to take on the MicroSteth as their term projects. I accepted because this way we can get a reading on the market with no expense. The $5000 to $10,000 a professional survey might cost could be better spent in promoting the MicroSteth.

I will keep you fully informed of my deliberations and the outcome of the market rsearch. Meanwhile, I have a job to do for you that you are paying me for, and I am anxious to get back to work.

Thank you again,
(signed) Simon Albert

ANOTHER PROPOSITION

A few weeks after writing the letter to Mr. Bates, Simon was interrupted at dinner by a telephone call from a Mr. Peter Rockwell of Rockwell and Co., members of the New York and San Francisco Stock Exchanges. Mr. Rockwell told Simon that he had heard about the MicroSteth and would like to speak to him about it before he committed himself to any other investment group. A meeting was arranged for the coming Saturday at the Rockwell and Co. offices.

When Simon arrived at the Rockwell office, he found five men waiting there for him. After introductions were completed a discussion began about the technicalities of the MicroSteth design and application. Then Mr. Rockwell called the meeting to order. He said:

"Gentlemen I think it is time for us to get down to particulars. Mr. Albert. My colleagues and I are convinced that your product idea has great merit and a good potential. Don't ask me how we know; we have our sources of information.

"Mr. Thompson, on my right, is a partner in Rockwell and Co., and he has special expertise in underwriting and in the promotion of worthwhile companies in the high-technology fields. Mr. Jompert, sitting beside him, is formerly vice-president for marketing of Alpha-Med, a leader in your field. He just resigned from Alpha-Med because he disapproved of being gobbled up in the merger with the agricultural chemical outfit. He is primed for a new venture such as the MicroSteth. Next to him is Mr. Rosen, also a former Alpha-Med executive. Rosen was their top manufacturing man. Mr. Morse is with our bank, and he'd like to take a part in the promotion too.

"Now Mr. Albert, we know that you are a loyal Bates employee and that Mr. Bates has made you several attractive offers. I think we can do better, and I'll tell you why. Bates is a generous man, but he has an unreasoning abhorrence of public ownership for his company. For this reason, we know he can't offer you the kind of deal your product deserves; that is, a plan for founding a public company with you as a substantial stockholder. According to our plan, you would hold a big block of stock for which there would be a public market. This is the way millionaires are made these days.

"I am now going to hand out copies of a proposal. It's rough and subject to revision, but it contains the main points of our offer. Allow me to read some of the main features aloud:

'1. A firm called the MicroSteth Instrument Corp. will be formed with a total capitalization of 1,000,000 shares of common stock.
'2. The initial subscriptions would be as follows:
    (a)   Mr. Albert, 100,000 shares for assignment of his invention and for his immediate services to the new firm as vice-president for engineering.
    (b)   Mr. Jompert for his joining the firm as vice-president for marketing and a cash contribution of $50,000—100,000 shares.
    (c)   Mr. Rosen for his joining the firm as vice-president for manufacturing plus a cash contribution of $50,000—100,000 shares.
    (d)   Rockwell and Co. for services and a cash consideration of $100,000—200,000 shares.

(e) The remaining 500,000 shares to be reserved for executive stock options (100,000) and for a public offering at a price of not less than $5 per share as soon as earnings prospects allow.

(f) The post of president would remain unfilled for the present and the three vice-presidents would function as if the firm was a three-man partnership.'

"I think these are the most important details. Salary, benefits, employment contracts, and stockholders' agreements all are covered in the document and can be modified in any reasonable manner.

"If things work out as I envision them, we can all make a nice bundle from this deal. I know that this is a big lump to swallow at one sitting, so why don't we break for questions and then adjourn. I will call each of you on the telephone and, when we are ready to move, we can reconvene."

CONVERSATION BETWEEN SIMON AND CONGRESSMAN SEYMOUR

SIMON: *What do you think, Dad? My head is spinning. I don't know what to do. I must decide, because my work is suffering, and Mr. Bates is pressing me for an answer.*

SEYMOUR: I think I see the whole picture, Simon, but after looking at your cost estimates (Exhibit A) there is one more possibility that comes to

---

Exhibit A   MicroSteth Cost Estimates

One-time Costs

Design engineering	$10,000
Tools and moulds for chassis	7,500
Cabinet and accessory tools	7,500
Microcircuit production tools	10,000
Inspection and production instruments	15,000
Transducer tooling	5,000
Manual writing and preparation	5,000
Labor and materials for ten handmade samples	15,000
Total one-time costs based on a production rate of 200 to 1,000 units per month	$75,000

Operating Costs

Material costs (200 to 1000 per month)	$ 85.00 per unit
Direct labor	20.00 per unit
Manufacturing expense	20.00 per unit
Selling expenses (exclusive of promotional outlays)	25.00
Total per unit costs	$150.00

Other Expenses

General and administrative expenses based on a production rate of 200 to 1000 units per month	$48,000
Direct costs as above	$150.00 per unit
G&A (200 a month)	20.00 per unit
Total cost	$170.00 per unit

my mind. Why not try to make it on your own? Then you would have 100 percent of the pie, not 10 percent. Suppose you raise $20,000 on your house. I could lend you $15,000 and perhaps your father could add another $10,000. That would give you $45,000 to start with. You could keep your present job for a while, and Adele could help out to keep expenses down. Perhaps you could keep the whole thing in the family. Then later, if the business prospers on a small scale, and the market is ripe, you might be able to place 10, 20 or even 30 percent of the shares with the public. In that way you would maintain a majority position and still have the advantages of a public market for your shares. Would you think of that? If your market estimates (Exhibit B) are reasonably correct, I think it could work out well.

Exhibit B   Sales and Profit Estimates

Market Estimate as a Function of Selling Price*

Price	Estimated Annual Demand	Revenue
$1,000	100	$ 100,000
500	1000	500,000
400	2000	800,000
300	9000	2,700,000
200	20000	4,000,000
100	100000	10,000,000

Estimated Buildup Time for Market Acceptance†

Years After Start-up	Cumulative (Light Promotion) (in Percent)	Cumulative (Heavy Promotion) (in Percent)
1	2	5
2	10	15
3	20	30
4	40	60
5	60	100
6	80	100
7	100	100

Light promotion is $10,000 + 10 percent of sales income per annum.
Heavy promotion is $100,000 + 20 percent of sales income per annum.

Profit Estimates

Direct costs	$150.00 per unit
G & A	20.00 per unit
	(based on 200 a month)
Total cost	
exclusive of promotion	$170.00 per unit

Profit before promotion at selling price of $250.00
$80.00 per unit
Profit before promotion at selling price of $200.00
$30.00 per unit

† * Based on student market research from Professor Albert's marketing research seminar.

EXCERPTS FROM A LETTER FROM SIMON TO PROFESSOR ALBERT

Dear Dad,

In the attached papers I have outlined all of the alternatives for exploiting the MicroSteth. It is obvious to me now that I have no real basis for preferring one over the other until Adele and I have a better idea of our goals in life. We discussed this in great detail and have come up with a tentative list of personal objectives:

1. To have a generous and steadily growing income.
2. To be able to have time to spend with my wife and children, particularly while the kids are young.
3. To build a substantial estate for the benefit of the children.
4. To have a substantial cash reserve in the event of family emergencies.
5. To have time, money, and energy to make more inventions similar to the MicroSteth.
6. To avoid excessive risks to present assets.
7. To have time, money, and energy for travel, education, athletic, cultural, and social activities.
8. To live a life reasonably free from excessive stress and strain.
9. To make a worthwhile contribution to the welfare of mankind and to the United States.
10. To leave some sort of mark on the world of my short existence on earth.

11. To always conduct myself in accordance with my ethical
     upbringing.

   Adele and I are planning to visit you during the recess. We'd like to
consult with you about how to proceed from here. I think I'm on to
a good thing and I'd like not to blow it.

---

1. *Prepare an analysis of this decision using one of the models in Chapter 5.*

2. *Prepare single-time and multiple-outcome matrices for each of the alternatives plus any additional alternatives that you may be able to conceive.*

3. *Prepare a valuation matrix from the outcome matrices.*

4. *Rank the objectives in order of their importance to Simon and Adele Albert. Would husband and wife have the same rank ordering? Compare the ranking of the objectives done by other persons. Are they the same or different?*

5. *How would you go about merit ordering the alternatives?*

6. *Which alternative do you prefer? Do you think your choice would coincide with Simon's? With Adele's? How did you come to your conclusion?*

CASE IV-II
Assembly Products' Staff Curtailment Problem

SUMMARY: A devastating fire in the main parts-fabrication plant causes a curtailment of production and customer shipments. A decision not to rebuild the plant makes a division-wide staff reduction inevitable. The assistant general manager is asked to prepare a layoff plan and to establish a set of retention criteria.

NEWS ITEM

BOMBER CRASH IN HOMETOWN PARK

December 27. A USAF bomber on a training mission crashed in the Hometown Industrial Park Sunday at 1:30 A.M. The bomber crew and the plant watchman are known dead. Damage to the park buildings has been estimated at over $25 million.

The fires started by gasoline spills from the crashed plane gutted the Convent Avenue plant of the Assembly Products Division of Conglomerate Corp. Because the plant was closed for year-end inventory, the usual night-shift personnel were not present. The only known person in the destroyed building was Amos Harrington, the night watchman. Mr. Waldo Armstrong, executive vice-president and general manager, when reached at his home, stated that the plant was a total loss and that production could not possibly be resumed for at least six months. The plant normally employs 1250 people. It is not known how the loss of the Convent Avenue plant will affect the company's production at its Norden Avenue factory.

Hometown's Mayor Robertson said that the disaster would damage the town's economy and would hurt small business people if 1250 of its residents were without employment. He expressed his relief that the loss of life was as low as it was, that the accident did not happen when the plant was running at full capacity.

Mr. Antonio Sorrino, president of the Metal Worker's Union local said, "I don't know how our people will manage with the plant shut down. The bad economic conditions brought about by the ineptness of Mayor Robertson's administration have cut reemployment opportunities. I am wiring the governor's office and Washington for emergency relief for our people."

TWX Armstrong to Headquarters

Convent Avenue plant totally destroyed. Insurance will fully cover losses. Destruction of tools and design drawings will prevent resumption for 120 days. Crash program to replace tools and develop outside sources begun. Finished goods inventories in warehouses and distributor's stocks will take care of 30 days customers' needs. Work in progress and Norden Avenue plant parts inventories available for 15 days production. Will advise day to day of further developments.

Armstrong

Excerpt from Conglomerate Corp. Board of Directors Meeting Minutes January 12, 197--

Mr. Peter Glover, Sr., board chairman, directed that the Convent Avenue Plant of the Assembly Products Division not be rebuilt. The division's cost data indicated that it would be more profitable for the corporation if parts were purchased from outside vendors and the insurance proceeds from the fire were used for general corporate purposes. An expenditure of $2 million was authorized for replacement of special tooling. Mr. Glover, Sr.'s motion was carried unanimously. Mr. Armstrong was authorized to proceed with the plan to restore full production at the Norden Avenue plant with purchased parts.

Excerpts of Verbatim Minutes of Special Meeting of the Executive Committee of the Assembly Products Division Held January 19, 197--

Those attending:
- Waldo Armstrong, Executive Vice President and
  General Manager
- Vincent Harris, Assistant Vice-President for Engineering
- Alvin Morrison, Assistant Vice-President for Purchasing
- David Stevens, Assistant Vice-President for Manufacturing
- Hubert Wolley, Assistant Vice-President for Manpower
- Peter Glover, Jr., Assistant General Manager
- Oscar Oliveri, Assistant Vice-President for Finance

ARMSTRONG: *Gentlemen. You've all read the board of director's resolution on the decision not to rebuild the Convent Avenue plant. We must accept that decision and proceed to plan our activities so that we can get back into production as soon as possible. Now I propose that we go around the table and give each of you a chance to report on his part of the overall plan. Why don't we start with you, Harris?*

HARRIS: We're working day and night to reconstitute the design drawings. Fortunately we had a full set of copies of the process drawings at the Norden Avenue plant, but they all have to be redrawn to make them suitable for outside procurement.

ARMSTRONG: *How about the drawings for special tools?*

HARRIS: All lost in the fire. We'll have to leave that to our suppliers. Our tool designs might not be proper for their machines anyhow. We've brought in a drafting service contractor to help us with the drawings. I think we can begin to issue final, checked drawings to purchasing in about a week, and we should be through in about three weeks.

ARMSTRONG: *Good, Harris. I'm sure you won't let us down. You all realize that nothing can happen until Harris' job is done. How about purchasing, Morrison?*

MORRISON: We've been getting a head start. The newspaper and radio reports of the fire brought a horde of salesmen to the purchasing department. Even though I have no final drawings to show them, I've been handing out sample parts to all comers and informal bids are beginning to come in. As soon as I can get official drawings, I'll get firm bids and delivery dates.

ARMSTRONG: *Good, Morrison. What's your timetable?*

MORRISON: I think I can begin getting parts in from temporary tools in about six weeks from date of purchase order. Parts from permanent tools will take about twelve weeks. We'll have to pay a premium for the initial shipments but, in the long run, I think we'll be able to bring in the entire bill of materials at a much lower cost than the Convent Avenue plant could.

ARMSTRONG: *That sounds pretty optimistic, Morrison. How about the assembly plant, Stevens?*

STEVENS: We're in good shape, boss. The Norden Avenue plant wasn't affected by the fire. Get in the parts and we'll run like a house on fire. Oops! That wasn't a good simile was it?

WOLLEY: Not so fast, Stevens. You're not getting off that easy. You're in trouble even if you don't realize it yet.

STEVENS: *What do you mean, I'm in trouble?*

WOLLEY: I think you've overlooked the plant-wide seniority clause in the union contract.

STEVENS: *What about it? The Convent Avenue plant was wiped out. That doesn't affect the Norden plant.*

WOLLEY: Oh no? You're so wrong. It affects you very much. By plant-wide, the contract really means division-wide. If you remember when we signed with the union we had only one plant. When we split up into two buildings, we put assembly in Norden and fabrication at Convent. We signed a memorandum of agreement with the union with the stipulation that plant-wide seniority covered all plants as one unit.

STEVENS: *Hell, man! Do you know what that means? We're in one hell of a mess. Most of the high seniority people work at Convent.*

WOLLEY: Right, pal. That means you'll have to lay off most of your people and retrain the Convent avenue gang to do the jobs that the Norden Avenue people are now doing.

STEVENS: *That's awful. That'll raise hell with my costs. The Convent Avenue people make almost 50 percent more.*

WOLLEY: That's right, Stevens. And you'll have to start your retraining program right away.

ARMSTRONG: *What should we do about the layoffs?*

WOLLEY: Stevens and I will have to get together with the union people and work this thing out. We'll work up a layoff schedule for all the people in the bargaining unit. There's one silver lining. The low seniority people aren't entitled to as much severance pay. If we had to lay off the old-timers it would cost us a fortune in severance pay.

ARMSTRONG: You do that, fellows. But I have another problem. I have orders from headquarters, right from Mr. Glover, Sr. to take immediate steps to cut back our overhead. With the Convent Avenue plant out of the picture permanently, our direct labor complement will be cut nearly in half. We must keep the ratio of indirect to direct expense in proper balance to preserve our profit margins. I'm afraid that will mean cuts in the indirect payroll in every department. And with Wolley's bad news about the plant-wide seniority clause in the union contract, which means a big jump in per-unit labor cost, we'll probably have to trim overhead more than I first thought.

WOLLEY: *How much, boss?*

ARMSTRONG: I'd say about half.

WOLLEY: *Half? Wow, that'll hurt like hell. I can hear the screams of anguish from all the department heads.*

ARMSTRONG: I know, but it can't be helped. I think we ought to cut a little deeper at first; then we can rehire a few people if we find that we cut too close to the bone. I have a distinct impression that we've lost some of the leanness we used to have. Maybe it'll be a good thing to shake everybody up a bit.

HARRIS: *What about my people? I need every man to get us rolling again.*

MORRISON: So do I. We have changed almost everything we buy. We used to buy tools, chemicals, and other materials. Now we have to buy components and finished parts.

STEVENS: And I have to retrain over a thousand people. I can't cut staff. I spent years in building the skills and quality consciousness of my people. We can't throw that all away.

ARMSTRONG: I know. Don't think I don't sympathize. But we have to face the facts of life. The fact we must face is that we must cut our indirect payroll to bring it into line with our direct payroll.

WOLLEY: *How about our old-timers? We have people who have worked for Assembly Products from the day old Mr. Pushkin opened up in that garage on Seneca Street. We just had an old-timer's dinner in which we told everybody, the press included, how much we appreciated their loyalty and hard work. We can't just cut those people off. And how about the young hot-shots we hired from the business school with such big promises? And the 100 minority-group workers we put on in the training program. How are you going to face the Chamber of Commerce on that one? Are you going to return your "Hometown Citizen of the Year" award? A layoff of the magnitude that you are suggesting will shatter the morale of the remaining people in the company and will raise hell with the local economy.*

ARMSTRONG: Its got to be, Wolley. I have my orders.

WOLLEY: We'll be undoing the work of ten years in staff development and community relations.

ARMSTRONG: It can't be helped. I know it hurts. I know you all have your favorites that you have trained to do things our way. I know none of you will be able to face the citizens in your community organizations. But facts are facts . . . I'll do one thing for you fellows. I won't ask you to prepare the execution list for your own departments. I'll have Glover, Jr., do the ground work. How about that Pete?

GLOVER: Whatever you say, boss. I've been thinking about how to handle this mess since you showed me the order from headquarters. I think I have a plan on how to proceed with the least sweat.

ARMSTRONG: Tell us about it.

GLOVER: What I propose is this. I'll prepare a set of personnel retention criteria, and we can all meet once again and decide how these criteria should be weighted. I'll consult with each of you and your staff on how each employee is to be rated on the criteria. Then we'll compute the retentions indexes for all employees. We'll divide the staff into three categories: (a) retain (40 percent), (b) retain or discharge with recall potential (20 percent), and (c) discharge with low-recall probability.

WOLLEY: *What criteria will you use?*

GLOVER: I don't know yet. I'll meet with you and work out an agreeable set of criteria, and we'll factor in your judgments on the importance of each criterion. Then, after I gather up all the personnel data, we can begin the scoring and calculation of the retention indexes.

WOLLEY: I don't like it. It sounds too impersonal and mechanical to me. Pete, I think you have an adding machine where you should have your heart.

GLOVER: I know it sounds that way, Wolley. But remember, what ever method you use, the result must be the same. Doing it in a different way won't save one job. I'd like us to do this unpleasant job as fairly and as humanely as possible. If you have a suggestion for a better way of doing it, I'll be glad to use your way.

ARMSTRONG: *Pete's right, Wolley. You are still having difficulty in facing up to the realities of this situation. Pete, go ahead with your plan. When do you think you'll be ready with the final results?*

GLOVER: In about thirty days.

ARMSTRONG: *That long? What do you propose we do meanwhile? Do we keep everybody on the payroll?*

GLOVER: Yes and no. I think we should recall everybody who is needed to get us rolling again. The others should be given their annual vacations right away. By the end of thirty days, our final retention choices can be made and notices can go out.

WOLLEY: *How about severance pay?*

ARMSTRONG: We'll follow company policy. Two weeks pay for every year of service for permanently discharged people.

WOLLEY: *Can we have any flexibility in the upward direction?*

ARMSTRONG: *I think we could do something in exceptional cases. What do you have in mind?*

WOLLEY: Nothing in particular. I just wanted to know how hard-nosed we were going to be. I have a special problem with people near retirement. They'll never be able to get other jobs in this town.

ARMSTRONG: Let me know the size of the problem. We'll try to work something out with early retirement.

OLIVERI: The severance pay and early retirement will be very costly if we lay off a lot of high seniority people.

GLOVER: True, but they're the highest paid, too. One factor balances out another.

OLIVERI: *Has anybody figured out what the severance pay policy will cost us?*

GLOVER: Not as much as we first thought, especially in the factory. Remember we have to keep all the high-seniority people and cut off the less senior. But for the overhead staff it may be more painful. I have a seniority distribution and salary range distribution for the nonunion staff. It looks like this:

Years of Service	Percent of Staff Involved	Average Annual Payroll Cost
25 and over	5	$17,000
20 to 25	10	14,500
15 to 20	15	13,000
10 to 15	20	12,000
5 to 10	20	10,000
1 to 5	25	9,000
0 to 1	5	8,000

ARMSTRONG: All right gentlemen. I think we've all got the picture. We have had a ratio of indirect to direct staff of about 1:2. That means we must cut at least 600 overhead people. I'll leave the details to you. Let's set a date of one month from today for making the final staffing decisions. Please prepare a statement of how you think your operation will be affected. Meanwhile, call back everybody you need to get us operating again. . . . Oh, yes; Pete. Let me see your plan for retention scoring before you go all the way with it. I'd like to test it with a few people who I am pretty sure will stay or have to go. I'd like to see how your scheme compares with my judgment.

---

1. Put yourself in Pete Glover, Jr.'s position and with the data and facts provided in the case prepare the following:
   (a) A set of decision objectives.
   (b) A set of retention criteria.
   (c) A set of criterion weights.
   (d) A method for combining the criterion scores.
   (e) The cut-off scores for the three categories.
   (f) A procedure for implementing the plan.
   (g) A set of justifications and explications for all of the above.
2. What do you think of Glover's way of approaching the retention and layoff problem? Would you do it differently? If so, how? If not, why not?
3. Are there any larger issues involved in this case that should be of concern to decision makers? Do you think that if the people at headquarters were made more aware of the consequences of their decision not to rebuild the Convent Avenue plant, they might reconsider? Do you think that they took enough of the important factors into consideration when they made their decision?

CASE IV-III
The Manager Who Made Too Much Money

SUMMARY: The annual earnings of the vice-president and general manager of Conglomerate Corp.'s Rare Metals Division are out of line with the earnings of the company's other executives. The president is trying to work out a satisfactory solution to the problem.

Homer Kingsley, age 45, is vice-president and general manager of Conglomerate Corp.'s Rare Metals Division, a position he has held for seven years. The division was formerly a small part of the Solid State Devices subsidiary which had been acquired by Conglomerate in 1960. At that time the rare metals business had been an unprofitable sideline, and serious consideration was given to abandoning that part of the business.

Gordon Rossiter, president of Solid State Devices, both before and after the acquisition, was convinced that the rare metals business had good profit potential providing that it was given good leadership and promotion, neither of which had there been time for before the acquisition. On his recommendation the rare metals group had been spun off from its parent, Solid State Devices, and had been given divisional status. An executive search organization was retained to find the best man for the top job of running the Rare Metals Division. They found Homer Kingsley, a graduate metallurgist, then doing a similar job for one of the country's largest manufacturers of solid-state devices.

To entice Kingsley away from his remunerative position, it was necessary to confront him with an irresistible offer. He appeared to be less interested in salary than he was in building an estate of considerable magnitude if he made a big success of the Rare Metals Division's business. He was willing to forego rewards if he failed, but he asked for large rewards if he succeeded. His confidence and aggressiveness proved appealing to Conglomerate's top management, and a mutually agreeable compensation package was worked out.

The package had four components:

1.   A salary of $18,000 per annum.
2.   An expense allowance of $5000 per annum.
3.   Restricted stock options for 25,000 shares of Conglomerate Corp. common stock at 95 percent of market price as of date of the contract, good for 10 years.
4.   A profit incentive based on the following formula:

$$10 \text{ percent of} \left[\begin{array}{l} \text{(net, before-tax profit contribution of the division)} - (15 \\ \text{percent of value of total assets used in the business)} \end{array} \right]$$

According to this complex formula, Kingsley would receive incentive payments only when his profit contribution exceeded the target rate of return expected on Conglomerate's assets used by the division. One of the restrictions of the stock option contract provided that he could exercise no more than 20 percent of the options in any one year, and then only in those years when his incentive payments reached or exceeded $10,000.

There was no provision in the employment contract for salary increases. If Kingsley was to increase his earnings, he would have to make his division very profitable by Conglomerate's very high standards. Moreover, this employment agreement was to be noncancellable by the company for five years, and it was to be renewable on Kingsley's sole option as long as he was able to (a) increase the division's *total* earnings each year over those for the previous year, *and* (b) earn back at least the target rate of return. If he failed in either of these two goals, the contract could be either terminated or renegotiated on six months notice by the firm.

The division's performance data, the incentive payments earned by Kingsley, and the market prices of Conglomerate's common stock are given in Table C–III.

On the first of April, 1969, the firm's outside auditors presented the Conglomerate Corp.'s board of directors with the fully audited financial state-

TABLE C–III   Rare Metals Performance Data

Year	Division Sales	Before-tax Profits	Total Assets Used
1961[a]	$ 5,521,000	$ (100,000)	$ 6,420,000
1962	7,350,000	237,000	6,200,000
1963	9,090,000	451,233	5,800,000
1964	12,720,000	1,500,100	8,900,000
1965	15,603,000	1,650,000	9,600,000
1966	18,560,000	2,427,000	12,800,000
1967	19,560,000	2,950,000	14,300,000
1968	19,100,000	2,500,000	14,000,000

Year	Earnings: Percentage of Assets	Incentive Earned	Share Prices[b]
1961[b]	(Deficit)	0	35⅜
1962	3.8%	0	39½
1963	7.8	0	42¼
1964	16.8	$16,500	30¾
1965	17.2	21,000	45⅛
1966	19.0	50,700	50⅛
1967	26.1	78,500	55¾
1968	17.8	40,000	45½

[a] Kingsley takes command at the end of 1961.
[b] Option price 34⅛.

ments for the preceding calendar year. In a note accompanying the financial report for the Rare Metals Division, there was a computation of Homer Kingsley's incentive earnings and the comment that because the division's earnings had fallen below the previous year's, the company now had the right, if it wished to, to renegotiate Kingsley's employment agreement. In his oral report to the board, the chief auditor reemphasized this point. The item was placed on the agenda for the May board meeting, and Mr. Barry Ovington, Conglomerate's president and chairman of the compensation committee, was asked to make whatever investigation he thought necessary to come to a decision on the Kingsley contract.

Ovington assigned the inquiry to Mr. Rossiter, who also sat on the compensation committee. He knew Kingsley well and had been a party to the design of Kingsley's contract. Rossiter was requested to prepare a recommendation for the May board of directors' meeting.

EXCERPT FROM MEMORANDUM: ROSSITER TO OVINGTON

Kingsley has done an outstanding job as manager of the Rare Metals Division, and there is no doubt that he should be handsomely rewarded. His salary and incentive earnings for the last three years were: $68,000, $96,000, and $56,000—not too much considering the performance of his division. In addition, he has realized substantial capital gains from his stock options.

Under ordinary circumstances, I would have recommended that we take no action on the Kingsley employment agreement unless Kingsley, himself, asked for changes. Conglomerate Corp. has done very well by Kingsley, and he has done well for us. It is very tempting to leave things just as they are; not to do anything to disturb a well-functioning operation.

Unfortunately, I uncovered one unsettling factor that I was unaware of before starting this inquiry. It appears that many of our division managers and subsidiary executives are resentful of Kingsley's large compensation. This resentment is greatest among our $50,000- to $75,000-a-year men in the divisions doing more than $25,000,000 annually. Several of these men claim that Kingsley's compensation is disproportionately large in relation to his sales and earnings contribution. Many of them contribute greater sales and profits than the Rare Metals Division and yet, either they earn less or they do not earn proportionally more than Kingsley.

I have also heard many derogatory remarks about Kingsley's

management practices. Some of these criticisms I attribute to jealousy, but I cannot overlook the claim that a good deal of the division's success is the result of the tremendous growth in the usage of certain rare metals and the simultaneous shrinkage in the supply of unprocessed materials. These two factors undoubtedly contribute to the high price levels of rare metals, and high prices and profits do permit everyone to overlook sloppy and inefficient management, if indeed this should be the case.

I am convinced that the sniping and envy is unfair and unjustified. But I believe these phenomena are symptomatic of general and widespread dissatisfaction with a perceived inequity in our compensation structure. This is something we did not consider when we made the original deal, probably because we had no idea that Kingsley would be so successful. The other executives correctly feel that their contributions are as meritorious or more meritorious than Kingsley's, yet their rewards do not reflect the situation fairly. Apparently the Kingsley contract's provisions are widely known and the perceived inequity, widely resented. If we are to avoid further disaffection among our key people, something must be done to correct any inequities that are present.

For these reasons, I shall recommend to the board of directors that we exercise our right to renegotiate the Kingsley employment contract and that we send him notice to that effect before the expiration of the six-month grace period.

---

1. *What do you think Conglomerate Corp.'s objectives are in this situation? How should the objectives be weighted?*
2. *Prepare a set of alternative courses of action that you think have some chance of succeeding in this problematic situation.*
3. *Which alternative compensation plan would you recommend that they offer Kingsley?*
4. *How do you think Kingsley would react to the prospect of the company's renegotiating his contract?*
5. *Are the other executives justified in their resentment of Kingsley's larger (relatively or absolutely) compensation?*

CASE IV-IV
What To Do About the Bribe Offer

SUMMARY: The marketing manager of an aircraft instrument manufacturer is approached by a "fixer" who offers a corrupt proposition for opening up a hard-to-sell account.

The Alpha Industries Division of Conglomerate Corp. designs, manufactures, and markets high-precision aviation instruments to commercial airplane makers and to contractors for the United States Department of Defense and for NASA. Although Alpha has a standard line of products used both for commercial and military applications, it also makes special instruments to customer order.

Joseph Harris, Alpha's director for marketing, has been fairly successful with the precision instrument line. Alpha is an approved supplier for every instrument user in the United States, Canada, and all NATO countries.

Unfortunately, as Joe Harris discovered quite early in his tenure at Alpha, there is a vast difference between being placed on a customer's approved list of suppliers and receiving regular orders. Alpha has been successful in obtaining a good share of instrument orders from some customers but, for others, Harris has not been able to progress beyond the sample-order stage.

One very large user, the Strange Aviation Corp. (name fictitious) proved especially baffling to Harris. They used thousands of instruments every year of exactly the types that Alpha supplied; Alpha's prices were competitive, but in spite of a repeated and intense wooing of the customer, Alpha received no more than sample orders from Strange Aviation, Harris' failure to break into Strange Aviation was proving to be an embarrassment because his boss, Clarence Penny, had taken a personal interest in Harris' progress with this account.

One day in March, Harris was attending an industry trade show in New York City. He was standing in Alpha's display booth answering inquiries when he was approached by a dapper-looking man of indeterminate age. The man said:

"I can see from your badge that you're Joe Harris. I've been looking forward to meeting you, Joe. My name is Marty Ackersen."

The two men shook hands, then Ackersen said:

"Joe, I'm here representing a client. I work as an industrial purchasing consultant for the Strange Aviation Corp. You sell them, don't you?"

"Yes, but not nearly enough," Harris answered.

"Would you like to sell them more than you now do?"

"I sure would."

"I'm glad to hear that, Joe. Suppose I look into my contacts at Strange Aviation and see if I can be of any help. Where can I reach you?"

"I'm here most of the day. At night I'm at our hospitality suite at the Hartford House."

"Good," Ackersen said. "And when do you close up shop for the night?"

"About midnight."

"Suppose I call you before twelve if I have anything. OK?"

"Sure Marty," Harris replied. "I'll look forward to hearing from you."

Ackersen departed and Harris finished his stint at the display booth. He had a solitary dinner and then resumed his duty in the hospitality suite. At eleven-thirty Ackersen called and asked Harris to meet him at the bar in the lobby.

They met there and retired to a secluded table in the cocktail lounge. After some desultory trade chatter, Ackersen looked squarely at Harris and said:

"Joe, I have a proposition for you. I spent a few hours today with the Strange Aviation people. I think we can work something out that will be good for you."

"Great," Harris answered. "Let's hear about it."

"Joe, I don't know how long you've been in this business, but I'm a real old-timer. I've learned that sometimes the straightforward and conventional approach to a buyer is less successful than the devious approach. I know that you've been trying to sell Strange Aviation for a long time without even getting to first base. Am I right?"

"Right," Harris answered. "So what?"

"So I'm the answer to your prayers. I have the instrument buyer in my pocket. I have him eating out of my hand."

"What do you mean?" Harris asked.

"He's my boy. I have him in my pocket. He'll do anything I ask. I'm his benefactor. He owes me a lot."

"Really? How will that help me?"

"I can get him to buy your instruments in place of someone else's."

"Good. Let's go." Harris said. "When do I get an order?"

"Not so fast, buddy. Hear me out," Ackersen said.

"Oh? There's a catch?"

"No catch, but there's procedure we have to follow."

"What is it?"

"It's simple enough," Ackersen said. "Here's what we'll do. You make an L3700 radar altimeter that Strange Aviation uses. Right?"

"That's right."

"And you sell it for $15,000 for the standard model. You charge a small premium for extras or for special customer specifications."

"That's right. Extra accessories and special testing can add as much as 25 percent to the cost."

"Good. Here's what we'll do. Strange Aviation's purchasing department will place orders for the L3700 instrument package, but they will use their own model number and they will add some trivial specifications that shouldn't cost much to meet. You quote them 15 percent more than the regular price for the standard model, $17,250 to be exact. When you get paid, you kick back the 15 percent premium to me. I split it three ways; $750 for you, $750 for me, and $750 for the buyer. We may be able to place orders for 100 altimeters a year plus some other instruments with the same kind of deal. That's a nice piece of change for everybody. And it's so simple. All you do is appoint me your special sales agent for the Strange Aviation account and pay me a 15 percent commission. What do you say, Joe? Isn't that a sweetheart deal?"

Harris stared at Ackersen but held back the harsh words he felt rising in his throat. He pretended to be thinking over Ackersen's offer, then he said:

"I don't know. We already have a sales agent for that account. If I cut him out after all the work he's put into the account, he'd get suspicious and complain."

"Why cut him out? Let him have his regular commission. Your regular price includes an allowance for his commission."

"That's true, but if I have to pay two commissions, there's bound to be questions. My boss would then get involved. I couldn't keep it quiet."

"Who's your boss, Clarence Penny?"

"Yes."

"Oh, I know Clarence very well. Why don't you talk to him when you get back. But don't say anything about your 5 percent cut. Tell him that we have to pay off the buyer and the buyer's boss. He'll understand that. I'm sure he's worked deals like that before himself."

"I don't know. Let me think about it," Harris said.

"OK, Joe." Ackersen yawned. "I'm getting tired. I've had a long day. I think I'll hit the sack . . . Joe, I'll call you in a week or so to get your answer. I'm looking forward to doing a nice piece of business for Alpha Industries as their special sales agent. And you'll be a hero, Joe, if we can pull the deal off. But remember, it's this way or nothing. You won't be able to sell anything to Strange Aviation any other way."

1. As Joe Harris begins to think of Ackersen's offer, what personal and organizational goals do you think he will perceive? What are his goal priorities?
2. Identify the interests that would be affected by this decision problem.
3. What alternatives are open to Joe Harris?
4. Diagram the decision process using the concepts and models developed in Chapters 3, 4, and 5.
5. Prepare an outcome and valuation matrix. Find the best alternative. How did you identify which was best?

V. SYNTHESIS

16. Which Choice Rule?

This chapter deals with the factors underlying the selection of a choice rule for merit ordering alternatives. The characteristics of the various rules are discussed. There is a possibility that the final ordering of alternatives will not be pleasing to the decision maker because of outright error, failure to capture the true criterion weights, or because of post-decision regret.

THE PROBLEM OF INFINITE REGRESS

In Chapter 14, a method was presented for estimating explicit criterion weights taking into account interest group priorities. An intermediate step was included that required estimating urgency weights to give expression to these priorities. Confronted with this paradox, the reader may ask with justifiable impatience, "What good is a method for arriving at an estimation of weights which requires that we make another estimate beforehand?"

A problem very similar to this arises when one seeks the answer to the question: Which choice rule shall we use? The obvious answer, if the methods presented in this volume are accepted, is (a) to define the criteria on which alternative rules arc to be evaluated; (b) to set up a decision matrix with alternative rules in the rows and criteria in the columns; (c) to insert numerical rating scores in the cells; (d) to assign weights to the criteria; and (e) to select a choice rule for finding which alternative is best. And how do wc select a choice rule for this purpose? We, define the criteria, and so forth, ad infinitem.

These logical anomalies are analogous to the two-mirror puzzle. Two floor-length mirrors are placed side by side about four feet apart with the reflecting surfaces facing, and a man places himself between them. As he looks into either mirror, he sees reflections of reflections of reflections. If we begin a logical argument with the definition of terms, we must then define the terms, and so on. Or, if we wish to test reason, we must use reason to make the test. Simply stated these are examples of the philosophical problem of *infinite regress.*

Logical puzzles of this sort are the bread and butter of logicians, Talmudic and ecclesiastical scholars, and perhaps even for intellectually inquisitive and playful decision makers. Fortunately, this apparent paradox, although temporarily distressing, ought not to prove disabling in the ordinary run of multiple-objective decision problems for a number of reasons:

1. In many instances, the intermediate steps that lead up to this kind of regression are of progressively smaller moment (convergence) and, therefore, errors at that stage have negligible effect on the final outcome. (When this is not true, of course, greater caution must be observed.)
2. For some, perhaps many, decision problems, one choice-rule alternative so dominates all others that its use appears obvious because it is the one that would be chosen whichever method is used. Thus the paradox is avoided altogether.
3. For some, perhaps many, decision problems, one criterion is so overwhelmingly important compared with others (it has a much higher explicit weight) that the selection is primarily univariate rather than multivariate. The choice among alternatives is made simply from a ranking of scores on the single criterion.
4. As a last resort, when all other escapes fail, we do as most mathematicians and pragmatic logicians do; we ignore the paradox and proceed as if it did not exist.

CONSIDERATIONS FOR CHOICE RULE SELECTION

A variety of factors should be considered before making a selection of an amalgamation rule (for ranking alternatives), a statistical mean (for computing figures-of-merit), or a satisficing rule (for classifying alternatives as "accept-reject"). Some of these factors arise from the specific conditions surrounding the decision-evaluation problem and are more-or-less independent of the technique being used. Others are more closely related to a particular methodology.

NEED FOR DEFENSE. When the decision is one that will affect many contending and vociferous interests and the eventual choice or ranking of alternatives will be subject to attack by powerful advocates of rejected alternatives, the rule used should be one that is capable of justification. (This will be especially true with alternatives close in merit, when the use of another rule will cause a formerly rejected alternative to be moved to top rank.) Under such trying conditions, many decision makers would like to keep the details of their decision-making process strictly secret. But, very often, when the stakes are large, secrecy may not be possible, at least, not for very long. If the decision must be documented, part of the presentation should be an elucidation of the rationale behind the particular choice rule being used.

CREDIBILITY OF THE CHOICE RULE. The amalgamation rule or statistical mean to be adopted in the particular case should be one that is readily comprehended by the decision-maker's clientele. The ultimate choice or ranking of alternatives should be credible, and the method of choice should be confidence-inspiring to the persons or groups that have the power to sabotage, resist, or frustrate the implementation of the decision.

URGENCY OF DECISION. Delays in arriving at a suitable amelioratory action can cause the accumulation of losses or other kinds of disutilities. In these cases, the decision maker will be subject to great pressures for an early decision. If the gain from further delay cannot be justified by improvements in decision quality, the more leisurely methods of choosing alternatives may be foreclosed. In such emergencies, the operative philosophy is: "Don't just sit there thinking; do something; do anything, but do something!"

TIME HORIZON. When the decision involves a sequence of time intervals and multiple-time matrices are used, one amalgamation method may be best for combining score sets for alternatives for a single time interval, and still another rule may be best for amalgamating cell entries through time.

WHO WILL BE DISCRIMINATED AGAINST. The inner logics of the various amalgamation rules and their related statistical means causes them to discriminate against some kinds of alternatives' score profiles and to favor others. If the alternatives are people or are reflections of particular interests, someone will inevitably be injured. So long as the decision maker has a choice of amalgamation methods, and as long as the rules treat different score profiles unequally, his actual choice may cause one set of interests to be favored over others. This discrimination happens whether or not the decision maker intends it to happen, or whether or not he is aware of it happening.

UNITS AND SCALES OF MEASUREMENT. If the circumstances dictate the use of natural, heterogeneous units for measuring scores of alternatives on multiple criteria, only the few rules that are compatable with those units can be used (for example, Rules Nos. 1, 2, and 4). The nature of the measurement scales and the ability to quantify criterion scores must be taken into account too, because non- or partially quantifiable criteria must be treated differently from the fully quantifiable.

OPTIMIZING OR SATISFICING. If we are looking for the best alternative in the set under examination, we use one of the optimizing rules; for one that meets the minimum standards of acceptability, we use a satisficing rule.

COSTS OF A LESS-THAN-THE-BEST-CHOICE. Some of the rules do not protect the decision maker against the possibility of making a catastrophic decision; others are so conservative that they rule out possibly attractive alternatives in favor of "safe" alternatives. If the costs of a less-than-the-best alternative being chosen are unacceptably high, the rule with the safer choice logic is better.

THE SEVERITY-LENIENCY CONTINUUM

The elements of the score set for a hypothetical alternative can be displayed graphically as a score profile as shown in Figure 16–1. A high score means that the alternative is strong on that criterion; a low score, that it is weak. Except for dominant and contra-dominant alternatives, we can expect that the alternatives in a set will have different combinations of strong and weak valuation scores.

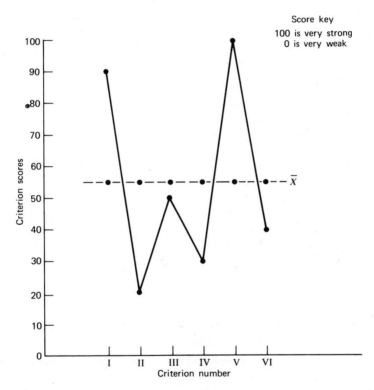

FIGURE 16–1. *A profile of scores for an alternative on six criteria. This alternative has a higher degree of profile scatter than would a hypothetical alternative with all scores falling on the dotted line.*

The discriminatory tendency inherent in an amalgamation rule or statistical mean arises from the operation of implicit weighting factors. Other things being equal, Rule No. 4 (the product rule) and Rule No. 6 (distance-from-perfection-rule) tend to discriminate *against* alternatives having higher profile scatter high and low scores in the profile). In contrast, Rule No. 5

(furthest-from-the-worst) discriminates *in favor* of alternatives with higher profile scatter. Rule No. 3 (sum-of-the-points) tends to ignore scatter altogether, and rates alternatives by the profile mean.

In some ways, Rule No. 5 may be viewed as the "patriot's rule." He loves his country so much and is so dazzled by its finer qualities (high scores on some criteria) that he overlooks entirely the country's shortcomings (low criterion scores). Rule No. 4, by similar reasoning is the "radical's rule." He is so obsessed by the shortcomings (low scores) that he completely overlooks any fine qualities. Rule No. 3, therefore, is the "liberal's rule." He neither overstresses weakness nor is he bedazzled by the strengths. Other examples of such polar attitudes are described in Box 16–1.

Box 16–1 Examples of Polar Attitudes

P_1 The *incumbent* seeking reelection to political office concentrates on his achievements and neglects to mention his failures.

P_2 The *challenger* seeking to unseat the incumbent publicizes the other's failures and downgrades his achievements, no matter how worthwhile they might be.

*   *   *

P_1 The *plaintiff* of a lawsuit seeks to assert his claim and belittles the merits of the defense.

P_2 The *defendant* seeks to deprecate the plaintiff's argument as being without merit.

*   *   *

P_1 The *hero* focuses on the goal to be achieved and ignores the personal risks of injury or death.

P_2 The *coward* is so overwhelmed by the dangers that he loses sight of the goal.

*   *   *

P_1 The *pathological personality* perceives no threat; for him it is the best of all worlds; he deprecates the possibility of disaster.

P_2 The *paranoid personality* sees threat in every event; all contrary facts are ignored.

*   *   *

P_1 The *gambler* says, "I feel lucky today. I know the odds are against me, but I feel in my bones that I'll win."

P_2 The *gambler* says, "I feel unlucky today. I'm sure I'll lose everything if I play today."

*   *   *

P_1 "I love her (him); she (he) is just perfect."

P_2 "My ex-husband (wife) is a terrible person."

*   *   *

P_1 There have been some bad side effects, but the new treatment has produced cures not possible by other means; adopt the new therapy in spite of its occasional side effects.

P_2 Although the new treatment has produced some cures not possible with other means, it has some bad side effects and, therefore, should not be released for general use.

*   *   *

P_1 The *gullible* person believes everything he sees in print regardless of the evidence of his senses.

P_2 The *doubter* believes nothing he reads regardless of the weight of the evidence.

Another example can help to dramatize these oddities in the choice rules and statistical means. Peter and James are two college students who are enrolled in the same classes in mathematics and history. Their course grades are as follows:

Course	Peter's Grades	James's Grades
Mathematics (3 credits)	92 (A)	72 (C)
History (3 credits)	52 (F)	72 (C)
Where A=4.0; B=3.0; C=2.0; D=1.0;		

The cumulative grade-point scores (figures-of-merit) for the two students using different amalgamation rules are:

Values Assigned to eta	Cumulative Grade Point Scores (FOM)	
	Peter	James
+3	0.0	2.0
+1	0.0	2.0
+½	1.0	2.0
0	2.0	2.0
−½	2.5	2.0
−1	2.8	2.0
−3	3.3	2.0

If the class rankings (and all the rewards associated with top rankings) were based on cumulative grade-point scores, Peter would outrank James when eta was negative; they would have the same class rank when eta was zero; James would outrank Peter when eta was positive. Which value one would use for eta depends entirely on the judgment and the attitude of the grading institution toward dull but steady performance compared with brilliant but erratic performance. The use of conventional arithmetic means for computing cumulative grade points would rate Peter (the hare) as equivalent to James (the tortoise).

Evidently, some amalgamation rules reward Peter for his high grades and are tolerant of his failures, whereas other rules have the opposite effect; they punish him severely for his failures and are not impressed with the high grades. The degree of overlooking of high and low scores appears to be related to the numerical values assigned to the parameter, eta.

Reasoning from the foregoing example, we can characterize rules or means based on negative etas as lenient, gentle, or tolerant of weakness in varying degrees; rules based on positive etas, as being severe, punitive, harsh, intolerant, or of weakness in varying degrees. This reasoning permits us to represent rules and means along a severity-leniency continuum as is shown in Figure 16–2.

Choice rules and statistical means that are punitive and harsh, that stress low scores and overlook high scores are placed at the severe end of the continuum. Those that are tolerant of the low scores and dazzled by high scores are placed on the lenient end. *Every choice rule or statistical mean can be placed somewhere on this continuum.*

Moreover, rules with indifference curves that are convex (bend away) with respect to the origin tend toward the severity pole; the degree of severity is roughly proportional to the amount of curvature of the indifference curves. Rules with indifference curves that are concave (bend toward) with respect to the origin tend toward the leniency pole of the continuum. The degree of leniency is roughly proportional to the amount of curvature.

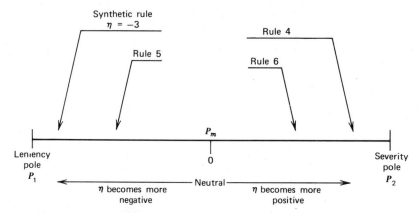

FIGURE 16–2. *Severity-leniency continuum for various numerical values of the parameter* η.

Another Example (Box 16-2)

The arithmetic means for the scores of Messrs. Able, Baker, Charles, and Davis, shown in Box 16–2, are all equal to 10.0. Thus, if we were to use the sum-of-the-quality-points rule (Rule No. 3), we would conclude that all four are equally meritorious. But are they?

Box 16–2 Figures of Merit for Four Men on Eleven Criteria

Criterion Number	Valuation Scores for this Man			
	Able	Baker	Charles	Davis
1	11	12	16	18
2	12	14	18	19
3	10.5	11	12	13
4	11	12	15	16
5	10.5	11	12	13
6	10	10	10	10
7	9.5	9	8	7
8	9	8	5	4
9	9.5	9	8	7
10	8	6	2	1
11	9	8	4	2
Average Deviation	0.91	1.82	4.17	5.09

Value of eta	Figures of Merit Computed from Choice Rules for These Values of the Parameter, eta			
	Able	Baker	Charles	Davis
+3	9.85	9.22	5.14	2.63
+2	9.88	9.49	6.66	4.48
+1	9.94	9.95	8.46	7.40
0	10	10	10	10
−1	10.05	10.20	11.20	11.70
−2	10.13	10.45	11.77	12.78
−3	10.17	10.59	12.65	13.46

Davis's profile contains both high (19 on criterion no. 2) and low (1 on criterion no. 10) scores. Would we be willing to trade off weakness on criterion no. 10 for strength on no. 2? Is Davis really just as good as Able?

We could only answer this question by exploring our attitudes toward the greater weakness of Davis compared to Able on some criteria, and the greater strengths of Davis on others. Two extreme possibilities are:

1. We could be strongly attracted by Davis's strengths relative to Able and very tolerant of Davis's relative weaknesses. If we felt that way, we might want to rate Davis higher than Able. This would be the equivalent of using a choice rule (or mean) with a negative value of eta. The size of the eta we used in forming our rule would be a reflection of the degree to which we were attracted to Davis's strengths and indifferent to his weakness, relative to Able.
2. We could be so repelled by Davis's weakness relative to Able that we choose to overlook Davis's high scores. In that case, we would want to rate Able higher than Davis. This would be the equivalent of using a rule with a positive eta. The size of eta would be a recognition of our repulsion from Davis's weakness and our indifference toward his strengths, relative to Able.

The man who chooses a rule (or mean) based on a highly positive eta acts as if he overreacted against weakness and underreacted toward strengths as indicated by high and low scores in the score profile. A man who chooses a highly negative eta to form the rule (or mean) acts as if he was overreacting toward strengths and underreacting against weaknesses.

If we identify subjects such as Charles and Davis as representing greater risks of failure because of their low scores (in spite of their high scores); and Able and Baker as lesser risks because of their absence of low scores (and high scores, too), we may also think of the choice rules as falling on a *risk-attraction, risk-aversion* continuum. Neutrality toward risk (P_m in Figure 16–2) would be placed at the midpoint of the continuum.

From the foregoing reasoning and examples, we can see that *whether or not he realizes it, the man who adopts a choice rule or statistical mean for a particular decision problem is expressing an attitude toward profile scatter in score sets. These are attitudes of severity or leniency or of risk-attraction or risk-aversion.*

If he has a free choice of modes for expressing this attitude toward profile variability and he has the absolute power to impose his choice on others, he is fortunate. But, if persons or entities undergoing evaluation have the knowledge and power to make or influence the choice of a rule (or mean), they can be expected to demand a choice rule that will tend to favor their cause relative to others less powerful, less knowledgeable, or articulate. Thus the Peters of the world can be expected to favor rules or means derived from highly negative values of eta; the Charleses and the Davises will argue the same way. But the Jameses and the Ables will push for rules or means based on highly positive values for eta. Formulas derived from etas that do not favor the advocate's position will be denounced as "unfair," "biased," or "discriminatory."

There are some implications for scientific research involved in the choice of an appropriate value of eta for evaluating alternatives. If important research conclusions are based on a ranking or merit-rating scheme and the ranking of alternatives could be altered with different etas, the researcher may be called on to justify his choice of eta, especially if his critics discover that a different value of eta would have materially altered the research results.

WHAT IF THE CHOICE RULE GIVES AN UNACCEPTABLE DECISION?

As a practical matter, there are countless opportunities for error, oversight, incorrect analysis, or distorted perceptions of the realities in making complex decisions that involve multiple objectives. But, if we do a thoroughly competent job in carrying out the various steps in preparing the multiple-criterion decision matrix, if the numbers we assign to alternatives on the various criteria are substantially correct, and if we use an *appropriate* amalgamation rule or statistical mean to rate or rank the alternatives, the final decision should be as good at it is humanly possible to obtain under the circumstances.

What then if, when we have completed the lengthy operations and computations described throughout this volume, we find that we are displeased with the alternatives chosen as best, or with their rankings? It is not unusual for a decision maker to say, "I know that your model identifies alternative no. 5 as best, but if I were making the choice by myself, I would place alternative no. 5 lower in merit than no. 7, which I really think is the best." Or he may be thinking to himself, "Dammit, I only went through this rigmarole to get documented confirmation for the alternative I really liked best, but the blankety-blank model gave me another alternative. How am I going to work myself out of this mess?"

One obvious explanation for noncorrespondence between the results from the use of a multiple-criterion decision model and from the use of intuitive methods is procedural or substantive error. An interest group may have been overlooked; the criteria may have been improperly defined, an important one may have been omitted, or some are redundant (and therefore counted twice); the explicit weights used may have been improper; the wrong amalgamation rule may have been used; arithmetic errors may have been committed. Careful recapitulation and cross-checking should help to uncover any of these outright errors.

Less obvious, perhaps, is the fact that by using multiple-objective models, we are taking into account factors that could not adequately be considered by purely intuitive methods. The unaided human mind is limited in its ability to simultaneously consider more than one objective at a time, particularly in times of stress. Thus, in many instances, the initial intuitive choice is cruder in the sense that it is more likely to have been swayed by predispositions, emotions, and other temporary, but irrelevant influences; and it is more likely to be focused on a single objective. *In the absence of procedural or substantive errors, the multiple objective methods described in this volume should, on the average, permit making superior decisions, evaluations, or ratings compared with ordinary intuitive, single-criterion methods.*

In Figure 16–3 are shown, schematically, the possibilities if:

1. You decide that the alternative you chose as best, by using one of the methods in this volume, is correct.
2. You decide that the choice made with the model is incorrect.

If you like the alternative chosen (or the rankings) and agree that it is correct, there are still two possibilities:

1a. Your model's choice and your intuition are both correct and your judgment is confirmed (but do not allow complacency to overcome your caution because);
1b. Both your judgment and the model's choice might be wrong. (Although the choice is satisfactory to you and you are tempted to adopt that alternative, both are wrong.)

If, on the other hand, you do not like or accept the results from application of the multiple-criterion model, there are four possibilities:

2a. The alternative chosen with the model is really the best of the lot and your intuition is wrong. (This possibility may be hard to take, but it should never be excluded from consideration.)

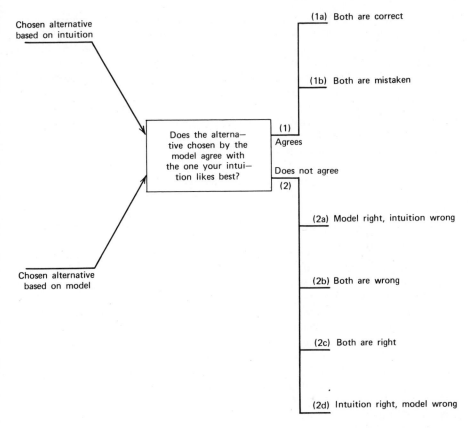

FIGURE 16–3. *Tree of possibilities when comparing the alternative chosen by the multiple-objective model with the one that would have been chosen by intuitive means.*

2b. Both your intuition and the model's choice are wrong. (Some other alternative in the set, neither your intuitive nor the model choice is the best; something went wrong in the analysis.)

2c. Both choices are right, both alternatives are good. (Somewhere in the decision process, one or more changes in preferences led to a divergence in the choices.)

2d. Your intuition is correct after all and the model's choice is a poor one (because of an error in the application of the model or because the same criteria, scores, or weights were not used in both cases).

The existence of the foregoing six possibilities implies that the process is not yet complete when the best alternative (or ranking) is found by use of a decision model. Considerable rechecking and verification is required; just how much depends on the magnitude of the decision consequences. Obviously, just because you like the choice made with a particular multiple-criterion model, this does not preclude the possibility of gross or subtle error. In fact, the Freudian psychoanalyst might suggest that there is no such thing as a true "error," but that all so-called errors are but subconscious attempts to influence the outcome of the process. The experience of the United States Bureau of Internal Revenue with errors in income-tax returns (which overwhelmingly favor the taxpayer) gives credence to the psychoanalytic view on error making. If there is any real danger of this unconscious bias, the only safe course is to have the decision reviewed by a disinterested third party.

Possibility 2d deserves some further discussion. Very often, for personal, political, or other unstated reasons, the criteria used (or their weights) for the decision matrix are not really the ones that the decision maker believes to be important. This inconsistency, in rare instances, will be the result of psychological factors such as denial, mental blocks, distorted perception, and subconscious preferences which, if Freudian psychoanalytic theory is applicable, can produce behavior without conscious motivation. A more likely reason for not using the real criteria or true weights is that to do so would not be socially or politically expedient.

The circumspect factory manager may not give a tinker's damn about the effect of his factory's effluents, stack gases, or noise pollution on the surrounding community, but it would not be in good taste for him to admit his indifference to cherished values too openly. By placing a high numerical weight on the criterion "To Be a Good Corporate Citizen" which is, in fact, false, he makes almost inevitable a disparity between the alternatives favored by the model in which this criterion is given high priority, and the one where it is afforded no weight at all.

The head of a military procurement agency that is making ready the placing of a large military hardware purchase may wish to preserve his reputation for integrity and the appearance of objectivity and impartiality. If he fears a congressional investigation, but he really wants to place the contract with a particular contractor and he knows in advance to whom he would like the purchase order to go, he must do a thorough job of obfuscation. To publicly admit his favoritism to one supplier would create a political scandal at the cost of his job and possibly his career.

The fact that a model exists for choosing among competing alternatives and that this model may be used to confuse rather than to clarify, to conceal rather than to reveal, is a matter of interest, because not only can these models be used for defending decisions but they can also be used for attacking them.[1] If the alternative being chosen seems totally at variance with the one that common sense indicates as best, the suspicion that the method has been so used (or misused) should not be dismissed without some thought.

If the person or organization making the decision or evaluation is forced to offer a complete explication of the decision steps, an astute investigator can easily detect any irregularities. Deceit or deliberate misapplication can be exposed, and correct procedures can be used in place of the incorrect. The ability to analyze and thoroughly explicate a complex decision involving multiple objectives provides an excellent framework for a thorough cross-examination by trial counsel in a search for deliberate or inadvertent errors. It is not difficult to visualize a trial proceeding or a congressional inquiry in which the department head, cabinet officer, military commander, or other high-level decision maker is called on to explicate his decision subject to the penetrating scrutiny of his adversaries. The methods developed in this volume can be used equally well by the attacker or the defender.[2] *We have provided a methodology that permits an escalation of the level on which complex managerial decisions involving multiple objectives can be debated.*

Post-Decision Regret and Dissonance[3]

After we have made a choice between two or more seemingly equally attractive alternatives (for example, whether to buy the flashy convertible, the two-door sedan, or the high-powered sports coupe), we may begin to experience a phenomenon that psychologists call "post-decision regret." The decision maker wonders, "Did I really make the best choice? I know that the alternative I chose has its strong points, but it also has its weaknesses. Wouldn't alternative no. 3 have been a better choice? Or no. 5?" He finds that he has become over-aware of the weaknesses of the chosen alternative and the strengths of the rejected ones. (Deep in his psyche, his eta values are wavering.) He finds himself vacillating in his conviction about the real superiority of the "best" alternative. The greater the stakes, the more fearful he may become, and the more he seeks confirmation and reassurance that the alternative he chose was really the best choice.

After a while, his doubts begin to wane and his confidence grows that his initial choice was really the best after all. *Dissonance sets in.* His inner psyche cannot accept the unpleasant proposition that he accepted an inferior alternative and rejected superior ones. He begins to refocus on the strengths of the chosen alternative and the weaknesses of the rejected ones. This is exactly the reverse of what was happening during the post-decision regret phase. Now he views the strengths of his choice as confirmation of the wisdom of his selection and views the weakness of the discards as further proof. He becomes more and more "locked in" on the chosen alternative and, with the passage of time, his earlier doubts disappear. He is now ready to do battle to defend the obvious wisdom of his choice against all doubters and all waverers.

Notes and References

1. See Case A-III, "Defending or Attacking the Executive Decision," for a paradigm of how an attack can be mounted.

2. Ibid.

3. Leon Festinger, *A Theory of Cognitive Dissonance* (Evanston, Illinois, Row Peterson Co., 1957).

Important Words and Concepts

Infinite regress
Convergence
Severity-leniency continuum
Discriminatory tendency
Profile mean
Profile scatter (variability)
Score profile
Risk-attraction, aversion
Cognitive dissonance
Post-decision regret

Questions for Review, Discussion, and Research

Review

1. What is the "problem of infinite regress"? Give some examples. What is its connection with the methods discussed in this book? How can one cope with the problem?

2. What are the criteria for selection of a choice rule or statistical mean for merit ordering alternatives?

3. When would one use a choice rule and when an equivalent statistical mean?

4. Why is profile scatter or variability in score-sets a factor to be considered in the selection of a choice rule?

5. What is a severity-leniency continuum?

6. What is meant by risk-attraction and risk-aversion?

7. What is the relationship between the curvature of indifference curves and place on the severity-leniency continuum?

8. Under what conditions would Peter be rated higher than James? Lower? The same?

9. Under what conditions would Able be rated higher than Davis? Lower? The same?

10. What is the applicability of the concept, post-decision regret, to multiple objective decision making? What is the relevance of cognitive dissonance?

Discussion

1. Would you expect persons who are the subjects of a multiple-criterion evaluation plan to have preferences about the choice rules used for merit ordering or for assigning figures-of-merit? If so, why; and are they justified? If not, why not?

2. What should a researcher or management consultant do if the ranking of alternatives (or subjects) under evaluation is significantly different with different choice rules? What do you think of the quality of research in which the research findings are materially altered if different rules are applied to combining elements of the score-sets?

3. What, if any, are the political, legal, and economic implications of the selection of a choice rule in an important multiple-objective decision or evaluation problem?

4. What should one do if he is displeased with the rankings of alternatives that result from the application of a particular choice rule or statistical mean?

5. What are the probable effects of using criterion weights as window dressing to please others?

Research

1. Search the literature for a multiple-criterion study (or use one of the cases in this volume) and test the results that are obtained with different choice rules based on both positive and negative etas.

2. Assume that you are the plaintiff's attorney (or his expert adviser) in an action that is attacking an important multiple-objective decision or evaluation. Prepare a plan for attacking the choices made by the defendant. Reverse your role and play the part of the defendant's attorney (or his expert adviser) and prepare your defense (and, if possible, your counterattack). (*Hint:* the decision might be the awarding of an important contract, the selection of candidates, the choice of a site, or any other you may wish to examine.)

17. Answers to the Four Questions

This concluding chapter presents answers to the four questions posed in the preface. The answers are based on the materials discussed in the preceding chapters.

EXPLICATION OF DECISION PROCEDURES

Is it possible to devise a decision procedure where despite the need for judgment, the procedure can be fully explicated and each step made defensible?

By breaking up a complex decision into its component parts, it becomes easier for the decision maker to explain and justify the final results. Although extensive and detailed explications are not always required, in situations where justification is needed, the ingredients can be assembled from the materials presented in the foregoing chapters.

The existence of an explication capability also serves the needs of persons who wish to inquire into the validity or equity of other's decisions to convince themselves that the decision was fairly made, that there were no gross errors or biases, that due diligence was exercised in assembling the data, and that the welfare of important interests were properly weighed. The natural arenas for such an inquiry are courts of law, formal legislative inquiries, administrative proceedings, public hearings, or executive committee meetings.

Although thorough explications of important decisions may appear desirable for many reasons, there are also reasons why persons or organizations may prefer to avoid preparing detailed explications. For example:

1. The procedures involve unacceptable expense and time delays plus irreplaceable scarce skills.
2. By imposing such procedures on subordinates, the higher-level administrator is, in effect, reducing the subordinate's power to act arbitrarily. (Many people see this as an attempt by the organization to increase its control over their activities, and they may perceive their instructions as

producing lowered personal status and autonomy. If so, resistance can be expected.)

3. The requirement that a full and honest explication be prepared (and, perhaps, published) reduces the ability to deceive, obfuscate, evade, or otherwise muddy the waters. (These latter are skills widely demanded in some political, diplomatic, business, and counterintelligence activities.)

4. The existence of a detailed record of an important decision can provide documentary evidence that can subsequently be used as material for an attack against the persons or organization involved in the decision.

5. A written record of the steps and data involved in an important decision can involve information of great value to enemies or competitors. (This danger makes installation of costly security and counterintelligence arrangements more necessary. The obvious risk is that these protective measures may be only partly effective.)

An Outline of a Full Explication

A full explication will contain most (if not all) of the following parts.

1. *Background.*   A statement of the background conditions giving information about the organization and the state of the environment along with the circumstances leading up to the specific decision(s); a statement of bias.

2. *Motivation for the Decision(s).*   A statement about the symptoms or conditions that made the status quo undesirable or untenable; of how the symptoms were detected; of what attempts, if any, were made by others to obscure or conceal the symptoms; of what standards were used to compare the then existing state with the desired state of affairs; of the extent of the deviation from the desired state; of the duration or any time dependency of the symptoms; of the cost incurred or other consequences of failing to make the needed changes.

3. *Diagnosis.*   A recapitulation of the diagnostic procedures; a detailing of the exclusive and inclusive hypotheses and tests used to eliminate or confirm hypotheses; the levels of causation and diagnosis explored; the final diagnosis and its limitations.

4. *Interests.*   A review of the persons, groups, factions, or organizational claimants (legitimate or illegitimate; favorable or adverse) that will be affected by the decision or by acts of omission or commission; a review of their power, trouble-making capabilities, the urgencies and priorities of their claims (immediately and in the short- or long-range future).

5. *Objectives and Criteria.*   A statement of objectives and the resulting criteria; a means-ends analysis of objectives to place them in their proper position in the goal hierarchy; their relative urgencies, priorities; the trade-offs that can be made; a statement of the time dependencies; a discussion of criterion purity.

6. *Identification of Alternatives.* A statement or listing of the alternatives including those that were summarily rejected as infeasible; the basis for rejection or nonrejection; any special precautions that were taken to be certain that all worthwhile alternatives were found and that none were overlooked.

7. *Factual Data on Evaluation of Alternatives.* A presentation of the factual data used in the evaluation of alternatives on all criteria; statements about assumptions used in forecasting or estimating alternatives' scores on criteria; statements concerning whether environment is one of certainty, risk, or uncertainty; basis for probability estimates and confidence levels; assumptions about the future in which the consequences of the alternatives will occur.

8. *Basis for Choice or Ranking.* Statements of basis for making choice or for merit-ordering alternatives; presentation of the decision matrix or matrices; basis for transformation of units; use of utility scales or other bases for numerical estimation of alternatives' scores on criteria.

9. *Quantitative Procedures.* Statements dealing with the quantitative procedures including estimation of criterion weights, transformation of data scales, longitudinal amalgamation, computational routines; choice rules or statistical means employed and the rationale underlying the choice of a rule or mean.

10. *Identification of Best or Alternatives' Rankings.* The presentation of the rank numbers or figures-of-merit for alternatives.

11. *Testing the Choice.* A statement of the testing of the choice against the symptoms, diagnosis, and the decision objectives.

12. *Unfinished Business and Miscellaneous.* A statement of any unfinished aspects of the decision process; the degree to which the decision leaves some symptoms only partially ameliorated; further recommendations of action intended to prevent future reoccurrences of symptoms; a statement of costs; a list of credits and acknowledgements.

INDIVIDUAL DIFFERENCES IN DECISIONS AND RATINGS

Why is it that men of good will, presented with identical alternatives and who agree on the essential facts in a problematic situation, still arrive at quite different choices of alternatives? What are the stages in the problem-solving processes that could give rise to this phenomenon? Where are the forks in the road?

If any one of the models presented earlier in this volume was universally adopted for making complex managerial decisions that involve multiple objectives, and henceforth all decisions and evaluations were made in a completely uniform fashion, there would still be countless opportunities for individual differences in decision outcomes. Instructors who teach by the case method in collegiate schools of business or in executive training programs find a wide diversity in problem solutions offered by the participants. The more complex and unstructured the problem, the more heterogeneous the backgrounds of the problem solvers, the more varied are the solutions. This finding should surprise no one because we know that each person brings to the attack on a specific problem his own unique background, propensities, special interests, frame of reference, and world view.

In a typical problematic situation we could expect that each person will see the problem in a different light. Moreover, even in the best circumstances, there will be information filters and traps that conceal some, give undue emphasis to others, and completely distort evidence that is essential to proper diagnosis.

There is a naive and simplistic hope implicit in the appointment of "fact finders" in labor disputes that if an impartial third party can find enough facts on which both labor and management can agree, the main basis for contention would disappear. Others hold that if only barriers to interpersonal and intergroup communication can be eliminated, conflict between the contending parties will be substantially reduced. At best, these two propositions are half truths.

Fact finding is analogous to the gathering of objective data for preparing the outcome matrix. All parties may be thought of as having identical decision criteria for evaluating alternatives, since if one party deems another's irrelevant, he can assign a zero weight to those criteria. But this is as far as fact finding can go, because beyond that stage, we become very subjective. We must make judgments on the following:

1. The utilities of alternatives' outcome scores: the shapes of the parties' marginal utility functions.
2. The trade-off ratios between pairs of criteria for each party; numerical criterion weights;
3. The attitudes toward profile scatter for each party which underlies the selection of a choice rule.

To hope that the contending parties in any negotiation or dispute will make identical judgments on utilities, marginal utilities, trade-offs, weights, or choice rules is unrealistic and hopelessly optimistic.

Thus, even if all parties can agree on the facts in a situation and they are able to communicate their thoughts and positions perfectly, their valuations and trade-offs will be highly individual. Goodwill alone is not enough to overcome differences in valuations or emphasis and is not enough to guarantee identical rankings of decision alternatives. Goodwill can be of inestimable value in arriving at a workable compromise, but agreement on the facts alone is a necessary but not a sufficient condition for agreement.

COMPUTERIZATION OF THE DECISION PROCESS

Is it possible to break down a class of multiple-objectives decision problems so that it can be programmed on a digital computer and thereafter so routinized that complex decisions can be made by computers?

The answer to this question is an unconditional "yes" for well-structured, repetitive, homogeneous decisions and a conditional "no" for poorly structured, one-of-a-kind decisions. The conditional rather than the absolute negative is used here because in, some instances, it may be possible to impose a structure on a loosely defined situation, or by making some unimportant simplifying assumptions, to treat a particular decision problem as if it were a member of a general class of structured problems for which programs are available. Whether such an effort is worthwhile depends on the economics and the amount of unreality introduced by the simplifying assumptions.

Certain kinds of decisions are readily adapted to computer methods. Profile matching in personnel selection or computer dating, portfolio selection in investment practice, vendor choice in industrial purchasing, media selection in consumer advertising, and multiple-attribute testing in production quality control are just a few examples of the kinds of decisions that are already automated or have potential for early computerization. Computerized methods are becoming available for remote medical diagnosis through symptom data banks and electrocardiography; for playing a rather good game of tic-tac-toe or chess. Both the medical and game applications involve many difficult choices among alternative strategies, and both are examples of repetitive decisions.

Of course, even in cases where the computer can be used to run through a simulation, it is necessary first to make a competent analysis of the decision and to supply the detailed information in properly encoded format that is required by the particular computer program. For example, suppose that there is a program for choosing an industrial distributor with which to place orders for small quantities of electrical parts. The memory bank will have been supplied information about the firm's experience with all approved distributors and with their ratings on delivery, quality, average costs, reliability, inventory levels, lines carried, and other pertinent factors, which data is presumed to be kept up-to-date in a routine fashion. Depending on the urgency of a specific order, the buyer would then have to insert numerical weights to reflect trade-offs among criteria (for example, delivery versus price); he would have to be certain to properly characterize the items to be ordered so that the appropriate distributor can be queried, and so forth.

However, there will be occasions when the decision maker is faced with one-of-a-kind, poorly structured problems with ambiguities, conflicting interests, political considerations, and with the need for more information than can possibly be obtained at reasonable cost in the time available. In these cases, greater reliance must be placed on the human mind and less on machines, no matter how sophisticated. For problems of this type, if machine methods can be used, it will be for parts of the problem only as, for example, in data handling or for numerical computations.

SIMULATION OF INDIVIDUAL DECISION PROCESSES

Can the decision processes of a particularly skilled administrator be simulated and reproduced so that he can delegate many of his complex decisions to subordinates with reasonable assurance that their decisions would not differ materially from those he would have made under similar circumstances?

This question is vital because it points directly to the heart of the difficulty with delegation of authority faced by many high-level administrators. In spite of the lip service given to executive overload and the ever-present need for delegation, many top administrators do not feel secure enough to allow their subordinates to learn to deal competently with their bosses' problems. For these executives, the foregoing question is either irrelevant or poses a threat. But, if we assume that the top man is sincerely trying to relieve himself of some of the stress and overload associated with making complex decisions, is it possible for him to do so? The answer to the question is conditionally affirmative.

The conditional is used in place of the unconditional because it is hard to believe that the unique decision-making ability of a great practitioner can readily be transmitted to less talented persons. But if we think of the top man as a teacher who (in the same sense that Andre Segovia undertakes to develop the latent abilities of students of the classical guitar) is willing to develop the abilities of his subordinates and to train younger men to step into his shoes, then the foregoing question is important.

The higher a person is placed on the executive ladder, the more ambiguous and complex, and the less structured are the problems with which he must cope; and the higher up he is, the more claimants his decisions must serve. While at a low level, the employee has one or, at most, two or three bosses, the top man has many more to whom he must answer.

The simpler, better-structured decisions are dealt with at lower levels in the organization and, in most cases, are handled better than they could be handled by higher level people. As the problems become more difficult and diffuse, where mere technical expertise is insufficient, where complex interactions between contending interests are of paramount importance, they are passed up the line to the upper reaches of command for solution.

In a model organization, each executive level would have incumbents with the competence to deal with their own problems, but not with the problems that occur at the next higher level. Their inability to deal with these higher-level problems stems not only from lack of access to the specialized information available only to higher executives. If this were the only reason, the man on the $(j-1)$ *st* level would be competent to deal with the jth level problem, if only he could get the lacking information. In the more typical case, it is not only information lacks that prevent the $(j-1)$ *st* man from doing as good a job as the jth does; there are other factors of importance such as greater skills, a different outlook, a greater sensitivity to multiple interests, a longer time horizon, and a greater ability to handle ambiguity and frustration.

How then does the administrator-cum-teacher go about the task of training his subordinates to make decisions as he, the master, would? One method is the time-honored but long-drawn-out apprenticeship during which the novice assists and observes the master in his work and gradually, through imitation and practice, learns to emulate the master's methods. Another is the "sink-or-swim" technique. The neophyte is placed in a position of higher responsibility and is left to his own devices to cope. Some succeed, some fail outright, others muddle through. The cost of the errors made can be high. The successful men are put through the trial again and again until they reach either the organization's top level or their own ceilings.

Both of the foregoing methods achieve the objective indirectly and, although effective, they are expensive and take a long time. One way to reduce the learning time is for the master to instruct the novice directly in his methods. But, to do this successfully, the master must know his own methods. This presents a new difficulty, because many, if not most, administrators do not really know how they make decisions. Therefore, an important prerequisite for the application of direct instruction is a greater self-knowledge of decision-making technique.

The "Outline of a Full Explication" presented earlier in this chapter is a good vehicle both for self-analysis by the teacher-administrator and for training subordinates, subject of course to modification and elaboration as indicated by the particular situation. The apprentice can use the outline to prepare a detailed checklist of decision steps and can thereafter assist his superior in working out the parts. By imposing the self-discipline and analysis needed to make a full explication of various decisions, the master learns about his own methods with the student's assistance, and the student learns from the master decision maker. In this way, the apprenticeship time can be shortened and the administrator can both upgrade his own and his subordinate's capabilities in making complex managerial decisions that involve multiple objectives.

APPENDIX

APPENDIX

COMPLEX CASES INVOLVING MULTIPLE OBJECTIVES

CASE A-1
George, III Gets Hit Again

SUMMARY: As the result of a long series of "muddling-through" decisions, the president of a large decentralized company faces a rebellion in a remote subsidiary.

General Background

My name is George L. Holden, III. I am a fifth-generation American (Boston 1916), and the only child of Adelaide (nee, Lawrence) and George Holden, II. I was educated in the Boston public schools and took by B.A. and M.A. at Harvard. After graduation in 1939, I entered my father's business (the Holden Manufacturing Company) as assistant to the president. My business career was interrupted briefly by service in World War II. I served with the United States Army and was discharged at the war's end with the rank of major in Military Intelligence. On my discharge in 1945, I married Mrs. Holden (nee, Annette Wilson Grant) and returned to Holden Manufacturing as executive vice-president.

From 1945 until 1960 the business prospered, but showed little real dynamism or growth. My father became less active as time went on and left more of the management load for me to carry. In 1960 he retired altogether and took my mother on an extended cruise around the world. I will not take any more of your time with the events before 1960, because they have little bearing on the main interest of this narrative.

In 1960, on becoming chief executive of Holden in fact and in name, I took stock of the company's standing in the industry and decided that we had reached a plateau. We were making a line of electromechanical components and assemblies which we sold to a broad cross section of American industry. We had enjoyed considerable success and good profitability, but we had missed out on several important opportunities, notably in the space and computer industries.

Early in 1960, our board members were approached by a number of Wall Street houses about converting Holden from a privately-held firm to a public company. At one of the presentations, I met Mr. James Stegman, a partner in an old-line, but recently revitalized, investment banking house. Mr. Stegman sold us on the idea of going public and on his house's handling the underwriting. Later Jim also argued with us about the desirability of corporate growth through the mergers and acquisitions route. We were reluctant to move in this direction, but we ultimately accepted Jim's advice and were successful beyond any of our expectations. From a sales level of $20 million in 1960 we moved up to $100 million by 1966 and then to over $300 million by

1970. We made some good acquisitions and some that proved disappointing, but by year-end of 1970, we had stabilized and trimmed and were doing very well indeed. By then we had twenty-five subsidiaries in the high-technology fields and had strong market positions in military, aerospace, home entertainment, data transmission, and the computer fields as component suppliers.

We ran a highly decentralized operation with powerful profit incentives for our subsidiary executives. It was by no means impossible for one of our top people to build an estate of over $1 million after only ten years of work—that is, if he delivered what was expected of him. Several of our men did that and more.

We developed a good formula for managing these dispersed operations, and we did not need a large headquarters staff. I didn't believe in having a large corporate bureaucracy that would interfere with the work of the operating people. We did need some headquarters people to coordinate the subsidiaries, to insure a uniform corporate image, and to present a united front to the financial community. From headquarters we controlled only finance, stockholders' relations, and industrial relations. I think that the advertising people became involved in subsidiary marketing now and then, but certainly no more than was absolutely necessary.

In all, we had seven functional vice-presidents on the corporate level: finance, research and development (technological), research (economics and marketing), marketing, manufacturing, industrial relations, and administration. Each of these people had his hands full with twenty-five subsidiaries but, because there was little interaction between the plants and all were well managed, the individuals of headquarters group were not too overworked. They had time to visit each plant at least once a year, and to talk by telephone to the plant people at least once in two weeks. Along with attendance at trade shows and industry functions; with our annual executive meetings at headquarters; and with regular, written reporting, communications were tolerably good between the "mother firm" and the "colonies." I use this metaphor deliberately, because as you will discover, some of our key people thought of our mutual relationships in this light.

Of course, we had our problems. Things went well for us, but I should not leave you with the impression that no troubles ever developed. We had our share of product obsolescence, competitive difficulties, trouble with tight money, program cancellations, a few large-customer bankruptcies, labor troubles, and all the others that make any executive's life tense and demanding. But our people were dedicated, and they knew their jobs well; so we coped, prospered, and grew. Unlike some of our contemporaries, much of our growth was generated internally from the application of good management, aggressive product promotion, creative planning and financing, and clever marketing.

In the rush of everyday business, the headquarters people could not afford to give a disproportionate share of their attention to the affairs of any one subsidiary; hence, we used the good selection of managers and "intelligent neglect" as our main management techniques. I guess you might say that we were lucky, too, because only one subsidiary gave us any major trouble. But even in this instance, at first the trouble wasn't very bad. But because their behavior violated my sense of propriety, it caused more expenditure of managerial energy than was justified. I, myself became so deeply involved emotionally in the imbroglio that, if I accept my doctor's opinion, it ruined my health. The subsidiary I am referring to was the RST Division, a 1962 acquisition, that in 1968 was doing about $20 million in sales.

RST Instrument Company Background

The troublesome subsidiary, our RST Division, was formerly the RST Instrument Company, a privately-owned firm that had acquired an excellent reputation in supplying electrical measuring instruments to government and industry. Its products were both proprietary and custom-designed to customer specifications. The firm had been founded and operated by two very good engineers, Eli Cairns and Louis Ahrens, both of whom, although married, were childless, and who had no heirs capable of taking over the business. The owners had been ill and had not been able to take active part in the management for many months when the situation came to our attention.

They had a superb business run by a very competent general manager, Morton Selfrige, aided by a loyal, creative engineering staff and middle-management group. This permitted the owners to run the business from afar, but as you know, this cannot work forever. In any going business, particularly in fast-changing technological fields, there are always hard decisions that cannot be put off indefinitely. RST's owners were either unwilling or incapable of facing up to these problems.

Jim Stegman uncovered the RST Instrument situation for us, and when he approached them about selling, Cairnes and Ahrens jumped at our all-cash offer. Our price was fair and in record time RST Instruments became a wholly-owned subsidiary of Holden Technological Enterprises, Incorporated.

One important fact did not come to our attention until much later. The RST management people had been dreaming about taking over the company when the owners retired, and a good workable plan had been devised to meet this objective. They had almost completed arrangements for a public offering that would have permitted the management people to pay off the two owners in cash and marketable stock, but then the 1961–1962 slump hit the stock market, and it was virtually impossible to float new issues. They tried unsuccessfully to find a reputable underwriter to handle their issue. This left Cairns and Ahrens without a deal to sell RST; so when our offer was presented, they almost jumped with joy. Their joy was not shared by the management group; these people were bitterly disappointed. One of them told me later, "We felt that we were being sold into slavery. We came so close to gaining our independence that we could almost taste it."

Cairnes and Ahrens remained with RST for three months to help with the ownership transition. Our troubles with the RST Division began with their departure.

As we customarily did when we took over a company—and we fancied ourselves old, experienced hands at that—we brought a headquarters team into Indianapolis (the RST plant was on the outskirts of the city), and they, went into every detail of the business. From what we could see, everything was in good order, just as represented in the negotiations, and we were satisfied. We held a celebration dinner and meeting for an entire weekend at a downtown hotel for RST management down to the foreman level. On Saturday night we also had the executives' wives in for a special pep meeting with good entertainment, flowers, and expensive souvenirs for the ladies.

I remember the closing portion of my afterdinner address to the assemblage. I said, "We are very pleased with RST and we think that RST and Holden have a wonderful future together. We like the way you have been doing things, and we plan practically no changes at this time. If changes are required in the future, they will have the purpose of expanding RST's operations and to meet the next leap in sales growth, and this will be good for every one of us. The only change we are contemplating for now is to bring in a Holden executive as a replacement for Mr. Cairnes and Mr. Ahrens, when they retire completely, . . ."

I am a very sensitive public speaker and I could see that, up to a point, I had been making a good impression on the RST people. They were nodding their heads in agreement with my statements. In my exhuberance and in my self-congratulatory mood, I had failed to notice the cool reception given to my last sentence about the upcoming appointment of a "governor-general." For a brief instant they all stared at me, and when I finished my statement and sat down, there was polite applause mostly, I suspect, from the Holden delegation.

Our Troubles with RST Begin

We took over RST in November of 1962, the owners left in February of 1963, and from that time until mid-1968, we ran through six Holden-appointed general managers. It was our unvarying practice after any acquisition to have, at the top, a man who we were confident would be unquestionably loyal to Holden. The best way we knew for accomplishing this objective was to hire him at headquarters, either from outside the company, or by promotion from another subsidiary, and, after a short indoctrination interval, to send him out to the plant. A successful manager could do very well for himself and his family if he were both competent and loyal.

When I announced our intention at the first meeting with the RST people, I had in mind a man from a smaller subsidiary who had caught my eye as a "comer." Much to my chagrin, my choice lasted only six months. As soon as he had settled into the new job, things began to go wrong. There were work stoppages, deliveries to customers were delayed, quality fell, and so forth. Word began filtering back to headquarters through a grapevine that the new manager was a dud. Although this didn't square with my previous experience with the man, I asked him to return to headquarters to be relieved. He refused to return and resigned instead. That was number one!

After that we through a retired infantry officer (eight months), a well-recommended controller type (one year), an overaged engineering type (nine months), and one or two hard-nosed characters, without the feeling that headquarters had any real control over what was happening at the RST plant.

Without going into any unnecessary detail about our failures with RST top managers, we had one hell of a time getting a semblance of control over the plant. The job was made more difficult because, throughout the five years, RST continued to be profitable; it showed reasonable growth in sales and return on investment. In fact, except for the annoying difficulty in getting control of RST at headquarters, RST was one of our jewels. It was my impression that they were determined to assert their independence from Holden's control by being competent and profitable, even if they were totally uncooperative in every other way, so that we would be reluctant to interfere with them. Of course, it worked out just the way that they had it planned. Each general manager we sent to Indianapolis we instructed very carefully not to "rock the boat," not to disrupt a well-running organization.

For a while we suspected that there might be some thievery going on at RST and that there was a conspiracy to cover up their actions by getting rid of any outsider if he could not be persuaded to join the conspiracy. We actually fired some of the managers because we thought that they had gone over to the "enemy." We were wrong about that. We hired a detective agency to infiltrate the plant and those of two main suppliers. We tried entrapment of buyers by bribery attempts; looked for systematic pilferage, embezzlement, falsification of expense accounts, and many other ways of stealing, crude or subtle. Our detectives tried to earn their fees by turning up something wrong, but what we found was no better or worse than was going on in our other plants. There was some petty thievery, but nothing of a large or systematic nature that could account for the reluctance of the RST management to permit outside interference (they defined Holden's emissaries as outsiders).

We were not getting hurt by this situation, but it was getting on my nerves. It became the subject of jokes and humorous comment. Every Holden intrusion was met by RST's people with sudden retaliation. I used to lie awake nights thinking about this humiliating problem.

Every time someone from headquarters intervened in RST affairs uninvited, something unpleasant happened and something different each time. Perhaps a key man would threaten to resign because he had been abused by the intruder; there might be a wildcat strike; or a customer delivery might be held up. No order from headquarters was deliberately disobeyed, but somehow our directives were applied in such a manner as to have bad results.

They were clever, so clever about their responses that our people became afraid that they might be blamed for causing trouble. They all developed clear cases of what a psychologist might call avoidance behavior. The worst case I remember was when, in response to a headquarters initiative, some deliveries were held up. I received a nasty telephone call from the president of the customer's firm in which he threatened us with an antitrust suit. Apparently they were competing with a Holden subsidiary for a government contract, and they were led to believe that Holden had interfered with their deliveries to embarrass them. Of course, we knew nothing of this, but it was not nice.

You may ask why we were willing to tolerate such a situation. Why didn't I take some kind of decisive action to quell this impertinence and insubordination? I remind you that we had twenty-four other subsidiaries to worry about, most of them equally or more important than Holden. RST was very self-sufficient, more so than some of the others. The easiest course was to leave RST alone as much as possible, especially when things went much better if we did just that. Moreover, this happened so subtly and over a number of years that none of us realized that this was not a series of unrelated events but a carefully calculated response to headquarters intervention into RST affairs. Perhaps we could have done something at any time, but we had more urgent things to do; perhaps if RST were located in the East instead of the less accessible Midwest, things might have been different. Travel to Indianapolis was a nuisance, and it accomplished so little that was worthwhile.

By the fall of 1968, when we had a fiasco in coordinating our centralized computer operations with RST's, the situation had reached a psychological climax with me at the vortex. I had become very touchy about the situation; I began to imagine that people were laughing at me for being so weak or foolish or indecisive. RST was the subject on the agenda of several board meetings, and there developed a cleavage between the "doves" and the "hawks." The doves urged that we leave well enough alone; the hawks wanted to take decisive action to crush the "rebellion" at any cost. Their position was, "Why should we put up with such nonsense?" Even Mrs. Holden used to comment about my mystifying inability or unwillingness to take what her bridge partners thought was decisive action to squelch those "pipsqueaks" in Indianapolis.

I was getting flack from another source, too. By that time I held only 10 percent of the Holden shares, and a group of public stockholders had elected two directors who were quite hostile to my administration. They were whispering that perhaps I was losing my grip (I was only 52 at the time) or that I was too much of a playboy, or that I was too involved in outside interests, and so forth.

Although I took the position at board meetings that this was a minor matter that did not merit the attention lavished on it, RST was beginning to act as a burr under the saddle, especially when they refused to cooperate with the labor negotiations we were engaged in with a union that was demanding national representation in all Holden plants. I finally agreed that I would take it on myself to resolve the situation once and forever. I announced that

I would try one more general manager, and if that failed, I would take some unspecified, but drastic action to put an end to the RST insubordination.

We Begin Remedial Action

Jim Stegman was a member of our board and, since he was instrumental in bringing the RST acquisition to us, he had a greater personal interest in our problem than the other directors. Jim and I had lunch together the day after a meeting, and he told me of a young man who might be the long-sought answer to the RST general-manager problem. The fellow's name was Thomas Jeffers, Jr.

Tom was a Harvard MBA who had graduated with highest honors. He had also excelled at college (CCNY) and was voted "Man most likely to succeed" by his class. He made an outstanding record with Stegman's firm, and it was rumored that he was looking for a greater challenge. Stegman thought that Jeffers would be after my job in a few years, but if that didn't worry me, why not interview Jeffers for the top job at RST?

I laughed about Jim's idea of Jeffers being a threat to my position and agreed to meet the man. Jeffers came to my office the next day, and we discussed his qualifications and ambitions. Frankly, I was terribly impressed with the man. At that time he had just turned thirty-five; he was tall, well built, and had a commanding presence. I was convinced that here was a man who would succeed in any job he chose to undertake.

I outlined the problem with RST withholding nothing. I asked him to consider that six otherwise competent men had failed before him. Did he care to risk a bad failure at this stage in his career? He asked permission to visit the plant before giving me his decision. I agreed.

Two weeks later, Jeffers called and asked for another appointment. When he arrived, he told me that he had made a thorough investigation of RST's prospects and that he was willing—even anxious—to take on the challenge. We talked some about compensation and worked out a satisfactory arrangement.

After the usual 30-day indoctrination interval, Jeffers left for Indianapolis. I was interested to learn that he had sold his house and his boat, had taken his children out of school, and had placed a binder on a house near the plant. Obviously, I thought, Jeffers was planning for a long stay at RST. This lack of hedging impressed me even more, because he obviously had so much confidence in his ability to succeed where others before him had failed.

In retrospect, I am convinced that he took the job in good faith and that he had intended to carry out the assignment as we had outlined it to him. I do not believe that he had any other motivation than success and an opportunity to rise to the top of the Holden organization. I suspect that Jim Stegman was not fooling when he laughingly spoke of Jeffers as an aspirant for my job. Jeffers was ambitious, and he had the ability to achieve his ambitions.

Jeffers' first request was a queer one. Before and after the sale to Holden, the RST organization had been run by Morton Selfrige. In actual fact, it was Selfrige who kept the division running smoothly when Holden-appointed general managers were dropping like flies. I knew about Selfrige, but never considered him for the top job at RST because I knew of his disappointment at not getting control of RST for himself, and I doubted that he could ever overcome his bitterness. I couldn't take him out of RST until I was certain that I had a good manager to replace him and, after the difficulty with RST began, Selfrige lost most of his luster for us.

Jeffers asked me to transfer Selfrige to a job as general manager of another subsidiary or to a position as assistant general manager of one of the larger groups. Jeffers praised him for his competence, but said that he (Jeffers) could never succeed at RST so long as Selfrige was there. Firing Selfrige would be a mistake, according to Jeffers, because it would be a loss to Holden, and it would probably damage morale at RST and, therefore, make his (Jeffer's) job more difficult. Selfrige's loyalty to Holden would be intensified, and his hold on RST's people loosened if he were in Boston or California instead of in Indianapolis.

Jeffers' argument made good sense to me, and I carried out his recommendation. We made Selfrige an irresistible offer as vice-president and general manager of a small subsidiary, and he accepted after some hesitation. Just as an aside, Selfrige did a superb job for us and became one of our key people. We did well for him too; I suspect that he is now working on his second million in personal assets.

Jeffers did a lot of other things at RST too, but most of them involved my corporate officers and, other than give them a clear sign to give Jeffers what he needed, I wasn't involved further.

The Outcome of My Remedial Action

Jeffers began his job at RST in January of 1969. RST disappeared from my consciousness as I turned to more pressing problems. Holden Technological Enterprises was being attacked by a small computer-software firm that was trying to acquire Holden stock for paper of dubious value. Their offer of convertible debentures and warrants, although spurious in my judgment, appeared to be irresistible to some of our stockholders. In addition, we had a little scandal in one of our plants. One of our overzealous chief inspectors had "adjusted" some measuring instruments which caused defective materials to be passed in inspection. Unfortunately, this was on a government contract and when one of the inspectors, who held a grudge against his chief, told the resident government inspector, all hell broke loose. The story broke in the newspapers and was blown up all out of proportion. We tried to present our side of the story, but the overall effect was poor. One consequence was a loss in 10 percent in the market value of Holden shares, which made the tender offer to our stockholders even more attractive. As a result of these two events, some of our outside directors had some unkind things to say about the company's management (they meant me, but they weren't ready to make an open break at that time).

Amid all of this intrigue at the home base, I received a telephone call from Indianapolis requesting that I visit the plant if possible. Jeffers asked particularly that I bring Jim Stegman along if I could make the trip. If not, he would come to headquarters with his executive team. There was something they just had to talk about. As it happened, I was scheduled to attend an industry meeting in Chicago, so I agreed to bring Jim along with me and to stop off at Indianapolis for a day.

I arrived on Tuesday morning and immediately was closeted with Jeffers. Stegman was to arrive at about lunchtime, and Jeffers and I had some business chitchat for an hour or two. He told me that he wanted to talk with Stegman and me at the same time and that his executives would also like to be present at the meeting. As soon as Stegman arrived, we all drove over to a nearby restaurant where Jeffers had reserved a private dining room. We had lunch, and I could see that everyone, except Jim Stegman and I, was full of suppressed excitement. Jeffers seemed the calmest of the RST crowd, but he, too, seemed different.

After the luncheon dishes were cleared away, Jeffers rose and addressed his remarks at Jim and me. What he said, in effect, was that the RST executives were in a state of open rebellion. For years they had expected to gain control over RST and they had been cheated out of the opportunity by pure chance. Now, because of a favorable combination of circumstances (for them, not Holden), they were able to demand that we set RST free, that we give it independence. Specifically they demanded that Holden divest itself of RST stock by a spin-off to Holden stockholders and that RST executives be elected to a majority of the seats on the new board of directors. If Holden refused to accede to these demands some or all of the following things would happen:

1. The key people would leave the company, either to go into their own business or to work for competitors. Although they recognized that Holden might take some legal action to protect some of the trade secrets, legal action would not guarantee survival of the business;
2. The trade union in the factory was very resentful of the absentee ownership by eastern capitalist interests and would strike if Holden refused to go along. A strike at this time would be disastrous because of the pressure of the urgent needs of several customers; some of whom, incidentally, were also competitors of other Holden divisions;
3. The adverse publicity produced by the rebellion would act to persuade the stockholders that Holden's management was no longer capable of managing effectively. A public relations firm was standing by with press releases telling the story of the "Declaration of Independence" of a "Colonial-like" subsidiary from the "Imperialistic Mother Company," lampooning the plight of George the Third by his reincarnated nemesis

Thomas Jeffers (the son), Jr. This publicity, they speculated, would damage Holden's position in the take-over attempt that it was desperately trying to frustrate.

On the other hand, Jeffers pointed out, there were some advantages to Holden in accepting the RST executives' demands:

1. A spin-off of RST stock at this time would be viewed by Holden stockholders as an extra dividend that should endear the Holden management to them and should hold off the raiders;
2. Because of plans for growth, new products, and pledges of outside support, RST stock should rise on the stock market, again pleasing the stockholders.

As a clincher to his previous arguments, Jeffers asserted that Holden had no choice but to accept if it wished RST to survive. The alternative was acceptance of the ruination of the company. Holden could not dispose of the subsidiary in any other manner because it could not deliver the management and other key people. There would be nothing of much value left to sell other than fixed assets and inventory.

Jim Stegman and I were flabbergasted at the audacity and perfidy of Jeffers' statement of their demands. We sat there stunned, unable to make an articulate reply. Running through my mind was the bitter thought that hiring Jeffers turned out to be a terrible mistake and that the dissidents on the Holden board would surely have a field day with this situation. Stegman recovered first and, in a strained voice, asked for time to think over the "offer." Then we left the restaurant and looked for a hotel room to stay the night.

After thinking about the matter for several hours, I decided that it would be impossible for me to give in to the RST executives' demands. My only alternative was to return to the RST plant and fire the entire bunch of traitors. Stegman tried to persuade me to wait, to stall for time until we could come up with something constructive, but I refused. The accumulation of difficulties, humiliations, and frustrations in my dealings with RST over the years welled up within me and caused me to act emotionally rather than rationally. We went back to the plant and convened all of the executives in the conference room. I delivered a bitter speech attacking the immorality of their demands, calling Jeffers a Judas, and working myself into a high emotional pitch. Then I told Jeffers I wanted to talk privately to him in his office.

I demanded that he tell me how the entire plot had come about. Jeffers told me quite candidly that the RST executives had never given up the idea of capturing control of the company, but Morton Selfrige, their leader, had never had enough courage to face a knockdown, drag-out battle considering the danger to their careers if they failed. One day, at a dinner meeting, one of the executives had had a bit too much to drink and had blurted out their imminent plans for wresting control of RST from Holden. All that they were waiting for was to decide whether to invite Jeffers to be their leader or to try to get rid of him as they had the other Holden-appointed general managers. Jeffers had become convinced that a divestiture of the RST Division was the only way to save the business from ultimate destruction and that his loyalty to Holden demanded that he take appropriate action to save the underlying values from loss, so he consented to lead the rebellion. He was convinced that, in spite of the unconventional manner in which this was being done, it would be consistent with the long-run interests of Holden. Needless to say, I disagreed violently with Jeffers, but I was at a loss as to how to handle the situation.

1. Identify the elements of the decision sequence that led up to the rebellion.
2. Was there any critical point where timely and appropriate action might have forestalled the crisis?
3. Identify the interests involved and discuss their objectives.
4. What do you think Holden's aims should be?
5. What criteria would you suggest that Mr. Holden establish for gauging the merit of the alternative ways for dealing with this crisis?
6. What alternative ways can you think of for dealing with this rebellion?
7. How would you go about ranking the alternatives for desirability or for choosing a particular course of action?

CASE A-II
An Emergency at the Orrin Electric Products Company

SUMMARY: An electrical appliance manufacturer experiences an epidemic of customer complaints about defects in a radio-phonograph. There is danger of a flood of returns that could undermine the financial stability of the firm. Emergency action is taken to find the causative factors underlying the complaints and to determine a timely remedial action that will forestall a financial disaster.

Background

The Orrin Electric Products Company (ORRINCO) is a producer and marketer of a broad line of electrical goods for the consumer and industrial markets. The home appliance division of ORRINCO, headed by Mr. Robert Orrins, son of the president and grandson of the founder, has in its product line various models of radios, radio-phonographs, tape recorders and players, toasters, hair dryers, electric shavers, coffee makers, warming trays, and mixers. The home appliance division of the company is profitable and has a reputation with its distributors, dealers, and customers for ethical dealings and superior quality in manufacturing and design. The electrical appliance business has always been highly competitive, seasonal, and sensitive to general economic conditions.

Analysis of sales volume by product line indicated to ORRINCO's management that a disturbing trend was emerging. The company's appliance sales, both absolutely and in market share, appeared to be in a declining trend. Analysis of the market situation revealed that a portion of the decline could be attributed to a drop in consumer demand for electrical appliances, another portion could be attributed to the tendency for dealers and distributors to carry smaller inventories, and a large fraction could be attributed to the inroads made by domestic and foreign competitors. The appliance markets were experiencing severe price cutting and the intensive promotion of low-priced, low-profit items by hungry, aggressive competitors.

Mr. Robert Orrin, as director of the appliance division, was asked by the firm's corporate management to make recommendations on strategies and programs for reversing the downward trend in ORRINCO's sales and the apparent "loss of magic" of the company's brands.

Mr. Robert Orrin presented several promotional proposals, one of which was very appealing to the management and was adopted for immediate implementation.

Description of the ORRINCO Promotion

The ORRINCO promotion was similar in concept to promotions that had been carried out by the General Electric Company and the Consolidated Edison Company in the New York Metropolitan market in the years 1938 and 1939. At that time a promotional merchandise package consisting of a radio-phonograph, a toaster, an electric iron, and a standing floor lamp were sold for a special price lower than the items would cost if purchased separately. The package was promoted by the utility company, and purchasers could pay for the merchandise over a period of time along with their electricity bills. Many thousands of merchandise packages were sold in this joint promotion.

The ORRINCO merchandise package was to consist of the following items:

Item	Normal Price
1 Portable radio-phonograph (stereo)	$ 69.95
1 Electric steam iron	14.95
1 Pop-up toaster	14.95
1 Electric percolator	12.95
Plus a choice of either a hair dryer or an electric frying pan	19.95
Total normal price	132.75
Special promotional price	99.95

The promotional package was to be offered to large-city electric and gas utility companies for resale through their showroom, offices, and by direct mail and telephone solicitation. At the time, ORRINCO's management believed that the electric utilities would be interested in this promotion because a buyer's use of the products would result in an increased usage of electricity. Also the 20 percent gross markup offered to the utilities was thought to be attractive, especially since they would only act as sales outlets and collection agencies. Inventories, delivery, and warranty repairs were to be handled by ORRINCO's regular authorized dealers.

It was suggested that the electric company sell the merchandise package for either $99.95 cash, or for $10 a month for twelve months. Because the merchandise would be sold only to regular electricity and gas customers, it was anticipated that credit losses would be minimal. A money-back guarantee was to be offered, but the customer would have to return the entire package for refund and not just one or two of the components of the package. It was believed that this type of guarantee would prevent customers from returning all of the merchandise because they might not be fully satisfied with one of the items.

Upon accepting an order from a customer, the local utility sales person was to notify the local authorized ORRINCO dealer who would then deliver the merchandise to the customer's home. The dealer would then present the delivery receipt to the utility company for payment. His cost was 10 percent under the utility company cost. This dealer's markup was considered reasonable because the dealer had no selling expense, paid no salesman's commissions, and had no credit problems because the utility paid all bills by the tenth of the month. The dealer was to be reimbursed for warranty-repair expenses according to a flat-rate schedule. After the expiration of the one-year warranty, the dealers would be the beneficiaries of further repair business.

The products that made up the promotional package were to be specially designed and manufactured for this deal and would in no way resemble the regular ORRINCO lines. It was believed that the extra costs for the design, production, and packaging of the products could be successfully amortized over the large quantities that would be sold.

ORRINCO's management was convinced that the combined prestige of the ORRINCO brand and the electric utility sponsorship backed up by the dealer organization would make this promotion a resounding success. Production plans were made for the manufacture of more than 500,000 sets of products to be sold over a six-month interval from March to August of the next year. Break-even was estimated to occur at a sales level of about 150,000 sets.

Retail promotion was to be accomplished by personal selling in utility company showrooms, by telephone and direct mail solicitation, by posters and billboards, and by newspaper advertising. These efforts would involve little extra expenditures of money because most of the big-city utilities already were large users of newspaper space, envelope stuffers, and billboard and poster space.

Because the products were relatively simple, no special training of installers and service people was thought necessary other than the usual service notes and instruction manuals that ORRINCO regularly supplied to its dealers and service stations.

Results of the Promotion

The promotion was enthusiastically received by several big-city utilities, by ORRINCO dealers, and by the public. Large numbers of these promotional packages were sold both for cash and on the $10 per month plan. The utility companies encountered little or no resistance to the slight extra charge for credit. ORRINCO, however, was hard pressed to meet the demand and was delinquent in delivery despite many hours of overtime work in the factories.

Warranty Experience

The company believed that its regular sales organization backed up by its dealer service departments would be more than adequate to handle the in-warranty repair load. This expectation proved to be substantially correct for every appliance except the radio-phonograph. For a number of unexpected reasons there was an avalanche of complaints about the performance, reliability, and serviceability of the radio-phonograph. Because this was the biggest and most costly component of the promotional package, there was a great danger that customers would decide to return the entire package and ask for refunds. In fact, this was beginning to happen, especially in cases where the dealers were slow in making repairs or when they were unable to keep the item in service because of repeated failures. It appeared, from preliminary reports, that a number of serious defects and inadequacies were present requiring that many of the outstanding sets be called back for correction. Both the utility company representatives and ORRINCO's management concluded that this problem was of too great a magnitude to be entrusted to the dealer organization.

Robert Orrin's Action

Robert Orrin realized early that he was faced with a crisis that could have important repercussions on the company's reputation for quality as well as its financial solvency. Not only would the company's products get a bad name, but the money-back guarantee could produce astronomical financial losses most of which would have to be borne by ORRINCO. It was also evident that, in this emergency, ORRINCO would have to take the initiative to correct the situation because it had the greatest stake in a favorable outcome.

After attending a "table-banging" session with his father, ORRINCO's president, Robert Orrin called an emergency meeting to which he invited the company's national service manager, Mr. Harry Dett, the engineering manager, Mr. Oswald Moran, the purchasing director, Mr. Edward Colin, the manufacturing manager, Mr. Ronald Kelly, the quality control manager, Mr. Martin Owens, and the division's staff consultant, Mr. Kenneth Peterson. A number of decisions were made at that meeting:

1. Intensive incoming inspection, in-process, and finished-goods quality control was to be instituted immediately to guarantee that phonographs now in production and in inventory would be free from any defects.
2. An immediate study of field failures and failure reports was to be made to ascertain the nature of the defects.
3. An immediate review of the design was to be made by the engineering people to ascertain if there were any unknown design defects that needed correction.
4. The service manager, Mr. Dett, was instructed to work with the staff consultant, Mr. Peterson, to immediately design an organization for the purpose of servicing the radio-phonograph in the field. The design plan was to be implemented as soon as possible and, until then, the service manager was to do the best that he could to alleviate the situation.

At the close of the meeting, Mr. Orrin requested that Mr. Dett and Mr. Peterson remain in his office for a further discussion of the repair organization.

Mr. Robert Orrin's Instructions and Comments

"I asked you gentlemen to remain behind to discuss our problem because you two will have a large part of the responsibility for saving all of our necks in this situation. As far as I can tell now, we have assembled and shipped about 300,000 of the RPS stereo phonograph-radios. Just how many of these are in customers' homes we have no way of knowing yet. We have received close to 100,000 warranty registration cards to date, but as you all know there is a lag in returning cards and some customers just don't bother. We don't know yet if there is a basic design defect in the sets or if there was one or more bad parts that were used. Perhaps some of the troubles can be traced to poor workmanship because of excessive overtime hours of work in the factory.

"You also are aware that the sets were sold with a money-back guarantee and ultimately we would be left holding the bag if many are returned for refund. This could cause a catastrophic money loss to say nothing of the loss in reputation and market position .

"We must do something to limit our losses and if possible turn defeat into victory. I say this because the merchandise promotion was a tremendous marketing success, and we could repeat it in various parts of the country in future years. I needn't remind you that a failure at this stage would probably shut off future promotions of this sort.

"The damage to our reputation for service would also be irreparable. We would lose the confidence of our dealers as well as our customers. Our stockholders—and I know you gentlemen hold shares and stock options—would be damaged financially. Perhaps the forward progress of ORRINCO would be impeded for years to come. Perhaps Ford, General Motors, and Chrysler can live down occasional shipments of cars with built-in defects; I don't think we can.

"I needn't also remind you that a disaster like this, if not prevented, would probably require finding one or more scapegoats. Undoubtedly many heads will roll if we cannot rescue ourselves from this potentially disastrous situation.

"There is a possibility that the troubles may be due to some defective materials that escaped our inspection. There may be latent defects that could not be discovered by routine inspection. This we shall know more about in time. Meanwhile, of course, we shall require that all defective materials be returned for credit. This means that your plan will not only require that new

replacement parts be made available at all points in suitable
quantities, but that defectives be returned for analysis and credit.
We may also be able to recover some of our money losses from
suppliers who shipped us defective materials: that is, if such is
the case, and we could prove it in a court of law.

"Above all, it is essential that every set that was sold remain sold.
This means that not only must the customer be satisfied but also
that the utility company's sales people must be satisfied. So long as
they are convinced that we have everything under control, they
will resist accepting the merchandise deals back for refund. They
will offer exchanges, or repair services. If they get the idea that
we don't have command of the situation, they are going to get
orders from their brass to call everything back and to refund the
customer's money. We shall get everything shipped back to the
factory, and they will ask us to reimburse them for their losses.
I shudder to think of what the consequences of such a calamity
would be for ORRINCO. The president, my father, is now enroute
to hold meetings with the bigwigs of the utility companies to assure
them that we shall take every measure necessary to correct the
defects. He is going to tell them not to worry: to hold the line and
not to panic. I pray that he is successful. Meanwhile, of course,
we must back up his promises with a repair organization.

"I envision that we must be prepared to give, at best, same-day
services; at worst, 24-hour service to any customer who reports
a defect. The utility people tell me that they are willing to ask the
customer to carry the sets into their local offices. For those who
won't or can't they will send out a utility truck or delivery truck on
contract to make the pickup. If anyone asks for a refund, the
utility sales people will first offer to replace the set right then and
there. This will cost us some money, but I know it will be small
compared with the cost of returned deals.

"Although this is an emergency situation, we must make every
effort to keep the costs down. Also, I think it would be wise to
consider making this a permanent organization. We can use the
best people as cadres to staff a permanent field force for backing
up future promotions of this kind. If we had had such a force
before, we would have caught the trouble before it reached this
dangerous magnitude. Our relying on a dealer organization may be
all right in normal cases, but with these mass promotions, the time
lag is too long for safety and our peace of mind. We need almost
instantaneous feedback of any untoward troubles in the field. I'm
afraid that future promotions will have to bear the burden of a

factory-paid service force instead of our usual dealer service efforts."

Communication from Harry Dett to Robert Orrin, Next Day

Dear Bob,

I'm sorry I couldn't get to talk directly with you today, but your secretary said you were in an important meeting with your father and wouldn't be available for several hours. This communication was dictated to my secretary on a dictating machine wired into her telephone so that you could listen to the tape without having to wait for the information to be transcribed by typewriter.

When I left your office yesterday with Ken Peterson, Ken and I agreed that we couldn't make much progress until we had more hard facts about the magnitude of our problem. Therefore, I flew out to the East to survey the situation at first hand. I now have a good deal of useful information and more is coming in hourly.

I called first on the utility sales department and they took me over to their warehouse where they had 100 radio-phono sets that had been exchanged for customers. There were some more in local showrooms, and they are being put on tracks and being shipped over to me here at the warehouse. With the help of two service men from our local dealer's service department, we have been examining all the defective sets. Although this is by no means a random sample, I think a few facts are beginning to emerge.

First, let me say that the workmanship on these sets is not up to our usual standards. Several of the sets had defects that were due to poor wiring, poor soldering, and solder splashes. Several also had various kinds of defects that we usually expect because of human error or random parts failures. About 25 percent of the defective sets had one or more defective tubular capacitors. These units carried the supplier code 235754-28. Please tell Marty Owens to look out for parts made by this supplier. Also alert Ed Colin to get in touch with the supplier.

As you may have heard, this city has been going through an unusual heat wave and has been experiencing unusually high humidity. The coincidence of abnormally high heat and humidity may account for the delayed appearance of the defects in the sets. I sprayed each set that we examined with high-temperature steam from an electric vaporizer (ORRINCO make) and several of the sets developed the characteristic defect. Those that reacted to the steam test were all of the above supplier's make. Capacitors from other suppliers did not exhibit this sensitivity to steam.

I suspect that the capacitors have defective seals and that they are absorbing moisture. This moisture absorption produces degradation in electrical characteristics and the accompanying failure of the equipment. Drying out the capacitors with blasts of hot but dry air eliminates the trouble. We shall continue to make this test on other sets as they come in, but I think that we have pinpointed at least one of the troubles.

I have no idea how many of these capacitors we used in our production. It is also possible that only a few defectives were put in our sets, but it is possible, too, that all were defective. I'm afraid that the only safe course is to open up every set that has these units and to replace them as a matter of safety. If we do this, and this is the only systematic source of defects, we may have the major part of the trouble licked. We shall then be left with a smaller number of random defects to cope with.

I will call you again when I have more data. Best regards

Harry.

Excerpts from a Later Communication, Dett to Orrin

"I have more complete information now based upon the detailed examination of more than 1000 RPS radio-phonograph sets in the Eastern market. There seems to be no doubt that the abnormal rate of defectives was caused by an undetermined number of defective capacitors. These defective components can be identified by supplier code but, more simply, by the blue ink used in printing the ORRINCO brand on the body of the units. There are six places in the circuit of the phono-radio where these capacitors could be used and each location produces a unique set of performance symptoms as follows (location numbers refer to symbols on circuit diagram):

c10	gargling sound
c12	distortion
c15	motorboating
c18	oscillation
c19	distortion
c21	gargling sound

If two or more defectives are found in a set, the symptoms are mixed and difficult to diagnose.

"Conversations with purchasing reveal the following. Of the release of 500,000 parts complements, 3,000,000 tubular capacitors were ordered in equal shares from three suppliers. The three suppliers parts can be identified by the supplier code numbers but, more simply, from the color of the ink used in printing on the body of the unit: for instance, supplier A, blue; B, red; and C, yellow. Therefore 1,000,000 units with the blue ink were ordered and about 60 percent have already been released from parts stocks to the production lines.

"Unfortunately, the parts from suppliers A, B, and C were not segregated in the stockroom but were mixed in the stock bins. This means that mixed batches were issued to the production floor. The mixtures could be anything from 0 to 100 percent blue units. It follows, therefore, that any single chassis could have 0,1,2,3,4,5, or 6 blue capacitors inserted, but all together no more than 600,000 blue capacitors have been wired into sets. Since we have already produced 300,000 radio-phonographs, there will be an average of two per set, but if a number of sets had as many as six blue capactiors installed, the number of potentially defective equipments will be much less than 300,000.

"We cannot at this time be certain that every blue capacitor is defective or, if defective, that the temperature and humidity conditions would cause an immediate failure. Engineering analysis has shown that the fault in the blue capacitors was caused by a defective hermetic seal brought about by a fault in the mould used to seal the units. Whether this mould fault occurred in every unit shipped us, we cannot tell. We do know that destructive examination of blue units in sets and in stock showed a considerable variation in the extent of the leakage of the hermetic seals. Some showed no faults at all, some showed wide gaps.

"The wide variation in the extent of the fault in the hermetic seals of the blue units and the wide variations in temperature and humidity in the regions in which our merchandise is sold, suggests that we are sitting on a delayed-action bomb. We can expect that, in the absence of any corrective action on the part of ORRINCO, the reports of failures will continue to pour in. The only consolation I can find is that the delay in failure gives us some time to take measures to rescue our reputations.

"I recommend that we undertake the following steps.

1. All sets in inventory be sequestered and opened up for examination. Any blue capacitors found should be replaced, and the set should be retested before returning it to stock.
2. All sets in dealer inventories should be treated as in no. 1 above.
3. All sets in the hands of customers should be recalled for modification, preferable at a point nearby to avoid excessive shipping and handling costs.
4. All sets that have been returned for credit should be reconditioned and returned to stock.

"Our service organization should be set up to accomplish these tasks based on a minimum estimate of 50,000 and a maximum estimate of 300,000 RPS units. Our statistical department is preparing a more probable estimate of the number of defective RPS sets based on probability computations.

"As I mentioned in my previous report, the number of random causes of failure in these equipments appears to be greater than normal. Our usual experience is that about 3 percent of shipped merchandise will exhibit some defect within the three-month warranty period. In the present circumstances I think the figure would be closer to 6 percent plus the added difficulties caused by excessive handling and the back-and-forth transportation to the shops with improper packaging. Therefore, I believe we should be prepared for an additional rate of 20 percent defectives from random causes, including, of course, considerable cabinet damage. Handling will cause all kinds of damage to the wood-finished cabinets."

1. *Identify the components of this complex multistage decision.*
2. *For each subdecision in the sequence, diagram the steps using one or more of the decision models, if applicable, from Chapters 4 and 5. If not applicable, develop your own model.*
3. *Identify the parts of the overall decision that involve diagnosis and trace through the steps using the information from Box 3–1.*
4. *Identify the interests involved and their relative urgencies.*
5. *What do you think of the way Robert Orrins handled the problem? Is there any advice you could offer that would help him in this problem or in preventing recurrences of this type of problem?*

CASE A-III
Defending or Attacking the Executive Decision

SUMMARY: This case is an exercise in historical fiction; historical in that the story is built around actual happenings; fiction because facts are used selectively. Some are changed, some ignored, and some twisted beyond recognition. The fictional characters utter the author's words and not necessarily those of any person living or dead.

The Atomic Energy Commission is called on to defend its choice of Weston, Illinois as the site for the 200-Billion electron-volt particle accelerator. A systematic attack is mounted in Congress against the decision and the commissioner's deputy (a fictional character) meets the challenge.

FACTUAL BACKGROUND

On December 17, 1966 *The New York Times* reported the choice by the United States Atomic Energy Commission of a site for installation of a 200-billion electron-volt particle accelerator. Of the hundreds of possible sites, the AEC had first cut the list to eighty-five and then had asked a special panel of the National Academy of Sciences to narrow the choice further. The panel recommended Weston, Illinois; Brookhaven, Long Island, New York; Ann Arbor, Michigan; Madison, Wisconsin; Denver, Colorado; and Sacramento, California. The AEC chose Weston as the best site.

The construction cost of the 200 BEV project was estimated as falling between 300 and 400 million dollars with an annual operation cost of about 60 million. Truly, this was a desirable acquisition for any state, for any congressional district.

Thus, when the AEC chairman faced the choice of a site for this attractive facility, he must have known that of a United States Senate membership of 100 and a House membership of 435, he could please, at most, two senators and one representative. Moreover, because the AEC is dependent on congressional committees for funds and other important matters, it was obviously essential that the AEC staff prepare a reasoned justification for what must inevitably be an unpleasant decision for 98 senators and 434 representatives.

As everyone expected, the choice of the Chicago suburb, Weston, Illinois, proved unpopular with the representatives of the rejected sites. Many unkind things were said on the floors of the House and Senate and in the press about the Atomic Energy Commission and The National Academy of Sciences. Long and detailed arguments were advanced on why a particular rejected site was superior to the Weston location, and the legislators from Illinois were equally forceful in their defense of the virtues of Weston. The Atomic Energy Commission published a detailed justification for its choice but did not offer any data on the evaluations of the rejected sites, and it did not withdraw its final choice.

THE CONGRESSIONAL INVESTIGATION*

The clamor from disappointed governors, state legislators, mayors, representatives, senators, and newspaper editors was so great that the chairmen of both the Atomic Energy Commission and the Joint Committee on Atomic Energy concurred that a public airing of the factors involved in the site selection decision was mandatory. To this end, a joint subcommittee was appointed and instructed to fully explore all aspects of the siting decision. The first meeting of the subcommittee was announced, and the AEC was "invited" to send a qualified spokesman with all minutes, records, reports, and other data that might help shed light on the decision process. The AEC was represented by a special deputy commissioner, and the subcommittee chairman designated a prominent Washington attorney as special counsel to conduct the interrogation of the witness.

The First Day

CHAIRMAN: *Will the meeting please come to order [bangs gavel repeatedly] Sergeant-at-Arms, please get everyone seated! Get those television lights lower, please; that's fine now. Mr. Deputy, are you ready? Counsel, are you? Fine, then let's begin the proceedings. [Deputy moves over to witness table; counsel picks up his papers.]*

COUNSEL: *Mr. Deputy, will you please tell the committee how you fit into the matter under consideration here.*

DEPUTY: Presently I am special deputy to the AEC chairman. I was brought into the commission because of my experience and training as a private consultant in the economics of location. When the bevtron site selection matter is closed, I expect to return to my private consulting practice.

COUNSEL: *And you have the authority to speak for the AEC chairman?*

DEPUTY: Yes, but at this time only for the purpose of discussing the siting decision. If any other matters arise that go beyond my instructions, I will have to ask for new instructions or, perhaps, someone else will appear on behalf of the commission.

COUNSEL: *Thank you, Mr. Deputy. Let us now move on to more substantive matters. Can you refresh the committee's memories on the process involved in the site selection?*

DEPUTY: Certainly. The commission made public a two-volume scientific

---

* Historical fiction begins at this point except where specific citations to factual data or to real persons and places are made.

report on the design considerations for the 200-billion electron-volt accelerator and solicited applications from localities in the continental United States. We received a rather large number of applications, some good, some not really suitable. The list appears in the record but I have copies for the committee members and the press.* We also established a number of siting criteria that could be used for the initial coarse screening of the applicant localities. I believe that these criteria also appear in the Congressional Record (Vol. 114 pp. 10108–9, May 9, 1966). Through the use of these preliminary criteria, we eliminated the obviously unsuitable site proposals and were left with 85 that passed the coarse screening.

COUNSEL: *At this point, was there any attempt at evaluation of alternative sites?*

DEPUTY: No. Site evaluation is a time-consuming and expensive process. It makes no economic sense to spend large sums of the taxpayer's money in evaluation of the sites that will certainly be eliminated because they fail on some important criteria. The initial process was a pass-fail; go, no-go test. If the site alternative was obviously unsuited, it was given no further consideration. For example, a site that is located more than 200 miles from a major airport, or 500 miles from a university with a high-quality physics department, or in the middle of a seismically unstable region, or where electric power facilities are inadequate and presently overtaxed, would be dropped at an early part of the decision process. The people in these unsuitable places will certainly be disappointed, but that cannot be helped.

COUNSEL: *And then what?*

DEPUTY Even 85 sites were too many. Before evaluation could begin in earnest, the need for a finer screening process became apparent. The National Academy of Sciences was brought into the deliberations and their people were requested to refine the criteria and to use the new standards in a second, finer screening of applicant localities.

COUNSEL: *What was happening at this time? Would you say that most of the 85 sites that survived the coarse screening were perfectly feasible locations and that the second, finer screening would eliminate feasible sites?*

DEPUTY: Yes, that is true. Probably many of the 85 sites were feasible, but you must remember, we look not only for a feasible site but for the best. The refined criteria were intended to help us find the best. We still had to decide on *one* site. If we were not to use some kind of a lottery, we needed to know which site was the most suited to the purpose.

COUNSEL: *Would you say that persons who criticize the final site choice are justified, that you rejected many perfectly adequate sites?*

DEPUTY: Their disappointment is understandable but not really justified. We approached the problem as that of finding a site that would be the best match of the various criteria. Only in this way could we serve the best

---

* *Hearings before he Joint Committee on Atomic Energy, Congress of the United States, Eighty-Ninth Congress,* Feb. 2: March 8, 9, 10, 11, and 15, 1866 Part 3, pp. 1626–1631.

interests of the nation as a whole as compared with the interests of a single locality.

COUNSEL: *What did the NAS come up with?*

DEPUTY: They eliminated all but six of the 85 sites. Those that survived the second screening were: Weston, Illinois; Brookhaven, Long Island, New York; Ann Arbor, Michigan; Madison, Wisconsin; Denver, Colorado; and Sacramento, California. The NAS people preferred not to go beyond this point. They merely stated that these six sites were superior to the rejected 79, and recommended the selection of one of them. I have brought along some copies of their report.*

COUNSEL: *I ask you the same question about these six site alternatives, were all six feasible—in this case—good acceptable sites?*

DEPUTY: Probably yes. But we still had to choose only *one* of six. Again we elected to try to discover which of the six was the best. Again we understand the disappointment of the five rejected applicant localities, but no matter which site we chose, there had to be five unhappy applicants.

COUNSEL: *And the commission decided that Weston, Illinois, a suburb of Chicago, was the best place in the continental United States for installation of the accelerator?*

DEPUTY: That was the choice. Weston was judged to be the best of all applicant sites.

COUNSEL: *The best of all applicant sites? Does that mean that there might have been a better place but that the people in the better place might not have applied? Did the commission make any independent surveys that might have disclosed a better location?*

DEPUTY: The commission did not make an independent survey, but we believe that every place that might be suitable was included in the initial applicant list. There is no ideal location that was not included.

COUNSEL: *You used he word, ideal." Was Weston an ideal location?*

DEPUTY: Ideal? I can't say if Weston was ideal; it was the best of all the applicant locations.

COUNSEL: *While we are on the subject of ideal locations, let me quote a few lines from the NAS report, I quote, "no ideal site had been proposed and . . . the eventual selection depended on balancing the various factors of physical properties and environment." Do you conour with that statement?*

DEPUTY: Yes. That is just what I said before. No one of the 85, or the surviving six was perfect or so superior to the others that it was the obvious choice. Some compromises were necessary.

COUNSEL: *My friend the professor, sitting at my side, suggests that no one site alternative dominated the others? Do you accept that statement?*

DEPUTY: Yes, I do. No site was dominant.

COUNSEL: *Now we have six possibilities, how do we find out which is best?*

DEPUTY: It was necessary to develop specifications for each of the criteria so that the six sites could be scored on the criteria.

---

* Report contained in *Hearings before the Joint Committee on Atomic Energy, Congress of the United States, Eighty-Ninth Congress,* February 2, March 8, 9, 10, 11 and 15, 1966 part 3, pp. 1633–1655.

COUNSEL: *And this was done for every criterion? Could you illustrate?*

DEPUTY: Yes we did this. *An example?* Well suppose we consider the factor *distance from a major airport.* We could measure the mileage between the site and the airport. A smaller distance would be preferred to a greater.

COUNSEL: *Could you elaborate on this? What is a major airport?*

DEPUTY: A major airport is one that can accept passenger jets like the 747 and has connections with the major cities.

COUNSEL: *Would you be concerned only with distance? How about travel time? Suppose that there were not good roads to the site?*

DEPUTY: Yes we would also consider travel time as well as distance. Among sites with nearly equal distances, the one with better roads would be preferred.

COUNSEL: *Suppose that the site were directly alongside the airport?*

DEPUTY: That would probably not be too good because of the noise and vibration of the new jets.

COUNSEL: *So closeness is not enough. In fact, a site could be too close?*

DEPUTY: Yes, that would have to be considered.

CHAIRMAN: *Counsel, you are not planning to explore every one of the criteria, are you? We do not have the expertise to contradict the experts on technical matters.*

COUNSEL: *No, Mr. Chairman. We can stipulate that the commission's experts know how to set up specifications and evaluate each site on each criterion. We have no desire to quibble on matters like this. Now, Mr. Deputy, I assume that you have evaluated each alternative site on all of the criteria and that you have set up quality or efficiency scores for each site. Is that correct?*

DEPUTY: That is correct.

COUNSEL: *We haven't discussed the criteria so far. Suppose that I had different criteria from yours? Wouldn't this be a problem?*

DEPUTY: Not at all. We can easily assume that every one involved has an identical set of criteria. If one of my criteria seems irrelevant to you, assign a weight of zero to it. If one of yours seems irrelevant to me, I assign a zero weight. For criteria we all agree are relevant, we both assign a numerical weight other than zero.

COUNSEL: *I see. That helps. But we don't all assign equal weights to all criteria, do we?*

DEPUTY: Not at all. Each person is likely to have an individual set of criterion weights.

COUNSEL: *But doesn't that mean that each person will make a different choice from among the alternatives?*

DEPUTY: Not necessarily, but it is theoretically possible.

COUNSEL: *Let us get back to the site scores. We said that we could not tell which site was best from the scores alone because a site might be good on one criterion but poor on another. And each site has its own peculiar set of high and low scores. No one is superior on all criteria. Is that correct?*

DEPUTY: That is exactly the case.

COUNSEL: *So the difference between site evaluations depends on the weights assigned to the criteria?*

DEPUTY: True.

COUNSEL: *And if I used one set of weights Brookhaven might be best; if I used another set, Ann Arbor might be best; and, in both cases, Weston might have been far from the best?*

DEPUTY: That is quite possible.

COUNSEL: *Did everyone at the Atomic Energy Commission who had a part in the decision have the identical weight set?*

DEPUTY: No, there was some disagreement.

COUNSEL: *Ah! And how was this disagreement resolved?*

DEPUTY: The weights were finally decided by a consensus. The assignment of weights is not very scientific. There is a great deal of judgment involved.

COUNSEL: *Do you mean to tell this committee that after all the scientific rigmarole, the final choice is based on a collective judgment?*

DEPUTY: If you put it that way, I suppose you are right. But the scientific evaluation is necessary in order to have numbers to weight.

COUNSEL: *But the difference in ranking of an alternative site is as much determined by judgment as by scientific investigation?*

DEPUTY: That is true, unfortunately.

COUNSEL: *Then is it possible that those judgments were swayed or influenced by extraneous matters, by biases, predispositions?*

DEPUTY: I can't speak about anyone's biases but my own. In my case, there was no bias or preference or outside influence. My only consideration was for the welfare of the nation as a whole, and I resent the implication. Not only that, but I will vouch for the integrity of every member of the siting task force.

COUNSEL: *I'm sorry. I didn't mean to cast doubt on your integrity or on the integrity of any member of your task force. I'm certain, as you are, that they are men of highest probity. But the fact remains, that in spite of the scientific facade, judgment is a major determinant of which of the six sites is chosen.*

DEPUTY: Yes, that is true; judgment does play a part.

COUNSEL: *And what if your scores assigned to each site were taken by the representative of, say, Brookhaven in New York, and he performed the calculations, what do you think would happen?*

DEPUTY: I know what I hope would happen, but human nature being what it is, I'm afraid that he would work it out so that Brookhaven scored highest.

COUNSEL: *And Ann Arbor? Or Sacramento?*

DEPUTY: The same would happen there. Ann Arbor would be given top rating by the Ann Arbor people; Sacramento, top rating by their advocates.

COUNSEL: *Well where does that leave us? It seems to this committee that the commission gave the impression that their site selection was based on unimpeachable, scientific grounds, that there was no possibility of hanky-panky or of exercise of influence, and now we discover that really the choice of a site is really just a matter of someone's opinion. Now I ask you, who's opinion decided that Weston was best?*

DEPUTY: I think you are placing the entire matter in an unfair light. Certainly informed judgments played a part in making the final choice, but it was a choice among good alternative sites.

COUNSEL: *Yes, but for the rejected sites it doesn't make any difference whether they are rejected in the first screening or the last. They are rejected. Is it possible that some of the 79 rejected sites (in the first screening) would have reached the top six or seven or some other number if someone's judgment had been different?*

DEPUTY: It is theoretically possible, but I don't think that happened. The rejected alternatives were properly categorized.

COUNSEL: *You think? Don't you know?*

DEPUTY: I think, I believe, I am convinced, but there is a small probability that one or more might have made the second list had some judgments been different.

COUNSEL: *And the rejected sites might have had a chance of being chosen as best?*

DEPUTY: I very much doubt that.

COUNSEL: *But it is possible?*

DEPUTY: Very unlikely.

COUNSEL: *I see that you will not say positively that it is impossible. I acknowledge your honesty, but I sympathize with the outrage of the rejected applicants. All this time the committee thought that our scientists were being scientific when we see that they are forced to rely on their too human judgment. Do you think that they are better qualified to make such judgments than, say, a member of the United States Senate?*

DEPUTY: That is pure conjecture. I prefer not to comment on your last question.

COUNSEL: *Of course, it was unfair of me to put you in such a corner. I apologize. Let me summarize to this point; the total number of sites was subjected to a coarse screening and 85 sites remained. Then the NAS people refined the criteria and applied them to the 85 and found only six that were worthy of further consideration.*

DEPUTY: Not quite true. The six were the best of the 85. Any site might be worthy of consideration, but remember we were seeking the best site from those that were offered for study.

COUNSEL: *Thank you. There were six sites that were found to be worthy of the top place and those six were subjected to a further, more severe testing and, by using scientifically derived scores and subjectively derived consensus weights, a final choice of which of the six was best was arrived at. Is that substantially correct?*

DEPUTY: Yes, that is substantially correct now.

COUNSEL: *And if I told you that I had given your effectiveness scores to each of the six representatives, you would not be surprised if each of them came up with a different choice?*

DEPUTY: I'm afraid my answer to that would have to be yes.

COUNSEL: *Was there any overt effort made to protect the task-force members from outside influence or bias?*

DEPUTY: Yes there was. In addition to the obvious measures of selecting persons of known integrity and superior scientific judgment, we did not permit the persons who made the evaluations to know the weights to be assigned to the criteria. Also, the task force was divided into groups, and no one group had access to all of the data. Nor were these individuals equally competent in all areas. We had transportation experts, geologists, sociologists, and so forth as consultants. Thus, the evaluation and weighting processes were so fragmented that the possibility of external factors entering in any meaningful way was small.

COUNSEL: *When you say meaningful, do you mean that a small change in a weight or a score might have shifted the choice from one site to another?*

DEPUTY: I really can't say. Since no one site was dominant, weight assignments made all the difference.

COUNSEL: *How were the weights developed? Were unimpeachable scientific methods used?*

DEPUTY: I'm afraid not. Weighting is still very much a matter of judgment of which criterion is more important than another, and how much of one can be traded off compared with another.

COUNSEL: *Very good. I'd like your opinion on a small numerical problem [moves to blackboard] Can everyone see this? Good [writes on board], I have two sites that I call site A and site B with evaluation scores on two criteria,*

	Criterion Scores	
Site	I	II
A	60	40
B	10	90

Notice that site A scores higher on criterion I than B, but lower on criterion II. Does this bear any similarity to the six site selection problem your task force dealt with?

DEPUTY: In a highly oversimplified form, yes, it is analogous.

COUNSEL: *Notice that if I added the points (60+40) or (90+10) the total points are the same for sites A and B. That means that sites A and B would be equally suitable, is that not so?*

DEPUTY: Yes, that is so.

COUNSEL: *Now if I weight criterion I heavier than II, site A would be preferred to B. And if I weighted criterion II heavier than I, site B would be preferred to A. Is that reasonable?*

DEPUTY: Yes, that is reasonable.

COUNSEL: *So in this special case, a small difference in emphasis of criterion I over II or vice versa, can shift the siting choice?*

DEPUTY: True.

COUNSEL: *And if the stakes were very high, say 300 millions in capital outlays and 60 millions per year in expenses; or high employment versus high unemployment, a slight shift in favoring criterion I over II, or II over I could make the difference between prosperity and disaster for a community?*

DEPUTY: Under the conditions you postulate, yes, that is a possibility.

COUNSEL: *Is this in any way similar to what happened in the siting choice made by the AEC?*

DEPUTY: Not exactly, but not completely different either, I'm sorry to say. None of the six sites given us by the National Academy of Sciences was obviously superior to any other and none obviously inferior. In that sense we could not choose from among the six until we applied criterion weights. Then a best choice emerged.

COUNSEL: *Was the best very much superior to the five next best?*

DEPUTY: Not really. The rankings could easily have been altered by small changes in criterion weights.

COUNSEL: *Now suppose, and I'm not suggesting that this really happened, that I knew in advance which of the six I wanted to be found best, could I shift the weights somewhat to accomplish my objective?* In my blackboard example, a shift of as little as 1 percent in the weights in favor of one criterion over another could have shifted the choice of sites.

DEPUTY: It's theoretically possible, but I don't think it happened in this case.

COUNSEL: *How can you be so certain? When the consensus was reached on weight assignment, how can you be so sure there was no favoritism? After all, the task force was made up of extremely gifted men, many qualify as geniuses, some undoubtedly have photographic memories. How can you be certain?*

DEPUTY: When you put it that way, I suppose that I can't be certain. But that didn't happen because the final siting choice was not made by the task force, but by the members of the commission, the "inner circle."

COUNSEL: *Suppose that the members of the "inner circle," as you call them, knew that Weston, Illinois had just received another very large government grant, and that the other five cities had not benefited from governmen grants or contracts for several years, do you think that would have made a difference?*

DEPUTY: I can't comment on that. That is a policy matter beyond my competence.

COUNSEL: *What if Weston, Illinois were found to have segregated schools and housing, would that make any difference?*

DEPUTY: My answer is the same. That would be a policy matter.

COUNSEL: *Let me change the form of the questions. If I told you that these two conditions had been found in Weston and then heard that Weston* was therefore reduced in rank in favor of Ann Arbor, Michigan, would you be surprised?

DEPUTY: No, I would not be surprised.

COUNSEL: *In spite of the fact that neither segregation in schools and housing nor equity in distribution of government grants was on the list of criteria?*

DEPUTY: Please don't try to push me into that corner. The NAS criteria were all based on the cost-effectiveness approach and on considerations of operational efficiency; political matters were not considered by the siting task force. If other, extraneous matters were introduced, they were factored into the choice process much later.

COUNSEL: *Were political considerations introduced?*

DEPUTY: I have no knowledge that they were.

COUNSEL: *Could you say positively that they weren't?*

DEPUTY: No, I could not say for certain. I just don't know.

COUNSEL: *Then the final choice was not made by the siting task force?*

DEPUTY: No, we just submitted our recommendations.

COUNSEL: *And what were your recommendations?*

DEPUTY: I'm sorry that I must decline to answer that question. My instructions require me to respectfully decline to answer on grounds of executive privilege.

COUNSEL: *If you can't or won't tell the committee in detail, can you tell us of the format?*

DEPUTY: Yes, we did something similar to a judge's charge to the jury: (a) If you think that capital cost is the most important factor, _____has the lowest on that; (b) If you think that operational costs are most important, _____is lowest on that. We prepared a number of suggested criterion weighting combinations and pointed out their logical consequences. The "inner circle" had only to decide which weighting combination best fit their considered judgments.

COUNSEL: *I submit to you that the process you describe is not really very scientific or even very objective. The siting choice was passed on to the inner circle of the AEC, and they could either accept or ignore the scientific findings.*

DEPUTY: True, they could if they chose to, but I don't think they did.

COUNSEL: *Do you know they didn't?*

DEPUTY: No I don't know for certain. But having the power to do so and actually doing so are two different matters. The siting task force did its job as directed. We were supposed to investigate the good and bad points of each site, to present sound data in understandable form to assist the commission in making its final decision.

COUNSEL: *Mr. Deputy, when the site selection task force completed their work, was there a final report to the commission?*

DEPUTY: There was, and it was a very large document.

COUNSEL: *Is it available for the committee's inspection?*

DEPUTY: I can't answer that question at this time. Its present status is that of a confidential internal report not for publication. The chairman would have to make a formal request to the AEC chairman.

COUNSEL: *Did the report contain detailed evaluations on each of the six alternative sites and every criterion?*

DEPUTY: Yes, both very detailed and condensed.

COUNSEL: *Why didn't the commission make the comparisons public?*

DEPUTY: Such a release would serve no useful purpose. We have prepared a detailed analysis of the Weston site choice and it is in the record (Congressional Record—House, Jan. 23, 1967 pp. 1145–1148). This in our judgment is sufficient.

COUNSEL: *What the committee would like to find out is whether the justification contained in the exhibit was made after the choice of the Weston site and is intended as window dressing to supply apparent justification for what was really a politically motivated decision.*

DEPUTY: I believe that the justification is correct and to the point. The choice of the Weston, Illinois site can stand on its own merits.

COUNSEL: *Very good, Mr. Deputy. You are a skilled and persuasive advocate. I'd now like to change the subject, if I may. Let us go back to the scoring chart. You did say that there were scores for each site on each of the criteria, didn't you?*

DEPUTY: Yes, and the scores were supported by considerable narrative and statistical materials.

COUNSEL: *Excellent. Now we have six alternative sites, a lot of criteria, and a set of criterion weights. Could we arrange the data in the form of a table, say, with the rows corresponding to the sites, the columns corresponding to the criteria, and the box formed by the intersection of a row and column, to a score?*

DEPUTY: Yes that is feasible.

COUNSEL: *And then we include numerical weights, and the table looks like this (Exhibit A)?*

DEPUTY: Yes that would work.

COUNSEL: *Now assuming that we can put numbers into all the boxes and weights to each criterion, are we finished?*

DEPUTY: No. We would now have to operate on the numbers in the table.

COUNSEL: *Ah, how would you do that?*

DEPUTY: We would add all of the weighted quality points and the site with the largest quality-point-score total would be the best.

COUNSEL: *Is that what the task force did?*

DEPUTY: Yes, in effect that is what we did; except that we made several tables, one for each weighting combination, and we did the computations on a computer.

COUNSEL: *Are you satisfied with that method?*

DEPUTY: Why, yes. *Do you see anything wrong with it?*

COUNSEL: *Well, I personally am no expert in this field, but the professor would like to ask you a few questions if the chair will permit.*

CHAIRMAN: *Any objections? Go ahead Professor.*

PROFESSOR: *Mr. Deputy, you said that you used the weighted sum of the quality points rule. Why did you do that?*

DEPUTY: Why not? That's the way we always do it.

Site	Criterion number												25	26	27	28	29	30
	1	2	3	4	5	6	7	8	9	10			25	26	27	28	29	30
Denver, Colorado																		
Ann Arbor, Michigan																		
Brookhaven, Long Island, New York																		
Madison, Wisconsin																		
Weston, Illinois																		
Sacramento, California																		
Weights																		

Exhibit A

EXHIBIT A.   Table of ratings of six sites on thirty criteria.

PROFESSOR: *But why add the points? Why not multiply them instead. Or why not sum the squares or square roots? What is so sacred about the arithmetic summation?*

DEPUTY: Why introduce additional complications? The sum method works well enough for our purposes. It gave us a good answer.

PROFESSOR: *Do you and your colleagues realize that the sum, product, squares, and square-root methods might give different results?*

DEPUTY: Now that you mention it, I suppose that is a theoretical possibility.

PROFESSOR: Let me demonstrate for the committee. Recall the simple problem Counsel put on the board yesterday.

	Criterion	
Site	I	II
A	60	40
B	10	90

Suppose, if we neglect weights for the moment, we use a simple sum. Then site A and site B are equal. If we use the product, site A is better than B. If we use the squares, site B is better than A. So it matters very much for this oversimplified case which method we use for combining these scores.

COUNSEL: *Thank you Professor. Mr. Deputy, do you concur with the professor's demonstration?*

DEPUTY: Yes, it is very interesting. I don't know if this would have affected our choice.

COUNSEL: *We now have another variable, do we not? We start with an ostensibly scientific evaluation with admittedly subjective weights. Now we have a choice of methods for combining weighted scores.*

DEPUTY: It certainly looks that way.

COUNSEL: *When you arbitrarily decided to use the sum of the quality points, weren't you introducing a hidden bias into the choice of sites?*

DEPUTY: I'm not sure, it's theoretically possible. But that was not our intention.

COUNSEL: *Professor, what kinds of biases do the different methods introduce?*

PROFESSOR: The differences are mainly in how the rules treat site profiles with extreme values. The product rule tends to be very severe on sites with profiles containing low scores and tends to deprecate compensating high scores on other criteria. In contrast, the squares rule tends to overlook low scores but gives greater weight to high scores even if a low scoring criterion might presage disaster. You might say that the product rule prefers sites with a dull glow whereas the squares rule prefers alternatives with a bright but flickering light. The sum rule falls somewhere in between the product and squares rule.

COUNSEL: *What might be the consequence in a particular site selection problem? Can you say?*

PROFESSOR: I can't say until I examine the actual data. But if a particular site scored very low on one criterion but quite high on others, it might get chosen over others even if the low scoring criterion might be the cause of a future disaster. This is more likely to happen if the squares rule is used, and is quite unlikely if the product rule is used. The product rule represents a state of pessimism, the worst might happen so let's protect ourselves against it. The squares rule represents a state of blissful optimism; only the best can happen, forget about low scores if the others are high enough. This is also true for the sum rule, but not to the same degree.

COUNSEL: *How does one know which rule to use?*

PROFESSOR: Since bias is inevitable, the best you can do is to select a rule with the correct bias and make it explicit.

COUNSEL: *Mr. Deputy, does this make sense to you?*

DEPUTY: Yes, I think so, but I would like to think about it for a while and, perhaps, rerun some of our calculations.

COUNSEL: *How long would that take?*

DEPUTY: A few hours, I think. If I ran over to my office now, I think I could have some answers by 3:00 P.M. this afternoon.

COUNSEL: *Mr. Chairman, can we recess until this afternoon?*

CHAIRMAN: I think not, Counsel. I would like Mr. Deputy to have a bit more time. Today is Thursday; suppose we adjourn over the weekend and reconvene Monday. *Any objections?* So ordered.

MONDAY

CHAIRMAN: *Will the committee meeting please come to order. Counsel, do you think you can finish your questioning today?*

COUNSEL: Yes, Mr. Chairman, unless something unexpected arises. We should be finished in an hour.

CHAIRMAN: Very well, proceed.

COUNSEL: *Mr. Deputy. Do you have any further testimony on the matter we were discussing at the end of the Thursday session?*

DEPUTY: Yes. I think I have made some interesting findings.

COUNSEL: *Will you please inform the committee?*

DEPUTY: After our meeting on Thursday, I called some of our task-force members together and discussed the problem of combining methods. We decided to rerun the data using different rules and to see what the results would be.

COUNSEL: *And did you do this?*

DEPUTY: Yes sir we did.

COUNSEL: *And what was the result?*

DEPUTY: I won't go over all of our findings because that would not add enlightenment, only confusion. We did redo all of the calculations for all weight combinations. But, I will report on the weight set that was used to select the Weston site. Will that do?

COUNSEL: *We'll see. Tell us about that one.*

DEPUTY: When we used the weighted sum-of-the-points rule, Weston, Illinois was the site with the largest quality-point total. When we used the product rule, Weston was the third choice; with the squares rule, it was the second choice. [This statement is greeted with loud noises.]

CHAIRMAN: *Order. Order. If we can't have some reasonable quiet I will have to clear the hearing room. Mr. Deputy, did I hear correctly? Weston was best only with the sum rule?*

DEPUTY: Yes, Mr. Chairman

CHAIRMAN: Well what the hell! . . . Oh. I'm sorry Counsel. I was carried away for a moment. You go ahead, please

COUNSEL: *Could you tell us which site was "best" with the other rules?*

DEPUTY: I respectfully decline to answer on grounds of executive privilege.

COUNSEL: *How can the committee find out?*

DEPUTY: I presented these findings to my superior, the AEC chairman. There will be a meeting of the Commission tomorrow morning. If there is to be any action to rescind the choice of Weston, Illinois for the installation of the particle accelerator, there will be an announcement at a specified press conference. If the decision is made not to rescind, I do not know whether there will be any special announcements made. Until then, my instructions are to make no further statements beyond an elaboration on the material covered up to Thursday, which is not still confidential.

COUNSEL: *Are you prepared to change any of your earlier testimony on the basis of your new findings or new instructions?*

DEPUTY: No sir, I am not.

COUNSEL: Very well, then, Mr. Chairman, I have no further questions of this witness.

CHAIRMAN: *Thank you, Mr. Deputy, for your excellent cooperation with the work of this special subcommittee. I do not know at this time if we shall require any further testimony from you. Until such time as we may wish to recall you, you are excused. Thank you again. Are there any other witnesses that wish to be heard at this time? No? It seems that until we hear that the AEC has rescinded or reaffirmed its choice of the Weston site, this subcommittee should stand adjourned.*

1. *Answer research question no. 2 of Chapter 16, using the facts presented in this case buttressed by additional reading of the cited government documents.*
2. *If instead of a congressional investigation, the action challenging the choice of the Weston site had been entered by representatives of one of the rejected sites in a federal court, how would the development of the attack and defense be different?*
3. *Prepare a detailed explication of the siting decision similar to that outlined in Chapter 17 by using the facts in the case plus material gleaned from the applicable government documents.*

CASE A-IV
A Scientific Breakthrough Is Presented to the World

SUMMARY: In this fictional case, the George Holden, II Foundation is sponsoring a seminar at which the results of an unorthodox scientific project will be announced to the world. Invited to the seminar are a cross section of the leadership of major American institutions. The participants are invited to offer their expertise on the problem of how to follow up on the scientific findings.

THE FIRST DAY

George Holden, III

Ladies and gentlemen, honored guests, I wish to welcome you to this symposium of the George Holden, II Foundation. Within my lifetime the discoveries and technological developments in fields such as nuclear physics and engineering have revolutionized our modes of transportation, energy production, and how we defend ourselves or fight our wars. Developments in solid-state physics have made possible a rapid development of computers which promise to irrevocably transform our personal lives and industrial technology. There is no doubt in my mind that without the early successes in semiconductor technology, such far-reaching developments as the large-scale computer and its offshoots; long-range guided missiles, and their relatives, would have been impossible. So we can all see how new and obscure discoveries can produce great changes in the human condition. We can envision great changes in products and industrial technology and in the quality of life. We can also envision terrifying weaponry that, if improperly used, could easily cause the extermination of human life on earth.

How many of you in this room tonight have had these thoughts? "If only we had another chance. If only we could forsee some of the long-range consequences of the new discoveries or the new technology. Perhaps then we would do things differently."

This symposium, in a broad sense, gives us all such a chance. I think you will concur with my judgment that the discoveries you will hear about here can have far-reaching ramifications. What will we do with them is the main question you are being asked to explore.

The ladies and gentlemen in this banquet hall are a cross section of the intellectual leadership of our great country. Two-hundred and fifty guests were selected from business, industry, and commerce, from law, government, and politics, from education, and letters, from the press, from the military establishment, and from many others. We were convinced that you wonderful people can help us find some of the answers. I know you will want to try.

At this time I would like to present the executive secretary of the George Holden, II Foundation, Dr. Russel J. Walsh. Dr. Walsh is the prime mover in the foundation's scientific work and this symposium is his brainchild. He has been in charge of all the arrangements, and he will inform you of the details of the program. Dr. Walsh. (Applause.)

Dr. Russel J. Walsh

Good evening ladies and gentlemen, I hope you all breakfasted well and are ready for an exciting experience. I promise you that none of you will remain untouched by what you will hear.

Now let us get down to the real business. I would like to introduce my distinguished colleague and friend, Dr. Zachery M. Deutch. Dr. Deutch did his undergraduate work at Columbia University where he graduated magna cum laude. He took his doctorate at Harvard. He is a practising clinical psychologist, being licensed in the state of New York, but his first love has always been research in "psi" phenomena, or what the layman calls extra-sensory perception (ESP) or mental telepathy. Dr. Deutch was an early contributor to this field through his work at Duke University, and he is a charter member and past president of the American Society of Psychical Research. He is also a foreign fellow at the Royal Society for Psychical Research, a rare award for a mere American.

Dr. Deutch has been working on his project for five years under foundation sponsorship. He has assembled a fine team of scientific assistants, some of whom you will meet here this week. His work has progressed to the point where we think it is ripe for public disclosure. Also, Mr. Deutch needs additional financing if he is to bring some of his discoveries to commercial fruition. The immense financial requirements are beyond the Holden Foundation's capabilities, although we have just signed a new commitment with Dr. Deutch and his colleagues to continue their theoretical work.

Now I'd like you to meet Dr. Deutch, the man, himself. Dr. Deutch!

Dr. Zachery M. Deutch

Thank you, Dr. Walsh. I think a good place to begin this discussion is with my early paper, "Speculations on the Failure to Achieve the Repeatable Experiment." A reprint of this paper has been delivered to you.

For centuries men have been convinced that they have the ability to communicate nonverbally, not only through gestures, facial expressions, postural changes or physical manifestations such as blushes, going pale, sweating, giving off odors, and the like; but also in a less easily defined way —through mental telepathy or ESP. Many still hold this to be true, but they have never been able to produce scientific proof to support their beliefs.

Thousands of experiments have been performed with inconclusive results. Permit me to cite one type of experiment as an example.

Two subjects, let us call them S and R, are seated at tables in two adjacent but isolated rooms, unable to see or hear each other. At a signal from a controller, S picks up a playing card from a randomly shuffled deck and concentrates on the value of the card—say, it's the king of diamonds. R, hearing the same signal and knowing from his instuctions that S is looking and concentrating, also concentrates and writes down his guess of what card S is looking at. At the next signal, S picks up a second card, concentrates; then R writes down his guess. This procedure is repeated over and over, ad infinitum, and the results are analyzed. If real communication occurred, R should have been able to make accurate guesses of the cards S saw. We could expect some correct guesses by chance alone even if no communication occurred. If imperfect communication occurred, the number of correct guesses should significantly exceed the number attributable to chance alone. Elaborate statistical tests are required to discover if the actual number of correct guesses is better than chance.

Some experimenters have reported better results than others. Some S's and R's give better results than others. If ESP ability is present, the experiments indicate that it is very, very faint and unreliable. Even the good results are good only in the sense that the number of correct guesses is statistically better than chance. No reliable experimenter has reported 100 percent correct guesses or even 80 or 90 percent in a repeatable experiment.

You might reasonably ask, if people do have this ability, why doesn't it show up in the card-guessing experiments? There are people who are willing to concede the possibility of the existence of ESP, but they point out that there is no reliable evidence that people have this sensory capability. We continue to hear reports from people whom we believe to be sincere and honest of ESP experiences, but the reported phenomenon cannot be replicated.

I have met people who told me of their psychic experiences. Some were my professional colleagues, men of probity, who, I am certain, would not wilfully deceive me. Even more disturbing to me was the inescapable fact that I, too, had some ESP experiences—at least, I think they were. But then, my many years of clinical practice had convinced me of the ability of normal, well-meaning people to practice self-deception.

This problem troubled me for years, but gradually some light began to appear. My paper, "Speculations, etc." was the fruit of the early years' cogitations.

Permit me to review my reasoning for you. First I ask you to accept, tentatively of course, that ESP is a real phenomenon. If you find this too hard, let me plead with you to temporarily suspend your critical faculties and allow that it might exist. Are you willing to do that, just for me? Good! Thank you for humoring me. (Laughter.)

Now I ask you to accept that if ESP really does exist, it is a communication phenomenon. By that I mean that for a successful ESP even to occur, there must be both a sender and a receiver. In fact, persons will probably be both senders and receivers, like walky-talkies. You send to me and I receive you; I send to you and you receive me.

Now, many people who believe in ESP also believe that these communication events can take place over long distances, perhaps miles or even many miles. One experiment was attempted in 1971 between earth and a moon-landing site.

If people do have this ability, we would expect to find some person-to-person variability. Some people would be more powerful senders, and some would be more sensitive receivers. Also we might reasonably expect their sending and receiving abilities to vary with various personal factors, such as fatigue, emotional state, state of health, ability to concentrate, and so forth. Also, since most people are not aware of ESP capabilities, they might be sending and receiving without any conscious awareness that they were doing so.

These considerations led me to a very important conclusion. *If people are always sending, and if transmissions can cover long distances, the channel or medium of transmission must be horribly overcrowded with hundreds or thousands of millions of simultaneous transmissions.* In the city of New York or in the cities of London or Tokyo, there might be eight to ten million simultaneous transmissions. In the entire United States, 200 million and in the world 2 billion. Thus the ESP channels, if they do exist, must be oversaturated with what I call *"Psi-Clutter" and this high level of clutter and background ESP noise saturates every individual's telepathic reception sensory apparatus.*

No wonder, then, that telepathic communication is not possible under ordinary circumstances even if the phenomenon is real. No wonder ESP experiments are nonrepeatable. Our ESP reception apparatus is clogged by the high level of psi-clutter making the deciphering of any single transmission most improbable. If a coherent transmission does ever occur, it can be only by the rarest of chances. A particular transmission may rise in intensity enough to be momentarily above the background clutter, and an occasional coherent message may get through, but surely this is not repeatable on demand.

This is an important idea, and I'd like to develop it further by using an analogy to radio reception, with which I'm sure you are all familiar. As you know the radio-frequency spectrum contains not only AM radio stations' transmissions, but also FM, television, aircraft signals, radar, microwave transmissions and many others, all being broadcast simultaneously. If we were to connect a sensitive crystal detector to a wide-band antenna and then connect the detector output to a high-gain audio amplifier with loud speaker output, we could expect to receive every transmission on the air simultaneously. Anyone who has witnessed this experiment knows that most of the time you get an unintelligible hash, but once in a rare while, an intelligible sound can be deciphered.

I think something like this happens every minute of the day with telepathic transmissions. But we are subjected to so much psi-clutter every hour of the day that we unconsciously "turn off" our reception faculties. If an occasional transmission does get through to us, we probably won't recognize it, because we don't believe it could happen. Instead we may say to ourselves, "Something just flashed into my mind, but it's slipped away. I can't remember what it was."

To cope with this problem, radio engineers use something known as "preselection." This is a technique by which the receiver *tunes in* to a desired transmission and simultaneously *rejects* all undesired ones. This is what we all do when we tune a radio to a station or switch on a television channel.

The human counterpart to the preselection process psychologists call, *selective perception.* It is the capability that permits me to discern my name being mentioned above the deafening noise of a cocktail party, or which permits me to pick out my grandchild on the stage at the kindergarten play from an undifferentiated sea of children's faces. It is the faculty that permits shutting out irrelevant stimuli which might otherwise saturate our sensory apparatus.

Perhaps people can be trained to selectively perceive telepathic communications. But we see no persuasive evidence that the ability is widespread. We should not be surprised at this lack of evidence. First, we have the psychological phenomenon of "denial" at work. If we refuse to believe that something exists, we will not see it even if it is right in front of our eyes. Also, we know that the faculty is almost completely unused, and in most persons it may have atrophied. For example, we know from clinical experience that a man who, blind from birth, has had his eyesight miraculously restored must be *taught* how to see, that is, to exercise some visual perception to prevent his visual apparatus from being overwhelmed by sensory overload.

If this capability does still exist in humans, it is probably vestigal, unused, untrained, and virtually saturated and jammed by psi-clutter. For all practical purposes, should not any reasonable person conclude that the capability is nonexistent?

Except that there may be rare moments when a particular telepathic transmission is of high enough intensity to override the background jamming by psi-clutter. This could happen, in theory at least, if many people simultaneously send the same message in some sort of *telepathic scream* and if the sensory apparatus obeys some sort of Weber-Fechner law, coherent transmission might conceivably occur.

There is suggestive evidence that something like this can happen. In a panic situation everyone in the crowd is operating at a high emotional pitch and is thinking or feeling, "run, run, escape, escape, let's get out of here." This panic seems to affect the other members of the crowd with an upward crescendo of emotional pitch. If ever the telepathic scream is operative, this is the situation!

And have you ever noticed how much easier it is to make an audience laugh than an individual in a one-to-one exchange. I often find myself laughing uproariously in a theater at humor that would leave me completely unmoved if I were by myself. This, too, may be the telepathic scream in operation!

There may also be rare moments when two people achieve such a close rapport in a highly emotional exchange that words or gestures are not necessary for communication to take place. This may happen between a mother and her nursing infant, or between lovers during their most tender moments. In a negative way, it may take place between two antagonists bent on doing violence to each other. In these cases we may have a combination of high-level transmissions and an increased sensitivity of reception. I wonder, also, if the feeling of group solidarity we sometimes experience is not an example of the telepathic scream on a small scale among the like-minded, "tuned-in" people who make up the group.

And now, I think we have some time for questions before the luncheon recess. Are there any questions?

QUESTION. Dr. Deutch. It is my impression that you are firmly convinced that telepathic transmissions and receptions do happen between persons. Do you have any notions on the physical nature of the transmissions? Are they electromagnetic radiations, or something of that sort?

ANSWER. We don't know the physical nature of the emanations. Our people have been working on several theories among which are the electrical and electromagnetic theories, but at present we don't even have a plausible speculation.

QUESTION. Then how can you possibly do any worthwhile scientific work on ESP if you are ignorant of the nature of the transmissions?

ANSWER. Our ignorance does create great obstacles, but we believe that some worthwhile things can be accomplished. It was possible for early investigators to do good work in optics without a full understanding of the true nature of light. Even the most primitive man can make good use of his eyes and ears without any understanding of the nature of sound or light.

It would be immensely helpful if we could understand more about the emanations, how they are generated, how they are decoded by the brain. But even without this knowledge we can do some work on a phenomenological basis. It has been a common experience in science for theory and full understanding to lag behind technology, sometimes for generations.

QUESTION. We sometimes hear of mentally unbalanced people saying that they hear voices in their heads. Are these telepathic experiences?

ANSWER. We don't know. Of course, we'd have to examine each case. But I can offer some thoughts on the subject. Suppose you were one of the natural sensitives who could really receive these messages and suppose you were told that only crazy people heard these voices. Wouldn't that tend to disturb you? After a while you might begin to question your sanity, and this might be a destabilizing experience.

Also, there is the possibility that certain people may develop abnormal sensitivity during periods of mental or physical illness, just as they might develop hypersensitivity to light or sound. Some mentally unbalanced people may actually be hearing voices in their heads that are bona fide ESP experiences. We don't know, but I think it would be wise to keep an open mind on this question until we can find out how real are the voices.

QUESTION. You claim that high population density tends to interfere with telepathic communication. Suppose I went into the middle of the Mohave desert with one companion, would I be able to have an ESP exchange with him?

ANSWER. I have no way of knowing for certain. We do have evidence that the level of psi-clutter is much lower far from population centers, in the desert, on mountain tops, in the ocean. This would be so if the intensity of the emanation tended to fall off as the distance from the sender is increased. This may be why some creative people are able to work better in such places, because their thoughts are less likely to be muddled by high levels of psi-clutter. We tried some experiments on a mountain top and in a boat in the middle of Lake Erie, but we still found high levels of interference from psi-clutter.

QUESTION. Do you think that primitive man was a better ESP subject than modern man?

ANSWER. Of course, we can only speculate on this. But, yes, there is high probability that primitive man relied more heavily on ESP because with very low population densities on earth, the psi-clutter must have been much, much lower. I know that the current theory of the origins of language hold that man developed language as life became more complex and the ordinary grunt or gesture could no longer suffice. An alternative theory is that the development of language was made necessary because the growth in population and the accompanying higher levels of psi-clutter made the ESP mode of communication increasingly unreliable.

Are there any more questions? If not, I'd like to leave you with two provocative thoughts. If it were possible somehow to provide a "quiet" environment with a negligibly low level of psi-clutter, might we then be able to achieve very reliable ESP communication between people? Alternatively, if it were somehow possible to magnify a particular person's telepathic emanations, in a manner analogous to the way my voice is being amplified by the public address system in this room, might we be able to have reliable ESP communication by overriding the ambient psi-clutter? In this afternoon's session, I will tell you of the progress that we have made on both of these fronts.

END OF MONDAY MORNING SESSION

AFTERNOON

Dr. Walsh

Good afternoon, ladies and gentlemen. I hope you enjoyed your luncheon. I could tell from the few snatches of conversation I overheard, that Dr. Deutch's talk this morning has stirred up a bit of controversy. I will not cut into Dr. Deutch's time any longer. But when he finishes the second part of his talk, please remain seated for a few minutes. We will have a number of items of business to discuss. Dr. Deutch!

Dr. Deutch

Ladies and gentlemen, I'd like to describe a series of experiments that our group performed a few years ago. These experiments have been replicated many times by independent investigators so that we are willing to accept the conclusions as valid.

In the experiment, we place a subject in a comfortable chair in a quiet room free from distraction. He removes his shoes and socks, and we attach a sensitive thermocouple to each big toe. The thermocouple terminals are connected to a sensitive, balanced bridge with a galvanometer attached. If both toes are at the same temperature, the galvanometer needle is centered. If the left toe has a higher temperature than the right, the needle moves to the left; if lower, to the right. We ask the subject to concentrate on making his left toe warmer than his right. If he succeeds, he is rewarded in some suitable manner. After a few hours of practice, most subjects begin to have some degree of control and, after one or two weeks of steady practice, some subjects develop complete mastery of this technique. We have then perfected a sensitive measuring instrument in human form. The subject can cause the needle to move left or right on command. He can do it on verbal command, in response to a light or sound, to the snap of a finger. We are now ready to ask the big question! Can he do it on telepathic command?

The results we obtained were encouraging. We reasoned: if the interference caused by psi-clutter was causing erratic results, what would happen if we could do the experiments in a shielded room insulated from psi-clutter. This caused our people to think about a quiet room, something analogous to the shielded rooms used by radio engineers to test sensitive radios or acoustical engineers to test microphones.

To make a long, tedious story short, after several years of trial-and-error work, we hit on a material that could be used as insulation against telepathic emanations, and we built a quiet room with it. It is a small room, only about eight feet by eight feet in floor area. We can put only a few people in it at one time, but it works spectacularly. For the RIGHT-LEFT toe-temperature experiment we can get 95 percent correct responses routinely, as compared with 50 percent outside the room. This we believe to be a scientific breakthrough.

Oh, I see some raised hands. Dr. Walsh, should I stop now for questions? All right, let's start here.

QUESTION. How is your quiet room constructed? What is it made of?

ANSWER. I can't answer your question completely because most of the details are confidential. I can tell you a few things, however. The room is a cavity in a very large mass of material; if I recall correctly, the mass is a cube measuring more than 100 yards on an edge. The structure is made up of hollow building blocks measuring two by three by three feet. The hollows are filled with our insulating material, the chemical and physical nature of which we must keep secret. The inner room is completely isolated from the outside. It has its own atmosphere supplied by oxygen tanks and its own power supplied by alkaline batteries. A crane is used to lift away a section to allow people to enter and leave the inner space.

QUESTION. How did you find the insulating material?

ANSWER. By trial and error. We tried many hundreds of materials before we found one that seemed to work.

QUESTION. Do you know how much attenuation the quiet room affords?

ANSWER. No, we don't. We know it is considerable, but as yet we have not developed a method for measuring the attenuation. When we do, we will be able to continue the search for better insulating materials and an optimal design. We need time, money, and manpower to pursue this avenue of research.

QUESTION. Did you do any other experiments in the room other than the hot-cold toe thing? (Laughter.)

ANSWER. Yes we did. And here I am taking the risk of losing my scientific detachment. We have done many interesting things but are not ready to publish any results. We have not yet had the time to design experiments to test many of the hypotheses that have occurred to us.

We have used the room as a lie detector. We have a few very sensitive people who can read the minds of some subjects. We have done a few tests with animals and find that they are much more sensitive than people. Our people have been running wildly and nonscientifically through experiments. When their excitement wears off, we expect to restore a little scientific discipline and do controlled experiments.

QUESTION. What you have told us seems incredible. How can we know its not a gigantic hoax? You could be a confidence man, Dr. Deutch. Or, are we being subjected to some kind of experiment to discover the limits to our credulity?

ANSWER.   I can understand and sympathize with your scepticism. You aren't the first person who has expressed disbelief. Unfortunately, time does not permit us to demonstrate the quiet room to every one of you. We can do the LEFT-RIGHT toe experiment and a few others at a demonstration tonight. And if Dr. Walsh agrees, we can demonstrate the quiet room to a small group. If you will select a committee of ten, I can have a helicopter fly us to the site tonight for a demonstration. We'll do a few simple lie-detector tests and an elementary mind-reading experiment.

QUESTION.   Can anyone do these things?

ANSWER.   Yes, but for naive subjects, until their telepathic perception can be trained, they do better under a mild hypnosis. This permits them to avoid distraction from the unfamiliar surroundings and from the inevitable hostility and fear the experience produces. It is very unsettling to discover that your inner thoughts are no longer private, that someone can see into your mind, or can implant ideas into your consciousness without your knowing it.

QUESTION.   At the end of the morning session, you mentioned something about amplifying a person's telepathic emanation and simulating a telepathic yell by synthetic means. Do you have anything to add about that work?

ANSWER.   Yes, but our work in that research direction is not as far advanced as the work on the quiet room. We are working on a transducer to convert telepathic emanations into electrical energy which then could be amplified without limit. We are also working on a transducer to convert electrical signals into telepathic emanations. We have had some minor success on the first part, in converting telepathic signals into electrical energy, but not on the second. We are trying and our people are confident that in time they will succeed, but at present we don't have enough resources to do much on this aspect of the research.

QUESTION.   Does that mean that the thoughts of one person could be implanted into the minds of many people without their realizing what was happening?

ANSWER.   Yes, that is one possible application, or if you prefer, a possible misapplication.

QUESTION.   May I ask a question of Dr. Walsh? Dr. Walsh. I for one have heard enough talk for one day. I'd like to see some of the demonstrations, and I'd like to hear the report of the committee of ten that we should appoint to visit the quiet room. I move we adjourn for the afternoon and witness the demonstrations.

Dr. Walsh

I think Dr. Deutch has pretty much finished his main presentation, haven't you sir? Yes, just as I thought. If the members of this symposium would like to adjourn to begin witnessing the demonstrations, would you please raise your hands? Good. The ayes have it!

I'd like to suggest one change in our procedure. Because many of you will be witnessing different demonstrations, and may not have time to see them all, I suggest that we reconvene here in the morning at ten o'clock for an hour or so. Then we can all listen to the reports on the demonstrations from the witnesses.

The foundation trustees are of the opinion that, unless you are all convinced of the validity of Dr. Deutch's discoveries, you will not be able to put your minds to the problems and opportunities they present. This must not be an abstract exercise in science fiction. The problems can be of deadly seriousness, and the opportunities may be beyond our present conception.

END OF AFTERNOON SESSION

MORNING OF THE SECOND DAY

Dr. Walsh

Ladies and gentlemen, may we please come to order? You have all heard the reports of the committees that witnessed the demonstrations. Verbatim copies of the reports will be delivered to your desks shortly.

I think that even the most sceptical among you must now be ready to concede that Dr. Deutch and his associates have made a fundamental breakthrough in the area of psychical research. The "quiet room" is a development of paramount importance and the still incomplete work on telepathic-to-electrical and electrical-to-telepathic transducers shows great promise.

Are we ready now to split up into panels to consider some of the issues raised or are there more questions? Yes?

QUESTION. I have a question for Dr. Deutch. Dr. Deutch, last night your associate, Dr. Webber, said something about a number of peripheral discoveries made by your group. Could you tell us about these?

ANSWER. Certainly. In the course of our investigations a number of things were discovered or developed as serendipitous by-products of the main effort. We are not certain where these will lead, but I agree that members of the symposium should factor this knowledge into their deliberations.

We have verified the psychokinesis phenomenon, that is, the ability of persons to produce actual physical and chemical changes in matter by psychic means in the quiet room. This faculty seems to be capable of being strengthened with practice and learning.

We have found that in the quiet room certain persons have the ability to produce physiological changes in other humans and animals. This phenomenon lends new credence to the advocates of psychic healing. We told you of the LEFT-RIGHT toe temperature experiments. We have witnessed other more spectacular experiments too. We have seen changes in blood pressure, pulse rate, intestinal motility, eye-pupil dilation, salivation, galvanic skin response, EKG changes, and others induced physically in the quiet room. The ability of healer and healee seems capable of being strengthened by practice and learning. We also found that a person's susceptibility to these psychical influences is heightened under hypnosis.

Some animals appear to have greater psi-sensitivity than others, and greater than humans. This may account for some animal behavior formerly attributed to instinct.

Infants cannot communicate verbally but seem to be sensitive telepathic receptors. We have been able to eavesdrop on mother-infant exchanges in the quiet room. The emanations are particularly intense during breast feeding and fondling of the infant by a loving parent or nurse.

QUESTION.   When one person implants a thought in another's mind, does that mean he can control the other's behavior?

ANSWER.   We don't know the answer to that question. It is possible to implant a suggestion in another's mind, but we couldn't be sure action would result. It depends on whether the receiver knows the origin of the thought and on his disposition to take action at the time.

QUESTION.   Suppose you are able to perfect your electrical to telepathic transducer and could produce extraordinarily high levels of ESP emanations, what could be done with it?

ANSWER.   The question relates to practical applications. I can think of a few; the panels will probably think of many more. An advertiser could reach his audience telepathically. An army could reach the opposing force or civilian population; a politician could reach the electorate. The ESP amplifier would be another means of mass communication and persuasion. However, if many machines were placed in operation at the same time, they would raise the level of psi-clutter to a hitherto unimagined height, psi pollution would result!

QUESTION.   Would a government have an advantage if they had exclusive rights to such a machine?

ANSWER.   Any party with exclusive right to the machine would have a great advantage over competitors.

QUESTION.   Is there any possibility that telepathic communications can be channeled in a manner analogous to radio frequency spectrum assignments?

ANSWER.   That's a very interesting question, and we are beginning to think along those lines. Our preliminary work in the quiet room has convinced us that there may be many different kinds of telepathic emanations. We hope someday to identify and classify them. This may take years of study, but I think we may find it possible to do just as you suggest someday. Really that's the only hope for ultimately overcoming the effects of excessive psi-clutter. Today, in our primitive state of knowledge, we are lucky to just transmit, detect, and read a transmission.

QUESTION. Suppose I think in French or Russian, would it be possible for someone who does not know these languages to read my thoughts or to respond to them?

ANSWER. I must answer this question from fragmentary knowledge. When the sender is in a heightened emotional state, this can be communicated regardless of knowledge of language. Some emotions are free of cultural or language content. But some persons are more verbal than emotional or visual in their thoughts. In these cases, the receiver may not be able to interpret the received messages. Thoughts and other mental processes are much more complex than we have realized in the past.

QUESTION. I notice that you and your colleagues are very casual about security. There are no armed guards and the committee of ten reported that there were no guards protecting the site of the quiet room. Considering the importance of your work and its potential value to a foreign power, shouldn't you be more security conscious?

ANSWER. That is one of the things that we are asking the panels to advise us on. Should we make a full and complete disclosure to the world press and to the world scientific community, or should we try to clamp security on the development. I think Dr. Walsh has had some contact with the Department of Defense on this matter. For the scientific staff this is a painful question.

Dr. Walsh

Yes, I have been in touch with the Central Intelligence Agency and other intelligence agencies of the United States Government. They would prefer if we kept quiet about this work and relied completely on government financing. They have offered fabulous sums of money to support the development for military purposes. While we have not rejected their offers, we have not accepted them either. The matter is open until we obtain the advice of the panel on military applications and security.

One important consideration relating to security should be brought to your attention. We had not intended to make a public disclosure of this matter, but Dr. Deutch and his associates have voted unanimously to do so. There is a serious security problem brought up by the CIA and the military intelligence people in charge of security clearances. This project would probably be given a top-secret classification. If so, few of the scientific staff would be given security clearance; as defined by the intelligence agencies, our scientists are all potential security risks. They have all, at one time or another, been denied security clearance. They are brilliant men but they have an internationalist outlook on science. As a practical matter, if the project were assigned top-secret classification, there is serious doubt that most of the present staff would be able to continue their work. If they continued their work independently, we would be just where we are now.

Now ladies and gentlemen, we have arrived at the end of the information and persuasion phase of our symposium and at the start of the analytical and predictive phase. The Holden Foundation has made a firm commitment to support the theoretical work of Dr. Deutch and his associates for the next five years. But as you can readily see, our resources are small compared to what would be needed to bring the work to fruition.

We at the foundation would not like to see funds allocated for socially undesirable ends. We would not like to see these discoveries developed to the detriment of the world's populations. You now have your chance to influence the course of development of these new and exciting discoveries. What do you think are its ramifications? What are its applications? In what ways can they be misapplied? What avenues should be exploited first? I leave those things to you.

Please make good use of this chance to influence the outcome. We may never have such an opportunity again. If we do not choose wisely, the developments may run away from us in spite of our good intentions. I pray the Lord give us the gift of wisdom.

This case can be used as an exercise in multiple interest-group decision making, utilizing role playing as the principal technique. The following procedural steps are recommended:

1. From a large participating group, individuals are selected to play the role of representatives of specific interest groups, for example of the ACLU, American Medical Association, American Bar Association, United States Central Intelligence Agency, United States DOD, National Association of Broadcasters, and representatives of political organizations, psychological organizations, advertising, industry, and others that might have an interest in Dr. Deutch's discoveries.

2. Assemble the representatives in a large room and divide up into special interest subcommittees (for example, civil liberties, business, and military applications). Conduct small group and large-group brain-storming sessions to develop possible applications, misapplications, products, side-effects, and the like from Dr. Deutch's development.

3. Develop a number of specific proposals for further action with reference to the new discovery. What interests are affected? How can the proposals be evaluated?

4. Prepare a number of written reports giving summaries of the committee deliberations to be assembled into a final report for the Holden Foundation.

5. Discuss the alternatives of full disclosure versus military secrecy; of moving the project to another country, for example, the USSR, or the People's Republic of China, or the United Kingdom or somewhere else.

Index